WHY RIVALS INTERVENE

Why Rivals Intervene

International Security and Civil Conflict

JOHN MITTON

UNIVERSITY OF TORONTO PRESS
Toronto Buffalo London

© University of Toronto Press 2023
Toronto Buffalo London
utorontopress.com
Printed in the U.S.A.

ISBN 978-1-4875-0827-2 (cloth)
ISBN 978-1-4875-3791-3 (EPUB)
ISBN 978-1-4875-3790-6 (PDF)

Library and Archives Canada Cataloguing in Publication

Title: Why rivals intervene : international security and civil conflict / John
    Mitton.
Names: Mitton, John, author.
Description: Includes bibliographical references and index.
Identifiers: Canadiana (print) 20220427674 | Canadiana (ebook)
    20220427712 | ISBN 9781487508272 (cloth) | ISBN 9781487537906 (PDF) |
    ISBN 9781487537913 (EPUB)
Subjects: LCSH: Intervention (International law) – Case studies. |
    LCSH: Civil war – Case studies. | LCSH: Security, International –
    Case studies. | LCGFT: Case studies.
Classification: LCC JZ6368 .M58 2023 | DDC 341.5/84 – dc23

We wish to acknowledge the land on which the University of Toronto
Press operates. This land is the traditional territory of the Wendat, the
Anishnaabeg, the Haudenosaunee, the Métis, and the Mississaugas of the
Credit First Nation.

University of Toronto Press acknowledges the financial support of the
Government of Canada, the Canada Council for the Arts, and the Ontario
Arts Council, an agency of the Government of Ontario, for its publishing
activities.

Funded by the   Financé par le
Government   gouvernement
of Canada   du Canada

Canadä

For mankind do not await the attack of a superior power, they anticipate it.
> – Thucydides, *History of the Peloponnesian War,*
> Book XI, para. 18

It is better to judge dispositions, not intentions.
> – Israel Defense Force Chief of Staff (1974–8) Mordecai Gur

When elephants fight it is the grass that suffers.
> – Kikuyu proverb

Contents

Tables, Figures, and Maps

Acknowledgments

I would like to thank the many people who have helped and supported me along the way. First on this list is Frank Harvey, mentor and friend. Also, the staff, students, and faculty over the years in the Department of Political Science and at the Centre for the Study of Security and Development at Dalhousie University, particularly Tracy Powell, David Beitelman, Brian Bow, and Ruben Zaiotti. Thanks as well to the staff, students, and faculty at the Centre for Military, Security and Strategic Studies at the University of Calgary, particularly Rob Huebert for his interest and his kindness. Thank you to the faculty and staff of the School of International Relations at the University of Southern California, particularly Patrick James, a role model in work ethic and generosity. Thanks to the entire Department of Political Science at Memorial University of Newfoundland. Thank you to Daniel Quinlan at the University of Toronto Press for finding a way. Most importantly, thank you to my family: the immediate – Heather, Susan, Ron, Julia, Harold, and Charlotte; and the extended – Ruth, Rob, Neil, Mary Ann, Laura, Brian, The Girls, and the entire Moffatt clan. There are others too numerable to name. I am incredibly grateful.

WHY RIVALS INTERVENE

Chapter One

Introduction

Many of the most prominent conflicts of the twenty-first century (Afghanistan, Libya, Syria, etc.) have been, at one time or another, characterized as civil conflicts subject to outside, third-party intervention. In the latter half of the twentieth century, the ideological and geopolitical struggle between the United States and the Soviet Union was defined, in part, by interventions and "proxy wars" in various corners of the globe. In the ancient world, Rome and Carthage were drawn into the first Punic War as a result of intervention in Sicily, in which each empire supported opposing sides (Mamertine and Syracuse) in a local dispute. The Peloponnesian War between Athens and Sparta, similarly, included local conflicts in which allies were supported by the two great powers; even the First Peloponnesian War in 460 BC was triggered, in part, by balancing support to Megara and Corinth in a local border dispute. "Intervention is as ancient and well-established an instrument of foreign policy as are diplomatic pressure, negotiations and war," wrote Hans J. Morgenthau (1967, 425), "from the time of the ancient Greeks to this day, some states have found it advantageous to intervene in the affairs of other states on behalf of their own interests [while] other states, in view of their interests, have opposed such interventions and have intervened on behalf of theirs." While the modern study of international war typically has been divorced from the study of civil conflict, this distinction belies important interrelations (both theoretical and empirical) that reveal themselves in the study of history and, in particular, the study of relations between antagonistic states – enemies or *rivals* – in the international system.

Understanding the international dimensions of civil wars represents one of the most important and pressing puzzles in the study of world conflict, one that spans diverse literatures in comparative politics and international relations (IR), and that requires a theoretical engagement that goes beyond merely identifying the correlated conditions of probabilistic intervention. More must be done to understand *why* states intervene in civil conflicts – that is, to identify and explore the causal mechanisms which trigger intervention in specific circumstances – particularly if the deleterious effects of prolonged violence that result from such interventions are to be mitigated or prevented. Civil conflicts that experience "balancing" or "dual-sided" interventions, in which each domestic faction is supported by an outside patron, are longer, bloodier, and more difficult to resolve than those that do not (Cunningham 2010; Hironaka 2005). To take the Afghanistan case alone, the death toll after nearly two decades of war stands near 240,000 (Crawford, Fiederlein, Rzegocki 2021) – this, in a conflict many recognize as exacerbated by Pakistani involvement that Western policymakers have been unable to dissuade despite prolonged and concerted effort. A better appreciation of the rationale and logic undergirding Pakistani behaviour is essential for improving policy in this instance; even more, an understanding of why certain countries are so committed to seemingly counterproductive interventions can be useful as new conflicts emerge.

This book focuses on the theory and practice of intervention in civil conflict by international rivals – that is, the phenomenon of two states, locked in a long-term and ongoing acrimonious relationship, intervening on opposing sides of a civil conflict occurring in another state. As mentioned, the empirical record – particularly after the Second World War – suggests that not only is this behaviour fairly common (at least 35 such conflicts occurred between 1945 and 2002); it also generates and exacerbates a significant amount of conflict, violence, and bloodshed in world politics. My primary research objective is to explain this behaviour and, in so doing, suggest ways the international community might prevent these types of interventions from recurring (or better manage their consequences).

I argue that international rivalry is an ongoing (continuous) strategic relationship in which the push of the past (experience and reputations), defined by war, conflict, and crisis, and the pull of the future (uncertainty), in which security and survival are the ultimate goals, trigger balancing behaviour vis-à-vis external civil conflicts. This dynamic affects how rivals intervene. Contrary to many standard interpretations of intervention, rivals are inclined to focus on the overarching international relationship. The immediate stakes of the civil conflict – the gains intrinsic to the country in question – are less relevant. More specifically, rivals will be less concerned with helping a particular side *win* and instead be driven by a desire to frustrate or block their rival's capacity to further its own interests. The animating motivation is the prospect of future confrontation, conflict, and war at the international level. The stakes of the civil conflict are considered through this prism, and other interests (including material gains, immediate security, and/or identification with domestic groups) are either irrelevant or sacrificed in favour of protecting long-term security vis-à-vis an anticipated opponent. For outside observers, this priority is puzzling; for states engaged in rivalry, it is largely inescapable.

This introductory chapter proceeds as follows. First, I briefly discuss the two key phenomena I address in the book – international intervention in civil conflicts and international rivalry – and reiterate the core argument of the book, which links these two phenomena (intervention and rivalry) via a proposed causal mechanism. I then summarize the research findings from the case study chapters. Finally, I offer a roadmap for the book as a whole.

International Intervention in Civil Conflicts

Civil wars are international events. Of the 150 civil conflicts that occurred between 1949 and 1999, 101 (or 67 per cent) experienced outside intervention of some kind (Regan 2000, 2002). As Balch-Lindsay and Enterline (2000, 618) have suggested, "external intervention in civil wars is nearly ubiquitous." Even those conflicts that do not experience intervention have consequences for other states by, *inter alia*, altering the international structure, destabilizing the region, and threatening to spill across borders (making them pertinent to the decisionmakers of proximate nations; see Kathman 2011).

The study of the nexus between international relations and civil war is not new and has progressed through several more or less definable stages, while nonetheless remaining generally marginal in the discipline. Not surprisingly, the early literature was significantly influenced by the dynamics of the Cold War, particularly American and Soviet involvement in the Third World. Given the implications of this involvement – and the apparent centrality of Third World proxy wars[1] to broader superpower relations – a subset of scholars became interested in the linkage between internal and external conflict, even as the majority of the academy continued to treat inter- and intrastate war independently (early exceptions included Rosenau 1964, 1969; and Mitchell 1970); a

---

1 I have opted to focus on "intervention," rather than simply "proxy war," as the former encapsulates a wider range of behaviour (up to and including direct military involvement) that is of interest to the theory I present. Put simply, all proxy wars are interventions but not all interventions are proxy wars.

practice that largely continues to this day (see the summary in Levy and Thompson 2010).

Although several quantitative analyses did appear during the last two decades of the Cold War (see, for example, Dunér 1983; Gurr and Duvall 1973; Pearson 1974a, 1974b; Rasler 1983; Tilemma 1989), a relative dearth of appropriate datasets and the persistent historical centrality of US-Soviet rivalry meant that historical and comparative case studies emphasizing the foreign policy dynamics, geostrategic incentives, and political preferences of superpower interveners continued to dominate the literature. With the end of the Cold War and the development and distribution of more comprehensive data on intervention, however, quantitative analysis (as elsewhere in political science) gradually rose in prominence, eventually becoming the standard approach in the analysis of external-internal linkages.

This shift in the literature was about more than just methodology, however. Also important was the proliferation of civil conflicts and the concomitant decline of interest in traditional state-to-state conflict (the focus of much of IR study during the Cold War). The result was a greater emphasis on civil conflict itself, as a subject to be studied for its own sake (see the discussion in Florea 2012). Scholars became particularly interested in, for example, the onset and/or causes of civil war (see Regan 2010), a focus embodied by the well-known "greed versus grievance" debate: whether civil conflict initiation was best explained by incentives for material gain or by identity concerns related to ideological/religious/ethnic characteristics.

The study of intervention, in this context, became largely about understanding the *consequences*, or outcomes, of foreign involvement. Scholars examined the effects of international intervention on the duration, severity, intractability, and/or outcome of civil war (see, for example, Collier, Hoeffler, and Söderbom 2004; Cunningham 2010; Elbadawi and Sambanis 2002; Heger and Salehyan 2007; Mason and Fett 1996; Regan 1996, 2002), as well as the conflict-resolution approaches interveners might employ to end them (Balch-Lindsay, Enterline, and Joyce 2008; Cunningham 2006; Lemke and Regan 2004). This literature established, in broad terms, that third-party interventions can prolong and exacerbate civil wars (for an exception, see Collier, Hoeffler, and Söderbom 2004), particularly if interveners do not have as their primary goal immediate conflict resolution (see, for example, Akcinaroglu and Radziszewski 2005; Cunningham 2010; Walter 2002). Hironaka's study of "never-ending" civil wars suggests that balancing, or as she calls them, "dual-sided" interventions are a major factor "extend[ing] the length and intensity of a civil war by pouring resources into opposing sides, adding more and more fuel to the fire" (2005, 131–2). The frequency of these competing interventions approaches that of interventions more generally; if, as suggested above, over two-thirds of civil wars since 1949 have experienced intervention of some kind, Hironaka notes that "almost half of all civil wars fought since 1945 saw external support given to *both sides of the conflict*," which is to say that balancing interventions and the deleterious effects they bring are endemic features of civil conflict.

In light of these established consequences, scholars began to focus on the potential *causes* of intervention (see, for example, Balch-Lindsay and Enterline 2000; Carment, James, and Zeynep 2006; Carment and James 1996). Much of this work, however, focused on the structure and/or characteristics of the conflict itself that might trigger intervention (for example, the presence or involvement of an ethnic kin-group). More recent work has examined the strategic environment facing potential interveners, and the possibility that the dynamic interaction between multiple interveners influences decision-making (see, for example, Aydin 2010; Aydin and Regan 2012; Findley and Teo 2006; Fordham 2008; Gent 2007, 2010; Mullenbach and Matthews 2008; Salehyan, Gleditsch, and Cunningham 2011). For her part, Hironaka (2005, 137) suggests that third-party intervention can be – to appropriate Clausewitz – interstate conflict by other means: "The proliferation of weak states and corresponding changes in the international community have led to the use of intervention as a means of pursuing interstate rivalry or aggression." This, essentially, is the phenomenon I explore in this book.

The claim that intervention can serve as a proxy for interstate conflict is made elsewhere. Balch-Lindsay and Enterline (2000, 620), for instance, note that interventions may be undertaken for reasons "wholly unrelated to the civil war itself," often having more to do with the choices of other third-party actors and geopolitical considerations related to the international environment. Such considerations figure prominently, of course, in studies of superpower intervention during the Cold War. Fordham (2008), for instance, found that American intervention was more likely in the event of Soviet intervention in the same conflict (see also Gent 2010; Lagon 1992; Mullenbach and Matthews 2008; Scott 1996; Yoon 1997). In her review of the literature on American interventions, Amber Aubone (2013) identifies systemic and dyadic variables as one set of explanations (along with internal determinants, domestic politics, and individual and organizational beliefs) that have received support through empirical analysis. As she explains: "The common assumption is that US intervention in civil conflicts during the Cold War was driven largely by the security concerns of containment and the motivation to be more powerful than its rival, the USSR" (Aubone 2013, 287). The influence of the "geographic and strategic environment," as Balch-Lindsay and Enterline (2000) identify it, is of course not unique to the superpowers during the Cold War; the salience of particular conflicts to particular dyadic relationships in the international system will likewise generate opportunities and challenges – and strategic sequences – that make balancing interventions possible and even likely.

In their overview of the literature on third-party intervention in civil conflicts, Linebarger and Enterline (2016, 99) note that, "while it is widely accepted that third parties are strategic actors within the context of a conflict, their strategic interactions with the broader international environment is a neglected area of study." They go on to identify "The World Politics of Intervention" as an important area of future research. Specifically, they suggest greater efforts be made to "connect civil wars to insights in the broader world politics literature" (106). This includes tying the decision to intervene to assessments of the international environment, ending the hitherto exclusive focus in the civil war literature on "the traits of the conflict or conflict-state" (108). By focusing on international rivalry, this book is among the first full-length, detailed examinations of the "World Politics of Intervention," and thus constitutes a needed step in the development of the literature on civil conflict intervention.

The extant literature has established that 'rivalry' is strongly correlated with the decision to intervene. For example, Findley and Teo (2006) find that a state was eleven times more likely to intervene if a rival state was supporting the government in a civil conflict, and four times more likely if a rival was supporting the opposition.[2] Yet recognizing that such a correlation exists does not illuminate the underlying cause(s) of the behaviour. What is it about rivalry that motivates states to intervene in this way, particularly given the enormous costs and risks associated with involvement in an outside civil conflict? Why would violence and war that occur in another country – often one with seemingly minimal immediate economic or strategic significance – trigger potentially risky entanglement?

Such questions are familiar to diplomatic historians. The legacy of Vietnam and other costly interventions (or "over-extensions") in

---

2 There are different sets of criteria for establishing that a relationship constitutes "rivalry" (X number of conflicts over X number of years, etc.), with obvious implications for the coding of rivalry as a variable and the resulting statistical analysis. Often, scholars performing quantitative analysis will check their findings against alternative formulations (see, for example, Colaresi et al. 2008).

"peripheral" conflicts befuddle many assessments of American foreign policy, particular those which assume that the national interest (defined in terms of power and/or security) is pursued in a broadly rational manner. Soviet involvement (1979–89) in Afghanistan, likewise, is recognized with hindsight as a harbinger of decline, the loss of resources and prestige resulting from the embroilment helping precipitate the final collapse of the USSR and the end of the Cold War. Each superpower, similarly, was guilty of pursuing involvement in an Angolan civil war for which neither ultimately could provide sound justification – that is to say, justification in terms of the strategic, economic, or humanitarian interests manifest in the conflict itself. Moving further back in history, the ill-fated Sicilian Expedition in which Athens sailed a great distance to involve itself in a dispute between the Italian city-states of Segesta and Selinus is generally considered a turning point in the Peloponnesian War, leading eventually to Athenian defeat at the hands of its Spartan rival. Most recently, as mentioned above, Western analysts and policymakers have expended great energy trying to convince leaders in Pakistan that its involvement in the war in Afghanistan – specifically, Islamabad's continued support for the Taliban insurgency – was odds with its own self-interest, an argument that, for decades, fell on deaf ears.

The forces of history are too variegated to allow for sweeping generalizations with respect to the motivations, causes, and determinants of such an array of international behaviour. The cases I investigate in this book are, as a consequence, necessarily selected with more limited scope in mind. Nonetheless, the questions with which this book is more narrowly concerned contribute to the broader body of knowledge about interventions throughout history. More specifically, I seek to *explain* what has been so commonly *observed*, both anecdotally and in the statistical literature. I move beyond the correlation and go into specific cases to determine the underlying cause of the decision to intervene and the strategic rationale by which the intervention was conducted. Given the strength of the correlation, an examination of the mechanisms and processes underlying rivalry intervention is justified, even demanded, in methodological terms (Beach and Pedersen 2013).

International Rivalry

In lay parlance, the meaning of the term rivalry is relatively well understood, and the designation has long been used in diplomatic history and foreign policy analysis. One understands that the United States and the Soviet Union were "rivals" during the Cold War; indeed, much of the literature summarized by Aubone, as elsewhere, references "rivalry" as a factor influencing American intervention. No further explanation or elaboration is required to justify this claim. Over the past several decades, however, a small but growing literature has focused on the study of rivalry as more than mere historical description or intuitive designation. Scholars have examined systematically relationships characterized by long-standing hostility and repeated conflict (for a summary, see Dreyer 2014). One of the key findings of this research has been that rivalry relationships produce outcomes that distinguish them from other dyadic relationships in the international system. As such, it is not sufficient merely to use rivalry as a case selection mechanism or independent variable, as the dynamics of rivalry might well be part of the causal process (or causal mechanism) by which certain phenomena occur – in this instance, civil war intervention. Given the statistical *correlation* between rivalry and intervention, and in the context of the shift towards international *explanations* for outside intervention described above, the present study focuses on how rivalry itself might trigger such behaviour.

A theory of rivalry intervention presupposes a theory of rivalry itself: an argument that rivals intervene because they are rivals would be meaningless. It is therefore crucial to unpack the dynamics that make "rivalry" a distinct type of international relationship. It is possible then to explore whether evidence in specific interventions supports the hypothesis that these dynamics explain the decision to intervene. The purpose is to link the dynamics of rivalry to the causal mechanism leading to intervention. This will (a) offer a better explanation of specific interventions; (b) suggest a causal process linking rivalry to intervention across time and space (albeit with the necessary caveats associated with generalization from a small number of cases); and (c) enhance the broader understanding of rivalry itself, with potential implications for other types of behaviour that occur in such relationships.

The fundamental insight of the rivalry framework is the intuitive notion that "conflicts and wars are related to each other" (Diehl 1998, 2).[3] That is, particular events (wars, conflicts, disputes) are not ahistorical but part and parcel of a larger and ongoing narrative. Despite some disagreement among scholars about how exactly to conceptualize and measure rivalry, several key observations have emerged.

---

3 While intuitive, this assumption was not always incorporated into studies of international conflict, which traditionally treated war atomistically, separating particular conflicts from their historical context. See, for example, Midlarsky (1989).

First, quantitative research has established that conflict and war occur disproportionately between rivals. Gary Goertz and Paul Diehl (1995, 32), for example, found that, "of militarized disputes, 45% occur in ... rivalries, and over half of the wars [in the international system] take place between ... rivals." The work of Goertz and Diehl (2001) on the war-proneness of rivalries offers powerful "prima facie" evidence that the study of rivalry is pertinent for scholars of conflict and war.

Second, as William Thompson (1995, 215) has observed, "[c]onfrontations between rivals ... work differently than confrontations between nonrivals." John Vasquez (1996, 532) highlights the fact that prior hostility alters how states perceive each other; in situations where there has been a significant level of prior conflict, "there is ... a tendency for all issues (and the specific stakes that compose them) to become linked into one grand issue – us versus them." As a result, states engaged in rivalry may allocate strategic value to a particular issue or stake to a degree far greater than would be the case in an isolated or non-rivalry confrontation (see also Vasquez and Leskiw 2001). Although I challenge Vasquez's psychologically based *explanation* for this behaviour (see chapter 2), the *observation* that rivalry confrontations play out differently than isolated or non-rivalry confrontations is crucial.

Third (and as a consequence of the above), all disputes in rivalry are related. Issues of high salience (such as disputed territory) might be important for the birth of rivalry, but hostility from such confrontations is carried over to influence subsequent conflicts, even ostensibly minor or insignificant ones. This dynamic might be particularly difficult for observers to appreciate, as it defies the assumption of discrete cost-benefit calculations on the part of a state. The true source of hostility might not be readily apparent, and in fact might lie in the distant past and/or a different geospatial location entirely. To take an obvious example, no account of the Siachen glacier dispute between India and Pakistan would be complete without an appreciation of the historical relationship between the two countries; an analysis predicated solely on the immediate strategic value, tactical advantage, and/or economic opportunity of the glacier (of which there is virtually none) would be almost farcical. The impasse makes sense only if one considers it as part of the broader rivalry between the two states, and thus connected to other disputes within it. The result is the appearance of greater hostility, and greater volatility with respect to any particular confrontation – a border incursion more likely to escalate, brinksmanship more likely to break down.

Collectively, the work on international rivalry has established the relevance and viability of the concept; these relationships are different, with observable implications for how states behave within them. And yet, a coherent conceptualization and theory of rivalry dynamics remains elusive. Put succinctly, why do rivals behave as they do and, relatedly, how can rivalry be linked explicitly to observed behaviour? Many treatments of rivalry dynamics are imprecise, listing several characteristics without identifying which are most fundamental, crucial, or determinative for rivalry behaviour. Thompson and Dreyer (2011), for example, suggest that "antagonism, mistrust, and threat expectation" combine to constitute rivalry: from a theoretical perspective, each characteristic suggests a different underlying process, whether emotional (antagonism), psychological (mistrust), or strategic (threat expectation). In this book, by contrast, I articulate a novel and parsimonious theory of rivalry dynamics.

I argue that rivalry is shaped by hostile past experience (a history of conflict) existing under conditions of imperfect information and international anarchy. In the absence of perfect information with respect to rivals' intentions, states rely, in part, on past behaviour in the relationship, leading them to anticipate future conflict. Given this expectation, rivals will be particularly sensitive to developments that might enhance another's strategic position. Any such change could alter the balance of power (whether globally or locally) in the *next* confrontation. Rivalry is fundamentally a relationship in which all conflicts are believed to be linked in an overarching competition that has the potential for violence. A state's security is therefore perceived to be threatened at all stages and in all facets of the relationship – which is to say, security concerns remain acute even in the interregnum between overt conflicts. It is for this reason that balancing interventions in civil conflicts should be considered in the context of the broader international relationship between two rival states. The proposed causal mechanism for intervention derives from the dynamics of rivalry: *decisionmakers anticipate the negative long-term security consequences – at the international level – of non-intervention and act accordingly.* Long-term security vis-à-vis a rival is, in this sense, "overweighted" in a state's calculations. This theory of rivalry and related explanation for intervention is fully developed in chapter 2.

Summary of Findings

In order to assess the argument, I examine three cases of rivalry intervention: the Indian and Pakistani interventions in Afghanistan (2001–21); the Syrian and Israeli interventions in Lebanon (1975–85); and the Soviet and US interventions in Angola (1975–6).

The India-Pakistan (Afghanistan) case is complex given that Indian and Pakistani involvement in Afghanistan stretches back many decades prior to the outbreak of war in 2001. Nonetheless, the American invasion shortly after 9/11 drastically altered the political structure of Afghanistan such that it is possible to bifurcate between the pre- and post-2001 eras and to speak meaningfully about new and distinct interventions during the latter period.

Following the overthrow of the Taliban, India began supporting the nascent Afghan government, largely through massive economic aid, including the development of major infrastructure projects. Pakistan, having initially supported the American effort against the Taliban, reversed course in late 2002, and subsequently began a prolonged campaign to support an emerging Taliban-led insurgency against the new Afghan government.

India's intervention on behalf of the new government was the product of several factors, including economic opportunities and a broader geopolitical interest tied to regional hegemony and the projection of Indian power. Also important, however, were rivalry concerns associated with the security threat tied to Pakistan's use of Islamic terrorism and militancy against India. The Pakistani decision to support the Taliban insurgency is more directly attributable to rivalry dynamics. Unlike the Indian decision, Pakistan's intervention ran *against* (rather than with) its other interests. The decision sequence leading to the 2002 reversal – along with subsequent evidence and the persistence of the policy – corroborates the presence of the proposed causal mechanism. Concerns about long-term security, given the anticipation of renewed conflict with India, drove Pakistan's policy in Afghanistan.

The Israel-Syria (Lebanon) case is similarly complex albeit for different reasons. Respective Syrian and Israeli interventions in Lebanon occurred over a period of roughly ten years, from the outbreak of the Lebanese civil war in 1975 through what is known as the Lebanon War from 1982 to 1985. The case therefore offers multiple decision points, in the context of changing circumstances, whereby the presence of the rivalry-driven causal mechanism can be assessed. Syrian attempts to quell instability in 1975–6 were linked to apprehension about a potential Israeli invasion of Lebanon (and the security consequences that would ensue). As it turned out, the intervention threatened to bring about this very scenario, given Israeli concerns about Syrian control of territory in southern Lebanon along the Israeli-Lebanese border. Later, the roles were reversed, as Israeli forces moved into Lebanon in 1982 and Syria reacted by supporting proxy forces to counter their presence.

The various iterations of these competing interventions are covered in the case study, but in broad terms the evidence suggests that both Israel and Syria were driven primarily by long-term security concerns vis-à-vis each other; the specific dispensation of political control in Lebanon itself was ancillary to such considerations.

The US-Soviet (Angola) case is more straightforward but nonetheless illuminating. Historians generally agree that US and Soviet involvement in Angola was tied to the broader Cold War relationship. The civil war in Angola that broke out in 1975 was geographically distant from both states, and the country had no major or immediate material or strategic implications for either side. There was a potential ideological dimension, insofar as the Soviets supported a stridently Marxist domestic faction (and publicly championed its support for Third World revolutionary movements more generally); but the evidence suggests that the underlying motivation for Soviet intervention had more to do with concern about Chinese and American influence in southern Africa. The US intervention was even more clearly motivated by rivalry concerns; US decisionmakers explicitly tied the imperative to balance the Soviet presence in Angola to potential long-term consequences for the ongoing security competition with the USSR. Failure to check Soviet influence in southern Africa, the logic went, might result in future, more direct challenges (owing largely to reduced American credibility), which could undermine US security by altering the global balance of power and potentially precipitate catastrophic all-out conflict.

The cumulative evidence therefore supports the argument that the causal mechanism triggering civil conflict intervention in these three cases was long-term security concerns generated by international rivalry. In addition to the *initial* decisions to intervene, the cases highlight the relevance of rivalry for the *development* of the interventions over time. In each instance, there was a sequence of action/reaction as rivals responded to the other side. Future work might specify precise explanations for these retaliatory and/or escalatory sequences – by treating them as iterated coercive encounters in the context of deterrence theory, for example. The observation, however, that there was some level of synergy between interventions – that rivals calibrated their interventions over time in relation to the other side's activities – is further evidence (suggestive, not dispositive) that rivalry was the key motivator in each state's decision-making calculus. More specifically, the evidence indicates that adjustments were generally consistent with the rivalry goal of intervention, rather than, for example, the *victory* of a particular domestic faction. This finding is important insofar as the basic (and logically most simple) assumption of many observers regarding such interventions was that support for a domestic faction was designed to help that faction overcome its domestic opponents. Rather than outright victory, interveners appeared content to muddle through, doing just enough to forestall victory by the other side. This dynamic was the source of domestic US opposition to the country's intervention in Angola, as members of Congress, and even of the administration who focused on African affairs reasoned that any support short of that necessary to achieve "victory" was pointless. The dynamic also shows the exacerbating role that rivalry interventions can play insofar as resolution of a civil conflict is delayed owing to interventions *intended* to balance, or to stalemate, rather than decisively to resolve violence.

Finally, in general terms, the case studies indicate that a common causal pathway operated across time and space. There are fundamental similarities in the development of each respective rivalry over time, in the decades preceding the interventions of interest. Perceptions within the rivalries were remarkably consistent; leaders and decisionmakers were wary, cautious, and concerned about the future – always believing that renewed conflict (future war) was possible, even likely – without displaying overt hostility, hatred, or other obvious signs of personal antipathy towards their opponent. The interventions themselves were justified primarily in defensive terms, as leaders repeatedly stressed the potential security consequences of inaction. Across three different instances of international rivalry, and the interventions of six international rivals in three separate civil conflicts, there is consistency with respect to the perceptions and priorities that drove the decision to intervene.

These findings generate important policy considerations for decisionmakers regarding ongoing civil conflicts and the perils of rivalry interventions under certain circumstances. Given its historical ubiquity, knowledge of the logic and process by which rivals intervene is an important foundation for the effective prevention, management, and resolution of civil war. In many instances, states (particularly the United States and its allies in NATO, including Canada) become involved in civil conflicts, or conduct international interventions, without realizing the implications – or, more precisely, the complications – stemming from the international or regional environment. Attempts to end or stabilize such conflicts risk being undermined by the obstinacy of actors whose motivations might be misunderstood or underestimated.

Roadmap of the Book

Here, I offer a brief overview of the course of the book, highlighting the key information and takeaways from each chapter.

In chapter 2, I articulate in greater detail my theory of rivalry and the explanation for rivalry intervention that flows from it. I argue that the dynamics of rivalry are explicable through reference to strategic interaction under conditions of international anarchy and incomplete information, and need not rely on emotional, psychological, and/or idiosyncratic explanations derived from lower levels of analysis. An important clarification in this regard is the distinction between *interpersonal* rivalry and *international* rivalry. I argue that the metaphorical invocation of the former has clouded analysis of the latter by introducing dynamics – specifically emotional and/or psychological biases – unsuitable and unnecessary for understanding state-to-state (as opposed to individual-to-individual) relationships. I translate the theory into a specific causal mechanism that, I posit, explains why rivals engage in offsetting or balancing civil conflict interventions. I then outline my methodology in examining the existence of the proposed causal mechanism. These methodological choices inform case selection, and so I explain the criteria and rationale for case selection, noting the various trade-offs that inevitably flow from such considerations. I close chapter 2 by discussing the evidentiary requirements, as well as the structure of the subsequent case studies.

Chapters 3, 4, and 5 form the empirical core of the book and present the India-Pakistan (Afghanistan) case. Chapter 3 discusses the overall history and development of the India-Pakistan rivalry, including the various wars and crises that occurred between 1948 and 2001. This history is relevant to my argument about intervention because it establishes the *context* in which each rival assessed the civil conflict in which intervention was contemplated. History – past experiences, prior interactions, and the reputations that formed as a result – is the basis for perceptions about the future that constitute the causal mechanism triggering intervention. Chapter 4 examines the Indian intervention in Afghanistan after 2001. Chapter 5 does the same with respect to Pakistani intervention, and assesses both interventions comparatively and in the context of theoretical expectations.

Chapter 6 presents the Israel-Syria (Lebanon) case. I begin with an overview of the development of the rivalry from 1948 to 1975, again setting the context in which the Lebanese conflict was considered. I then explore the details of the competing interventions: a ten-year period of conflict in Lebanon saw iterated interventions by both rivals in what was an ongoing crisis. The case therefore offers multiple decision points, on both sides, relevant to unpacking each rival's decision-making processes. I conclude the chapter by comparing these interventions with those in the India-Pakistan case.

Chapter 7 presents the US-Soviet (Angola) case. Again, I begin with an overview of the rivalry of the two superpowers from the immediate post-war period up until 1975. I then examine their interventions in the Angolan civil war of 1975. In the concluding section, I evaluate the findings of this case in the context of both the India-Pakistan and Israel-Syria cases.

In chapter 8, I summarize and unpack the research findings as a whole. I revisit the expectations and arguments articulated in chapter 2 and reconsider them in the light of the evidence contained in chapters 3–7. I evaluate the overall strength of my argument in light of this evidence, and extrapolate implications for the development of knowledge on rivalry and intervention. I note potential avenues of future research given my research findings. Finally, I conclude with a discussion of policy implications, connecting the book's findings with the practice of international politics.

Rivals behave in ways that are both unexpected and predictable. As regards intervention in civil conflict, their motivations – perhaps counterintuitively – are largely determined by international security. The international community, keen on moderating the length, intensity, and consequences of civil wars, will need to understand these motivations – knowing both where they originate and, equally important, how powerful they are.

Chapter Two

A Theory of Rivalry (Intervention)

In this chapter, I present my theory of rivalry intervention: the common pressures that dominate international relations and politics – particularly the absence of an unbiased governing authority to manage relations between states effectively – combine with the informational inferences derived from past experiences and international reputations in ways that encourage defensive balancing behaviour vis-à-vis civil wars. States are expected to display and communicate a primarily defensive, future-oriented logic with respect to the decision to intervene, emphasizing the history of confrontation with their rival and the potential strategic danger of allowing the rival's intervention to go unchecked. Embedded in this argument is a conceptualization of rivalry itself – which is to say, a theory of rivalry is revealed through the development of a theory of rivalry intervention.

The argument that rivalry causes intervention raises the question: what is "rivalry"? Below, I sketch two alternatives. The first, following much of the extant rivalry literature, foregrounds psychology and emotion. Hatred and misperception, this perspective argues, are at the heart of rivalry. I call this approach *pathological rivalry*. I subsequently develop my own argument about rivalry, emphasizing structural and strategic dynamics. I call this approach *rational rivalry*. The point is not to present two theories that subsequently will be tested side-by-side against empirical evidence; rather, the juxtaposition helps elucidate the logic of rational rivalry and highlights the ways in which it challenges existing scholarship on international rivalry.

I then turn to the narrower argument regarding rivalry interventions in civil conflict, specifying (and graphically representing) the causal mechanism that links rivalry to intervention. I end the chapter by outlining the case-study methodology I employ to examine this explanation.

Pathological Rivalry

The language of psychology and emotion pervades discussions of rivalry in international relations. This is mirrored by the general trend in the field, described by a 2017 special issue of the prominent journal *International Organization* as the "Behavioural Revolution in IR." This approach foregrounds what Kenneth Waltz famously termed the "first-image" of IR theorizing: the individual level of analysis. It suggests that individual psychology, cognition, and/or emotion drive the practice of international politics, as leaders and decisionmakers confront situations and interpret (or, more often, *mis*interpret) information through processes of the mind. A first- or even second-image (which would include *social* psychological principles) approach to international rivalry would argue that hatred and hostility – as products of individual psychological and emotional processes and intersubjectivity between actors – drive rivalry behaviour.

In this section I sketch a behavioural theory of rivalry that emphasizes psychology and emotion as the causes of perceptual distortion and pathological antagonism between states. This discussion serves as a point of comparison and foil for my own theory of rivalry, subsequently articulated, which moves towards what Waltz deemed the third-image – that is, the structural imperatives of the international system itself. Although many in the rivalry literature allude to first- and second-image factors (in particular, emotional hatred and intersubjective, social, hostility), the clearest and most consistent articulation of this approach comes from John Vasquez (2009; Vasquez and Henehan 2001) and Brandon Valeriano (2012).

The basic premise of pathological rivalry is that rivalry is a distortion of, and deviation from, rational decision-making. As Valeriano (2012, 13) writes:

> Some states are actually "addicted" to conflict with other states. The image of another state as an enemy endures in the relations between the states and in the minds of the elites and the mass public. Despite any information that may cause a re-evaluation of the relationship, rivals typically are stuck in the situation because of the traits exhibited by addicts. Rivals tend to be impulsive, to be socially disconnected from each other, and to exhibit compulsive conflictual behavior. These are all traits one would expect to find in drug addicts, not responsible international actors. Rivalry as a situation is the height of irresponsible international behavior.

Importantly, this attitude (or addiction) adheres to "elites" (as well as to members of the mass public), which is to say it infects individual decisionmakers and distorts their ability to craft "responsible" foreign policy.

Vasquez (2009, 79), likewise, suggests that, in rivalry, "a major motivation behind actions is psychological hostility, i.e. more emphasis is placed on hurting or denying something to the other side than on gaining something positive for oneself." This focus – harm to the other side above any potential gain for oneself – is the crux of the psychological/ behavioural distortion foregrounded by the pathological rivalry explanation. The impulse defies a fundamental precept of rational behaviour, which Vasquez uses to distinguish rivalry from typical competition.

The key difference is that between a conventional *cost-benefit* calculus (in which an issue or point of contention is evaluated with respect to the costs and benefits related to particular outcomes) and an *affect* calculus (in which the *identity* of the opposing actor establishes preferences with respect to potential outcomes). The result is conflict, competition, and even war in circumstances under which a cost-benefit calculation would be expected to produce none. "Rivalry is essentially an irrational project," Valeriano (2012, 138) writes, "that defies normal power or balance considerations."

The key to rivalry, therefore, is to understand the psychological basis of negative affect between states, rooted in the hatred and hostility that stem from repeated conflict. The result is a relationship "characterized by selfishness, relative positions, mistrust, hostility, and animosity" (Valeriano 2012, 14). Behaviour in rivalry is primarily a function of these factors; leaders are overcome by their hatred for the rival state, and act as though blinded by this impulse. Each successive conflict only increases this animosity over time, amplifying the distortions associated with rivalry. Concrete stakes (including territory or political influence in another country) are infused with symbolic significance, making them indivisible and rendering resolution all but impossible.

This cycle forms part of the underlying structure of pathological rivalry, as it moves beyond the purely psychological to explain the genesis of rivalry (perpetually conflictual relationships) by reference to inherited systems of beliefs, worldviews, and/or norms. Pathological rivalry contends that a belief in realpolitik is the underlying condition that promotes conflict and generates competitive spirals, as bellicosity is met with more aggression and hawkish predilections dictate responses in kind. Which is to say, the pressures of the relationship itself do not determine that states behave in this way; they do so because of the inherited wisdom (norm) of power-political behaviour (displaying resolve, using force, etc.). The recourse to this type of response exacerbates and reinforces psychological hostility (rather than resolving it): "One of the great ironies of human interaction … is that conflictive (i.e. negative) acts are intended to change issue positions, but instead change affect. Typically, if an actor tries to resolve a disagreement on a salient issue by punishing another actor, this will generate hostility rather than any shift in issue position" (Vasquez 2009, 83–4). Note again that the basis for this contention is the psychological effect of interpersonal interaction (we know that punishment results in hostility between individual *human beings*), which is then applied to the interaction between states (or state leaders). A conflict arises and is handled according to the precepts of realpolitik, this response provokes realpolitik from the other side, and these conflictual interactions generate hostility that results in a focus on the identity of the opponent (negative affect), leading the stakes to be infused with symbolic significance and eventually uniting all issues of contention into one single overarching issue: us versus them.

With respect to civil conflict intervention – the phenomenon of interest in this book – pathological rivalry offers two possibilities.[1] First, one might expect rivals to conduct balancing or offsetting interventions for essentially offensive purposes. Psychological hostility and hatred would cause leaders to seize an opportunity to attack their rival's interests in whatever capacity and location possible. The perception of an exposed position with respect to a rival's involvement in an external civil conflict would present an opportunity to damage, bleed, or disrupt the rival (recall that *harm* is the overriding interest with respect to a negative-affect calculus). This explanation accords with the aggressive hostility that characterizes many of the descriptions of rivalry in the literature, including the "addict" characterization offered by Valeriano.

The second possibility relates to a defensive motivation, and stems from the "paranoia" that is often described as a psychological effect of rivalry. Leaders might be concerned that their rival's involvement is a conspiracy against their own interests, or a prelude to more direct confrontation (this might particularly be the case in regional rivalries, where the relevant civil conflict is proximate to both nations). This possibility hews more closely to the rational theory of rivalry outlined below, and therefore will be more difficult to distinguish than the offensive,

---

1 Neither of these, it should be pointed out, was articulated directly by Vasquez, Valeriano, Leng, or any other scholar operating in this tradition. Their work on rivalry did not engage directly the question of civil conflict intervention. I therefore extrapolate logically consistent expectations given their conceptualization of, and explanation for, rivalry itself.

aggressive variant of pathological rivalry. Paranoia and exaggeration are, in a sense, in the eye of the beholder. An actor might find it prudent to err on the side of caution, while outside observers might ascribe paranoia for what they perceive as an exaggeration or overestimation of threat. Yet, if such behaviour is consistent between rivalries – that is, across space and time – how useful is it to describe defensive motivations in rivalry as distortions of the individual psyche, as opposed to functions of the structural situation that confronts it? Indeed, it might be that expressions of "paranoia," in the form of exaggerated threat estimations, are the micro-foundations of a structural situation that *generates* them.

This suggests a potential synergy or synthesis between micro and macro approaches – in this case, between pathological rivalry and my rational theory of rivalry. After all, any macro theory *requires* some kind of micro-foundation, which in the social sciences involves the behaviour of individuals who act (and can only act) according to their perceptions of reality. It would be nonsensical to suggest that states conduct balancing interventions in the absence of human activity to bring them about. From a micro perspective, the paranoia and threat exaggeration observed in rivalry is a pathology; from a macro perspective, they might be the predictable consequences of pressures at the international level.

Nonetheless, the level at which the analysis begins is important. The same phenomenon, approached from different perspectives, yields alternative interpretations and, with them, divergent policy recommendations. Recall Valeriano's contention above that a change in attitude is necessary to forestall the onset and perpetuation of rivalry: abandon realpolitik, and the negative consequences that ensue will be avoided. Of course, Valeriano recognizes, as do others who adopt this view, that this is much easier said than done, and is cautious as to how realistic such an attitude change might be. Yet this analysis of rivalry suggests that it is at this individual level that policy change should be pursued. This focus is a natural outgrowth of pathological rivalry: the theory ends where the theory begins, with the preferences, beliefs, and attitudes of individuals. If individual belief systems are the starting point for, or the trigger of, the subsequent conflict spiral that creates rivalry – if they begin the process by which psychological hostility is subsequently fostered and compounded – this places the causes of rivalry beyond the structure of conflict, which would make international relations tragic, and places it in the minds of men and women, making it ironic: *if only decisionmakers could see the light*. Again, the only remedy is to make this apparent and to hope that, in so doing, entrenched belief systems with respect to power politics can be transcended or abandoned.

Consider the following example offered by Stein (2013, 383), which, although not apropos civil conflict intervention or rivalry per se, again illustrates the basic logic of the behavioural approach while also implying an overlooked alternative explanation:

> In 2009, Israeli and American leaders had access to almost all the same data and evidence on Iran's nuclear program … Yet American officials estimated a much longer time horizon – five years – for the development of a nuclear weapon by Iran than did Israel's officials who estimated a year or two. The difference in threat perception is not explainable by the evidence but by the higher emotional loading of the likelihood of an Iranian bomb for Israel's leaders that shaped threat perception.

In this reading, Israeli leaders were "emotionally loaded" vis-à-vis the Iranian nuclear program, and therefore distorted evidence to arrive at a more pessimistic appraisal of the situation. Why the discrepancy with the American assessment, however? One or two years as opposed to five? Is this explainable merely by reference to different levels of "emotion"? How could this possibly be measured? By contrast, reference to the relative danger (given geographical proximity) and the associated existential implications, along with the history of Israeli-Iranian competition in the region, suggests Israel had compelling strategic reasons for being more concerned than were their American counterparts: the implications (costs) of being *wrong* were simply much higher. Although this insight also fails to explain the precise discrepancy in time horizon (how many years is an "existential threat" worth?), it is a superior explanation because it *precedes* and *specifies* the causes behind the "emotional loading" foregrounded by behavioural analysis. It is more satisfactory because it does not reduce serious, sober individuals (to say nothing of the intelligence apparatuses that inform them) into emotionally charged imbeciles.

Rather than searching for the consistency of rivalry behaviour in the *a priori* belief systems of particular leaders (or in the cognitive, psychological, and emotional processes that result from repeated conflict), the theory I outline below emphasizes the structural conditions of the international environment that lead, however tragically, to rivalry behaviour between broadly rational actors, even those that might be defensive or status quo with respect to their intentions.

Rational Rivalry

The ultimate intent of the theory I present in this chapter is to examine the *causal mechanism* or *process* linking international rivalry to civil conflict intervention. The theory is not a general theory of intervention: intervention is subject to equifinality, meaning there are multiple causal pathways by which a state can be motivated (or induced) to intervene in a civil war. In this book, I take as my focus one potential pathway, but the theory is not meant to predict when intervention will occur; rather, the theory establishes and elucidates the putative mechanism linking rivalry to intervention through historical case studies, which are particularly useful when linked to quantitative research that has already established a correlation between two phenomena.

The import of the theory extends beyond the parameters of simply the cases I examine. Since, as I make clear below, the mechanism purported to connect rivalry to intervention – put succinctly for the purposes of exposition: strategic concern for the future – is inherent to the relationship of rivalry itself,[2] broader behaviour within rivalry (that is, beyond intervention) is potentially illuminated. This has significant implications for future research. The causal mechanism I identify here might be found elsewhere, and the theory that purports to explain this mechanism could be applied to other forms of behaviour in international politics. In short, I reveal a theory of rivalry through the development of a theory of rivalry intervention.

Interpersonal versus International Rivalry

I begin by drawing the distinction between *interpersonal* and *international* rivalry. In this book I develop a theory of the latter, while, as noted, extant treatments of rivalry between states have often been muddled by familiarity with, and reference to, the former.

In the study of IR, states typically are categorized with respect to their material capabilities (great power, major power, minor power, etc.), but it is also useful to categorize *relationships between states* according to their *perceptual* dynamics (friends, enemies, allies, rivals, etc.). After all, material capabilities are relevant only relative to other states in the international system. War and peace, moreover, can be understood most fundamentally in dyadic terms even if, as is clear empirically, multiple states often interact in complex webs of relations, including wars and conflicts (consider, for example, the multiple overlapping alliances involved in the First World War). Nonetheless, a conflict involving

---

2 This is to say that *rivalry* is the mechanism linking rivalry to intervention, a formulation that is not tautological if one recognizes that "rivalry" is a concept imposed on reality for the purpose of analysis. It is the underlying conditions, or dynamics, of rivalry that are of interest – that both make the concept and generate the behaviour associated with it.

multiple states is composed, logically, of sets of interacting dyads.[3] The moment a state "acts" internationally, it minimally involves at least one other state. The most basic building blocks of international relations are therefore dyadic relations, and theorizing about them is (or at least should be) fundamental to the study of international relations.

I posit rivalry to be a basic feature of the relations between certain states. This is because the existence of rivalry – more specifically, the threat implied by the prospect of future conflict with a rival – amplifies precisely the dynamics of international anarchy that result in confrontation between states. The concern for survival as the ultimate goal – in the sense that, without it, the pursuit of any other goal is impossible – is particularly acute when a state is assessing the intentions of a rival. The fundamental reality of self-help means states must act to protect themselves in the face of this threat; and the function of power as the means by which to secure one's survival means not only direct war, but the overarching balance between the two rivals will be of constant concern. Hence rivals move to balance, block, frustrate, and offset each other's interests and/or gains. Understanding international rivalry *on its own terms* – which is to say, absent recourse to analogy or metaphor, which often muddies rather than clarifies its unique characteristics – is necessary for appreciating its relevance to broader considerations of international relations.

All states at all times stand in various relations one to the other. In a useful abstraction, Arnold Wolfers (1962) conceptualized these relations as existing along a continuum between extreme enmity and extreme amity. With respect to the former, he wrote: "Enmity reflects the existence of a conflict of interests. *Peace is threatened at that stage of the conflict when physical coercion, by one side or both, becomes a practical possibility"* (Wolfers 1962, 30, emphasis added). It is this latter consideration – the possibility of physical confrontation – that, I suggest, is most important. Conflicts of interest are essentially ubiquitous and exist even between nations whose relationship approaches "extreme amity," such as the United States and Canada. Yet, as Wolfers implied, such a disjuncture threatens peace only so far as physical violence is considered possible. It is precisely this possibility that is most severe – not necessarily objectively, but *subjectively,* in the perceptions of state leaders – in the context of rivalry. Rivalry, in this sense, is the *acute possibility* of war and violence as perceived by the parties involved.

---

3 Even if two states are simply attacking a common enemy and have no direct interaction, the relationship between the two can be described in terms of their shared and/or conflicting interests.

It is similar, in this way, to the "friend-enemy" distinction made famous by German political theorist Carl Schmitt. As Schmitt's ([1928] 2007, 32) definition maintains, "the political," at its most fundamental, takes the form of an antithesis between "friend" and "enemy" where "the ever present possibility of combat" between "fighting collectivities" exists. It is the group itself, moreover, that defines the enemy; the designation is public and political, not private or personal: "The enemy is not merely any competitor or just any partner of a conflict in general. He is also not the private adversary whom one hates. An enemy exists only when, at least potentially, one fighting collectively of people confronts a similar collectivity" (Schmitt 2007, 28). This distinction is key. The use of the individual pronoun is somewhat misleading: in reading Schmitt, it is clear that the actors to which this decision apply are political collectivities, not individuals. Political enemies, in other words, stand in relation to each other as group entities. For Schmitt, the decisive political entity in the twentieth century was the nation-state, an assumption we might reasonably carry forward to the twenty-first. Political enemies are therefore states; this enmity exists between the units themselves (as states *qua* states) and not between the individuals that comprise either collectivity.

The basis of this confrontation between states is explicitly existential: "Each participant is in a position to judge whether the adversary intends to negate his opponent's way of life and therefore must be repulsed or fought in order to reserve one's own form of existence" (Schmitt 2007, 27). While competition or rivalry in, for example, the economic sphere can be about material gain or profit, political rivalry (or enmity) between states is about *survival*. Again, this is not to say that the basis for disagreement need initially be existential – that is, borne out of a desire to destroy one's opponent. As Schmitt maintains, conflict can have its origin in any sphere of activity or with respect to any goal or interest of the political units involved. It is only once the conflict approaches real violence – and therefore the possibility of "negating" an opponent in the ultimate sense – does the disagreement (or conflict of interest) become political.

This violence need not even approach "total war," as it became known in the twentieth century, in which the negation of the enemy becomes the focus of an entire society and in which the question of survival becomes most acute. Indeed, the advent of nuclear weapons has largely forestalled the development of such conflicts, meaning any question as to the implications of total war – while not irrelevant – is less fundamental to global politics today than it was in a previous era, at least for the moment. The concern here is with the *threat* or *possibility* of violence: the perception that one's own existence as a political unit *could be* endangered by the aggression of another. Ironically, therefore, the existence of nuclear weapons actually amplifies this condition; despite the logical impossibility of their use, the prospect of nuclear annihilation – the speed with which it might be unleashed by the push of a button – generates intense anxiety and concern. As the Soviet-American rivalry demonstrated, direct large-scale violence of any kind need not occur for states to be enemies in this ultimate sense.

Schmitt's definition of the political enemy is useful as a foundation for understanding the conceptualization of rivalry I offer in this book. The key distinction is that between personal/private hatreds on one hand and public/political rivals on the other. Wolfers (1962, 25) recognized the common difficulty in making this differentiation: "Terms like 'amity' and 'enmity' – even more, terms like 'friendship' and 'hostility' – must be used with caution in discussing interstate relationships. These terms are taken from the universe of interpersonal relations and they convey a sense of emotional involvement. In contrast, diplomatic postures of amity and enmity do not depend on emotional conditions and may in fact contradict them." Which is to say, the private enemy and the public enemy are not one and the same, and the characteristics of the relationship that define one or the other – though often described with a similar vocabulary – are different as well.

Schmitt (2007, 27–8) attempts to pre-empt any confusion or conflation in this regard: "The friend and enemy concepts are to be understood in their concrete and existential sense, not as metaphors or symbols, not mixed and weakened by economic, moral, and other conceptions, least of all in a private-individualistic sense as a psychological expression of private emotions and tendencies." The propensity to discuss international rivalries in the language of interpersonal rivalries pervades both diplomatic history and more recent treatments of the rivalry concept in IR. This leads to a form of the pathetic fallacy, in which group entities such as states are said to "hate" or "despise" one another despite the fact that such emotional conditions apply only, it should be obvious, to individuals. Although the role of emotions in IR has been examined usefully in the literature (for a recent treatment see McDermott 2017), and my argument ought not to be considered a decisive refutation of its applicability in other contexts, the point is that understanding a concept such as rivalry – despite its so often being couched and described in interpersonal language – need not invoke emotion as an explanatory variable.

Of course, one can speak of the "mood" of a nation with respect to general public sentiment; it is certainly a reasonable course of inquiry to examine general attitudes of citizens – or even those of elites and political leaders – in other nations, both in the abstract and vis-à-vis counterpart individuals. Even more, these attitudes might well influence certain dimensions of public policy or shape the way foreign policy towards a particular country is formulated. Personal animosity between decision-makers, likewise, can be of considerable influence, particularly in the context of crisis negotiation. Yet such analysis should not stand in for, or obfuscate, an analysis of international rivalry in which the political, not the personal, is emphasized. This basic distinction between rivalry as an international phenomenon between group-entities (states) versus rivalry as an interpersonal (emotional, psychological, individual) condition underlies this book as a whole. With this distinction in mind, we can now turn to the specific dynamics that generate perceptions and behaviour in rivalry.

Rivalry as "Continuous Negotiation"

States in rivalry have interacted in the past and expect to do so again in the future. Whatever they do in the present is affected by (the perception of) this reality. The concept is simple but powerful. It is similar to "continuous negotiation" as defined by Thomas Schelling (1960) in his famous "Essay on Bargaining." "To study the strategy of conflict," Schelling wrote, "is to take the view that most conflict situations are essentially bargaining situations" (5). The emphasis is on explicating the way two or more actors interact such that the behaviour of one is contingent on the behaviour of the other (or others). The purpose is to outline, in broad terms, "a tactical approach to the analysis of bargaining" (21) in which the strategic (or interdependent) is emphasized.

The terms "bargaining" and "negotiation" might be confusing here; one should remember, however, that Schelling included within these terms precisely the type of geopolitical conflict that was occurring then between the Soviet Union and the United States. His point was, in effect, that the type of strategy related to such conflicts was fundamentally similar to other forms of competition – say, between labour unions or even individuals on the street. "Negotiation," in this sense, is a broad term, far beyond the narrow and conventional usage denoting the crafting of a deal around a table, that can include military crises, threats, and other forms of international conflict. The crucial factor is the interdependence of actions, the action-reaction sequence denoting "negotiation" and the totality constituting the "bargaining" situation. "Continuous negotiations," Schelling (1960, 30) wrote, are "a special case of interrelated negotiations [occurring] when the same two parties are to negotiate other topics, simultaneously or in the future." This recognition implies an ongoing relationship, one in which future conflict is assumed and, even more important, in which *present behaviour is conditioned by this knowledge.*

In the context of such negotiations, Schelling underscored the importance of reputation in the bargaining process. What a state has done in the past sets the parameters of the present relationship. Even more, the *staking* of a reputation is a tactic available in the present negotiation "to persuade the other that one cannot afford to recede, one says in effect, 'If I conceded to you here, you would revise your estimate of me in our negotiations; to protect my reputation with you I must stand firm.' The second party is simultaneously the 'third party' to whom one's bargaining reputation can be pledged" (Schelling (1960, 30). This logic, moreover, can cut both ways: the *protection* of one's reputation – particularly if it has been at stake in the past or might be perceived to be at stake in the present – is a powerful motivating factor. In the context of continuous negotiations, in which parties interact (and, just as important, expect to interact) over time, concerns about how one's actions will be perceived – backing down, failing to follow through, showing weakness, showing toughness, etc. – are about more than just the present confrontation (negotiation) and the stakes involved in it. Schelling's concept, therefore, is particularly useful for explicating the strategic logic related to these types of ongoing relationships.

In sum, understanding rivalry as a continuous (hostile) negotiation is helpful for establishing its strategic parameters: past interactions and the anticipation of future interactions define the present bargaining situation, amplifying the relevance of reputation and altering how actors otherwise would be expected to behave in the context of a one-off or isolated encounter.

Reputation and Rivalry

Reputation is key to Schelling's conceptualization of continuous negotiation and is similarly relevant to the idea of rivalry developed here. Reputation influences the perceptions of actors with respect to potential future behaviour. Which is to say, past behaviour influences not only perceptions regarding likely behaviour in the context of a specific, ongoing crisis or conflict, but also in hypothetical and as-yet-uninitiated conflict. Reputation is the basis for hostile perceptions such as those observed in the rivalry literature. The atmosphere of enmity that characterizes rivalry is the product of the accumulation of experience between rivals that leads them to expect continued hostility, and

the concomitant recognition that one's own reputation will be important in future confrontations and crises. I argue that such perceptions of
hostility are not "emotionally loaded," in the interpersonal-individualistic
sense of the term – although it is possible that the specific individuals
involved might "hate" their rivals in this way – but rather are the reasonable and predictable result of the search for relevant information
and the imperative to be prudent in international politics.

For international rivals, repeated conflict and hostility lead, in part, to
an inference of malign intentions that might not be made in other circumstances, all else being equal. The reputation of Egypt in the eyes of Israel
is markedly different than that of the United States, given the respective histories of the states involved – to put it more categorically, because
Egypt is a rival of Israel and the United States is not. In this sense, a
"rivalry reputation" is somewhere between a specific and a general reputation (on this distinction, see Harvey and Mitton 2017): it applies across
time and between crises, much like the latter, but is nonetheless localized
(or "specific") to interactions within the rivalry itself.

There is a tendency to dismiss historical reasoning (reputation, historical analogies, etc.) as shortcuts or convenient but inaccurate "heu-
ristics" in the decision-making process (see, for example, Press 2005;
Stein 1985; Yarhi-Milo 2014). In many instances this assessment is valid,
particularly insofar as leaders draw disproportionately on "vivid" historical cases in which they were directly involved or for some other
reason not primarily tied to the actual similarities between situations.
It is not disputed that individuals reacting to new information search
for cognitive consistency by conforming evidence to pre-existing beliefs
and worldviews. What is often overlooked, however, is that in certain
circumstances it is *perfectly rational to do so*. Robert Jervis's (1976, 117)
admonition that "scholars too often apply the labels of closed-
mindedness and cognitive distortion without understanding the necessary role of pre-existing beliefs in the perception and interpretation of
new information" continues to hold.

While distortion is certainly possible, the process can be justified
because "balanced attitude structures do not reveal irrationality if the
cognitive consistency can be explained by the actor's well-grounded
beliefs about the consistency existing in the environment he is perceiv-
ing" (Jervis 1976, 119). In the context of international relations, enduring relationships with particular states (whether conflictual *or* amicable) offer "well-grounded" parameters for such consistency. Sensing
deception from someone who has deceived in the past, or inferring
aggression from someone who has aggressed before, is rational in a
context of incomplete and imperfect information. Reference to past

experience "would decrease accuracy *if data were completely unambiguous* or if all states of the world were equally probable. But since the evidence always permits multiple interpretations and because theories developed from previous cases must provide a guide to the explanation of new information, the influence of expectations on perception is not only consistent with rationality, but is 'essential to the logic of inquiry.' One can be too open-minded as well as too closed to new information" (Abraham Kaplan, quoted in Jervis 1976, 154; emphasis added). Absent this process, actors would confront each new situation, each new piece of information or evidence, *de novo* – which is to say, they would discount relevant information, thereby significantly *decreasing* the probability of accurate perception: "Intelligent decision-making in any sphere is impossible unless significant amounts of information are assimilated to pre-existing beliefs" (145). Indeed, this process of reasoning is fundamental to the very "scientific process" that is often heralded as the apotheosis of rationalism (see Jervis 1976, 156–62).

The key consideration is that relying on past behaviour and/or reputation is not in and of itself a decision-making distortion, and does not, therefore, necessitate explanation from a psychological or cognitive perspective. All that need be relaxed is the assumption of complete or perfect information (or "unambiguous data") – a situation which fits extremely well with the reality of international relations under conditions of anarchy (more on this below). Particularly in the context of rivalry – which by definition includes a history of interaction between states – inferences informed by past experience can be subsumed within a rationalist framework.

Jervis (1976, 120) himself seems to recognize as much when he says, by way of example: "If you think the Russians are aggressive, there is nothing irrational about viewing their suggestions with suspicion – not only will you know of previous attempts at deception, but the belief that the Russians are adversaries implies, by definition, that you should be skeptical of their proposals." To rely on past experience, to infer intentions based on rivalry reputation – which is to say, a reputation developed through experiences within the relationship – is a process that need not be explained by emotion, enmity, hostility, or hatred. It is, rather, a largely unavoidable (and broadly predictable) basis for interpretation between states locked in a pattern of repeated disputes, confrontations, and crises.

In recent years, a spate of work on reputation in IR has responded effectively to earlier scholarship that had cast doubt on the concept as a useful variable in the study of international politics (critical works include Hopf 1994; Mercer 1996; Press 2005). Harvey and Mitton

(2017) explicitly address these criticisms and, through empirical analysis of post–Cold War American coercive diplomacy, demonstrate that reputation is an important component of credibility, which in turn constitutes one of several prerequisites for successful deterrence. Much like the theory developed in this book, this approach treats past behaviour as *information* that shapes, in part, the perceptions of an adversary. Marc Crescenzi (2018) takes a similar approach, positing that what states do (their behaviour and actions) serves as information that other states use to overcome uncertainty in international politics. Crescenzi's theory of reputation is much broader than the one I present in this chapter, as he applies it to both conflict and cooperation across the international system. Harvey and Mitton focus on reputation in the context of coercive diplomacy, but also treat the concept expansively by considering both its "general" (established over time and with respect to behaviour vis-à-vis third parties) and its "specific" (established within a protracted crisis vis-à-vis an adversary) manifestations. My treatment of reputation here, by contrast, is consciously bound by the rivalry domain.

In this way, my approach is similar to the work of Van Jackson (2016), who explores the influence of reputation in the context of the US-North Korea rivalry. Tracking the development of this rivalry across several crises, Van Jackson concludes that reputational considerations were important for understanding the initiation of crises, the response to such challenges, and the development of expectations in the rivalry over time. Exploring reputation in the context of rivalry is helpful, Van Jackson argues, because it specifies the conditions whereby reputation is most relevant. In the iterated and ongoing rivalry between the United States and North Korea, expectations about behaviour mattered both in and between crises. Of course, Van Jackson explores only a single rivalry, so it is important to qualify the applicability or generalizability of his findings. Yet this exploration of "rivalry reputation" suggests an important advance in the reputation debate (and one I similarly seek to make in this book). A "rivalry reputation" falls somewhere between a general and a specific reputation. It is less broad than the former, applying to the interaction between particular actors and not necessarily transferring to interactions with states outside the rivalry dyad; yet it also applies across time and between crises, meaning it has broader scope than a within-crisis, specific reputation.

Other approaches in the recent wave have less in common with my own. Much excellent work has been done, for example, on individual-based reputation and its potential consequences for the conduct of international politics. Danielle Lupton (2020), for one, highlights the ways in which reputation adheres to specific national leaders, with important implications for how resolve is ultimately assessed in the context of an international crisis. Keren Yarhi-Milo (2018) applies concepts from psychology to address the possibility that different leaders – depending on their psychological disposition – might have different attitudes about the importance of maintaining a reputation for resolve, with obvious consequences for when the states they lead might initiate conflict. Joshua Kertzer (2016) takes a similar approach, using laboratory and survey experiments to identify the conditions under which individuals will or will not fight to protect their reputation for resolve, and applying those social-psychological insights to historical cases of great power intervention. Finally, Roseanne McManus (2017) analyses leaders' statements of resolve, and additionally argues that hither-to underappreciated domestic political dynamics also play a role in adversaries' perceptions.

The uniting feature of this body of scholarship is an emphasis on first- and second-image variables: individual psychology, social psychology, and domestic political factors. The contrast with my structural, third-image approach is, therefore, clear. Nonetheless, there is no reason to claim that the approaches are mutually exclusive or that one refutes or necessarily contradicts the other. Decades ago, Huth (1997) pointed to the duelling possibilities that reputation might adhere to states or to individuals. The latest wave of reputation research suggests that scholars have become less interested in solving this "debate" and more focused on demonstrating the *multiple* ways reputation can influence international politics, depending on the domain of interest. My contribution to reputation research comes by incorporating state-based reputation into an explanation of a specific empirical phenomenon in a bounded milieu (intervention in rivalry). It less "settles" the reputation question than cumulatively adds another brick to the expanding foundation of research demonstrating the concept's importance for various aspects of international politics.

Rivalry under Anarchy and the Search for Security

While it might be rational to infer intentions from past experience, reputation is insufficient for explaining how and why states *act* as a result of these inferences. Perceptions of the past help determine the parameters of the milieu – put another way, they help the state *recognize* that it is, in fact, engaged in a "continuous negotiation" – but do not in themselves motivate states in one direction or towards one response or course of action over another.

Charles Glaser (2010, 84), while not concerned with rivalry per se, suggests in his *Rational Theory of International Politics* that "a world history that has experienced high levels of conflict results in states often starting their interactions with information that opposing states are likely to have malign motives [and] creates a tendency for a continuation of conflict relations." The reason, according to Glaser, is that " variation in the state's information about the opposing state's motives can produce variation in the severity of the security dilemma and in the state's choice of strategy" (83). The link between perceptions of intentions and state behaviour *requires* assumptions about the goals states have, as well as the conditions of the international environment in which they operate. Both of these elements are the domain of mainstream IR theory, but are surprisingly neglected in much of the rivalry literature.

I have already discussed the condition of uncertainty and the relevance of reputation for overcoming it. But following from this, the paramountcy of survival and the reality of self-help to secure it offer the animating assumptions behind the theory of rivalry intervention. Ultimately, most authors in the rivalry tradition *begin* with materialist assumptions, particularly insofar as territorial disputes are identified as key drivers of rivalry behaviour. Yet these ostensibly rationalist frameworks seem unable to account for the supposed "distortions" associated with rivalry perceptions.

Whatever other interests a state might have, they must above all continue to exist in the international system. While obvious, this basic fact conditions states to privilege survival above all other values (Mearsheimer 2001). Given the nature of rivalry, moreover, there are likely no other settings or relationships in which the very existence of a state is more challenged or endangered. Intuitively, it is difficult to imagine that a concern for survival has any bearing on Canada's relationship with, or perception of, the United States, even in the face of massive power asymmetry that makes it possible, at least hypothetically, for the latter to annex the former. Given the long and established history of amicable relations between the two countries, it is reasonable to assume that Ottawa is not strategizing ways to ensure Canada is not invaded or can defend itself in the event of such an invasion (although such war plans did exist, it should be noted, as recently as 1921 [Lippert 2015]). Yet, for international rivals, the precise opposite is true. Given a lengthy history of inimical relations, it *is* reasonable to assume that rivals will be overwhelmingly concerned with strategizing ways to ensure their own survival in the event of war.

The security dilemma, which ultimately reduces to uncertainty regarding other states' motivations and intentions, is in this sense largely "solved" by rivalry, albeit it in an alarming way (see Jervis 1978 for a more complete discussion of the concept in the context of the theory developed in this chapter). While it is true that intentions are, in the end, "ultimately unknowable" (Mearsheimer 2001, 45), given what has been termed in the philosophy of science "the other minds problem" (Jackson 2011), this does not mean that states do not use whatever information is at their disposal to discern these intentions to the best of their ability. The result of such assessments subsequently influences behaviour. David Edelstein (2002, 12), for example, writes: "In the infrequent case where states are confident that another state has either benign or malign intentions, formulating appropriate strategies is straightforward … if State A confidently believes that State B has malign intentions and State B has the capability to harm State A's interests, then State A employs predominately competitive strategies meant both to balance and deter State B." Importantly, these "competitive strategies" are necessitated by State A's overwhelming desire to survive; the nature of anarchy means international politics is a self-help system – a combination of malign intentions and sufficient capabilities to inflict harm demands that even an inherently peaceful and satisfied state respond by, as Edelstein suggests, balancing or deterring its potential opponent.

In the context of a rational framework modelled on continuous negotiation, in which the push of the past and the pull of the future combine to generate certain strategic imperatives, rivals behave in predictable ways owing to basic pressures that exert themselves on decisionmakers in the international environment. The simple assumption here is that survival and security are a state's fundamental goals. The key consideration is how states evaluate potential threats and the information they use to make these evaluations. The nature of rivalry, as a continuous hostile negotiation, serves to amplify the concerns of the security dilemma – or, put another way, allows "State A to confidently believe that State B has malign intentions." Given the imperative of survival, this is predictable, as is the behaviour that results from it: a concern for preventing an unfavourable change in the relative position or status quo between the two rivals.

This means that outwardly aggressive behaviour can in fact be defensive in origin. Intervention into civil conflict, for example, can be spurred by essentially defensive, not expansionist, goals. Balancing can occur not just through alliances or arms buildups (as typically conceptualized), but also through low-grade conflict itself, short of all-out war, such as in proxy conflicts or offsetting interventions designed to fore-stall advantage accruing to a rival.[4] This might well result in escalation or conflict spiral, as states respond to perceived aggression in kind, but the initial motivation is nonetheless defensive. (To be clear, this does not mean that states engaged in such behaviour are themselves entirely defensive – they might well have aggressive/offensive intentions more broadly – but rather that the apparently aggressive act of intervention or proxy war can be predicated on concern for long-term security.)

Situating the Theory

In keeping with the general trend in IR away from grand theorizing, I do not explicitly situate the theory articulated above under any grand paradigmatic umbrella. Nonetheless, the basic orientation of the theory, along with many of its underlying assumptions, does place it within the tradition of realism (broadly) and neorealism (more narrowly). For example, the theory makes the following assumptions, each of which is drawn from a neorealist understanding of international relations: the structure of the international system is anarchic, meaning states must look out for themselves; states value survival, and are therefore acutely concerned with security; the intentions of other states can never be known with absolute certainty, nudging states towards pessimistic appraisals of those intentions in the name of prudence (in light of the preceding two assumptions); and, finally, states can be treated as broadly rational actors (see Waltz 1979 for the paradigmatic exposition of neorealist theory). At the same time, my theory moves beyond basic structural assumptions, emphasizing, through its incorporation of reputation and past experience, the importance of subjective *perceptions* through which structural reality must be filtered. As with the work of Edelstein (2002), cited above, the key *problematique* becomes how states assess intentions (Edelstein also builds from an essentially neorealist foundation). The interpretation of available information is how any actor – whether a state or an individual – makes determinations about

---

4 For a historical discussion of intervention as an act of balancing on the European continent, see Gulick (1955, 62–5). As an expostulation of the logic associated with intervention-as-balancing, Gulick quotes Lord Henry Brougham, Lord High Chancellor of Great Britain (1830–4), who wrote: "Wherever a sudden and great change takes place in the internal structure of a state, dangerous in a high degree to all neighbours, they have a right to attempt, by hostile interference, the restoration of an order of things safe to themselves; or, at least, to counter balance, by active aggression, the new force suddenly acquired" (quoted in Gulick 1955, 63).

the reality which confronts it. Understanding the assessment of intentions – that is, improving upon the rather simple third assumption that states simply assume the worst – mandates a focus on that process: how does an actor interpret information? In tackling this question, the final assumption – about the basic rationality of states – is unpacked.

Over the past several decades, a significant volume of work from an array of theoretical perspectives has engaged these considerations. At one extreme, ardent structural (neo)realists believe that states simply assume that other states are aggressive and will act accordingly; the implications of anarchy and the concomitant necessity of self-help combine with the "other minds problem" to produce worst-case assumptions (Mearsheimer 1995, 2001; Rosato 2015; Waltz 1979). So-called defensive realists moderate this position somewhat, arguing that states that are not aggressive can effectively communicate or "signal" their benign intentions and that, crucially, the targets of such signals can recognize and appreciate them (Glaser 2010; Schweller 1996; Taliaferro 2000/01). In other words, two states that are fundamentally "security seeking" (that is, neither aggressive nor expansionist) can overcome the propensity for mistrust inherent in the structural condition of international anarchy. This argument is reflected in formal rationalist approaches that emphasize the role of "costly signalling": actions that credibly reveal a state's intentions because no rational state with different intentions would undertake them – examples include investing heavily in defensive weapons to signal benign intent or issuing public threats and/or mobilizing military forces to signal resolve in a crisis (on costly signalling, see Fearon 1997; Fuhrmann and Sechser 2014; Jervis 2002; Kydd 2005; Slantchev 2005). The focus of this work is on the strategic "bargaining" that occurs between states, typically in the context of direct security crises. Particularly given rational incentives to misrepresent resolve and/or strength (so as to improve one's position in the bargaining situation), the assessment of intentions remains very difficult, albeit not impossible.

Because states seek *security*, not power per se, the primary cause of conflict is the security dilemma, defined by Robert Jervis as a situation whereby "the means by which a state seeks to increase its security" – by, for example, building or developing arms or by entering into security alliances with other states – "decreases the security of others" (Jervis 1978, 169). By virtue of the security dilemma, even defensive or status-quo states can find themselves engaged in conflict. The lack of perfect information – precluded because of the "other minds problem" as well as the incentives for aggressive states to hide or lie about their intentions – means the security dilemma can never be resolved entirely, even if it can be mitigated significantly through a variety of means, including by signalling, as noted above, and in situations where defensive technology predominates in the military balance between offence and defence. Central to the security dilemma are perceptions as to adversaries' future intentions. If this question could be solved with absolute certainty, defensive (status-quo) states would be able to avoid conflict.

Despite the difficulty, therefore, states spend considerable resources attempting to ascertain other states' intentions. Edelstein (2002) argues that states employ a "portfolio" of indicators to assess intentions that includes both domestic signals (regime type, personality of leaders, social identity, etc.) as well as behavioural signals (past behaviour, alliance commitments, arms procurements, etc.). Yarhi-Milo (2014), for her part, suggests that leaders are subject to multiple cognitive and psychological biases that lead them to privilege certain types of information (particularly "vivid" experiences in which they were involved directly) when assessing an adversary. Her work builds on the tradition of applying psychological principles to IR made famous by Jervis (1976), who emphasized the role of "misperceptions" in the assessment of intentions. This approach examines the various cognitive and psychological biases that prevent the straightforward and uniform assimilation of information. Strong prior beliefs, motivated reasoning, wishful thinking, defensive avoidance, loss aversion, and other biases undermine the ability of state leaders to assess their opponents accurately (see Jervis 1976; Lebow and Stein 1989; Levy 1997; McDermott 2004; Shore 2014; Stein 2013; Taliaferro 2004; and for a specific discussion of perceptions in rivalry, see DiCicco 2011). Levy's (1992, 1997) "prospect theory" explicitly leans on leaders' perceptions of future losses and/or gains, highlighting the ways in which such perceptions shape decisions about potentially risky international behaviour (for example, initiating – or not – an international crisis). Starting from an *ex ante* "baseline," leaders do not make purely rational decisions, but rather are beset by psychological biases; their baseline means they prefer what they already have to what might possibly be gained. Taliaferro (2004) applies these insights to great power intervention specifically, arguing that such risky behaviour is tied to leaders' loss aversion regarding relative power and prestige. Recent work similarly has foregrounded international status and the attendant concern states have for their relative position as shaping a state's foreign policy (see Murray 2019; Ward 2017).

While the various approaches propose different explanations and highlight different underlying dynamics, there is a common recognition that assessing intentions in IR is *difficult*. Structural and offensive realists go so far as to argue that it is impossible, or in any case irrelevant: given international anarchy, worst-case assumptions will prevail. Defensive realists suggest that the worst-case baseline can be overcome, with the bargaining literature forwarding costly signalling as a mechanism by which intentions can be communicated credibly. Psychological approaches question the empirical veracity of such mechanisms by noting the various individual-level biases that preclude accurate perception.

My argument overcomes these difficulties by focusing on the perception of intentions in a *specific* type of international relationship: rivalry. The structural realist position is too broad, and cannot explain the empirical observation that many states do cooperate and trust one another – that is, do not make worst-case assumptions. Defensive realists and formal rationalist approaches overemphasize direct interactions and present behaviour; the assessment of intentions also occurs outside specific crises or bargaining situations (i.e., beyond "signalling") and when states are not attempting explicitly or expressly to communicate their intentions to an opponent. Psychological approaches are, in a sense, too complicated: the emphasis on individual-level biases and the associated difficulties of accurate perception risks obfuscating the patterned, systematic assessments that can and do occur at the international level. Put differently, the theory I outline *does not need* social psychological principles in order to explain how states perceive one another in the bounded context – rivalry – in which it operates. The perceptions can be derived from the situation in which states find themselves. It might be, as mentioned above, that the micro-foundations of the theory are related to social psychology – that leaders and decisionmakers are influenced by past interactions to infer malign intentions because of some psychological process. However, an explanation that focused on such a process would be redundant, *because the behaviour is consistent with basic rationality*. This was suggested by Robert Jervis himself, the doyen of social psychology in IR, in the passages from *Perceptions and Misperceptions* (1976) quoted above. Indeed, the strength of the theory I present here is precisely its ability to account for differentiated assessments of intentions – *pace* more straightforward structural realism – while maintaining the parsimonious assumption of basic state rationality.

A juxtaposition with Taliaferro's (2004) explanation for great power intervention – although he does not address intervention into civil conflict per se – is also illuminative. Both Taliaferro and I explain intervention by reference to a concern for potential loss, including the loss of relative power that translates into a loss of security. My theory, however, suggests that such concern is a rational response to the parameters of the strategic environment. Taliaferro, by contrast, accounts for the motivating concern in psychological biases that distort rational decision-making.

Finally, it is worth briefly exploring the theory's relationship to another major theorical approach in IR: constructivism. In many ways, the nature of rivalry – even as it is described in this book, predicated as it is on structural assumptions – lends itself to a constructivist approach: there is an apparent mutual constitution of the rivalry relationship and the construction over time of hostility between actors. In this vein, Valeriano (2012, 30–1) takes an explicitly constructivist approach to rivalry, arguing that "[h]istory, culture, and tradition do matter for rivalry onset." Thies (2008), likewise, highlights the social construction of rivalry in Latin America, suggesting that states have adopted rivalry "roles" and established a regional "Lockean culture of anarchy." This formulation explicitly draws on Wendt's (1999) well-known "social theory of international politics," in which a state's perceptions of another state's intentions are the product of the historical relationship between the two, and of the "deeds" – actions – that constituted that relationship over time. As will become clear in the case study chapters in this book, the conceptualization of rivalry I offer consciously incorporates the history of conflicts and crises that occur between states. The constructivist approach to rivalry is correct to emphasize this history, as well as its consequences for how rivals perceive each other.

Yet my theory of rivalry is not entirely constructivist, for a very important reason. Although the history of conflict between states is important for how they perceive each other – and for the sense that future conflict is likely, which leads to defensive behaviour – hostility is not the *mere* product of those interactions. Rivalry is not, as Wendt might argue, "what rivals make of it" – or, as Hopf (2010) audaciously suggests in another constructivist conceptualization of rivalry, an unthinking reflexive "habit" adopted over time. Instead, it is a product of the strategic realities – including the anarchical structure of the international system and the absence of perfect information about other states' intentions – in which states find themselves. This is a key distinction: rivalry is an objective situation, not entirely reducible to intersubjectivity. Valeriano, as mentioned before, believes the solution to rivalry is the transcendence of "power-political" thinking: rivalry is what rivals make of it, meaning it can be overcome by a shift in how it is understood. I am not so optimistic: rivals are compelled to perpetuate rivalry because of the strategic situation in which they find themselves. Again, rivalry is tragic, not ironic; it cannot be solved by rivals' recognizing its futility, but is perpetuated by a cycle of mutual antagonism, rather than constructed whole cloth from that antagonistic history.

The purpose of this book is not to adjudicate among these various theoretical approaches nor to resolve the debate on the assessment of intentions in IR. Rather, I propose an explanation for a specific empirical puzzle: civil conflict intervention by international rivals. My explanation's contribution to the broader debate is its focus on the role that perceptions of intentions plays in the context of international rivalry. Within this bounded domain, I argue, systematic and rational assessments of available information lead to perceptions that a rival is likely to harbour hostile intentions. In a sense, rivalry "solves" the security dilemma, removing uncertainty as to the nature of the opposing state. It is here that the relevance of past behaviour and reputation comes into play; given that rivalry is – by definition – a relationship in which states have experienced past confrontations and crises (and typically, though not always, direct war), this history is particularly influential in terms of how a state overcomes the condition of incomplete information that obtains in the international system.

A Causal Mechanism Explanation for Rivalry Intervention

Taking the theory of rivalry outlined above, I now turn to a specific explanation of rivalry intervention in civil conflicts. The argument is predicated on a proposed *causal mechanism* linking rivalry to intervention: the perceptual dynamics described above shape rivals' decision-making process in determining whether or not to intervene. Causal-mechanism-based explanations are specifically designed to link observed correlations; they specify the "trigger" between X and Y (Mahoney 2000). The mechanism posited here is that conditions X (past interaction, expectation of future conflict, and international anarchy) should produce Y (a balancing intervention) because of M (concern for the future and the need to ensure security/survival).

Figure 1 provides a visualization of the explanation for rivalry intervention. To the left, we see the onset of rivalry. Because rivalry initiation is not the focus of the argument, I include only two basic components here: *political shocks*, identified by the rivalry literature as a virtual necessary condition for onset (Goertz and Diehl 2001); and an *initial crisis*, given that, by definition, rivalry must begin with a hostile interaction. Note that the beginning of a rivalry can be ascertained only in hindsight – obviously not all crises result in a situation of rivalry; rather, they offer the *potential* for rivalry to subsequently emerge – hence the label proto-rivalry, a term used by Goertz and Diehl (2001). Also necessary is a succession of following crises and conflicts through which the condition of rivalry (and the associated perceptions of the states within it)

Figure 1. Visualization of an Explanation for Rivalry Intervention

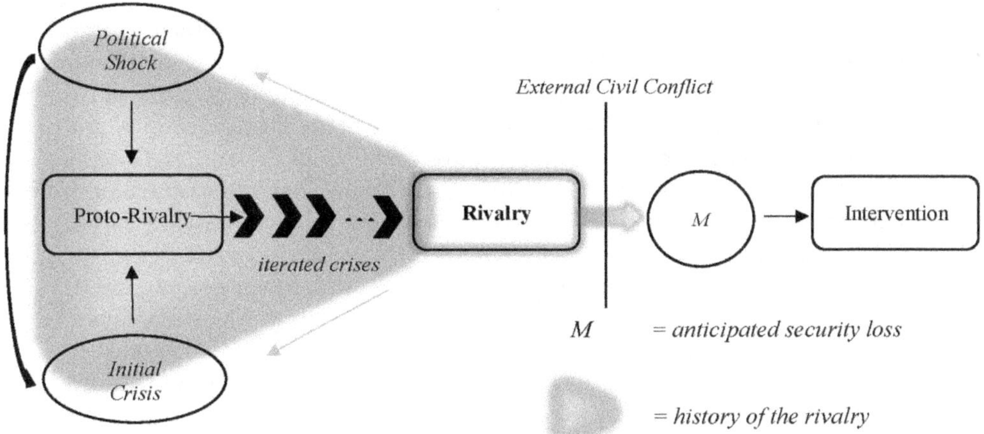

is created. While the argument makes no specific causal claims regarding necessary or sufficient conditions for the genesis of rivalry, and therefore potentially omits other relevant variables,[5] the existence of these crises, their circumstances and outcomes, are the context in which rivals consider an external civil conflict (the vertical line in the figure). The weight of this context is indicated by the blue cone that filters into rivalry. The light blue arrows similarly indicate rivals' search for information about each other's intentions in looking back over this history and these experiences. The rivalry itself is, in a sense, the culmination of this history. Confronted by an external civil conflict, intervention is triggered by the mechanism M of *anticipated security loss*. Rivals *anticipate* (or expect) that failure to intervene will result in a loss of security in the future. Given that renewed conflict with a rival is assumed – that is, the security dilemma is "solved" by an assumption of malign intentions – unchecked intervention will result in an unacceptable shift in the balance of the rivalry. This proposition should apply regardless of whether the rival is the stronger or weaker side. For the former, it would mean the potential loss or diminution of an existing advantage; for the latter, the exacerbation of an existing disadvantage.

---

5 The arrow connecting the political shock to the initial crisis is the recognition that the former typically triggers the latter.

The Case Studies

As discussed in chapter 1, the quantitative literature has established that the presence of rivalry is strongly correlated with balancing civil war interventions (see, for example, Findley and Teo 2006; Gent 2010; Hironaka 2005; Mullenbach 2001; Mullenbach and Matthews 2008; Wolak 2014). In methodological terms, the "cross-case" and generalized effects of rivalry (condition X) on intervention (outcome Y) have been examined. This book cuts in where this approach leaves off, focusing instead on the within-case and causal relationship between X and Y. Given this objective, I conduct a series of case studies using within-case, process-tracing methods. The purpose of these case studies is to evaluate the posited causal mechanism or pathway linking the presence of international rivalry to the decision to intervene in a civil conflict. The case study method is suitable for this purpose because of its inherent sensitivity to mechanisms and processes, as opposed to effects or correlations.

The India-Pakistan (Afghanistan) case is a good fit as a potential pathway case. The relationship is a consensus rivalry, meaning it appears on all six of the rivalry lists provided by Colaresi, Rasler, and Thompson (2008) between two regional powers. The civil conflict into which intervention occurred is proximate to both states. Finally, it is both historically and policy relevant as a recent crisis with significant Western involvement. Given these characteristics, I selected Indian and Pakistani intervention in Afghanistan (2001–21[6]) as my initial case study.

The second case builds on the initial one by examining the causal mechanism at work under broadly similar circumstances – that is to say, to increase confidence in the findings of the India-Pakistan (Afghanistan) case, I looked for a case that matched along several key dimensions. Again, the leverage obtained by selecting such a case is incremental but nonetheless important. In order to fulfil this function, I selected Israeli and Syrian intervention in Lebanon (1975–85). As with India-Pakistan, the Israel-Syria relationship is a consensus rivalry. Further, it is a rivalry between two regional powers, with intervention occurring in a proximate conflict. Israel enjoyed a relative power

---

6 Although Pakistani and Indian involvement in Afghanistan has continued post-2021, the victory of the Taliban in August 2021 marked a distinctive new phase in the country such that the 2001–21 period can be separated meaningfully for analytical purposes. Nonetheless, while I focus on this phase, the lessons regarding Indian and Pakistani competition in Afghanistan are germane to understanding Afghanistan under the present Taliban regime, much as Indian and Pakistani competition influenced the Taliban's first period of rule from 1994 to 2001.

advantage over Syria (as India does over Pakistan), but the two were nonetheless recognized to be military competitors. As in the South Asian context, religion was an important dimension of the Israel-Syria relationship (Jewish/Muslim for the latter, Hindu/Muslim in the former). To the extent that the India-Pakistan (Afghanistan) case reveals solid evidence that the proposed causal mechanism plausibly links rivalry to intervention, additional evidence as to the operation of this mechanism in the Israel-Syria (Lebanon) case establishes, at a minimum, that the mechanism travels, albeit potentially only under specific circumstances.

Having established narrow applicability and plausibility, the next step is to look further afield to assess whether the proposed mechanism has wider purchase. After all, international rivalries come in a variety of shapes and sizes; as a concept, rivalry is believed to obtain between states irrespective of religious, ethnic, or ideological character or whether the states are proximate (regional) or distant (global), etc. Certainly, the proposed explanation does not contain qualifications as to the type or character of the rivalry necessary for it to be operative.

As such, the third case I selected is Soviet and American intervention in Angola (1975–6). The US-Soviet rivalry was global, as opposed to regional, with the intervention of interest occurring in a geographically distant rather than a proximate civil conflict. Similarly, it was a basically symmetric rivalry between two major international powers for which ideology, not religion, was the primary underlying cleavage. These differences obviate some of the key potential confounders that were common to the India-Pakistan (Afghanistan) and Israel-Syria (Lebanon) cases. If the proposed causal mechanism similarly operates in the US-Soviet (Angola) case, confidence increases that a common causal link between rivalry and intervention exists across time and space.

In sum, my case selection proceeds according to criteria designed to maximize theoretical development regarding the causal mechanism (link) between rivalry and civil conflict intervention. I therefore selected cases in which both X (rivalry) and Y (dual-sided intervention) are present. The progression from one case to the next similarly expands confidence as to the generalizability of the proposed explanation. The first case establishes the existence of the proposed causal mechanism; the second confirms its existence in a similar setting; the third broadens the parameters of potential applicability by investigating the mechanism in a much different context. The increase in confidence that occurs with each case is incremental, but important.

In each of the cases, I examine the *anticipated process* connecting rivalry to civil conflict intervention (for a discussion of anticipated process tracing, see Rohlfing 2012). This approach is particularly well suited for the type of causal inference that is required. Conventional process tracing is typically associated with mapping *realized processes* – that is, processes that have actually come to pass empirically and can be tracked as a sequence of events (X1 → X2 → X3 → X4, etc.). Anticipated processes, by contrast, have to do with "the considerations that actors make before coming to a decision and/or committing a specific action. The consequences that actors expect will unfold if they take a specific action that account for their performing the action that results in the outcome" (Rohlfing 2012, 154). In other words, how did decisionmakers assess the situation facing their state, and what was their thought process with respect to the actions they believed necessary to confront that situation? In the choice between action/non-action (or intervention/non-intervention), what was the *anticipated process* associated with each alternative? Determining these perceptions is key to understanding why particular decisions (including the decision to intervene in a particular civil conflict) were made.

Because we are dealing with the decisions of leaders and policymakers to intervene, the appropriate place to look for evidence is in the diplomatic and historical record. In addition to contemporaneous primary documents (such as transcripts of meetings, internal memos, etc.) and public statements (in newspapers, official releases, interviews), one can also examine the memoirs and writings of the relevant leaders and decisionmakers. Ultimately, the extent to which decisionmakers acted according to the logic of my theory can be adjudicated by reference to what they said, wrote, and otherwise indicated regarding their thought process vis-à-vis intervention. Such documents can be supplemented by secondary historical analysis in which scholars have commented on, and provided their own interpretations of, leaders' decision-making rationale, keeping in mind potential biases of particular scholars and the possible distortions that can result from preferred interpretations.

At the same time, however, one can make inferences about the reasons behind interventions by tracking the practice of intervention, indirectly inferring motivation from the nature, scope, and conduct of the intervention itself. An intervention for the purpose of protecting security in rivalry is likely to be conducted differently than one designed to, *inter alia*, resolve conflict, secure a particular outcome for one or both sides of the conflict, or for reasons related to domestic politics. Rivalry interventions will be more concerned with blocking, frustrating, or damaging a rival's (or its proxy's) aims than with helping a particular side "win" or achieve more narrowly defined goals.[7] Similarly, the development of the intervention over time, and the extent to which there is synergy between the competing interventions, or the justifications associated with escalating/de-escalating involvement, can offer indirect evidence of state motivations. If the underlying theory is correct, in other words, there should be observable implications with respect to how the interventions were conducted.

Ultimately, it is the *combination* of both decision-making evidence (how decisionmakers arrived at and justified the decision to intervene) *and* non-decision-making evidence (what the intervention actually looked like) that help support the theory. The latter increases confidence in the probative value of the former because it decreases the likelihood that statements by decisionmakers about their motivations for intervention were disingenuous, instrumental (for public consumption), or inconsequential; while the former increases confidence in the latter because it guards against the danger of inferring "revealed preferences" simply on the basis of behaviour (George and Bennett 2005).

While anticipated process tracing constitutes the method for within-case inference, the purpose of conducting multiple case studies is to facilitate comparison across cases, thereby enhancing the applicability of the findings to a broader population of cases. While even a single case study is implicitly concerned with the broader population of cases implied by the demarcation of a single instance of an event, inferential leverage is enhanced by the inclusion of several cases that track and examine the same process in different contexts. Even if each individual case study is primarily concerned with elucidating the within-case process linking a particular rivalry to a particular intervention, cross-case evaluation (and therefore generalization) is possible so long as each case is conducted with the same goals in mind.

The progression of each follows roughly the same pattern in an effort to facilitate comparison. The India-Pakistan (Afghanistan) case is spread over three chapters because it is both the initial pathway case and a contemporary case with less available historical research – meaning more

---

7 It must be noted that these types of observations would also be generally consistent with Pathological Rivalry; as the purpose of the book is not the explicit comparison of my theory with Pathological Rivalry, however, that each piece of evidence does not offer a definitive test between the two is not fatal. My hope is that the preponderance of the evidence and the underlying logic of the theory will be persuasive to readers, rather than a point-by-point adjudication between competing theoretical claims.

original work (evidence collection, analysis, etc.) was required. None-theless, the key components of each case study are roughly as follows:

1. Nature of the rivalry: a brief discussion of the origins and basis of the rivalry.
2. Crises and conflicts: a brief overview of the history of the rivalry, highlighting the key events that established the relationship and, crucially, informed the perceptions that rivals have of each other.
3. Perceptions prior to intervention: a statement and analysis of how rivals perceived each other at the moment intervention in the relevant civil conflict was contemplated.
4. The civil conflict: a brief discussion of the civil conflict in which intervention occurred.
5. The rivalry explanation: an analysis of the interventions in terms of my theoretical expectations.

Although there is some variation within the cases (including the use of case-specific subheadings for the purpose of readability), the main headings of each case follow this outline.

In addition to a common structure, the cases are guided by general questions related to the *decision-making process* (again, the key variable to be explained is ultimately the decision to intervene), including:

- How did decisionmakers evaluate the relevant civil conflict?
- What broad perceptions did they have of their rival's intentions at the time intervention was being contemplated?
- What concerns did they reference, in public and in private, regarding the possible consequences of action/inaction (intervention/ non-intervention)?
- What arguments did they provide in support of intervention?
- What does the practice of the intervention – how it was conducted and how it played out over time – logically say about possible motivations?
- How did rivals justify their decision to intervene after the fact?
- Were decisionmakers motivated by hatred of each other, seeking to block and punish each other at any opportunity?
- Alternatively, was the decision to intervene predicated on straight-forward assessments of immediate interests (economic, security, etc.) or, as rational rivalry would predict, were decisionmakers primarily concerned with the long-term security implications of unchecked inter-vention and the strategic advantages that would accrue to their rival?

This list of questions is not exhaustive, nor is each question addressed in the same way in each case chapter. Part of the strength of the process-tracing approach is its ability to incorporate multiple and disparate types and sources of evidence to build a particular case – a common analogy is that of a police detective piecing together available clues to reach a conclusion. While each case study must grapple with the specific evidence that is available, the general focus is on unpacking the decision-making process. One can track how each state perceived the other, how they evaluated potential intervention, and what the comparative motivations for becoming involved in the relevant ongoing civil conflict ultimately were. To the extent that such evaluations and motivations are consistent in terms of the perceptions and thought processes leading to intervention, cross-case comparisons can incrementally increase our confidence as to the common operation of a particular causal mechanism across time and space.

Key Terms

Before continuing, I briefly characterize and define two key concepts pertaining to the argument I present in this book: civil conflict and intervention.

Civil Conflict

The argument asserts that rivals intervene in ongoing "civil conflicts." What is meant by this term? James Fearon (2007, 3) defines civil war as "a violent conflict within a country fought by organized groups that aim to take power at the center or in a region, or to change government policies." Whether violence constitutes "war" or "conflict" typically turns on a threshold number of battle-related deaths. In a more comprehensive definition, for example, Doyle and Sambanis (2000, 2006) consider a civil *war* to be an armed conflict that meets the following criteria: (a) the war has caused more than 1,000 battle deaths; (b) the war represented a challenge to the sovereignty of an internationally recognized state; (c) the war occurred within the recognized boundary of that state; (d) the war involved the state as one of the principal combatants; and (e) the rebels were able to mount an organized military opposition to the state and to inflict significant casualties on the state. Gleditsch et al. (2016), meanwhile, specify twenty-five battle deaths (in one calendar year) as the marker of civil *conflict*, with the further condition that at least one of the combatants be the government of a state.

For present purposes the parsimonious definition offered by Fearon is sufficient. The three civil conflicts (Afghanistan, Lebanon, Angola) that serve as case studies in this book are typically and generally identified as such. In each instance, two or more organized groups (including the nominal government) fought for power and/or control of territory. The theory I present should apply to all such cases, provided the other boundary conditions related to the theory are present. Which is to say, the size or scope of the civil conflict should not affect whether balancing intervention occurs, so long as the case satisfies the condition of organized groups using violence to vie for power, authority, and/or territory.

Intervention

Similarly, the argument is that rivals "intervene" in these civil conflicts. What type of behaviour satisfies this condition? The definition of intervention I use follows that developed by Regan (2000, 2009), and summarized by Linebarger and Enterline (2016, 96) as follows:

> [T]hird party intervention is the use of an actor's resources to affect the course of a civil conflict (Regan 2000: 9). These resources may be spent in a variety of ways that include, but are not limited to the following: (1) diplomatic methods, which can include mediation, arbitration, or the use of international forums (Regan 2000; Regan and Aydin 2006; Regan, Frank, and Aydin 2009, 6–7); (2) economic intervention, including sanctions, inducements, and foreign aid (McNab and Mason 2007); (3) the deployment of peacekeepers (Fortna 2004); (4) covert or overt support for one of the warring factions in the form of funds, sanctuary, and weapons (Salehyan 2009; Salehyan, Gleditsch, and Cunningham 2011); and, (5) direct military intervention (Balch-Lindsay and Enterline 2000; Balch-Lindsay, Enterline, and Joyce 2008; Mason and Fett 1996; Mason, Weingarten Jr, and Fett 1999).

As with the discussion of civil conflict offered earlier, the scope of this definition means that an expansive range of activity is consciously included within the parameters of the theory. Indeed, each case study exhibits different types of behaviour or policy that nonetheless satisfy at least one element of the definition.

Conclusion

In this chapter, I have conceptualized rivalry as a "continuous negotiation" in which present behaviour is informed by the past and conditioned by the future. Using past behaviour to infer intentions is a rational response to a condition of incomplete information. The rivalry solution to the security dilemma is to act competitively. These concerns constitute the link – the causal mechanism – between international rivalry and civil conflict intervention. In order to assess this argument, I examine three historical cases: India-Pakistan (Afghanistan); Israel-Syria (Lebanon); and US-Soviet Union (Angola). While any conclusions about the generalizability of my proposed explanation must be tempered by the realities of small-N qualitative research, to the extent that a consistent causal process appears to operate across the three selected cases the argument and evidence I put forward should increase our understanding of a complex international phenomenon.

Chapter Three

The Indian-Pakistani Rivalry

In the next three chapters, I examine my proposed explanation for rivalry intervention in the context of Indian and Pakistani intervention in Afghanistan. As I show, conventional assessments of the rationale motivating the two countries to become involved in Afghanistan could benefit greatly from a more nuanced understanding of rivalry dynamics. Pakistan's calculus, in particular, is better understood through the future-oriented defensive prism I outlined earlier. That view better accounts for the persistence and obstinacy displayed by Pakistani decisionmakers, while refuting idiosyncratic explanations that emphasize paranoia, emotional hatred, bureaucratic interests, and other factors implying mere incompetence or malevolence on the part of Islamabad.

Before examining intervention in Afghanistan directly, however, I begin, in this chapter, by providing the relevant background of the overarching rivalry itself. First, I describe the nature of the rivalry. The *basis* of a specific rivalry can take a variety of forms, while the underlying *dynamic* of rivalry – the defensive motivations for behaviour in the rivalry context – is consistent across time and space. Second, I offer a brief history of the crises, conflicts, and wars between India and Pakistan over the preceding decades. Given the centrality of past interactions to the concept of rivalry as offered in this book, familiarity with the pattern and development of the rivalry is necessary to appreciate the influence such interactions had (and have) on perceptions of present circumstances and, even more important, expectations of future conflict. This discussion sets the context for the chapters that follow, in which the competing interventions in Afghanistan by these long-standing international rivals are directly engaged.

The Nature of the Rivalry

The rivalry between India and Pakistan is first and foremost territorial: the partition of British India in 1947 immediately triggered competition over particular tracts of land as well as a contested border. It is also religious: the specifically Muslim character of newly created Pakistan was the basis of Pakistani nationalism and the fundamental feature of the country itself. Juxtaposition with Hindu India quickly became a core component of national identity. Although India was and continues to be avowedly secular, Hindu nationalism is nonetheless a feature of its domestic politics, and the relationship with Pakistan is often viewed through a religious lens. Finally, the rivalry is "positional" (Colaresi, Rasler, and Thompson 2008) in power-political terms, as each country is a significant economic and military power in the South Asian region – even if India is generally dominant in this regard and has extraregional power-political ambitions that Pakistan cannot similarly pursue. Given the scope of this positional competition, the rivalry can be characterized as regional (as opposed to global, as in the case of the US-Soviet rivalry discussed in chapter 7). The content of the rivalry is therefore a mélange of territorial, religious, and strategic (at the regional level) dimensions. Each dimension plays a role in defining the parameters of the relationship; they constitute the stakes, as it were, of what is being contested.

Outwardly, this can lead to assumptions regarding the purported motivation of specific behaviour. Religious divisions resonate, to varying degrees, with both citizens and decisionmakers alike. Passion, hatred, and other nakedly human emotions (jealousy, revenge, even forgiveness and compassion) are natural corollaries of religious identities. Moreover, territorial disputes are tinctured with religious connotations. The question of control over Kashmir typically is couched in terms of Muslim irredentism and Pakistan's desire to claim territory inhabited by its co-religionists. More generally, conflict and competition between India and Pakistan are often considered to contain a religious component, either overt or implicit.

The prospect of regional influence, and the strategic and economic opportunities that correspond with advancing national interests, similarly suggest motivations for expansion and even offensive, aggressive behaviour. Gaining access to energy markets in Central Asia is a motivation for both countries, as is military power projection with respect to both land and (particularly in the Indian case) sea. New Delhi and Islamabad act to expand, enhance, and enlarge their economic and strategic interests. Like all states, the pursuit of such interests forms the basis for much of their foreign policy. These motivations inevitably influence the rivalry, but are not in themselves conditions of it. *The important consideration is that neither India nor Pakistan is exclusively defensive in terms of its outward orientation.* Yet, even if the basis of such behaviour is not rivalry, it relates to the rivalry insofar as each state's behaviour is interpreted by the other through a rivalry lens. Thus, the momentum of rivalry, or the perpetuation of it, is potentially fuelled by behaviour that is largely inevitable, and anyway incidental to it. To argue, as I do, that rivalry is defensive is not to suggest that rivals behave only defensively; rather, the component of the relationship that is attributable to rivalry – that makes such relationships *distinct* from other dyadic relationships in the international system – is that motivated by defensive concerns. Rivalry is present when defensive concerns become dominant and produce behaviour inexplicable from a more straightforward cost-benefit analysis – that is, behaviour that differs from what it would have been in the absence of this dynamic.

Territorial considerations also feature prominently and suggest powerful incentives for conflictual behaviour. Territorial integrity is the *sine qua non* of modern statehood. Territorial disputes are a powerful predictor of both war and rivalry (Huth 1996; Vasquez 2009). A contested piece of land is an immediate and tangible point of contention, doubly so when laden with religious significance, as is the case on the subcontinent. But not all rivalries are territorial, and not all territorial disputes result in rivalry. They are therefore not reducible one to the other.

All of the above suggests varying dimensions of the India-Pakistan rivalry. All such dimensions undoubtedly contribute to how the rivalry plays out, and any accurate discussion of the relations – and conflicts – between the two countries generally would require some consideration of each. Moreover, for comparative purposes, it is helpful to juxtapose the nature of the India-Pakistan rivalry with that of Israel-Syria (chapter 6) and the US-USSR (chapter 7). Each rivalry is different in terms of the dimensions that provide its content, yet each is united in the underlying dynamic of rivalry within which this content operates. The point is to avoid stripping away the historical complexity of a particular case while nonetheless extracting what is consistent between cases separated by time and space. Religion, territory, regional power – each characterizes to varying degrees the exchanges between India and Pakistan; the product of these exchanges has been rivalry, with an emergent logic of its own. If rivalry is about the expectation of future conflict, it is assumed that conflict likely will break out because of one of these three dimensions.

What pattern of exchanges led to this rivalry? Again, the narrative is important in what it reveals about the development of perceptions and reputation between the rivals. I make no causal claims linking one crisis or conflict with the next; rather, my purpose is to illustrate and establish that these crises and conflicts have had a cumulative effect on how the rivals perceive each other and, consequently, on what they anticipate the rival might do in the future. It is these perceptions, I argue, that ultimately determined the two countries' behaviour (and policy) vis-à-vis Afghanistan.

Crises and Conflict, 1947–2001

In 1947, centuries of British colonial rule on the subcontinent came to an end, and with it the creation – in a process that was by all accounts rushed and on occasion haphazard and arbitrary – of the two sovereign nations of India and Pakistan. The two countries were born in bloodshed, as internecine violence and massacres between Hindu and Muslim communities – particularly in the province of Punjab, which a large segment of the new border bisected – raged tit-for-tat between dislocated populations. The two countries quickly found themselves in confrontation, as the question of territorial control over the region of Jammu and Kashmir could not be settled definitively.

The creation of the two countries was thus the genesis of war over disputed territory. Two key elements identified by the rivalry literature – a political shock (partition and the birth of the two countries) and a territorial dispute (the First Kashmir War) – were present for the birth of the India-Pakistan rivalry (on political shocks, see Goertz and Diehl 2001; on the importance of territorial disputes, see, in particular, Vasquez 2009). It is not surprising, then, that the India-Pakistan dyad is often cited as an "archetypal" rivalry and invoked as a clear example of the underlying concept. The relationship is included on virtually every list of international rivalries, no matter the coding or selection criteria (Geller 2005; Goertz, Diehl, and Saeedi 2005; see also Colaresi, Rasler, and Thompson 2008).

The rivals have fought four wars and undergone numerous crises and lower-level confrontations. The First Kashmir War was never formally resolved, as neither Pakistan nor India was satisfied with the status quo that had been established. The years following the war were punctuated with additional crises, including two (in 1956 and then more significantly in 1965) over the Rann of Kutch, a disputed territory in the marshlands along the southern border. The Second Kashmir War, in 1965, began similarly to the first, with Pakistan supporting a cross-border infiltration of guerilla fighters – supported by a limited number of regular troops – in an effort to set off an internal uprising against

Indian rule. The infiltration succeeded in creating small-scale chaos and violence but little else – no major uprising was triggered, and Indian forces eventually were able to quell the unrest.

Six years later, the rivals were at it again. Unlike the two wars over Kashmir that preceded it, the Indo-Pakistani War of 1971 was initiated by India, which seized on the vulnerability generated by a political crisis in Pakistan to score a significant blow against its rival. Civil unrest in East Pakistan[1] precipitated Indian involvement (the use of air cover) on the side of guerillas fighting against the Pakistani government. Pressured by this escalation, Pakistan conducted an air attack on India's northern air bases, formally beginning the international war on 3 December (Dixit 2002). Indian victory was decisive, the effects on Pakistan devastating. East Pakistan became the newly independent nation of Bangladesh, resulting in the loss of roughly 15 per cent of Pakistan's territory and, even more alarmingly, nearly 60 per cent of its population (Sathasivam 2005). The dismemberment of their state and the "blitzkrieg" tactics of the Indian armed forces were to have a lasting effect on the calculations of Pakistan's military planners.

Although not a direct conflict or crisis between India and Pakistan per se, the Soviet invasion of Afghanistan in the winter of 1979 constituted another important event in the evolving South Asian security situation. The primary outcome of the invasion was to solidify the superpower alignment of both India (pro-Soviet) and Pakistan (pro-US) respectively, with the Americans in particular investing heavily in Pakistan's military capabilities.

Robert Wirsing (2007) details a personal anecdote in this regard. While chairing a public seminar at Islamabad's Institute of Strategic Studies in the early 1980s, Wirsing listened to a speech by the head of Pakistan's air force, Air Chief Marshall M. Anwar Shamim. The topic was the Reagan administration's sale of forty F-16 combat aircraft to Pakistan, a deal designed to augment Pakistan's capabilities with an eye to the Soviet presence in Afghanistan: "In the course of Shamim's remarks, he showed a slide of the F-16's combat range. The concentric circles depicting its range were drawn over India, to Pakistan's east, not over Afghanistan, where the proxy war to free Pakistan's western neighbour of its Soviet invaders was then at its height. Shamim's tacit acknowledgement that the F-16 purchase was done with India fixed

---

1 At partition, two "wings" of Pakistan were created, West and East, separated by over 1,000 miles of Indian territory. This geographical incongruity was from the outset a source of anxiety for India, as it presented the possibility of a two-front war against a single enemy.

indelibly in Pakistani minds struck me at the time as curiously symptomatic of an infirmity in that era's U.S.-Pakistan strategic alliance" (Wirsing 2007, 152).

This "infirmity" presaged the American experience in post-2001 Afghanistan, as its ostensible partners in Islamabad would remain fixated on the Indian enemy to the detriment of the American anti-insurgent effort. Planning for future conventional combat with India overrode other considerations – then, as later, the United States appeared unable to grasp the logic of this calculation or the strength of the imperative from the Pakistani point of view.

In 1984, a brief military confrontation occurred over control of the Siachen Glacier, a remote and forbidding strip of territory that forms part of the Himalayan mountain range. The Siachen dispute highlights the continuous and ongoing nature of the India-Pakistan relationship. A minor military skirmish over a relatively unimportant and remote piece of territory makes little sense in the context of an isolated, one-off confrontation. The salience of Siachen can be appreciated only by recognizing that it constitutes not a distinct crisis or episode of conflict, but rather a visible flare, following an initial outburst at partition, of a conflict that has never ended.

In the fall of 1986, a series of Indian military manoeuvres initiated the so-called Brasstacks crisis (Wirsing 2003). The ostensible goal of the manoeuvres was to assess Indian military capabilities and to implement new organizational tactics recently developed by leaders in the Indian armed forces. Many Pakistani observers, however (both then and even now), maintained that ulterior – even aggressive – motives underlay the exercises (Bajpai 1995). Little direct evidence exists to suggest India planned to parlay the exercises into overt military aggression, yet many analysts nonetheless agree that India was keen to send a warning message to Pakistan, given Islamabad's increasing support for Sikh separatists in the Punjab. Thus, as Ganguly (2001, 85) notes, "embedded in the Brasstacks military exercise was an element of coercive diplomacy."

In the end, India could not assuage Pakistan's concerns adequately, despite assurances from the highest level of the Indian military as to its benign intentions, and so Islamabad opted to extend ongoing military exercises past their previously scheduled end date in order to maintain military preparedness in the border region (Ganguly 2001). Thus, each country, conducting ostensibly benign military exercises, aggravated fears in its counterpart to the point of a stand-off along the border. Tensions eased, finally, only after extensive high-level discussions and, crucially, the negotiated withdrawal of troops from the border region.

Throughout the 1990s, tensions over Kashmir continued to plague relations. The flaring of an internal political crisis in the region in late 1989 touched off an international crisis that threatened to spill over into war, with accusations of fomenting unrest levied at Pakistan and concomitant military manoeuvres generating yet another stand-off between the two militaries (Wirsing 2003). In April 1990, as India increased its troop presence in Kashmir to quell a rising insurgency – again believing Pakistan was to blame for much of its intensity – Islamabad mobilized forces in the region and began calling up military reserves, declaring it was ready to "meet the challenge" posed by Indian forces (Ganguly 2001, 94; see also Fair 2014).

In 1999, Pakistani troops crossed the Line of Control in the remote and icy Kargil region of Kashmir, and seized a series of Indian military outposts. India declared the move a clear breach of the Simla Agreement reached after the 1971 war (Wolpert 2010), and sought to regain the outposts through the use of force, including extensive aerial bombardment (Operation Vijay) and ground assaults on surrounding Pakistani positions. Indian forces then attempted to regain the outposts directly by mounting difficult and treacherous charges up the mountains, incurring heavy casualties but eventually pushing Pakistani forces out (Ganguly 2001).

Just a few years later, relations reached another low ebb, as massive military mobilization led to what many analysts consider a near-miss nuclear exchange. In the wake of Kargil came an increase of insurgent and terrorist activity in Kashmir, fomented, if not controlled, by Pakistan and its Inter-Services Intelligence (ISI) agency. In December 2001, a terrorist attack on the Indian parliament prompted New Delhi to mobilize military assets to the border (Operation Parakram), and threaten retaliatory consequences against Pakistan itself if Islamabad failed to deal with terror groups operating from its soil (Raghavan 2009). Islamabad responded in kind, positioning its own troops and military assets along the border, precipitating a stand-off involving approximately one million soldiers belonging, ominously, to two nuclear weapons states (Ganguly and Kapur 2010).

In May 2002, another attack – this time on an Indian army camp – aroused more anger in New Delhi, which now threatened an even broader military retaliation than the one initially planned; not just targets and territory in Kashmir, but those farther south (including in the Thar Desert) were now reportedly in play. This generated increased anxiety in Islamabad, with several officials intimating that the nuclear option was being considered as possible retaliation for any such attacks (Davis 2011).

Perceptions in 2001

The above narrative provides context for the case study of intervention in Afghanistan covered over the next two chapters. By 2001, New Delhi had over a half-century of behaviour informing its assessment of Pakistan's intentions and objectives and, just as important, its understanding of the tactics Islamabad was likely to employ to achieve them. At the turn of the twenty-first century, these perceptions were not those of unremitting hostility: a more accurate description would be a generally *pessimistic* interpretation of likely Pakistani motives and future behaviour. Which is to say, Indian officials were not deliriously warning of imminent Pakistani aggression; rather, they were resigned to the possibility of ongoing hostility in the form of the continued pursuit of long-standing Pakistani goals related to Kashmir, Islamism, and regional economic and security interests. In particular, India was wary of the *tactic* Pakistan had used consistently in the pursuit of its objectives: low-grade and clandestine support for Islamist groups in an effort to undermine Indian security. As Chris Ogden (2013, 45) observes, "the association between Pakistan and their use of terrorism against India has entrenched itself within Indian security perspectives." In several conflicts (including both Kashmir wars), Pakistan used irregulars as the "tip of the spear" before escalating to conventional confrontation. As the balance of power shifted more decisively in India's favour, Islamabad's support for terrorists became a stand-alone tactic designed to induce "death by a thousand cuts," a phrase used by Indian officials[2] and widely promulgated by analysts.

From a balance-of-power perspective, Stephen Cohen, writing in 2003, found India's continued preoccupation with Pakistan "puzzling." "It would seem that India," he writes, "seven times more populous than Pakistan and five times its size, and which defeated Pakistan in 1971, would feel more secure," before noting that "this has not been the case and Pakistan remains deeply embedded in Indian thinking" (Cohen 2003, 32). Cohen speculates that this preoccupation is predicated on the belief that Pakistan has never accepted the parameters of partition, and therefore retains its designs on Kashmir in particular, and on the rest of India's Muslim population more broadly, as the culmination of the country's Islamic mission. There might be truth to this, but where does the evidence for this preoccupation – Pakistan's continued

---

2 WikiLeaks, "Prime minister discusses Iran, Afghanistan with codel Berman," 21 April 2009, https://wikileaks.org/plusd/cables/09NEWDELHI782_a.html.

desire to revise the status quo – lie? Cohen provides a partial answer: "More recently," he writes (in 2003), "Pakistan has served as the base for Islamic 'jihadists' who not only seek the liberation of Kashmir, but the liberation of all of India's Muslims" (Cohen 2003, 35). This, more than anything, reinforces perceptions regarding Pakistani intentions. India is concerned about Pakistan because it believes Pakistan to be aggressive; its evidence for this aggression is largely the behaviour Pakistan has exhibited over the course of several decades, and during the 1990s in particular.

Several episodes at the end of the 1990s further entrenched these perceptions. The development and detonation of a Pakistani nuclear bomb in 1998 changed the dynamics of the rivalry; as many have subsequently noted (and as Indian officials themselves recognized), a nuclear deterrent afforded Islamabad more room to manoeuvre in terms of its provocations, both conventional and otherwise. The Kargil incident shortly thereafter demonstrated Pakistani boldness in this new context. Combined with recurring Kashmir crises throughout the 1990s – as well as, of course, the more distant but still relevant memory of multiple direct wars and conflicts – the turn of the millennium offered a threat environment to Indian decisionmakers that set the parameters for how they would consider developments in Afghanistan. I pick up these assessments in the next chapter. For now, it is sufficient to emphasize the relevance of past interactions and reputations for behaviour over the course of the entire rivalry. Whatever the broader public attitudes between the populations or the private resentments of individual elites, there remain systematic reasons for apprehension. Described as "paranoia" by others, India's concerns regarding Pakistan are prudent by its own estimation.

From Islamabad's point of view, the progression of the rivalry arguably has been even more formative. Several of the wars and confrontations resulted in decisive defeat for the Pakistani military. In both 1948 and 1965, Indian military forces pushed towards Pakistani territory, putting in artillery range major Pakistani cities, including Rawalpindi. In addition to the simple humiliation of military defeat, this underscored the vulnerability of Pakistani territory to Indian forces surging at various points from the east. As Sathasivam (2005, 153) points out – and as Pakistani decisionmakers are well aware – "most of Pakistan's population, industry, and arable land are located within 300 to 400 kilometers from the India-Pakistan border. This places all of Pakistan's major population centers, as well as all of its conventional military assets well within the strike range of India's combat aircraft and ballistic missile forces." Similarly, retired Indian general V.R. Raghavan (2001, 94) notes that a decisive Indian thrust at the "waist" of the country could allow it to be "strategically split." These realities are well understood by Pakistan's military planners. "From its very inception," writes Thomas Perry Thornton (1999, 171), "Pakistan was an 'insecurity state' that perceived itself not only as small and disadvantaged but as on the defensive against a real and present threat, with its survival at stake." Such immediate apprehension was the product of the situation the new nation found itself in – adjacent to a larger, more powerful neighbour with which there were territorial disagreements – *and* the experience of almost immediate war over said disagreements. This confluence reinforced Pakistani perceptions as to its "insecurity"; subsequent confrontations further entrenched them.

The most formative and decisive experience might well have been the 1971 war, in which Pakistan was not only resoundingly defeated but fractured territorially, an entire wing of the country effectively partitioned by virtue of Indian military interference. The scope of the Indian victory was alarming, from complete superiority in air and ground forces to naval domination at far remove from the ostensible heart of the battlefield. The reach of Indian forces during that conflict left a lasting impact on Pakistani perceptions. As Kapur (2011, 71) notes: "Pakistan's defeat in the Bangladesh war was devastating. The Indians had vivisected the country, creating Bangladesh out of the former East Pakistan. In addition, they had captured approximately five thousand square kilometers of territory and ninety thousand prisoners[.] Bangladesh ... proved that India could in fact decisively defeat Pakistan on the battlefield. This was a shattering realization for Pakistani leaders."

Also relevant are the tactics by which India effectuated its military victory. New Delhi initially supported the Mukti Bahini rebel group in East Pakistan, offering sanctuary, assistance, and eventually covering artillery fire for cross-border rebel attacks against the Pakistani military. Tactically, this necessitated a Pakistani response, which then brought India directly into the conflict. For Islamabad, this experience suggested an Indian willingness to employ and support local militants as a prelude to direct confrontation. Islamabad's contemporary focus on perceived Indian meddling in Balochistan – the strength of which has long confounded India, Afghanistan, and NATO – is perhaps more understandable in this context. An internal independence movement potentially receiving support from New Delhi presents an analogue to the Bangladesh experience. Again, the trauma of the 1971 war cannot be overstated – psychologically for individuals, whether public or elite, to be sure, but also in terms of its existential challenge to *state* security.

The loss of over half a state's population and one-sixth of its territory is essentially a brush with death, a bullet by the ear: Pakistan is understandably more suspicious than others as to the "benign" intentions of the rifleman who fired the shot.

More generally, the repeated crises and confrontations shaped Pakistani expectations with respect to Indian military responses. That is, they established a clear baseline of hostility on the part of New Delhi and a willingness to settle crises decisively, if necessary. Sathasivam (2005, 11) summarizes Pakistani perceptions in this regard:

> India['s] central role in separating East Pakistan (Bangladesh) from the rest of Pakistan has cemented within the minds of many Pakistanis the following belief: not only does India not have any intention whatsoever of relinquishing any part of Kashmir as the result of some political negotiations process, India is actually looking to taking away [*sic*] from Pakistan additional pieces of territory in the future until there is nothing left of Pakistan. The belief that India's long-term strategic goal is the destruction of Pakistan is a core element of Pakistan's post-1971 national psychology.

Now, it might very well be (in fact, it is likely) that India does *not* harbour the long-term strategic goal of destroying Pakistan. Yet Islamabad's belief to this effect is rooted not in "emotion" or "paranoia," but rather in the tangible *experience* Pakistan has acquired over the course of the rivalry, with the 1971 war, in particular, looming large. Discerning intentions in international relations is one of the most insoluble problems states face, a fact reflected by the lengthy and ongoing scholarly attention paid to the issue, both before the work of Robert Jervis and even more systematically afterward. Incomplete information, the other-minds problem, and the reality of self-help under international anarchy mean states use whatever means are at their disposal to assess intentions and interpret that information pessimistically. Given the stakes involved (state survival), the lessons of 1971 could not but engender extreme caution and apprehension on the part of Islamabad.

This experience prompted, it is worth noting, the initiation of Pakistan's nuclear program in 1972. Pakistan's then-president (and future prime minister) Zulfikar Ali Bhutto convened a meeting of the nation's nuclear scientists and engineers just two weeks after the war and exhorted them to develop the bomb as quickly as possible, having said the nation would "eat grass" if necessary to make it happen (Amin 2000, 78). That the decision was linked to the 1971 defeat is clear (see, for example, the discussions in Ahmed 1999 and Cheema 1996), and further underscores the effect of the rivalry (specifically, experience within the relationship) on determining threat perceptions. A nuclear deterrent was considered a necessary capability in terms of forestalling Indian aggression and addressing the imbalance in conventional military power that had been laid bare by the events of 1971 (Spector 1984). The proximity of this decision to the outcome of the war supports the inference – articulated in the extended quotations from Kapur and Sathasivam above – that Pakistani perceptions were powerfully shaped by the war's outcome. This is not to suggest that Islamabad is fundamentally in support of the status quo with respect to the relationship – the consensus among analysts and scholars that Pakistan is the revisionist power in the rivalry is basically correct, as it maintains an interest in seizing and controlling Kashmir and pursues antagonistic policies to that effect. But this does not obviate the basic lesson that Pakistani leaders have drawn from decades of conflict: that military confrontation with India is possible, even likely, and potentially devastating.

In the context of the balance of power Cohen references, Pakistani concerns regarding India are perhaps more immediately appreciable. A large, militarily dominant, nuclear-capable neighbour is likely to unsettle the security of any nation. For Pakistan, rivalry dynamics amplify these concerns. "Pakistan fears Indian aggression," writes Zafar Jaspal (2011, 54–5). "India's military victories over Pakistan including the partition of East Pakistan in 1972 reinforce fears that India seeks to keep Pakistan weak and subservient. India's preponderant size, resources, technological advancement, and military superiority give credence to its threats to make Pakistan a vassal state, if not eliminate it altogether. Pakistanis perceive that their identity, territorial integrity, and independence are under constant threat from India." These fears remained influential up through the 1990s. The prospect of Indian aggression was particularly acute as a threat given the structural realities of the balance of power between the two states. It is understandable, therefore, that Pakistan is typically considered particularly "paranoid" vis-à-vis India, specifically in places such as Afghanistan (see chapter 6). Again, this reinforces the extent to which rivalry dynamics are not separate from, or independent of, more straightforward balance-of-power considerations. Rather, they intermingle with these realities and together shape perceptions of intentions. Pakistan's concerns regarding India are predicated on the objective threat a large, powerful neighbour represents, amplified by the history of interactions between the two states. In terms of assessing likely Indian behaviour, the possibility of conflict is weighted with the existential consequences of a repeat of the 1971 war. This necessitates, as far as Islamabad is concerned, constant vigilance to protect against Indian encirclement. (Recall that, as mentioned above, the development of a nuclear weapon was and is justified almost exclusively in defensive terms.)

Not all interactions between the rivals, of course, have been conflictual. The Indus Water Treaty of 1960 is but one example of sporadic cooperation.[3] Repeated rounds of peace talks, initiatives, and summits have brought various leaders together at different times.[4] Economic cooperation, similarly, has been steadily, if not always successfully, pursued, to say nothing of the civil society and public linkages that occasionally have brought together members of each population. The Lahore Declaration of 1999 saw Indian prime minister Atal Behari Vajpayee and Pakistani prime minister Muhammed Nawaz Sharif "sharing [their] vision of peace and stability between" the countries, as well as announcing their "commit[ment] to the objective of … nuclear disarmament and non-proliferation," all while agreeing to "intensify their efforts" to resolve issues such as Jammu and Kashmir and "refrain from intervention and interference in each other's internal affairs" (Lahore Declaration 1999). And yet the Kargil conflict promptly followed, just as, similarly, the Simla Agreement of 1972 was followed by Indian nuclear tests and associated tensions in 1974, and the Tashkent Declaration settling the war in 1965 failed to prevent war in 1971.

We see in this pattern of interactions the influence of reputation, both over specific issues and over time. Lessons from individual crises informed tactics in the short term: Pakistan's decision to launch Operation Gibraltar – and thereby initiate the 1965 war – was partially a product of Indian "pusillanimity" in the Rann of Kutch episode earlier that year (Ganguly 1999, 160). Even more important is the rivalry reputation over the years as general proclivities and behaviour reinforced the perception on both sides that its rival was hostile: for India that Pakistan retained its revisionist designs vis-à-vis Kashmir, and for Pakistan that India could threaten it strategically through the use of superior conventional military force. Again, the suggestion is not that the tangible conflicts of interest that remained were irrelevant. Quite the opposite: that outstanding issues remain is a necessary condition for the continued hostility we observe. Yet it is the *combination* of these extant issues and the reputation both states developed as a result of the

---

3 The treaty outlines the procedures and mechanisms for cooperation regarding each country's use of the Indus River; see Indus Water Treaty (1960).

4 In addition to formal war settlements following 1965 and 1972 (Tashkent and Simla, respectively), mutual peace initiatives have been launched at regular intervals over the entire span of the relationship, roughly two per decade. See the discussion in Rajagopalan (1999).

conflicts they produced that serves to maintain the fundamental incompatibility between the two nations. Which is to say, suspicions between New Delhi and Islamabad are outsized beyond what should have been the case given the scope and salience of the outstanding issues.

This point is made forcefully by Thornton (1999, 184) in his assessment of Pakistani foreign policy just prior to the millennium:

> Pakistan's mixture of ambitions, goals, and threat assessment has been out of balance. In fact, Pakistan has faced very little threat in its history ... The focus on the India threat was no doubt warranted at first, and the events of 1971 were painful reminders of its potential, but for a quarter-century now India has been a status quo power and its threats have mostly been in response to Pakistani activities. Preoccupation with India has led Pakistan into costly debacles such as the misbegotten 1965 war, waste of budgetary resources, and policy choices that were probably counter to its values and broader interests.

The associated policy recommendation is, of course, for Islamabad to adjust its priorities and re-evaluate its threat perceptions vis-à-vis New Delhi. Yet such an adjustment is unlikely – at least in the short term – given Pakistan's experience over the past half-century. Confident peace with India might well be desirable, but because Pakistan *also* retains ambitions regarding Kashmir – along with the general desire to promote its interests by expanding its economic power and political influence, as all nations do – it knows that India might react, presumably aggressively given the history.

Most fundamentally, as a function of geography, anything Pakistan does will be of interest to India, a reality that Pakistani decisionmakers obviously recognize.[5] Even if Islamabad were to renounce any and all priorities that might possibly antagonize New Delhi – that is, adopt a foreign policy the explicit purpose of which is to project benign intentions, to the point of near inactivity internationally so as to preclude misperception – the basic strategic vulnerability outlined above, combined with past experience in the rivalry, would demand caution and scepticism. Thornton (1999, 185) himself recognizes as much when he writes: "[N]o Pakistani military planner could assume that India presents no security problem to Pakistan," and elsewhere that, "India will

---

5 Kenneth Waltz (1959: 183) invokes Jean-Jacques Rousseau to make the same point in a different context: "The states of Europe [Rousseau] writes, 'touch each other at so many points that no one of them can move without giving a jar to all the rest; their variances are all the more deadly, as their ties are more closely woven.'"

inevitably remain the principal determinant of Pakistani policy just as the United States is for Canada or Mexico" (186). This last comparison is illuminative; it is largely because the United States is not a rival (in the sense employed in this book) of either Canada or Mexico that such inevitable preoccupation can proceed along more amicable lines; the history of – which is to say, the reputations developed within – each respective dyad suggests cooperation or, if conflict, then confrontation short of military means.[6] The history of the India-Pakistan dyad suggests precisely the opposite, meaning the inevitable preoccupation of proximity is coloured by the possibility of violence.

This applies equally to New Delhi, of course, even if the "existential" dimension is less acute – although not absent, given Pakistan's nuclear capability. Yet the insurgency in Kashmir remains a major issue for Indian security, as does the threat of Islamist terrorism more broadly – a point reinforced by high-profile attacks in the heart of major Indian cities, such as New Delhi in 2001 and Mumbai in 2008, but recognized over the course of decades of Pakistani-sponsored guerilla and terrorist activity. Nor have conventional attacks from Pakistan completely dissipated. As evidenced by the Kargil episode, Islamabad's acquisition of nuclear weapons capability even seemed to augment, rather than diminish, this possibility (Ahmed 2000). Moreover, it is in the context of Islamabad's demonstrated revisionist ambitions that rivalry reputation informs Indian decisionmakers. Given its past behaviour, New Delhi can assume that Islamabad has not abandoned these aims; given this assumption, past actions provide a clue as to how it is likely to pursue them in the future. (For example, India adjusted its security policy and preparedness following the Kargil incursion.) Thus, while India is less concerned with being overrun militarily, it is wary of opportunities by which Pakistan might continue or augment its long-standing policies of supporting unrest in Kashmir, targeting India more broadly using state-sponsored terrorism, and potentially employing conventional forces to hurt or bleed India to supplement or consolidate the gains achieved by the first two tactics.

It is in this vein that Afghanistan has strategic relevance. As Christine Fair explains, "Pakistan has raised and supported several militant groups such as Lashkar-e-Taiba, Harkat-ul-Mujahideen/Harkat-ul-Ansar, and Harakat-ul-Jihad-al-Islami, among others, which operate in India. *All have trained in Afghanistan*, with varying proximity to the

---

6 Power asymmetry also exists, of course, between India and Pakistan (see Paul 2005), although clearly not to the same extent as between North American neighbours.

Taliban and by extension al-Qaeda. *Consequently, India is pre-eminently interested in ensuring that Afghanistan does not again return to being a terrorist safe-haven as it was under the Taliban"* (Fair 2010, 7–8, emphasis added). This theme of regional terrorism finding incubation in Afghanistan would feature heavily in Indian assessments of its security interests from 2001 onwards.

Pakistan, by contrast, is focused on retaining "strategic depth" in Afghanistan. William Dalrymple (2013) outlines the basic logic:

> The idea had its origins in the debacle of 1971, when, in less than two weeks, India crushingly defeated Pakistan in their third war ... According to the Pakistanis' narrative, the dismemberment of their country – which they blame on India – made it all the more important to develop and maintain friendly relations with Afghanistan, in large measure in order to have a secure refuge in the case of a future war with India. The porous border offers a route by which Pakistani leaders, troops and other assets, including its nuclear weapons, could retreat to the northwest in the case of an Indian invasion.

In both instances, these perceptions and associated priorities are predicated on experiences of the rivalry and the reputation for behaviour that has been established between the two states. For both India and Pakistan, concerns are future oriented; past conflict portends continued conflict and present policy is contemplated in the shadow of an ominous future. Given these origins – and the concomitant pressure to err on the side of caution given the nature of the international system – such perceptions will be "sticky" and difficult to change. As a baseline, I argue, they serve as powerful motivators of behaviour. In 2001, both Indian and Pakistani decisionmakers had long-term concerns about vulnerabilities in the rivalry. They were not paranoid or emotional in this regard, but conditioned by decades of history and experience. This is the nature and effect of international rivalry.

The War in Afghanistan

In the course of writing this book, in August 2021, a final withdrawal of remaining US and coalition forces from Afghanistan precipitated sweeping Taliban victory over Afghan National Security Forces (ANSF). The ominous trend manifest over the preceding years – the Taliban insurgency's reclaiming large swaths of territory in the south and southeast – culminated in a defeat for the Afghan government many had come to forecast as inevitable. Even as the war sputtered on over its last decade, attempts to understand this ultimate failure[7] occupied policymakers and analysts alike. (The war's end might, indeed, signal the moment for academics to take up this baton in earnest.)

Consistent across many of these assessments was the perfidious behaviour of America's nominal ally, Pakistan. Islamabad's continued support for elements of the Taliban insurgency undermined first NATO and then US-led efforts to stabilize the country. "The inability to stop [Pakistan's] covert interference in Afghanistan," wrote noted author and regional expert Steve Coll (2018, 667), was the "greatest strategic failure of the American war." Amrullah Saleh, former head of Afghanistan's intelligence services (2004–10), highlighted what he considered the naive belief that Pakistan might "change" – that is, give up its own regional ambitions and security agenda – as the fundamental error of US and NATO strategy (Wittmeyer 2013). While other factors were also mentioned – Roland Paris (2013), for example, noted the "surfeit" of possible explanations for failure, from the illegal drug trade to institutional incompetence (see also Waldman 2013) – the Pakistani problem, as it might be called, loomed large.

Civil war has been the reality in Afghanistan for decades. Soviet withdrawal at the end of the 1980s precipitated conflict among various factions in the early 1990s, each vying for control of, in particular, Kabul, the capital. One of these groups, the collection of Islamist "students" known as the Taliban, emerged as a dominant force in the mid-1990s, seizing control of Kabul in 1996 and acting as the nominal ruling government of the country (Maley 2002). Yet this control was not uncontested, with opposing factions, such as the Northern Alliance – a Tajik-dominated collection of disparate military groups – maintaining an active resistance against them and controlling territory of their own in the north and northeast (Saikal 2004). The American-led post-9/11 intervention dramatically reordered – inverted, destroyed – this prevailing political order. Taliban rule in Kabul ended. Crucially, the United States allied with the Northern Alliance in this effort – even using Northern Alliance fighters as the "expeditionary force" tasked

---

7 The term "failure" here is meant to describe an outcome far short of what was envisioned – a strong, centralized Afghan government in control of a secure and stable country – when the Bonn process was initiated in 2001. It should not be taken as a dismissal or indictment of the myriad achievements associated with improving the lives of millions of Afghans – including women and girls – and the sacrifices of the soldiers who brought these improvements about, even if only, tragically, temporarily.

with seizing the capital, a decision that would have significant consequences for how the subsequent conflict played out. From a relatively isolated group with little control over territory, the Northern Alliance was suddenly in the ascendency – many of its members went on to occupy prominent positions in the post-Taliban government (Maley 2002; see also table 2). Even more important, the Taliban was no longer in control, but would later emerge in the form of an insurgency.

The key dynamic is the 2001 US-led inversion of the power structure in Afghanistan. Pre-2001, the Taliban was the central government fighting off a challenge to its authority, primarily from the Northern Alliance. Post-2001, the Taliban was itself an insurgent group, challenging the authority of a new central government, created at the Bonn Conference of 2001, supported by the United States and its international partners, and heavily influenced by former elements of the Northern Alliance. The war that began in 2001 thus marked a significant disjuncture from the civil conflicts of the 1990s, both in scope – particularly as the Taliban regrouped, reorganized, and re-emerged as an insurgency – and in orientation.

For decisionmakers in Islamabad and New Delhi, the situation demanded a re-evaluation of existing policy. Islamabad, which had largely supported the Taliban government during the 1990s, had vocally – and controversially for many elements within Pakistan – supported the US invasion. If it wanted to continue its support for the Taliban, Islamabad would have to do so more or less covertly; it would also mean supporting an insurgency, rather than a centralized, ruling government. For New Delhi, which had offered moderate support to the Northern Alliance during the 1990s, the question became one of whether or not to support (and if so, at what level) the new central government against an ongoing insurgency. For both countries, a status quo had been upset; determining the parameters of the new state of affairs in Afghanistan – most crucially, who would be in power in Kabul over the long term – became a vital issue. Clearly, the United States and its allies would not stay forever, even if they stayed longer than many anticipated. The future of the region and whose interests would be protected and promoted in Afghanistan were therefore at stake.

For New Delhi as for Islamabad, the war in Afghanistan offered both opportunities and threats. In the context of their rivalry, I argue that the latter were decisive in the formulation of strategies and policies vis-à-vis Afghanistan. Concerns regarding the long-term consequences of the conflict, and what certain outcomes might mean for the ability of the rival to imperil its own security, dictated their respective responses.

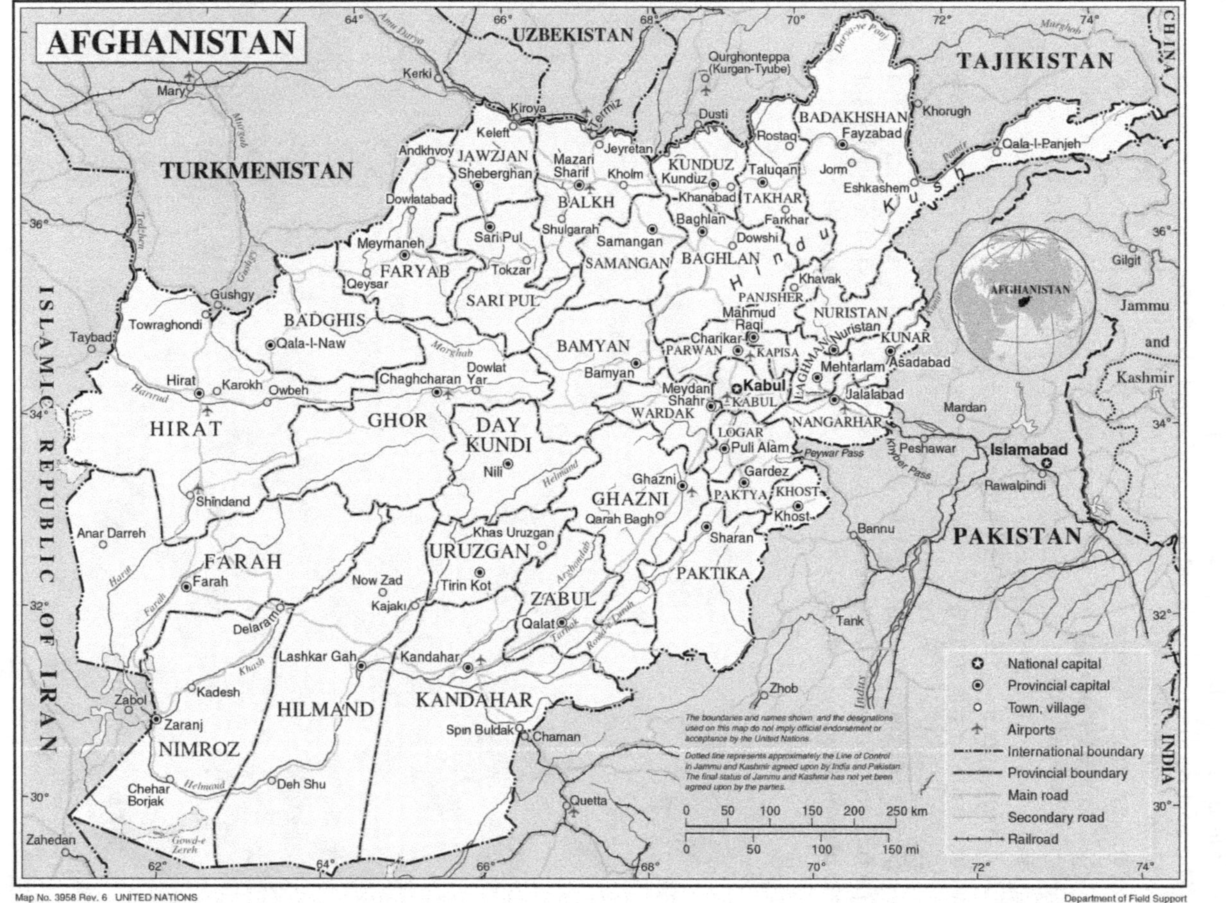

Map 1. Afghanistan

Source: United Nations, Map No. 3958 Rev. 7, June 2011.

Security concerns were not "emotional" or "irrational" or "paranoid"; they were predictable and procedurally rational.[8]

The end of the war – or, rather, the end of the most recent phase of the longer conflict in Afghanistan that preceded the 2001 US invasion and has continued since the 2021 US withdrawal – offers new opportunities to assess and to test the arguments I put forward. At the very least, one would expect Indian and Pakistani competition to continue in Afghanistan, although the precise form and severity of this competition will depend on the particulars of the new dispensation of power and influence under the reconstituted Taliban regime. These considerations are beyond the purview of the chapters that follow. Instead, I focus on the period of conflict from 2001 to 2021, highlighting the policies and practices of the two South Asian rivals that played such a significant role in how the war unfolded and how, ultimately, it ended.

---

8 Rational, if not necessarily *accurate*; states and state leaders can and certainly do make mistakes in their assessments. Correct or not, however, assessments have nothing to do with whether or not they are procedurally rational.

Indian Intervention in Afghanistan

With the history of the rivalry in mind, we can now move to the core of the India-Pakistan case study: their competing interventions in Afghanistan. Pakistani and Indian behaviour in Afghanistan can be best understood, I argue, through the lens of international rivalry. This does not mean that rivalry is the sole motivating factor driving foreign policy decision-making on either side; rather, focusing on the logic associated with rivalry helps to explain much of the rivals' behaviour. Myriad additional factors are relevant, including economic opportunities, immediate security concerns (for India in particular), ethnic motivations, bureaucratic interests (for the Pakistani military-intelligence apparatus, for example), political dynamics, corruption, personal jealousies and agendas, and so forth. There is no intent to deny or obscure the complexity of this reality. Yet, also operating are the broader, long-term contours of a political-security relationship at the strategic level – one that invokes existential considerations for both India and Pakistan as sovereign political communities, as *states* in the most fundamental sense of the term. In addition to, and overlapping with, the obvious and predictable consequences of a civil conflict occurring in close proximity – a concern for political influence, economic opportunity, immediate security implications, etc. – *rivalry* considerations associated with the India-Pakistan relationship itself require unpacking. More specifically, the war in Afghanistan, and the opportunities it has presented for both countries in a variety of domains, has triggered concern about the long-term consequences for the rivalry. In anticipation of future conflict, gains achieved in that theatre are potentially threatening. Explanations that do not include this rivalry dynamic are incomplete: as I demonstrate here and in the next chapter, rivalry considerations have been *decisive* and *dominant* in shaping the two rivals' interventions. Playing the long game mandates behaviour largely inexplicable by exclusive reference to the immediate context.

Given the nature of this case, the available evidence largely consists of secondary reporting and the inferences one can make through observed behaviour. In some instances, interviews with political officials, military leaders, and other decisionmakers have been collected and published, giving some level of direct insight into the rationale associated with the broad policy orientations of both countries. Also useful are the diplomatic cables released by the organization WikiLeaks as part of its "Cablegate" document release. Although the communiqués are between US officials – specifically, reports by the US embassies in New Delhi and Islamabad back to the State Department in Washington – they contain candid and classified assessments of Indian and Pakistani policies and strategic interests, as well as many direct or paraphrased quotations from senior Indian and Pakistani officials regarding a range of relevant issues, including Afghanistan. These communications are typically private, meaning they are stronger evidence of true sentiment or rationale than public statements that might be tailored for public consumption. A potential weakness, however, is that statements might be moderated for Washington's approval or calculated to win US support for certain policy preferences. The available cables roughly cover the period between 2004 and 2010, meaning that, even if the initial decision points in 2001–2 are not discussed, many of the subsequent policy decisions vis-à-vis Afghanistan and, even more important, the rationale and justification for these policies, are referenced (for a discussion of the use of WikiLeaks in political science and IR, see Michael 2015; O'Loughlin 2016).

India in Afghanistan

It should be noted that Indian involvement in Afghanistan did not begin in 2001. Both the broad historical ties that bind the region together[1] and more contemporary geopolitical considerations related to security and economic interests mean that New Delhi has consistently interacted

---

1 In cultural, ethnic, linguistic, and religious terms, the peoples of India, Pakistan, and Afghanistan share significant linkages and common history. The Mughal empire that ruled South Asia between the sixteenth and nineteenth centuries had Central Asian roots and included most of modern-day Afghanistan, Pakistan, and India. Going back even further, the Indus Valley Civilization of the Bronze Age spanned a similar geographical area. Today, all three countries invoke "familial" metaphors to describe even contentious ongoing relationships. See Kenoyer (1991).

with, and cultivated influence in, Afghanistan. Although the period immediately following partition was relatively quiescent in bilateral terms, by the 1970s the realities of global great power politics impinged inexorably on political and strategic dynamics in Central and South Asia. Both India and Afghanistan began to tilt towards the Soviet Union, each in its own way, due to antagonisms related to Pakistan (and driven partly by Pakistan's concomitant entry into the American orbit). In 1979, however, the relationship was significantly fractured as an anti-communist uprising in Afghanistan gave way to Soviet invasion. (India reluctantly supported the Soviets in this endeavour.) During the decade of Soviet intervention, New Delhi conducted clandestine and covert operations – coordinated by the Research and Analysis Wing (RAW), India's intelligence service – against Pakistani interests in the country (Islamabad was supporting *mujahideen* fighters against the Soviet Union; see chapter 5). The descent of Afghanistan into full civil war during the 1990s saw more concerted Indian efforts – given the close cooperation between Pakistan's ISI and various Islamist groups – to counter Pakistani influence in the country. As the Taliban gained control with aid from ISI, India began cultivating a relationship with the Northern Alliance, the Taliban's primary challenger (Maley 2002).

For India, the key consideration during this period was the connection between Islamism in Afghanistan and instability in Kashmir. Pramit Pal Chaudhuri, foreign affairs editor for the *Hindustan Times* and a member of India's National Security Advisory Board, summarizes the policy logic that obtained at the time: "[U]ltimately the game is how do you make Afghans strong enough to fight Pakistan … If Pakistan were to be bogged down, it will be fine by [India]. And [India] will get another five to ten years of relative peace on [their] border with Pakistan" (quoted in Paliwal 2017, 122). In other words, the defeat of the Taliban was not the primary goal for New Delhi, but rather the frustration of Pakistani influence. Further, such an outcome was desirable not for its own sake – as a way of punishing Pakistan, or exercising some sort of cathartic revenge, or even as an offensive tactic to "bleed" Pakistan to change the relative balance of power between the two nations – but rather for the perceived security gains to be achieved insofar as a bogged-down Pakistan might be distracted, or have resources diverted, from the Kashmir issue and the India-Pakistan border more generally. As an Indian military official was quoted saying in March 2001, explaining India's support for the Northern Alliance: "The situation in Afghanistan cannot be ignored as it impinges directly on the … Kashmir insurgency" (quoted in Bedi 2001).

This context is relevant for understanding the dynamics of Indian involvement in Afghanistan following the US invasion in 2001. In the aftermath of 9/11, the United States toppled the Taliban regime with only a few troops on the ground by essentially supercharging the Northern Alliance and using it as an expeditionary force. This meant that Northern Alliance personnel were well positioned in terms of the post-2001 Afghan power structure, and that India, given its historical support for the Northern Alliance, was by extension in a good place to exert expanded influence in the country. Yet New Delhi's relationship with the Northern Alliance was almost entirely instrumental. It took initial advantage of the connection in terms of cultivating post-invasion influence, but moved away as soon as it was expedient. Although both India and the Northern Alliance were happy to see the Taliban overturned, India never shared the Northern Alliance's goal of a Tajik-dominated central Afghan government; in the long term, the mitigation of instability and extremism probably would require some form of involvement by the Pashtuns, considering their demographic dominance in Afghan society (Pant 2012). To the extent that Pashtuns would be an integral part of the new provisional government, India was eager to cultivate new relationships. Those elements of the Northern Alliance – for example, leaders such as Younus Qanooni and Abdullah Adbullah – who would be politically involved would be useful. Others – in particular, militant elements, long supported on the battlefield – became less relevant to Indian aims and were largely dropped. The new focus was on the emerging post-Taliban government.

The negotiations at the Bonn Conference in 2001 involved, in particular, how the Northern Alliance would share power with other elements and groups within Afghan society. While the Northern Alliance was the most powerful faction represented at Bonn – other factions represented exiled Afghan elites of the so-called Rome Group, such as the "royalists," loyal to the deposed king Zahir Shah, and Pashtun tribal leaders of the Peshawar Group, neither of which controlled much, if any, territory – the international community believed that a broader-based government would be necessary for stability. For the Northern Alliance, the long-standing opposition force fighting the Taliban and fresh off of victory in Kabul, where it had reclaimed the various ministries, palaces, and barracks, the prospect of relinquishing some of its newfound control was unlikely to be popular (Dobbins 2008). Indeed, prominent Northern Alliance leader Burhanuddin Rabbani urged his followers to boycott discussions; this exhortation was ultimately ignored, but there was genuine concern that talks could unravel.

During the negotiations, India was not automatically in favour of the Northern Alliance's preferred positions. On the question of who would lead the new government, for example, the Indian delegation supported Hamid Karzai ahead of potential Northern Alliance candidates, with New Delhi more generally reorienting its support towards the new government and Ahmad Wali Massoud, younger brother of deceased Northern Alliance leader Ahmed Shah Massoud, expressing frustration with this move (Paliwal 2017, 198). Lalit Mansingh, Indian foreign secretary between 1999 and 2001, acknowledged that "it is … true that India scaled back its military support to anti-Pakistan elements in Afghanistan after 9/11" (quoted in Paliwal 2017, 11).

Again, this underscores the extent to which India's alignment with the Northern Alliance during the 1990s was a marriage of convenience; the broader aim was always the mitigation of Pakistani influence so as to limit or prevent Islamabad's ability to export and promote destabilizing Islamist violence throughout the larger region. When the Taliban fell in 2001, the best way to achieve such an outcome was to bolster a strong central government resistant to extremist ideology and Pakistani control. Continued support for the Northern Alliance might have offered certain military advantages insofar as a government led by the alliance would have been more unremittingly hostile to the Pashtuns and, by extension, Pakistan. But India knew that Tajik control of Kabul would enflame rather than subdue instability in the country, and so shifted policy accordingly. To sum up New Delhi's basic position: keep Pakistan out, but do so in a way that builds Afghanistan up, rather than merely keeping preferred partisans in charge. For this reason, New Delhi endorsed the makeup of the Afghan government that emerged from Bonn.

Table 1 is a list of the 2002 provisional government members by position, with each member's ethnicity and political affiliation noted.

As this list makes clear, the Northern Alliance certainly remained the most influential group in terms of sheer numbers within the provisional administration. Yet several key positions – most obviously the prime minister's role, but also Finance and Reconstruction – went to members of the Rome Group. Similarly, the composition was multi-ethnic, with eleven Tajiks offset by six Pashtuns, six Hazaras, and assorted other ethnic groups in smaller numbers. Of course, India was merely an observer and unable to dictate terms, but this outcome was largely in keeping with its stated preferences at the time, as outlined by those familiar with the negotiations (see Dobbins 2008). The historical relationship with the Northern Alliance offered New Delhi clear influence – particularly with Abdullah Abdullah as foreign affairs minister and Mohammed Qassem Fahim in charge of defence – while the multi-ethnic and diverse affiliation composition furthered India's aim of a broad-based and stable central Afghan government.

Although the 2001 Bonn Conference set the parameters for the new Afghan government, its biggest and most important benefactor was the

Table 1. Composition of Afghan Provisional Government, 2002

Position	Name	Ethnicity	Political Affiliation
Prime Minister	Hamid Karzai	Pashtun	Rome Group
Women's Affairs	Sima Samar	Hazara	Rome Group
Defence	Mohammed Qassem Fahim	Tajik	Northern Alliance
Planning	Muhammad Mohaqqeq	Hazara	Northern Alliance
Water and Electricity	Shaker Kargar	Uzbek	Northern Alliance
Finance	Hedayat Amin Arsala	Pashtun	Rome Group
Foreign Affairs	Abdullah Abdullah	Tajik	Northern Alliance
Interior	Younous Qanooni	Tajik	Northern Alliance
Commerce	Seyyed Mustafa Kazemi	Hazara	Northern Alliance
Mines and Industries	Muhammad Alem Razm	Uzbek	Northern Alliance
Small Industries	Aref Noorzai	Pashtun	Northern Alliance
Information & Culture	Raheen Makhdoom	Persian	Rome Group
Communications	Abdul Rahim	Tajik	Northern Alliance
Labour & Social Affairs	Mir Wais Sadeq	Tajik	Northern Alliance
Hajj (Pilgrimage)	Mohammad Hanif Balkhi	Shiite	Independent
Martyrs and Disabled	Abdullah Wardak	Pashtun	Northern Alliance
Education	Ghulam Muhammad	Hazara	Rome Group
Higher Education	Sharif Faez	Tajik	Northern Alliance
Public Health	Suhaila Seddiqi	Tajik	Independent
Public Works	Abdul Khaliq Fazal	Tajik	Rome Group
Rural Development	Abdul Malik Anwar	Tajik	Northern Alliance
Urban Development	Abdul Qadir	Pashtun	Northern Alliance
Reconstruction	Muhammad Amin Farhang	Tajik	Rome Group
Transport	Sultan Hamid Sultan	Hazara	Northern Alliance
Return of Refugees	Enayatullah Nazeri	Tajik	Northern Alliance
Agriculture	Seyyed Hussein Anwari	Hazara	Northern Alliance
Irrigation	Mangal Hussein	Pashtun	Peshawar Group
Justice	Abdul Rahim Karimi	Uzbek	Northern Alliance
Air Transport & Tourism	Abdul Rehman	Nuristani	Rome Group

Sources: *Guardian* 2006; *PBS Frontline* n.d.

United States. For all intents and purposes, the Americans were in control in Afghanistan, particularly in the early years of 2001–3. Nonetheless, Hamid Karzai's government (first the interim and then the constitutional, after the elections of 2004) was officially the sovereign authority, and immediately began cultivating diplomatic and international relationships in an effort to boost the (re)construction and development of the country. From the outset, India was a major donor. Significant outlays of financial and development assistance defined the early years of India's support for Kabul post-2001, moving towards more specific security assistance over time. (Direct security involvement – including, for example, the introduction of Indian military personnel – was resisted by both Kabul and New Delhi, recognizing the likely implications for Pakistani behaviour.)

In the broadest sense, India's approach to Afghanistan post-2001 was to support the central Afghan government. In response to a question posed in the Indian parliament (the Lok Sabha) in December 2001, Minister of External Affairs Jaswant Singh summarized the government's belief that "the future government in Afghanistan should be broad based, with equitable representation of different ethnic and religious groups" – an emphasis driven by a desire to incorporate Tajiks and other ethnic groups sympathetic to India and to limit, as much as possible, the dominance of Pashtuns (without excluding them entirely, for reasons noted above), a group with historical links to Pakistan and the dominant ethnic group among the Taliban. He further stated that the "future political structure in Afghanistan should not be allowed to export terrorism or extremism." To this end, New Delhi underscored the "importance of reconstruction and rehabilitation in post conflict Afghanistan," pledging an initial "line of credit of approximately US$100 million for post conflict reconstruction and rehabilitation work in Afghanistan" (India 2001). That same month, doctors and technicians were dispatched to help set up field hospitals for those heavily wounded in the early fighting (Fair 2010). In a short period, the initial commitment would expand significantly, as the scope of the reconstruction requirements became clear and the realities of the new environment in Afghanistan presented themselves to New Delhi. By the end of 2002, India's commitment had reached approximately US$500 million in aid and reconstruction money (Pant 2012). As Prime Minister Vajpayee declared in a parliamentary debate in November 2001, India would pursue "a maximum possible role" in Afghanistan in the years to come (*Asian Times* 2001).

New Delhi quickly moved to re-establish a heavy diplomatic presence in Afghanistan; the embassy in Kabul was immediately reopened, as well as consulates in Kandahar and Jalalabad (Hanauer and Chalk 2012).[2] Consulates in Herat and Mazar-e-Sharif – major commercial

---

2 The alacrity with which such diplomatic links were pursued is striking; as early as November 2001, with significant portions of the country still under Taliban control, India – against the urgings of the United States – "dispatched a team of intelligence officers, diplomats, and doctors" to Bagram airbase, recently seized by Northern Alliance forces (with American support) "to restart diplomatic links with Kabul" (Paliwal 2017, 181).

centres in the west and north – shortly followed. No longer reliant on the Northern Alliance for local intelligence, India used its new footprint to develop "an independent understanding of intra-Pashtun political and tribal dynamics" (Paliwal 2017, 176). This reflected New Delhi's belief that a stable Afghanistan would require Pashtun support, necessitating a drift from the Tajik-dominated Northern Alliance.

In February 2002, New Delhi welcomed Hamid Karzai on an official state visit. In meetings with Prime Minister Vajpayee, the two sides discussed specific reconstruction projects and cooperative activities, in particular in the fields of education, health, information technology, transportation infrastructure, industry, and energy (India 2002). Direct Indian involvement in the security sector was also contemplated. For many, given the historical relationship with the Northern Alliance, it seemed like a natural arrangement, and New Delhi was willing to contribute in this regard – willing, as Foreign Secretary Shivshankar Menon later told his American counterpart, to do "whatever it can to help Afghanistan,"[3] including helping to raise the Afghan National Army. The international community demurred, however, deciding in 2002 at a conference in Geneva that regional actors should be precluded from the security domain (Paliwal 2017). The Indian army was disappointed, but the leadership in New Delhi did not press the point. There was a recognition that such involvement might harm rather than help the Afghan government, given Islamabad's likely reaction. As a senior Indian diplomat explained, "nobody serious in the Indian government is thinking about boots on the ground [in Afghanistan]," adding that no one in the government would "want to do something that the Afghans viewed unfavourably."[4] Only if asked by the Afghan government, the diplomat suggested, would India become involved in security affairs.

Instead, Indian leaders doubled down on, and reiterated their commitment to, supporting the economic and political development of Afghanistan. Indian officials emphasized that their interest in Afghanistan was

---

3 WikiLeaks, "FS Menon tells USDP Edelman India will empower Karzai, wait for new govt in Bangladesh," 20 November 2006, https://wikileaks.org/plusd/cables/06NEWDELHI7870_a.html. This commitment was reiterated again and again by Ministry of External Affairs Joint Secretary Dilip Sinha; see WikiLeaks, "PM's Kabul visit: Terrific opportunity to work with India on Afghanistan," 2 September 2005, https://wikileaks.org/plusd/cables/05NEWDELHI6797_a.html.

4 Quoted in WikiLeaks, "Afghan military donations: GOI ready but needs a push from GOA," 15 February 2006, https://wikileaks.org/plusd/cables/06NEWDELHI1171_a.html.

"a peaceful, prosperous, stable and moderate Islamic state."[5] To be sure, this type of language is often diplomatic boilerplate – Pakistani officials, for example, said similar things throughout the same period. Unlike Pakistan, however, India's activity largely indicated a genuine desire for its professed goals – which is to say, deed followed word. The Indians pursued their objectives through a variety of projects, broadly consistent with the early discussions conducted with Karzai.

Infrastructure, in particular, was a focal point. The bulk of Indian aid was directed towards a series of significant infrastructure projects:

- The new Afghan parliament, built at a cost of US$90 million and completed in 2015 (*Hindustan Times* 2015).
- The 218-kilometre Zaranj–Delaram road (US$135 million), which connects Afghanistan's main Ring Road to the Iranian border, completed in 2009; New Delhi persisted in its construction efforts despite repeated Taliban attacks against Indian workers, allegedly coordinated by ISI to discourage Indian involvement in Afghanistan.[6] The road's construction was significant not only as a major piece of domestic transportation infrastructure, but insofar as it also provided a route for goods entering Afghanistan via Iran (and vice versa), thereby bypassing Pakistan. Additional smaller road construction projects included 58 kilometres of inner-city roads (40 kilometres in Zaranj, 10 kilometres in Gurguri, and 8 kilometres connecting Gurguri to Razai) (India 2009).
- The 202-kilometre 220 kV Double Circuit Transmission Line from Pul-e-Khumri to Kabul and a 220/110/20 kV substation at Kabul (approximate cost US$111 million), which helped bring electricity to Kabul and the surrounding areas (Pant 2016); India also constructed additional power substations in Charikar (Tanha 2015).
- The Salma Dam power project, intended to provide irrigation for approximately 80,000 hectares of land in Herat province and electricity to thousands of homes in the area. Construction stretched over a decade, facing constant security challenges. The final cost was significantly over budget (approximately US$290 million, against an original estimate of US$111 million), but the first water began churning in 2016, whereupon the dam was renamed the Afghan-India Friendship Dam (Swami 2011).

---

5 WikiLeaks, "Under Secretary Burns meets Indian Prime Minister Singh," 11 June 2009, https://wikileaks.org/plusd/cables/09NEWDELHI1209_a.html.

6 ISI officers allegedly offered between US$15,000 and US$30,000 as reward for the killing of "Indian nationals working in Afghanistan" (*Guardian* 2010).

These projects constituted the foundation of India's development efforts, but they were supplemented by dozens of other, smaller contributions across a range of sectors and areas "including infrastructure, communications, education, healthcare, social welfare, training of officials, including diplomats and policemen, economic development and institution building," all of which the Afghan government identified as "priority areas" (D'Souza 2007, 833; for a comprehensive overview of Indian development activity see Mullen 2017). From humanitarian assistance in the form of nutritional programs for Afghan youth, to private sector cooperation projects and development loans, to major food assistance (US$100 million of wheat to help address food shortages), the scope of Indian activity in Afghanistan has been considerable (D'Souza 2007). The announcement, in 2017, of a "New Development Partnership" between the two countries saw India commit to 116 new "high impact" development projects in thirty-one Afghan provinces (Roy 2017).

By 2017, annual Indian aid to Afghanistan had increased in stages from an initial commitment of US$100 million in 2001 (Mullen 2017) to as much as US$2 billion, with an additional US$1 billion committed (*Business Standard* 2018). This level of aid placed India fifth overall in terms of bilateral donors to Afghanistan, behind only traditional international donors the United States, the United Kingdom, Japan, and Germany (Price 2013). The aid increases, moreover, came in the context of rising security challenges, often with Indian workers and personnel as the explicit targets of terrorist attacks (*Hindustan Times* 2010).

In addition to bilateral aid, India supported the Afghan government through a series of preferential trade agreements, the first of which was signed in 2003 (Hanauer and Chalk 2012). Further agreements, as well as "memoranda of understanding of cooperation" in a variety of fields helped spur private business development (Pant 2012, 7). In November 2011, the state-owned Steel Authority of India led a consortium of public and private Indian companies through a successful bid for mining rights in three Afghan provinces – a deal which included an "800-megawatt power plant and 200 kilometers each of road, rail and transmission lines," and was said to be worth US$10.8 billion (Timmons 2012). Bilateral trade between the two countries, unsurprisingly, rose after 2001, though it remained significantly lower than might have been expected given the cooperative relationship between Kabul and New Delhi and the bilateral agreements that were initiated. The 2003 agreement offered Afghanistan significant duty concessions – sometimes as high as 100 per cent – on thirty-eight dry fruit products. In 2011, India removed customs duties on all Afghan products except alcohol and tobacco

(India 2015).[7] In 2014, however, India ranked second (behind Pakistan) in exports for Afghan goods (with a 28 per cent share of total exports) and just fifth in imports (at a measly 1.4 per cent share) (United Nations Special Programme for the Economies of Central Asia 2016). A major reason for this low figure was the issue of transit rights across Pakistan, which Islamabad refused to grant over the years. In an attempt to overcome such difficulties, India was the driving force behind Afghan membership in the South Asian Association of Regional Cooperation. New Delhi believed that Afghanistan's inclusion in the association would alleviate "issues relating to the transit and free flow of goods across borders in the region … thereby leading to the greater economic development of Afghanistan and the region as a whole" (Pant 2012, 10). Afghan membership would "complete … the South Asian identity," said MEA official Preeti Saran to her US counterparts in 2005.[8] Overall, New Delhi's official development aid was supplemented by concerted simultaneous efforts to bolster private sector connections in strengthening the Afghan economy.

India initially avoided direct involvement in the security sector, but this gradually changed, particularly as the international community's commitment to Afghanistan waned. In 2008, in the aftermath of both the attack on the Indian embassy in Kabul (60 dead) and the devastating terrorist attack in Mumbai (166 dead), which were believed to be aided and/or orchestrated by ISI, Indian officials hinted to their American counterparts that the standing policy not to be involved in security matters in Afghanistan "may be under review."[9] In 2009, the US embassy in New Delhi noted in a communiqué to Washington: "Indians are well aware how allergic Pakistan authorities would be to an enhanced police training program but are also convinced that such a program is urgently needed by the floundering Afghan state."[10] In October 2011, India and Afghanistan signed a strategic partnership agreement, the first between Afghanistan and another country. As part of the deal, New Delhi agreed to "provide light weapons, as well as training in

---

7 According to the Indian government, "Major Indian exports to Afghanistan are man-made filaments, apparels and clothing accessories, pharma products, cereals, dairy and poultry products. Afghan exports to India primarily comprises of dry and fresh fruits" (India 2015, 3).

8 WikiLeaks, "India getting serious about SAARC," 5 April 2006, https://wikileaks.org/plusd/cables/06NEWDELHI2323_a.html.

9 WikiLeaks, "India scenesetter for Special Representative Holbrooke," 12 February 2009, https://wikileaks.org/plusd/cables/09NEWDELHI268_a.html.

10 WikiLeaks, "Holbrooke-Mullen visit to India: Afghan police training," 16 April 2009, https://wikileaks.org/plusd/cables/09NEWDELHI747_a.html.

[counter-insurgency] and high-altitude warfare, to the Afghan army, police, and air force" (Hanauer and Chalk 2012, 22). This marked a significant shift, particularly insofar as these arrangements were broadcast to media and members of the international community. Some training of Afghan forces in India had occurred in 2007, and the Indian army had transferred a limited amount of defensive military equipment (armoured checkpoints and watchtowers) to the ANSF, but such activities were always downplayed and kept small for fear of antagonizing Islamabad (Pant 2016). By contrast, the 2011 agreement provided for "regular foreign office consultations and strategic dialogue" between the two countries, with Indian defence minister A.K. Antony declaring "India's commitment to building the capabilities of the Afghan National Security Forces" (D'Souza 2014, 393). The agreement was followed by subsequent Indian affirmations as to the expanded scope of their overall involvement in Afghanistan: "Our approach of high-level political engagement and broad-based development assistance in a wide range of sectors," declared Minister of External Affairs S.M. Krishna in the spring of 2012, "which have been identified by the Afghan government as priority areas for reconstruction and development, will not only continue but is set to intensify" (India 2012). By 2013, India was training over 1,000 Afghan troops (Price 2013). As NATO ended its combat mission in 2014, there were expectations that India would continue to step up in the security realm. In 2015, India provided four Mi-24 helicopter gunships to the Afghan air force. In 2018, it underwrote the purchase of an additional four Mi-24 helicopters from Belarus (Laskar 2018). These transfers marked the first provision of lethal weaponry and, in conjunction with the growing and expanding training relationship, indicated that New Delhi was indeed expanding the scope of its security involvement in Afghanistan.

In summer 2017, during his articulation of the new US strategy in Afghanistan, US president Donald Trump suggested that India might do even more in Afghanistan (Clary 2017). This possibility greatly irked Islamabad – in September, Pakistani prime minister Shahid Khaqan Abbasi told the Council on Foreign Relations that "any political or military" role for India in Afghanistan was unacceptable (Council on Foreign Relations 2017), yet nonetheless suggested the possibility that, as the United States drifted out, India might have ramped up in Afghanistan. As journalist Simon Tisdall remarked in 2011, albeit disparagingly, New Delhi had decided to "underwrite and, in effect, guarantee Hamid Karzai's [now Ashraf Ghani's] feeble Afghan government."

What is important to keep in mind, of course, is that this goal and its associated activities were a means to an end: enhanced security through the curtailment of Pakistan's ability to employ its Islamist proxies. Which is to say, development aid and support were not altruistic. Further, the specific character of India's policies was reflective of its expectations about Pakistani behaviour – expectations derived from experience within the rivalry. There was a strong belief among Indian officials that an Afghanistan beholden to Islamabad would serve as a hotbed for continued radical activity, threatening Indian security both in Kashmir and in the broader region. This possibility was particularly troubling in the context of assumed future confrontation over Kashmir. Destabilization could foment insurgency in the disputed territory and, as in the past, also lead to direct Pakistani military involvement. The period of Taliban rule in the late 1990s supported this perception. India was "by far the largest regional donor" (Mullen 2017, 6), outstripping even Russia and Iran to a considerable degree. To be sure, economic opportunities were a major consideration, as was the desire to project Indian power more generally, as New Delhi pursued its ambition to become a great power. Indeed, analysis of Indian aims in Afghanistan typically foregrounds three basic dynamics: economics, security, and regional influence, the latter often tied to ambitions regarding power projection and great power status (see, for example, the discussions in Hanif 2009; Pant 2012; Pattanaik 2012; and Price 2013).

It is worth discussing each of these dynamics briefly. Ultimately, I do not argue that rivalry considerations were the sole motivator for Indian behaviour; other considerations were quite clearly part of the explanation. Yet the dynamics of rivalry shaped Indian perceptions such that their behaviour was not what it otherwise would have been, given other incentives and interests. Which is to say, a complete understanding of, and explanation for, Indian behaviour is impossible without reference to international rivalry.

Economic Opportunities

As alluded to above, India had (and has) real economic interests in Afghanistan. Foremost among these is access to energy-rich Central Asia, with Afghanistan serving as conduit and corridor. As a potentially crucial component of a broader energy-related competition with China, as well as a means to reduce dependency on Middle Eastern oil, India "prioritized the region" (Joshi 2010, 22). Speaking in 2005, then-president A.P.J. Abdul Kalam explicitly linked energy considerations to Indian foreign policy (Kiesow and Norling 2007). Afghanistan was key to such efforts. As Shashank Joshi (2010, 22) explains: "India is ... desirous of Tajikistan's uranium and natural gas, has invested in Uzbek production facilities, and retains interest in a natural gas pipeline from Turkmenistan. Afghanistan furnishes a diplomatic and logistical foothold in the heart of the region." Construction on the Afghan portion of the long-awaited, and chronically fraught, Turkmenistan-Afghanistan-Pakistan-India (TAPI) pipeline finally began in 2018 (Gurt 2018). Ghani, Abbassi, and Indian minister of external affairs M.J. Akbar were all present at a groundbreaking ceremony in February 2018. Of course, a similar ceremony already had occurred in 2015 for the Turkmenistan portion, and the project continued to face delays and setbacks due to recurring security concerns and disagreement between, in particular, India and Pakistan about how the pipeline should proceed (Basu and Mishra 2018). As of 2022, progress on completion remained slow and rife with ongoing security concerns (Basu 2022). The difficulties associated with the pipeline underscore the extent to which clear mutual interest can be obviated by security concerns.

In addition to energy, Afghanistan was a potentially lucrative hub for regional trade in other goods, both as a target and, again, as a transit corridor. As mentioned, the volume of trade between India and Afghanistan was substantially lower than it could have been; once again, Pakistan played a spoiler role in this regard by systematically denying transit rights that would have allowed Indian-Afghan trade to traverse Pakistani territory. The Afghanistan-Pakistan Transit Trade Agreement (APTTA), signed in 2010 and renewed in 2016, explicitly excluded India, as Islamabad signalled its continued objection to Indian inclusion, even though Pakistan stood to benefit economically from transit activity (Syed 2016). India then sought alternative routes for trade with Afghanistan – in particular, entry through Iran via the Chabahar Port, which New Delhi and Tehran explored and expanded in the final years of the war (Haidar 2017).

Ultimately, India stood to gain from access to, and transit across, Afghan territory. Indian diplomat T.C.A. Raghavan opined in 2007 as to the "the untapped potential of the large Indian market for Afghan goods," citing the "need to open the borders for trade between Afghanistan, Pakistan, and India."[11] The realization of such possibilities, however, was contingent on quelling instability in Afghanistan (as the TAPI experience made clear), underscoring the import of India's development activity and the first-order concern for security. In a discussion in 2006 between US and Indian officials, "[Indian Ministry of External

---

11 Quoted in WikiLeaks, "India's contribution to Afghan reconstruction," 7 November 2008, https://wikileaks.org/plusd/cables/08NEWDELHI2874_a.html.

Affairs Joint Secretary Dilip] Sinha concluded that until the security situations in Pakistan and Afghanistan are addressed, 'there will be no investors for anything,' no roads, no pipelines, even though the market exists for goods and energy."[12]

Regional Influence, Global Power Projection

From a broader strategic perspective, many analysts pointed to Indian involvement in Afghanistan as an important "test case" for India's ambitions as a regional and, ultimately, global power (Fair 2012). India was keen to exert its regional dominance as a signal to China – and others – that it had arrived as a major player on the global stage, capable of wielding influence in its own geographic backyard. In this sense, extending influence into Central Asia constituted the land-based parallel to India's much-publicized naval foray into the broader Indian Ocean; as with power projection on the high seas, dominating events in Afghanistan helped legitimize Indian claims to great power status. (For assessments of India's ambitions in this regard, see Fair 2010; Mohan 2006; Pant 2010; Ogden 2011; and Tadjbakhsh 2011.)

Exerting influence in Afghanistan was considered to be an important component of realizing these aspirations. It also meant that, once engaged, New Delhi was reticent to cede the influence it had accrued. As former Indian army deputy chief of staff R.K. Sawhney explained in 2011, "India cannot afford to beat a retreat from Afghanistan if it wants to remain a major regional player" (quoted in Hanauer and Chalk 2012, 13). Indian professor and national security commentator Bharat Karnad, in lamenting India's continued reliance on US security efforts in Afghanistan and arguing for more robust Indian security engagement, noted that "free-riding offers relatively poor and weak countries or states, unwilling to adequately invest in their own defence, security without sweat, but it is something a would-be great power, such as India, should eschew" (Karnad 2009).

T.V. Paul (2005) has described the structural "asymmetry" in the relationship between India and Pakistan. This asymmetry is reflected not merely in economic and military terms, but also in the corresponding scope of each state's foreign policy interests. For India, in particular, involvement in – even domination of – Afghanistan as part of its regional environment constituted a reasonable foreign policy goal.

---

12 WikiLeaks, "MEA provides A/S Boucher with tour d'horizon of India's regional relationships," 13 April 2006, https://wikileaks.org/plusd/cables/06NEWDELHI 2496_a.html.

A July 2008 diplomatic cable from the US embassy in New Delhi references this orientation: "Indians are increasingly more interested in their promising global future than in their tumultuous regional past."[13] Thus, even had there been no security- or rivalry-related concerns in Afghanistan, India likely would have been involved in the conflict.

Security Concerns

Similarly, even if rivalry had not been a factor – which is to say, if the dynamics of India's relationship with Pakistan had not been implicated in what was happening in Afghanistan – straightforward and immediate security concerns would have been present. In reality, of course, it is impossible to extricate such concerns from the history between India and Pakistan and of South Asia more generally; but conceptually the point is that, if one imagines a world in which all else is the same, save the history of rivalry, and instead India and Pakistan had had peaceful relations over the decades, New Delhi still would have faced security challenges emanating from a proximate civil conflict. Put another way, keep all else constant but remove rivalry as a variable. The literature on the international consequences of civil wars (see, for example, Kathman 2011) underscores the extent to which conflicts can destabilize regions, whether rivalry is present or not. There is a contagion effect, such that civil violence spills across borders, destabilizes neighbouring and proximate countries, and even increases the probability of international conflict (Gleditsch, Salehyan, and Schultz 2008). Any explanation that foregrounds rivalry as a factor for intervention must take this contagion effect into account and take as evidence not just the *fact* of intervention but also its shape, scope, and justification.

India's domestic problems with terrorism and insurgency – not just of the Islamic variety but also with Sikh and Maoist separatist movements – makes New Delhi sensitive to such tactics and the possible spread of instability across borders. Keeping peace in the region is therefore a stand-alone security interest. So too is mitigating the destabilizing consequences of the drug trade, as opiate addiction is a significant issue in India, particularly in the Punjab region (Majumder 2017; Sharma 2011).

The key consideration for the present analysis is whether New Delhi perceived its security concerns in Afghanistan as (a) primarily

---

13 WikiLeaks, "Cool heads prevail in response to Kabul attack," 25 July 2008, https://wikileaks.org/plusd/cables/08NEWDELHI2047_a.html.

exogenous to, or (b) driven by, Pakistani *intentions and behaviour*. Below, in adumbrating the effects of rivalry on Indian calculations, I make the case that Indian security concerns were bound inextricably to New Delhi's perceptions of Pakistani intentions and the associated consequences for the future of the international relationship – the rivalry – itself. Yet the alternative is worth briefly considering. This alternative, it should be noted, is not predicated on the argument that Pakistan's historical support for Islamism and the Taliban were irrelevant to Indian concerns vis-à-vis Afghanistan. It is undeniable that New Delhi feared the spread of Islamist violence from Afghanistan to Kashmir and India proper, and that it blamed Islamabad for supporting these forces in the past. Instead, the alternative suggests that it was this fear, *irrespective of Pakistan's involvement*, that drove India's response: its intervention in Afghanistan.

There is disagreement, after all, as to the extent to which Islamabad actually controlled or influenced the Taliban insurgency at all (I address this point in chapter 5). Further, when complicity was acknowledged, it was occasionally blamed on "rogue" elements within ISI, and therefore not directly attributable to the Pakistani leadership (see the discussion in Rashid 2009). If India believed that Islamabad was not directing, supporting or instigating Islamist activity, it would be more difficult to argue that Indian concerns in Afghanistan were rivalry related. Even if India blamed Pakistan historically for the emergence and spread of extremism on the subcontinent, its concerns now might no longer be tied to perceptions about Pakistani intentions. Ganguly and Kapur (2009), for example, liken Pakistan's support for Islamist militancy to the situation of the "sorcerer's apprentice," suggesting that, having been created by Islamabad, militancy was now out of Pakistan's control and spreading on its own – a contention given credence by the emergence of the "Pakistani" Taliban and its targeting of the Pakistani state (see also Behuria 2007). Or perhaps Islamabad's continued involvement with such forces was incidental to Indian concerns – the danger lies in the spread of the ideology and the groups that perpetrate violence in its name, whether supported by Pakistan or not. Again, this would make it difficult to argue that the international relationship with Pakistan was responsible for Indian behaviour in Afghanistan.

The distinction is not trivial. At issue is the causal mechanism triggering Indian intervention. It is also easy to confuse, given that, as mentioned, Islamist militancy in South Asia quite clearly has been linked to Pakistan historically. But if the weapon outgrew the wielder – if the apprentice broke free of the sorcerer – then it cannot be argued that

India was motivated by rivalry concerns per se. Put another way, was the primary threat the Taliban, or was it Pakistan, with the Taliban serving as proxy? Is the *anticipated process* – the perception regarding the future that constitutes the causal mechanism, the trigger, leading to intervention – at the sub- and transnational level (militancy) or the international level (state-to-state relationship with Pakistan)? The three basic possibilities are as follows:

– *P1.* India's primary security concern vis-à-vis Afghanistan: *Islamist militancy (Pakistani involvement irrelevant, incidental and/or secondary)*
– *P2.* India's primary security concern vis-à-vis Afghanistan: *Islamist militancy as a tool of Pakistani foreign policy*[14]
– *P3.* India's primary security concern vis-à-vis Afghanistan: *equal weight between Islamist militancy in and of itself,* and *Islamist militancy as a tool of Pakistani foreign policy*

In each case, India is concerned with Islamist militancy and the possibility that it might spread to Kashmir and elsewhere, endangering Indian territory and interests. P1, however, does not have an international rivalry dimension, while in P3 rivalry is equally weighted with direct concern over militancy, potentially rendering the cause of the decision to intervene indeterminate. In P2, by contrast, rivalry concerns are primary and dominant.

I pick up the case for P2 below, while also eliminating P3 insofar as the evidence clearly demonstrates that rivalry concerns were dominant and therefore not equally weighted. But the evidence for P1 is worth discussing as well. There is no question, for example, that Indian concerns about the spread of Islamist militancy were genuine and not "merely" predicated on Pakistan's employing such militancy in the pursuit of other aims – for example, as a prelude to conventional military confrontation or as an alternative means to achieve Islamabad's goals vis-à-vis Kashmir, etc. In 2007, Raghavan voiced specific concern about "Talibanization" "creeping into the Punjab" and the "serious implications" this would have for India.[15] While he "bemoaned" Islamabad for not

---

14 Note that these possibilities relate to India's *primary* security concern *as it relates to the decision to intervene*; it is almost certainly the case that *both* Islamist militancy in and of itself *and* as a function of Pakistani policy were of concern to New Delhi. The point is that P1 is a non-rivalry mechanism related to security concerns from a transnational threat, while P2 is consistent with the rivalry explanation.

15 Quoted in WikiLeaks, "Tour d'horizon with incoming MEA Joint Secretary for Pakistan, Afghanistan, and Iran," 2 May 2007, https://wikileaks.org/plusd/cables/07NEWDELHI2101_a.html.

doing more to quell this phenomenon, his concern clearly lay with the perceived dangers of "Talibanization" (Islamic fundamentalism) itself. Similarly, in a 2008 conversation with then-US senator John Kerry, Prime Minister Singh lamented Pakistan's weak counterterrorism policies but highlighted as his main concern the consequent dangers of "Talibanization." He noted that Pakistan had been largely responsible for creating and supporting such forces in the past, but seemed worried that Islamabad might have lost its ability to control them. Absent "control at the source," he suggested, victory in Afghanistan might prove elusive, and ultimately the forces of Talibanization would threaten both Afghanistan *and* Pakistan over the coming years.[16] In December 2008, Prime Minister Singh suggested that the threat was region-wide, telling the Americans "there can be no concessions with terrorists. The terrorists operating against India were the same as those operating in Pakistan and Afghanistan."[17]

Of course, the target audience of this message might be relevant for understanding its tone and content – the United States has been consistently concerned about Islamist radicals taking control in Pakistan, largely because of the country's nuclear arsenal. Singh might have been playing up these fears to gain diplomatic support from the Americans. Later comments by Indian national security advisor M.K. Narayanan might be interpreted similarly, when he exhorted the United States to downplay talk of an "exit strategy" lest it embolden the insurgency simply to "wait out" US withdrawal. "We must win [in Afghanistan]," he said, "to stop the forces of extreme religious ideology from gaining ground. If Afghanistan is lost, Pakistan will definitely go."[18] Similarly, Indian diplomat Dilip Sinha warned against a premature US exit from Afghanistan, stating that it would embolden "fanatics ... and the result will be very bad for the region."[19] Again, the possibility that "Pakistan will go" – be overrun by extremists – is an abiding American fear; by invoking it, Narayanan and Sinha were perhaps trying to ensure continued American commitment to the cause in Afghanistan. Indeed, concern that the United States might leave prematurely preoccupied Indian policymakers, as I discuss later.

---

16 Quoted in WikiLeaks, "PM Singh tells codel Kerry re Pakistan: Enough is enough," 16 December 2008, https://wikileaks.org/plusd/cables/08NEWDELHI3165_a.html.

17 WikiLeaks, "PM Singh urges McCain codel to deliver tough message to Pakistan," 3 December 2008, https://wikileaks.org/plusd/cables/08NEWDELHI3054_a.html.

18 Quoted in WikiLeaks, "NSA Narayanan meets with U/S Burns," 12 June 2009, https://wikileaks.org/plusd/cables/09NEWDELHI1228_a.html.

19 WikiLeaks, "Indian views on Afghanistan: Eager for increased USG coordination, wary of Pakistan scheming, skeptical on R/R," 21 February 2010, https://wikileaks.org/plusd/cables/10NEWDELHI334_a.html.

Nonetheless, Singh's, Narayanan's, and Sinha's assessments are in line with the "sorcerer's apprentice" possibility, P1.

There is recognition among analysts that Islamic militancy and terrorism constitute a core threat to India's security. Evaluating the alacrity of Indian support for US intervention in Afghanistan in 2001, Brahma Chellaney notes that "New Delhi's action to extend full military support came voluntarily and enthusiastically … India belongs to that class of antiterror allies whose cooperation is driven by dire need, *for Islamic terrorism threatens to tear apart its pluralistic fabric*" (Chellaney 2001/2, 100, emphasis added). The emergence and growth of jihadi terrorism in the 1980s and 1990s meant that by 2001 the threat had reached fever pitch: "India's interests in Afghanistan after the terror strikes of September 11, 2001," writes Shanthie D'Souza (2014, 382), "need to be viewed in the context of its concerns over terrorism emanating from the extremely volatile Pakistan-Afghanistan border and spilling into India. A strong, stable, and democratic Afghanistan would reduce the dangers of extremist violence and terrorism destabilising the region." Christine Fair (2011, 181) points out that extremism tears at "India's domestic social fabric" by attracting disaffected members of India's domestic Muslim population and turning them against the state. Which is to say, the problem in some ways has metastasized beyond even a simply Pakistani-based (let alone Pakistani-directed) threat as the ideology itself has spread across the region.

Can India's intervention in Afghanistan be explained by such concerns alone, or primarily? Was the security threat from Islamic militancy and terrorism – irrespective of Pakistan's role – so acute that New Delhi believed it necessary to prevent a return of extremist rule in Kabul in the form of a Taliban or Taliban-influenced government? Was the scope of India's intervention explicable absent reference to perceptions regarding future Pakistani behaviour?[20]

---

20 It is important to clarify that this possibility – P1 – is *not* one that typically is foregrounded with respect to Indian behaviour. It is not a "conventional wisdom" that I am attempting to refute. Rather, scholars and analysts generally recognize that Pakistan's role is important. The point is that they do so without being logically clear as to these distinct considerations (Islamism itself; Islamism as a tactic employed by Pakistan within the rivalry) with respect to India's threat perception. Which is to say, they muddle them together, even as each points to slightly different motivations for Indian behaviour. I tease out each consideration, and foreground the rivalry dynamic as being more important for Indian calculations. In doing so, it is important to consider the logical alternative – that Islamism alone is the key – and to assess the evidence with these competing possibilities in mind. The point of addressing – and dismissing – P1 is that doing so logically supports P2. It anticipates the criticism that my argument regarding the centrality of Pakistan for Indian calculations overlooks the possibility that Indian behaviour has been driven primarily by other security considerations.

The answer to these questions is no. Although concerns over Islamic militancy and the possibility of the return of a radical Islamic regime in Kabul *were* motivating factors for Indian policy, they were *tied to* Indian perceptions about Pakistani behaviour and concern over Pakistani intentions. For India, as Foreign Secretary Shivshankar Menon told the United States in 2009, it is "more of a PakAf problem than an AfPak one."[21] To complete the extended quotation from D'Souza (2014, 382) above, she goes on to conclude that "New Delhi's worries [about extremism] are linked to its view that Pakistan's objective in Afghanistan is to assure itself of 'strategic depth' by reinstalling a pliant Taliban regime." Brahma Chellaney (2001/2, 101), equally, suggests that "India was disappointed that the US antiterror campaign" in Afghanistan after 2001 "targeted the child fathered by Pakistan, the Taliban, but not the procreator." The reason for such disappointment, he argues, was the Indians' knowledge that "[t]he terrorists in Afghanistan have only one escape route from their mountain hideouts – eastward into Pakistan where they can easily blend with fellow Pashtuns. Some of these terrorists could then move to Kashmir with Pakistan's encouragement or connivance. If that happened, India will face greater terror attacks, including major cities." Writing in 2001, this analysis was remarkably prescient, given that Taliban fighters did indeed escape to the mountainous Pashtun regions along the Pakistan-Afghanistan border, and that Indian cities did suffer major terrorist attacks in the subsequent years (Mumbai in 2006 and 2008, most prominently). Chellaney's assessment is echoed in the words of an Indian intelligence officer who, speaking in the *Times of India* shortly after the American invasion in 2001, lamented that "[t]he US, in its immediate self-interest, is going after only the grandson (Osama bin Laden) and son (Taliban) of terrorism, apparently overlooking the hyperactive grandfather (Pakistan)" (quoted in Sharma 2001). Similarly, a summer 2008 meeting between Karzai and Indian officials, in which the threat of "Islamic extremist networks" was emphasized, ultimately shifted to a discussion of Pakistan's role: "Indian and Afghan intelligence consistently point to ISI involvement in regional terrorist attacks, stating, 'terrorism is the product of ISI.'"[22] Thus, New Delhi remained, at the time it was contemplating policies vis-à-vis post-2001 Afghanistan, fixated on the parent (Pakistan), not the child (the Taliban).

---

21 Quoted in WikiLeaks, "Codel Berman discusses bilateral, regional issues with Indian foreign secretary," 22 April 2009, https://wikileaks.org/plusd/cables/09NEWDELHI 804_a.html.

22 WikiLeaks, "Karzai to visit India, be greeted with open arms," 1 August 2008, https://wikileaks.org/plusd/cables/08NEWDELHI2111_a.html.

The international relationship between India and Pakistan – the rivalry, its history and its implications – was inextricable from Indian security interests in Afghanistan.

The Rivalry Explanation

I argue that rivalry dynamics provide the most compelling explanation for India's behaviour in Afghanistan. This is not to deny that economic opportunities, ambitions to project regional and global power, and immediate security interests were (and are) also motivating factors for New Delhi. Rather, the scope, scale, and intensity of India's intervention in Afghanistan is explicable fully only by recognizing the amplifying effects of the India-Pakistan rivalry. This distinction is key. India's intervention was overdetermined given interests related to economics, power projection, and immediate security outlined above. Which is to say, I am not arguing that *absent* rivalry India *would not* have intervened in some way in Afghanistan. There are multiple causal paths leading to intervention; as with many social phenomena, occasionally these causal paths or mechanisms will overlap in a particular case. The point with respect to India's intervention is that it would not have proceeded *as it did* absent rivalry dynamics. By excavating evidence of rivalry considerations in Indian decision-making, I augment confidence in the general explanation for intervention developed in this book.

The scope of the development aid that was provided – in particular, in humanitarian and human capacity (training, scholarships, etc.) terms – is significantly more than was required to pursue, for example, purely economic opportunities. India prioritized a comprehensive relationship with Kabul intended to support and solidify all sectors of the emerging Afghan state. New Delhi even relinquished oversight and control of its aid efforts, in contrast to most international donors, allowing its funds and associated programs to be monitored and administered primarily by the Afghan government and other local actors (D'Souza 2014). Again, India had real economic interests at stake, but they were not primary or paramount. New Delhi engaged in a range of activities not directly related to securing available economic gains.[23] Similarly, the projection of regional power certainly played a role in New Delhi's

---

23 One could argue that India's development aid was larger and more comprehensive
than would have otherwise been the case in the absence of rivalry; this, however,
is a difficult counterfactual to prove. Instead, one can infer from the broad range of
non-economic activities (related to security and political influence, for example) that
economic considerations *alone* did not motivate Indian behaviour.

calculus, particularly in the context of its well-known global power ambitions. Yet to the extent that such a motive pushed Indian involvement in Afghanistan, it was logically secondary to security concerns; being the dominant player in one's own backyard presupposes that one can quell regional instability, and that one's own security is firmly protected. Further, given that New Delhi's primary competitor for influence in Kabul, over the long term, likely will be Pakistan, power projection was and will be tied to India's regional competition with Islamabad.[24] Pursuing either economics or power projection was *contingent on* and *implicated by* the ongoing relationship with Pakistan. Nor does the available evidence indicate that either economics or power projection was a primary goal for Indian intervention; statements from Indian officials repeatedly foregrounded the security domain as the main motivator for Indian behaviour.

These security concerns, moreover, were inextricably bound to the international relationship with Pakistan. Islamic militancy is seen as a creation of, and a weapon employed by, Islamabad. The fear is that Islamabad will leverage Islamic militancy to foment further unrest in Kashmir and elsewhere, and that Taliban control or influence in Afghanistan will allow Pakistan to incubate and foster additional Islamist elements for this purpose. As discussed earlier, Pakistan's use of militancy as a non-conventional, indirect method of attacking India is believed to be both useful on its own, as part of the "thousand cuts" strategy, and as a complement to potential conventional operations, as evidenced in the Kashmir wars and in the Kargil episode of 1999, a recent vivid experience for Indian policymakers in 2001 and shortly thereafter.

The centrality of Pakistan for Indian calculations in Afghanistan is reflected in the statements and perceptions recorded in diplomatic cables by the American embassy in New Delhi. Further, Indian officials quite clearly considered security in Afghanistan to be directly connected to security in the broader region. Which is to say, they were not worried about Pakistan's merely endangering their interests in Afghanistan, but also, and primarily, with the implications for Indian security *in general*; the competition for influence in Afghanistan was considered explicitly to be part of the overarching and ongoing (continuous) relationship with Pakistan.

In reading these documents it is easy to understand how the words "paranoia" and "obsession" might surface in analytical appraisals of

---

24 Although other countries – including Russia, Iran, and China – will also be a factor, geographic and ethnic realities, along with the history of the region, suggest a predominant role for Pakistan.

Indian strategic thinking vis-à-vis Pakistan in Afghanistan. Indian officials expressed comparative and consistent scepticism – indeed, pessimism; one cable describes an Indian official as "relentlessly negative" – in the face of their more ambivalent American counterparts. When Foreign Secretary Menon hinted at Pakistani duplicity by suggesting "the problem … has to do with where the threat in Afghanistan is coming from," his American interlocutor – Assistant Secretary of State for South and Central Asian Affairs Richard Boucher – "assure[s]" him "that [Pakistan's president Pervez] Musharraf considers the Taliban a threat … and … is determined to deal with the problem."[25] The consistency with which this pessimism is held is remarkable; multiple officials, at different levels of government, maintain a more or less uniform focus on Pakistan as India's primary threat. Of course, this might be (and to a degree almost certainly is) a function of discipline within the regime – speaking with a "single voice" diplomatically – yet it is nonetheless illuminative and consistent with the thesis that such pessimism is determined by rivalry at the international level. Although one political party, the Indian National Congress (INC), controlled parliament for all the years for which the cables are available – and we are consequently denied the "natural experiment" of comparing the language of different parties and presumably, ostensibly, different ideological orientations to see if attitudes towards Pakistan or perceptions regarding Afghanistan shifted accordingly – it is worth noting that the INC traditionally has been dovish and conciliatory (by Indian political standards) towards Pakistan. The Bharatiya Janata Party (BJP), which won the election in 2014, is a right-of-centre party more traditionally associated with tough talk about Pakistan. That INC officials were so persistently focused on the Pakistani security threat, therefore, is more revealing than if the BJP had been making similar statements – it is a harder case for the dovish party to be hostile than the traditionally hawkish one. Further, Indian policy towards Afghanistan was consistent post-2014: the trajectory for increased security involvement had already begun under the INC – for example, in the 2011 strategic partnership agreement – and was carried forward by the BJP. Throughout this period, New Delhi remained "committed to [doing] whatever it [could] to help Afghanistan."[26] Going

25 WikiLeaks, "Boucher and Menon tour d'horizon: Pakistan, Bangladesh, Nepal, Sri Lanka, and North Korea," 14 November 2006, https://wikileaks.org/plusd/cables/06NEWDELHI7767_a.html.
26 Foreign Secretary Menon quoted in WikiLeaks, "FS Menon tells USDP Edelman India will empower Karzai, wait for new govt in Bangladesh," 20 November 2006, https://wikileaks.org/plusd/cables/06NEWDELHI7870_a.html.

further back, similarly, when the BJP was in power from 1991 to 2004, it was in charge of India's initial post-2001 policy. Public statements at the time suggest a basic perception of the Pakistani threat consistent with attitudes revealed in the diplomatic cables. In October 2001, for example, India's Ministry of External Affairs (MEA) released a statement, as part of discussions with Russia on the future of Afghanistan, contending that the driver of Islamic terrorism in South Asia was "the sponsorship and support such terrorist groups have been receiving from certain countries that use terrorism as an instrument of policy" – a clear reference to Pakistan (*Times of India* 2001). The theory of rivalry I present in this book would not expect to find significant differences between the policies of various Indian political parties. In broad terms – minor differences inevitably occur; the point is determining whether the basic orientation shifts in a fundamental way – the consistency of the Indian approach to Afghanistan, first through a BJP administration, then the INC, before shifting back to the BJP post-2014, reflects a foreign policy continuity in keeping with the theory's expectations. The trajectory of the intervention and the basic thrust of the justifications invoked in explaining it seemingly have been immune to the hawk/ dove, right/left divide.

Of course, it is not simply the focus on Pakistan that is relevant, but even more so the way in which Indian officials were preoccupied. The expectation of the theory is that states will be concerned about how present realities affect future security. Drawing on experiences within the rivalry and the consequent reputations for behaviour that form, states view present circumstances through the prism of anticipated future crises. In this way, the theory suggests that concern about, and preoccupation with, an international rival is *not* "paranoid" or "obsessive," but predictable. (The implication here is that any state in comparable circumstances would behave similarly, thus obviating the convenient if problematic admonition, typically implicit, that the Indians or Pakistanis are uniquely "crazy" in this regard.) How do the available statements conform to these expectations?

There is a clear belief among Indian officials that Taliban control of Afghanistan would constitute de facto Pakistani control of Afghanistan, and that this would lead to significant security challenges in the future. There is a recognition that Pakistan's established pattern of supporting Islamic militants in Kashmir and elsewhere will continue (a reputation for such behaviour has been formed), and that India will be perpetually imperilled as a result. Pakistani-backed terrorism hangs "like the sword of Damocles" above India's head, according to Foreign Secretary

Dilip Sinha.[27] Pakistan's use of Islamist terrorism, moreover, is generally believed to be a component of its broader revisionist aims on the subcontinent – the use of the term "strategic terrorism" captures this belief well:[28] it is not incidental to, but a core component of, the ongoing rivalry. This perception is underscored again and again by statements that insist Islamabad is in control of the Taliban insurgency and could "turn off the tap" any time it wished.[29] (As discussed above, the notion that India perceived the insurgency to be anything *but* directed and controlled by Islamabad is untenable in the face of the available evidence.) The import of Indian developmental and, increasingly, security activities was tied to perceptions about what a Pakistan-controlled Afghanistan would mean for long-term Indian security. The "nightmare scenario," according to Ambassador K.C. Singh, was the prospect of "permanent sanctuary in Afghanistan" for Pakistani-directed Islamic radicals. "We do not want *another* century of instability," Singh explained.[30] This reference to "another" implies a previously existing one. The understanding that a sanctuary for Islamism would result in instability was predicated on the experiences of the past several decades and on Pakistan's reputation for exploiting Islamism.

It must also be noted that the Indian perception that Islamabad was supporting the Taliban in Afghanistan and perpetuating Islamic militancy in the region more broadly was based on real and tangible evidence – which is to say, it was not imaginary or lacking foundation.[31] On the former score, the American intelligence community largely concurred (see chapter 6). On the latter, similarly, there was an acknowledged – that is, more broadly than just in New Delhi – history and pattern (ISI links to the 2008 Mumbai attack, for example; see Burke 2010). Yet, as with all evidence, it must be *interpreted*, and herein we see

---

27 WikiLeaks, "AS Boucher and Foreign Secretary Saran talk civ-nuke, Nepal, China, Pakistan, and terrorism," 11 August 2006, https://wikileaks.org/plusd/cables/06NEWDELHI5609_a.html.

28 WikiLeaks, "Indian counterterrorism experts urge greater Indo-US cooperation, criticize Pakistan," 18 December 2006, https://wikileaks.org/plusd/cables/06NEWDELHI8387_a.html.

29 Ibid.

30 WikiLeaks, "Indians offer bleak assessment of Afghanistan and South Asian region during CTJWG," 2 March 2007, emphasis added; https://wikileaks.org/plusd/cables/07NEWDELHI1051_a.html.

31 If it were illusory, of course, there would be a more legitimate reason to question the basic rationality of Indian perceptions. Instead, Indian concerns are grounded in reality. "Just because you're paranoid," wrote Joseph Heller in *Catch-22*, "doesn't mean they're not after you."

again the consequences of rivalry. More or less the same evidence was treated differently by, for instance, India and the United States. Recall again the example provided in chapter 2 in which American and Israeli intelligence officials, presumably with access to the same or similar information, offered slightly different appraisals as to the imminence of the Iranian nuclear threat – the former, not facing an existential threat, pushed the time horizon further than the latter, for which the possibility of being wrong is significantly more acute, to put it mildly.

A similar dynamic is at play here: the United States was more willing to believe that Musharraf was legitimately ambivalent about the Taliban insurgency. The Americans knew there were real historical linkages and that certain elements within the Pakistani government/military apparatus – namely, ISI – might have maintained operational relationships with militants. Yet they also allowed for the possibility that the political leadership might not be directing such behaviour but genuinely desired to crack down on the militancy problem, perhaps somewhat handcuffed by the domestic unpopularity of explicit cooperation with the international coalition in Afghanistan. Consequently, the United States was more sanguine about the prospects of Pakistani cooperation – even as optimism waned over the years as little change occurred. For New Delhi, there was no ambivalence; Musharraf, it contended, was in control of ISI, as "the organization is a disciplined part of the military structure of Pakistan,"[32] and Musharraf himself, an army officer widely held responsible for the Kargil incursion (see Rajghatta 2002), had "spent his entire adult life plotting, planning and executing schemes to undo India."[33] Even as Pakistan shifted from a military to a democratic regime in 2008 – at least nominally a reason for optimism with respect to Pakistani bellicosity – Indian officials were dismissive, saying that "real power" adhered with the military and ISI, particularly on the issues of India and Afghanistan.[34]

Once again, the history is illuminative. Over the decades, Pakistan has oscillated between military and democratic rule several times: in the 1960s under General Ayub Khan; in the 1980s under General Zia ul Haq; and in the late 1990s under Musharraf. Each reversion to democratic

---

32 WikiLeaks, "Indian counterterrorism experts urge greater Indo-US cooperation, criticize Pakistan."

33 WikiLeaks, "India cautiously optimistic after Pakistan general election," 21 February 2008, https://wikileaks.org/plusd/cables/08NEWDELHI542_a.html.

34 WikiLeaks, "Mixed sentiment among Indians over Zardari government, welcoming possible along LOC," 16 October 2008, https://wikileaks.org/plusd/cables/08NEWDELHI2722_a.html.

rule – while clearly triggering many significant micro differences – did little to alter the fundamental contours, the tone and tenor, of Pakistani foreign policy as it relates to India. Whatever promises the Americans were hearing from the Pakistani leadership (Musharraf, Asif Zardari, or otherwise), New Delhi remained committedly sceptical. As described in a cable from 2010, "The Indians tolerate [the US] message about the importance of resuming a robust dialogue with Pakistan. *However, to the Indian mind, India has been the target of numerous conventional and unconventional attacks since Pakistan's inception.*"[35] Which is to say, history is a powerful instructor, and New Delhi was unwilling to trade tangible experience for "cheap talk." So, when evidence emerged that ISI was not only supporting militants in Afghanistan but also directing them to target Indian citizens and assets specifically (Walsh 2010), India was understandably less credulous than the United States as to Pakistan's avowed commitments to reform.

The point is they were not objectively *wrong* as to these assessments – and therefore "wrong" in the *substantively* rationalist sense – because it was, ultimately, extremely difficult if not impossible to know for sure what Pakistan's intentions actually were, just as the *precise* time horizon for an Iranian nuclear weapon is largely unknowable to American and Israeli intelligence. Assessing these intentions requires using whatever information is at hand to formulate a best guess estimate as to what they actually might be. This is the irreducible nature of all such assessments in international relations. States engaged in rivalry have a vivid historical experience upon which to draw – vivid, in particular, because it involves security competition, often conflict and/or war, which implicates the very basis of a state's existence as a state, which is to say survival. This means India interprets available evidence differently than does the United States when it comes to Pakistani intentions. Indian decisionmakers do so not because they are "emotionally loaded" or "psychologically hostile" towards their Pakistani counterparts and the Pakistani state, but for reasons tied to the international relationship between the two countries and the various imperatives present in the international system. The process is therefore *procedurally* rational.

This interpretation is further supported by the importance New Delhi attached to achieving its aims in Afghanistan across a range of domains: economic, strategic, and immediate security. All are real, and all offered incentives and justifications for Indian involvement in

---

35 WikiLeaks, "Scenesetter for Under Secretary McHale visit to India," 27 January 2010, https://wikileaks.org/plusd/cables/10NEWDELHI151_a.html.

Afghanistan. As potential *explanations* for this involvement, however, none is sufficient. The tenacity with which India pursued its objectives in Afghanistan belies any of these singular explanations. The implications of "losing" Afghanistan – of essentially acquiescing to Pakistani influence in the form of resurgent or renewed Taliban control – were too great, precisely because they invited *long-term* security consequences. (Recall the "century of instability" New Delhi is so keen to avoid.) As the security situation in Afghanistan deteriorated over the years, New Delhi's commitment grew. "The cost of losing Afghanistan is too great for India," former Indian high commissioner in Pakistan Gopalaswamy Parthasarathy told his American interlocutors in 2006 as the insurgency intensified. Parthasarathy was commenting on the increase in Indian aid that had recently been announced, bringing the total at that time to US$650 million.[36]

This dogged commitment to "victory" in Afghanistan – that is, the preclusion of Pakistani dominance – is reflected in two other themes present in the available US diplomatic cables. First, there is a constant concern about the potential of US withdrawal. New Delhi recognized that an American departure might result in victory for the Taliban, and therefore were highly motivated to forestall such a policy decision by Washington. Second, and relatedly, the prospect of negotiations with the Taliban was largely anathema to Indian thinking, insofar as they saw the Taliban almost exclusively as a Pakistani proxy.

These sentiments are also prevalent in the record of public statements made by Indian officials. In May 2011, as the July 2011 deadline for the drawdown of US troops set by US president Barack Obama drew near, Prime Minister Singh reiterated India's commitment to Afghanistan prior to a visit to Kabul and meetings with newly re-elected Hamid Karzai: "We cannot remain unaffected by developments in Afghanistan. We take a long-term view of our partnership with Afghanistan ... India's commitment to assisting the people of Afghanistan is enduring and has weathered many storms" (India 2011b). Around the same time, an Indian official was quoted as saying: "Nobody committed to the security and stability of Afghanistan would want precipitous withdrawal of forces" (Parashar 2011). The comment was in reference to "speculation that [the death of Osama bin Laden] might spur a euphoric US to expedite the process of troop withdrawal ... and allow Pakistan to run amok in a strategically crucial country" (Parashar 2011). In December 2011,

---

36 WikiLeaks, "Indian counterterrorism experts urge greater Indo-US cooperation, criticize Pakistan."

India's delegation to the International Afghanistan Conference in Bonn – marking the ten-year anniversary of the Bonn Conference, which established the new Afghan government – exhorted the international community to stay the course (India 2011a). Again, New Delhi was clearly concerned that the international community – the United States in particular – might abandon Afghanistan and leave it (let it "slip back") to the forces of Islamism that had predominated throughout the 1990s.

The subject of negotiations with the Taliban was similarly fraught, with New Delhi staunchly opposed when the idea first surfaced around 2008–9. The common refrain from Indian officials was the impossibility of distinguishing "good" Taliban from "bad." Any negotiations might allow for the return of the very Islamist (and Pakistani-backed) elements New Delhi had been so keen to keep out. Nonetheless, as the realities of the situation shifted, and as the United States clearly signalled its intent to draw down and eventually withdraw, the prospect of stability through such negotiations softened the Indian position. As Shashi Tharoor, Minister of State for External Affairs in 2009–10, stated at the time: "New Delhi has come around to accepting dialogue with those Taliban elements who are prepared to renounce violence ... But New Delhi is wary of those who, under Pakistani tutelage, might pretend to be reborn constitutionalists, but seize the first opportunity after the American withdrawal to devour the regime that compromises with them" (quoted in Paliwal 2017, 213). Recall, again, that Indian's overarching aim was to produce a competent, stable, and multi-ethnic central Afghan government. If talking with elements of the Taliban were able to accomplish this, New Delhi was willing to acquiesce. Indian foreign minister Salman Khurshid specified that "this process must be a broad-based Afghan-led Afghan-owned reconciliation process, within the framework of the Afghan constitution ... This dialogue must involve all sections of the Afghan society and armed opposition groups, including the Taliban" (quoted in Parashar 2013). India remained on guard, however, as the statement from Tharoor makes clear. Apropos concrete plans for peace talks with the Taliban that were then being pursued by US officials, Khurshid stated: "We have from time to time reminded all stakeholders about red lines that was [sic] drawn by the world community and certainly by the participants should not be touched, should not be erased and should not be violated" (quoted in Bagchi 2013a). The "red lines" referenced here are the preconditions – including the renunciation of al-Qaeda and acceptance of the existing Afghan constitution – that had been established during the George W. Bush administration for any discussions with the Taliban. The Obama team had largely abandoned these preconditions; New Delhi saw them as essential.

India was similarly disheartened that talks might include members of the Haqqani network, the Taliban grouped linked to the bombing of the Indian embassy in Kabul, and derided as "opportunistic" efforts (quoted in Bagchi 2013b) on the part of Islamabad, which was coordinating efforts along with Washington. Khurshid was clear that "the reconciliation process must not undermine the legitimacy of the Afghan State and Government and the political, social and economic progress witnessed in Afghanistan over the past decade, to which members of the international community have contributed in great measure. I may emphasize here that India's Afghanistan policy does not have an exit policy" (quoted in Parashar 2013). This statement underscores New Delhi's apprehension as to the international community's commitment to Afghanistan. Indian decisionmakers were willing to engage in peace talks, but feared that negotiations might serve as cover for an international exit. The rest of the world might be able to go home, but India was part of the neighborhood – its security was immediately implicated, meaning it did not have the luxury of looking for a way out.

In 2018, Afghan president Ashraf Ghani publicly invited insurgent groups, including the Taliban, to participate in peace negotiations. A statement from the MEA "welcomed the Afghan government's call to armed groups to cease violence and join [the] national peace and reconciliation process that would protect the rights of all Afghans," but went on to reiterate that "there can be no compromise with terrorism and action must be taken against those who continue down the path of violence and those who finance them and provide safe havens and sanctuaries" (India 2018). This last portion was a clear reference to continued concerns about Pakistan, and suggests that New Delhi's acceptance of negotiations that included members of the Taliban was not a reversal of previous policy but rather an adjustment as to the means for achieving long-held goals. A stable Afghanistan not beholden to Islamabad was, is, and will be the primary concern for New Delhi. All of the developmental efforts and vocal support for the Afghan government do not obscure the fact that this is the focus. When it comes to negotiations with certain elements of the insurgency, the public stance not to distinguish between "good" and "bad" Taliban was less principled than it was calculated. Paliwal (2017, 215–16) reports that, although the official line remained opposed to negotiations with the Taliban, internal discussions within the Indian government recognized that dealing with some elements of the Taliban might be inevitable. The point is illuminative. Discouraging negotiations early on was designed to forestall the return of Islamist elements. As the central government strained under the pressure of the insurgency, however, New Delhi was pragmatic in its outlook, gradually opening to the possibility that some members of the Taliban might help deliver the stability that was seen as all-important, provided these members were not directly beholden to ISI and Pakistan.

My analysis of India's intervention in Afghanistan suggests the following puzzle: if the rivalry explanation is basically correct in suggesting that New Delhi's concerns were related primarily to long-term security and potential future conflict with Pakistan, why was the Indian response not *more* assertive in Afghanistan? Why did security involvement remain limited, and even as it increased, why did New Delhi still largely resist and rule out the introduction of military forces, for example? Put another way, if India saw the security implications of an Afghanistan beholden to Islamabad as so acute, why was its response – particularly given its military superiority on the subcontinent – not decisive? This question becomes even more acute in the wake of the Taliban victory in August 2021: even as it became clear that the forces of Islamism would take control of the country once again, there was no shift in the basic Indian position of no "boots from India on the ground in Afghanistan," as Defence Minister Nirmala Sitharaman stated in 2017 (*Hindustan Times* 2017). Although beyond the purview of this case study, New Delhi's position following August 2021 has been consistent in this regard. India has expressed concern over the destabilizing consequences of the Taliban victory, offered humanitarian support, and convened a regional security dialogue in which proximate countries – including Russia, Iran, and five Central Asian states[37] – issued a joint declaration urging for a multi-ethnic, stable Afghanistan that would not serve as a hub for terrorism in the region (*Economic Times* 2021).

The reason for New Delhi's relative caution about direct military involvement is the nature of the rivalry between India and Pakistan. India's intervention was primarily *defensive* in nature. The concern was with its own long-term security. As the larger, more powerful, status quo state in the rivalry, India had no need to engage in offensive measures against Pakistan. Moreover, any overtly aggressive move into Afghanistan – the introduction of significant numbers of Indian troops, for example – inevitably would threaten Islamabad, prompting a reaction, thereby further undermining the very security Indian policy was designed to maintain and protect. New Delhi was aware of this. Former Indian ambassador to the United States Arun Singh outlined the

---

37 Kazakhstan, Kyrgyzstan, Tajikistan, Turkmenistan, and Uzbekistan.

thinking well: "Any major foray in security assistance or a security role could be counter-productive ... Pakistan would ratchet up its support to Taliban and Haqqani network [*sic*] citing India's presence" (*Print* 2017). Even though New Delhi considered Islamabad's apprehensions to be ill-founded, it could not but recognize the likely reaction to any direct Indian security involvement in Afghanistan. As such, New Delhi's policy had to skirt the line between (a) offsetting and minimizing Islamabad's role in Afghanistan, while (b) remaining restrained enough to avoid triggering a more vociferous Pakistani response – the added dynamic of Islamabad's nuclear capability was relevant in this regard as well. The import of *a* was a condition of rivalry: the belief, predicated on history, past behaviour, and reputation, that Islamabad would exploit Islamist militancy in pursuit of revisionist aims. The import of *b* was predicated on an appreciation of Pakistan's policies and its clearly stated and expressed aversion to India's presence in Afghanistan.

New Delhi's overriding concern about potential US withdrawal is appreciable in this context. As long as the Americans remained engaged in Afghanistan, India could be confident that a return to Islamist, Taliban rule would be precluded. India could allow the United States to be the engine and guarantor of its own preferences, thereby removing the need for direct Indian security involvement and the consequent possibility that such involvement could further destabilize the region by prompting a major Pakistani response. Thus, Indian officials worked hard to convince their American counterparts to keep their country engaged in the fight against the Taliban. New Delhi then supplemented these efforts by providing significant financial and developmental aid intended to foster long-term stability through the creation of a viable Afghan state. As the bulk of the international coalition began to draw down in 2014, India had to increase slightly its security cooperation with Kabul, recognizing that a failure to do so might undermine the gains that had accrued since 2001. They remained wary of going too far, lest Pakistan felt too threatened and responded accordingly.

Similarly, initial aversion to negotiations with the Taliban gave way to pragmatic recognition that such negotiations might be necessary. This shift would not have occurred had New Delhi been motivated by offensive or power-projection concerns or if it believed that the Taliban alone, not Pakistan, was the primary security threat in Afghanistan; keeping the Taliban out then would have been the predominate interest. Instead, India was willing to countenance diminished influence in Kabul, if it meant a stable Afghanistan. (The initial post-2001 decision to shift from the Northern Alliance to the multi-ethnic Bonn-created government also reflected these priorities.)

Of course, alternative interpretations are possible for observed Indian behaviour. Allowing the United States to do the heavy lifting – and lobbying aggressively for it to continue doing so – is also consistent with explanations that foreground economic or narrow security interests; likewise for the Indian position on peace negotiations with the Taliban. Yet the statements made by Indian officials – both public and private – seem to support the rivalry explanation ahead of the alternatives. Again and again, Indian decisionmakers and diplomats emphasized (a) their desire to prevent Afghanistan from once again becoming a host to Islamism and associated violence; (b) their perception that Pakistan was perpetuating and controlling the insurgency for the expressed purpose of making this happen; (c) their belief that Pakistan would exploit such a situation to further destabilize Kashmir and the region more broadly in pursuit of Islamabad's established and demonstrated revisionist aims; and (d) their commitment to forestall this outcome through extensive development efforts and, increasingly, as the United States and others stepped back, security involvement. Taken collectively, these observations support the rivalry interpretation. Moreover, statements from Indian officials are buttressed by actual Indian behaviour and policy: deed followed word. Almost immediately after the toppling of the Taliban, India emerged as a major supporter of the new Afghan government. This support was wide ranging and comprehensive, clearly intended to cement the new regime in Kabul and solidify its control over Afghan territory. As the insurgency emerged and the security situation was challenged, New Delhi steadily increased its support, becoming the largest non-traditional donor to the embattled country. Training missions were emphasized as capacity building became a priority. Understandable reticence about direct security involvement gave way to the transfer of military equipment, the signing of a strategic partnership, and training of the ANSF. New Delhi made it clear that it planned to remain heavily involved in Afghanistan; for India, there was no "exit policy."

We see here the consequences of the *anticipated process* expected by the theory of rivalry I develop in this book. Indian decisionmakers considered the consequences of a destabilized and Pakistani-influenced Afghanistan, and anticipated that this would lead to security problems down the road ("another century of instability"). This anticipation, this belief, was the catalyst for the Indian intervention in Afghanistan – or, rather, the catalyst for the *specific* intervention (its shape, scope, purpose, and scale) that has been observed since 9/11.

Chapter Five

Pakistani Intervention in Afghanistan

In this chapter I examine Pakistan's intervention in Afghanistan. First, I demonstrate that Pakistan was engaged in Afghanistan post-2001, despite its proclaiming that it was not. I then evaluate the decision-making logic underpinning this behaviour. Pakistan's intervention offers strong support for my argument, as decisionmakers appeared to be primarily motivated by long-term security concerns related to the perceived threat from India: the consequences of ceding influence in Afghanistan to their rival were too ominous for Islamabad to abide.

Pakistan in Afghanistan

Two overarching Pakistani interests in Afghanistan have prevailed since partition: mitigation of Pashtun nationalism and mitigation of Indian influence. Although other interests – including economic opportunities in Central Asia and tactical and strategic opportunities related to revisionism in Kashmir – are also germane, the core security motivations tied to the Pashtun and Indian questions have been the driving force behind Pakistan's behaviour. These concerns are to a large extent connected with one another. Unrest along the Afghan-Pakistan border due to Pashtun irredentism is perilous in the context of anticipated and expected conflict with India in the East, and their confluence raises the possibility of a two-front war. The effects of rivalry are clear: wars and conflicts with India loom over Pakistan's perceptions of the importance of Afghanistan. Also pertinent is the extent to which the rise of the Taliban in the mid-1990s represented the culmination of decades of effort (often covert) on the part of Islamabad to cultivate a friendly regime in Afghanistan, largely as a bulwark against the security concerns noted above. This helps explain Pakistan's reluctance, post-2001, to abandon its erstwhile proxies.

The nature of Pakistan's relationship with the Taliban is important for understanding Pakistani behaviour post-2001. Declassified US diplomatic cables published by the National Security Archive at George Washington University in 2007 offer insight into Pakistan's involvement with the Taliban regime between 1994 and 2001. Barbara Elias, in summarizing the release, notes that the documents "clearly illustrate that the Taliban was directly funded, armed and advised by Islamabad itself" (Elias 2007b). For example, a document from November 1996 notes that Pakistan's "Frontier Corps elements are utilized in command and control; training; and when necessary – combat" alongside the Taliban (Elias 2007a).

Insight as to American perceptions of Pakistani rationale is provided by an October 1995 cable entitled "Pakistani Afghan Policy: Anyone but Rabbani/Massoud – Even the Taliban." This last qualification ("*even* the Taliban") is meant to highlight the reluctance – supported by Pakistani statements offered in the cable – associated with Islamabad's support for the radical group. The latter's "obscurantist" views were "repugnant" to most Pakistanis, according to then-Pakistan ambassador to Afghanistan Qazi Humayun. Despite this reluctance, however, the emergence of the Taliban as the most viable alternative to the Rabbani government and Tajik forces of Ahmad Shah Massoud compelled Pakistani support ("*anyone* but Rabbani/Massoud"). This again illustrates that forestalling Indian influence in Kabul (Massoud, in particular, was seen as sympathetic to, if not reliant on, New Delhi) was Islamabad's overriding concern, rather than, say, ethnic or religious affinity with the Taliban or the belief that the group would be a ready proxy for Pakistani interests more broadly. Which is to say, again, that support was perceived as the best of bad options – as *reactive*, rather than proactive support for a willing and pliant proxy. As Elias concludes, the records "represent the most complete and comprehensive collection of declassified documentation to date on Pakistan's aid programs to the Taliban [between 1994 and 2001], illustrating Islamabad's firm commitment to a Taliban victory in Afghanistan" (Elias 2007b). In his 2006 memoir, Pervez Musharraf (2006, 203) recounts the basic logic, as he saw it, underpinning Pakistan's continued support for the Taliban during this period, consistent with the evidence from the released cables: "If we had broken with them, that would have created a new enemy on our western border, or a vacuum of power [in Afghanistan] into which might have stepped the Northern Alliance, comprising anti-Pakistan elements." By the turn of the century, Pakistan's commitment to Taliban victory had proved effective. The Northern Alliance was relegated to small pockets of territory in the north. Islamabad had attained its goal of a sympathetic – if not totally pliant – Afghan regime, one that was derived from, and had the general support of, the Pashtun ethnic group, while also being devoid of influence from India.

The events of 9/11 forced the Pakistani leadership – specifically President Musharraf – into a deep reconsideration of established policy. In the context of President George Bush's dramatic "with or us or against us" ultimatum, further underscored by the threat from then-deputy secretary of state Richard Armitage to "bomb [Pakistan] back into the stone age" if they chose the latter (*BBC News* 2006; see also Musharraf 2006, 201), Musharraf opted to break ranks publicly with the Taliban and align Pakistan with the US invasion of Afghanistan. He explained this decision to the Pakistani people in a televised address on 19 September 2001.[1]

The speech is illuminative for the justifications that were offered as well as the reluctant tone in which it was delivered.[2] While easy to dismiss as the genuflections of a secular leader making an unpopular decision in the face of a conservative, religious population, subsequent events lend the words portent. (Years later, Selig Harrison [2006] would lament that the speech, delivered in Urdu, went largely unnoticed in the United States.) Noteworthy in particular is the ambivalence of the support offered to US aims – hardly signalling the "unstinted cooperation" Musharraf had pledged to US Secretary of State Colin Powell just a few days earlier (Sipress and Mufson 2001) – the hedging with respect to opposing the Taliban, and, tellingly, the broadside attacks against India. The latter is particularly revealing insofar as India was essentially a peripheral player with respect to the immediate response to 9/11 and the US ultimatum vis-à-vis the Taliban in Afghanistan. New Delhi had, as Musharraf notes, offered its full support for American efforts, yet it was far too early to determine what, ultimately, the Indian role would be, either in any US military operation or in the long-term future of Afghanistan. For Musharraf, however, Indian involvement was not peripheral but the central consideration in determining Pakistan's appropriate course of action. Again, the focus on India in the context of this speech can be interpreted in multiple ways: playing to anti-Indian sentiments in the population; evidence of paranoid and psychological hostility towards India on the part of Musharraf himself and/or the Pakistani leadership more broadly; or as a reflection of long-term strategic concern about potential Indian involvement in Afghanistan. A fourth possibility is, of course, some combination of the

---

1 For the full text of the speech, see Musharraf (2001).

2 An address at the United Nations in New York two months later was only slightly more placatory; see United Nations (2001).

three – indeed, this is almost certain, as no narrow explanation is likely to run unmingled. Yet if one concentrates on the *content* of the speech itself, long-term strategic concerns are clearly central.

Although the usual caveats apply with respect to the veracity (or evidentiary value) of such public statements,[3] notice the ordering of Pakistani priorities, in which "security of the country [against] external threat" is listed as paramount. This priority, in particular, is used to justify the abandonment of the Taliban ("I give top priority to the defense of Pakistan, Defense [*sic*] of any other country" – for example the Taliban regime in Afghanistan – "comes later" (given the translation, this could also mean "after" or as second priority). More generally, the Taliban are given sympathetic treatment, with Musharraf emphasizing Pakistani efforts to support the regime diplomatically over the preceding years. Overall, the speech suggests that the decision to side with the Americans was a reluctant one, necessitated by circumstance and dictated in the final analysis by core security concerns – with the requisite and rote references to the integrity of Islam.

This initial decision point in the post-2001 era is an important one, and worth exploring in greater depth. The first consideration is whether Musharraf's declared break with the Taliban was reflected in actual Pakistani policy or was simply public posturing masking continued clandestine support. Given the nature of the US ultimatum, some have argued that Musharraf's "decision" was anything but – that he was instead forced to adopt a public position against his will and, consequently, that private Pakistani policy (support for the Taliban) remained unchanged from the pre-2001 era. Fair (2017, 136), for example, argues that Pakistani duplicity "should have been apparent as early as November 2001, when Pakistan's military executed the Kunduz airlift, in which it evacuated thousands of Taliban leaders and their al-Qaeda associates, along with their Pakistani advisers from the armed forces and the Inter-Services Intelligence Directorate ... just as US special forces operating with ... the Northern Alliance were about to take the city." Ahmed Rashid (2001), for his part, reported that, in late September 2001, up to five ISI officers travelled to Kandahar to aid the Taliban in their preparations for the

---

3 These caveats should not be overstated, however. While recognizing the "common criticism ... that public speeches may not reflect the 'true' personal beliefs of leaders" Jonathan Renshon (2010: 179) nonetheless points to "recent evidence that suggests that the public statements of leaders may reflect their true beliefs to a greater extent than skeptical observers would predict." Renshon cites his earlier study (2009) which indicated strong convergence between the public and, presumably more "accurate," private statements of John F. Kennedy during his time as president.

American attack. In October, ISI allegedly supported the cross-border provision of weapons and ammunition to Taliban forces (Frantz 2001). Such activities have led some to argue that Musharraf's pledges were empty and his support of the Taliban unbroken (see, for example, the discussions in Abbas 2014; Bird and Marshall 2011; Fair 2014, 2017; Nadiri 2014; Rubin 2015). Conversely, it is possible that Pakistan did, at first, break legitimately with the Taliban only to reverse that decision later on (see, for example, Hussain 2005; Jones 2008; Reidel 2011; Sirrs 2017).[4] Below, I present evidence of Pakistan's support for the Taliban from 2002 onwards.

Parsing the alternatives is important. Continuity across the pre- and post-2001 eras – that is, a policy of support for the Taliban unbroken by the US intervention – would be *more* consistent with alternative explanations in which emotional and psychological factors override rational considerations, or with bureaucratic interpretations of Pakistani behaviour in which the parochial interests of, in particular, the military and intelligence apparatuses override centralized decision-making processes.[5] Given the dramatic disruption of US intervention – the "political shock" that it constituted – a dogged commitment to established policy would have been unlikely had Islamabad actually pursued broadly rational decision-making processes. Indeed, the contention that Pakistan's Afghanistan policy was "captured" by hardliners in the military establishment keen on perpetuating their own institutional interests is offered as an explanation for such putative continuity (Fair 2014). Similarly, insofar as a failure to adjust policy given the new reality in Afghanistan suggests the absence of a rational (re)evaluation, one might conclude that Pakistan's Afghanistan policy was beholden to non-rational impulses, including emotional and/or psychological pathologies. Antagonism towards India, therefore, might have overridden other concerns, leading to the sacrifice of other interests (including, potentially, security) in order to maintain an anti–Northern Alliance stance – which, given American support for that group, would have become a de facto anti-American

---

4 It is important to point out the significant overlap between the two positions in terms of historical detail and evidence. There was, and of course always would be, the maintenance of, for example, personal relationships between Pakistani officials (particularly ISI operatives) and Taliban/insurgent leaders. The question is whether these relationships, even up to and including minor operational cooperation, constituted top-down Pakistani policy.

5 Christopher Darnton's (2014) conceptualization of rivalry is itself predicated on such "parochial interests," whereby the military establishment – he looks at cases in South America – perpetuates rivalry in order to maintain its share of scarce government resources.

stance. Focused on its enemy, beholden to the "negative-effect calculus" of emotional rivalry, Islamabad simply might have been willing to cut off its nose to spite its face. Likewise, such a continuity would call in to question the structure of the present case study – that a "decision" to intervene in Afghanistan post-2001 was made at all; instead, such a decision would have been made in the 1980s (or earlier) and simply maintained. This would undermine (or render superfluous) the proposition that Pakistan was engaged in a "balancing intervention" in Afghanistan. On the other hand, if the evidence shows that a genuine re-evaluation in fact did occur, this would bolster an explanation based on broadly rational decision-making processes. Of course, such an evaluation might have merely confirmed present policy; continuity, therefore, would not be fatal to a rational rivalry explanation. Still, the evaluation might have resulted in a course change, constituting visible evidence that the (re)evaluation took place and lending support to the rational rivalry explanation.[6] Crucial, in either case, is the actual rationale by which the decision was – or, perhaps, was not – made. What inferences about this thought process can be drawn from the available evidence?

Significant tactical and material support was offered to the United States in the early prosecution of Operation Enduring Freedom, including "over-flight and landing rights for US military and intelligence units[,] access to some Pakistani ports and bases[,] intelligence and immigration information, [and the facilitation of] logistical supply to military forces in Afghanistan" (Fair and Jones 2009, 167). Much of this support was considered crucial to the American effort (see the discussion in O'Hanlon 2002). According to Bruce Reidel (2011, 67), Pakistan "immediately evacuated the Pakistani advisers among the Taliban in Afghanistan and cut off supplies to the Taliban army. The impact on the cohesion of the Taliban forces was devastating: they collapsed rapidly under the weight of American air power and a Northern Alliance revitalized with CIA support and money."[7] An American diplomat affirmed this dynamic at the time, reflecting that, "[w]e did not fully understand

---

6 Such support, it is worth emphasizing again, would be suggestive rather than definitive. It is possible that the re-evaluation occurred, or could have occurred, along non-rational – emotional, psychological, bureaucratic – lines. The strength of the argument in favour of my preferred explanation rests not on any single decisive piece of evidence, but rather on the accumulation and logical interpretation of multiple observations.

7 Note that this interpretation is in stark contrast to the one offered by Fair above, in which such evacuations were seen as evidence of Pakistani duplicity. Key to adjudicating between the two interpretations is the extent to which primarily Pakistani advisers were evacuated or whether there were also large numbers of Taliban and al-Qaeda fighters. Nadiri (2014, 141) concurs with Fair's assessment,

the significance of Pakistan's role in propping up the Taliban until their guys withdrew and things went to hell fast for the Talibs [*sic*]" (quoted in Frantz 2001). Islamabad also deployed military assets to the Durand Line to close off potential infiltration routes – indeed, many al-Qaeda fighters were captured by Pakistani forces as they attempted to cross the border (Frantz 2001; see also Berntsen and Pezzulo 2005; Fair 2004). Owen Sirrs (2017, 226) describes cooperation between the CIA and ISI during this period, particular in the tracking and capture of high-profile al-Qaeda operatives. As Fair and Jones (2009, 167) suggest, "US officials widely praised Pakistani contributions in this period." These moves obviously fractured the relationship between Islamabad and the Taliban, with Hassan Abbas (2014, 119) reporting that "[Taliban leader] Mullah Omar was very annoyed with Pakistani leaders for siding with the US in the military campaign in Afghanistan. Pakistan had practically ditched the Taliban in October 2001 and had even handed over the Afghan ambassador in Islamabad to the US, in the process violating all diplomatic norms." There were those on the Pakistani side who were also opposed to the decisions being made, not only among the public but also within the ranks of the military-intelligence establishment (Fair 2014). Such criticisms indicate that Pakistan's policy in practice reflected the official line.

On balance, the evidence suggests that a real break or shift did occur in the immediate aftermath of the US ultimatum (Paliwal [2017, 162] describes it as a "breathtaking tactical U-turn") – a fact often distorted by subsequent events, in which Pakistani duplicity colours recollections of the period. In the context of what we now know about Pakistani

---

writing that the airlifts "evacuated not only Pakistani military officers and intelligence personnel, but also Pakistani and Afghan members of the Taliban movement," citing it as "early evidence of Pakistan's posture of accommodation vis-à-vis the Afghan Taliban." The source of this information, however, is a piece by the journalist Seymour Hersh (2002), which, in fact, is ambiguous as to whether the evacuation of Taliban fighters was the explicit purpose of the airlifts or whether Pakistani advisors took it upon themselves to "[bring] their friends with them," in the manner of the American evacuation of Saigon in 1975, whereby South Vietnamese nationals were, contra official orders, loaded onto fleeing helicopters. The parallel is obvious: there was a fear that the approaching Northern Alliance – bolstered by American airpower – might slaughter Taliban fighters (as the South Vietnamese "collaborators" feared communist retribution). In this formulation, Islamabad might have primarily wished to get its own people out, at which point, inevitably, many Taliban fighters nonetheless found themselves on fleeing aircraft. This alternative explanation also might help account for why the United States not only approved the Kunduz airlifts, but allowed them to proceed while American forces were positioned to stop them, as Hersh reports.

support for the insurgency from as early as 2002 onward, it is easy to assume that a break did not occur – that assurances of support for the US intervention were as hollow as subsequent reassurances that no support was being offered to the insurgency. This interpretation obscures a more complex reality whereby Islamabad did shift, or at least reset, its relationship with the Taliban and provided a modicum of support for American activities. The point is not that Pakistan flipped overnight from comprehensive support for the Taliban regime to full-throated and committed support for the American intervention against it and back again just a few months later – throughout the period, Islamabad's approach was reluctant, cautious, and, as I discuss below, in fact remarkably consistent as to the factors that drove its policy in Afghanistan.

The decision to side with the United States was nonetheless controversial within the Pakistani military establishment. In a high-level meeting convened in the days after the 9/11 attacks, several top officials challenged Musharraf, pushing for Pakistan to resist the United States and sustain support for the Taliban regime. Among this group was ISI director Lieutenant General Mahmood Ahmed. Musharraf resisted – the dissenters were in the minority – insisting that there was "simply no choice" (McCarthy 2002). One source describes how he attempted to convince the sceptics: "Musharraf eventually silence[ed] the dissenting generals by suggesting that if Pakistan [did] not agree to the US demands, Pakistan's long-time enemy India [would] gladly take the place of Pakistan in assisting the US."[8] Tellingly, those opposing the decision were swiftly marginalized. Following the meeting of ISI officers with Taliban fighters in Kandahar in late September 2001 – an incident which allegedly left Musharraf "infuriated" (Rashid 2001) – Ahmed was removed as ISI director and replaced by the more moderate Lieutenant General Ehsan ul-Haq.[9] Other dissenters from the meeting – for example, Lieutenant General Muzaffar Usmani, Lieutenant General Jamshaird Gulzar Kiani, and Lieutenant General Mohammad Aziz

---

8 See History Commons (n.d.). This account was corroborated by journalist Steve Coll: "After putting off [US Ambassador to Pakistan] Wendy Chamberlin on [September] 13th, Musharraf jawboned his generals and admirals, as well as his civilian cabinet, newspaper editors, and politicians, to prepare them for what he regarded as a necessary swerve in Pakistan's foreign and security policy. The essence of Musharraf's argument during these critical days was: *If Pakistan did not manage this moment of crisis to its advantage, India would*" (Coll 2018, 54, emphasis added).

9 CIA Islamabad station chief Robert Grenier described General ul-Haq as representing "new, more moderate leadership" in ISI, which he now believed was willing to "cooperate fully with the CIA in the war on terrorism" (quoted in Coll 2018, 90).

Khan – were pushed out or reshuffled into less prominent roles (McCarthy 2002). These and other personnel decisions indicated a desire to purge ISI of elements believed to be overly sympathetic to the Taliban cause (Grove 2007; Rashid 2001; Woodward 2002).

Recognizing again the obvious caveat that decisionmakers have incentives to distort (particularly post hoc), and are not to be considered completely trustworthy even as they describe their own decision-making processes, Musharraf's personal account of this historical moment colours in some of the justifications contained in the 19 September speech. According to Musharraf, he considered multiple factors in assessing the pros and cons of breaking with the Taliban and siding with the United States, even as he demurred as to the level of influence Pakistan actually had over the Taliban regime – "after the Taliban came to power, we lost much of the leverage we had had with them." There were economic considerations, for example, as well as a perceived opportunity to "eliminate extremism … and flush out foreign terrorists" in Pakistani society. Musharraf nonetheless makes clear that broader geostrategic considerations were paramount. These included the dangers of an American military attack – the possibility that Bush, Armitage, and company might make good on their threat – as well as the opportunities that would be afforded India should Pakistan resist the Americans in Afghanistan.

Perceptions regarding Indian behaviour loomed large. Even at that early stage, New Delhi's willingness to aid the Americans was a source of concern.[10] If Pakistan refused the Americans, Musharraf believed that India would take advantage of an improved relationship with them to undermine Pakistan's interests in Kashmir and in the region more broadly. With respect to the former, he worried that "the Indians might be tempted to undertake a limited offensive there" – at the very least, they would entrench a status quo Islamabad still wanted revised. Further, Musharraf worried about Pakistan's nuclear assets – only recently tested and established – believing that both the United States and India harboured designs of relieving his country of what it now considered necessary implements of deterrence against Indian military superiority.

---

10 Steve Coll's (2018, 55) account of a 15 September conversation between Ambassador Chamberlin and Musharraf highlights what Pakistani priorities were here:
   "Allowing American planes to overfly Pakistani territory would be 'no problem,' Musharraf said, but he asked for the US and Pakistani militaries to map out specific air corridors. 'We are concerned that India might try to intrude into airspace the US wants to use – we are sensitive about our nuclear installations.' Musharraf said the United States should tell India to 'lay off and stay off.'"

Finally, justifying Islamabad's erstwhile support for the Taliban, despite reservations as to both the character and, ultimately, pliancy of the regime, Musharraf hints at the rationale undergirding Pakistani decision-making vis-à-vis Afghanistan overall: the Taliban were supported so as to forestall "a new enemy on our western border, or a vacuum of power … into which might" step "anti-Pakistan elements."

Although offered here retrospectively, these concerns logically apply to how Musharraf and the Pakistani leadership considered Afghanistan following this initial decision point. The break from the Taliban occurred only in the face of "new, more deadly" concerns – the American threat, not to be dismissed lightly as the twin towers smouldered – which underscored the ultimate tenuousness of the shift; as realities changed and time passed, the decision clearly was subject to re-evaluation. Pakistan has had a long history in Afghanistan, bound by geography and memory, and was therefore unlikely casually to abandon an orientation grounded in those realities. It did so, rather, given, as Musharraf describes it, a "dispassionate … analysis" that considered the "well-being … and best interests" of the country.[11] Which is to say, there remained a broadly rational process in which security concerns were paramount: was the Taliban "worth committing suicide over? The answer was a resounding no." The decision at this moment was – reluctantly, ambivalently[12] – to support the United States and break with the Taliban. Nor were American requests too burdensome or decisive in this regard; they largely required passive, logistical support (access to bases, overflight clearances, etc.) and desistance as opposed to assistance (curtail already-existing support for the Taliban). Moreover, as Musharraf points out, the Americans provided some benefit to Pakistan itself (targeting of al-Qaeda operatives inimical to the Pakistani establishment, certain economic advantages). This allowed for "Islamabad's approach to Afghanistan in 2001–2002," according to Owen Sirrs (2017, 227), to be "wait-and-see" – that is, to shift and reconsider existing policy pending new information as to how realities in Afghanistan played out following the American intervention.

It did not take long for a re-evaluation to occur. As early as 2002, there is evidence of renewed Pakistani support for what was then a

---

11 Note that this inference is not based on the word of Musharraf alone, but also in the context of Pakistan's observed and established behaviour at the time: undercutting Taliban military effectiveness by removing advisers, deploying Pakistani military forces to the border, etc.

12 Musharraf would later tell Bruce Reidel (2011, 67) that the decision was "agonizing."

re-emerging Taliban force.[13] By 2003, the group had established itself in rural areas in the south and east of Afghanistan (Jones 2008). In some ways a striking replay of the Taliban's first decisive victories of the mid-1990s, Pakistan played an important role in this resurgence. "In 2003, ISI began creating a new Taliban," Sirrs (2017, 227) reports, "capable of filling the power vacuum [in Afghanistan] and securing Pakistan's interests." The modes of this assistance and support were myriad and are explored in greater detail below.

First, however, it is important to consider the *decision* to renew support for the Taliban – or, more precisely, to lend support, leveraging, to be sure, established relationships dating to the late 1990s and before – to the "new" Taliban insurgency. This is the crux of this case study: having suspended support for its Taliban client, what caused the Pakistani leadership to initiate a new intervention, in 2002–3, that – as anyone familiar with the realities of the Afghanistan war now recognizes – would have devastating consequences for stability in the region?

Unpacking this further, we can identify the following turning points over the relevant period pertaining to Pakistani decision-making:

– T1) American threat/ultimatum regarding the Taliban and impending American intervention in Afghanistan.
– T2) Decision to acquiesce to American pressure by cutting ties with the Taliban.
– T3) American/coalition intervention.
– T4) Decision to offer support for the emerging Taliban-led insurgency.

Although simplified, this timeline is useful for understanding the logical sequence of decision points for Islamabad. Both T1 and T3 are *events* or *actions*, each triggering a subsequent *decision* – T2 and T4 – by the Pakistani leadership. I have already shown that the US threat led to the decision at T2: Pakistan begrudgingly recognized that its interests

---

13 In addition to more straightforward evidence – statements, actions, reported behaviour – there are also more subtle indications as to the shift that occurred around this time. For example Gall (2014, 68) reports that, in the first couple of years after 9/11 – roughly the time frame in which Pakistan was committed to breaking with the Taliban – Friday sermons in the mosques of Quetta (the Pakistani city that would become the site of the Afghan Taliban leadership during the later insurgency) "emphasized Musharraf's policy of 'Pakistan First.' There were men from Pakistani intelligence present, and some mullahs were even arrested for talking out of line." A few years later, however, as Islamabad shifted its policy, "speakers began openly urging the faithful to go wage jihad in Afghanistan," a message Pakistani intelligence no longer felt it necessary to curtail.

were best served by bending to American will in Afghanistan. (This does not mean that Pakistan necessarily was compelled by the threat of American military action against it; just as important were the *rivalry* implications – what the American ultimatum meant for Indian involvement in Afghanistan.) Yet, as the timeline suggests, something changed such that the actual American and international intervention led to a new decision – T4 – essentially to reverse T2 and instead support a new and emerging Taliban, this time in the form of a guerilla insurgency targeting American and coalition (later NATO/ISAF) troops and, importantly, the new Afghan government that the intervention had created. Note that the insurgency's emergence roughly coincided with the creation of the Bonn Conference government in 2002; its acceleration from roughly 2004 onwards likewise coincided with the first Afghan election that year, which affirmed Hamid Karzai as president, entrenching what Islamabad saw as an Indian-influenced regime. The key consideration, therefore, is the effect of T3 and its aftermath. What happened as a result of T3, or in the intervening time between T3 and T4, that culminated in the decision at T4?

To answer this question, we can revisit the logic associated with T2. Presumably, and particularly given their relative proximity in time, the basic rationale and thought process employed at T4 was the same as that applied at T2 – after all, much remained constant, including the leadership. We know that at T2 there were two overriding Pakistani concerns: (1) US military action ("the onslaught," as Musharraf describes it); and (2) India's potential role in Afghanistan. Recall that the first dynamic mentioned following Musharraf's invocation of the "national interest" was the possibility that India would take advantage of any Pakistani hesitancy by aligning with the United States, using it as a pretext or opportunity for some type of aggression against Pakistan – an offensive in Kashmir, concretization of the status quo in Kashmir, or perhaps most alarmingly, seizure of Pakistan's nuclear assets. Musharraf allegedly used the spectre of Indian cooperation with the United States to convince sceptics in the military establishment that Pakistan should instead take the initiative and side with American demands. The Indian bugaboo similarly featured in public statements made at the time, helping to convince citizens at large that Pakistan should side with the United States. As Bruce Reidel (2011, 67) summarizes, "Musharraf put it succinctly – Pakistan's policy derived from its concerns about India. There would be no role for India in the Afghan war." While the US threat was not irrelevant, as it helped to tip the scales towards cooperation, the Indian dynamic was likely decisive. The rivalry-associated *advantages* – cooperation with the United States would forestall otherwise-unchallenged Indian participation and the potential dangers that would result – made it unnecessary to defy the American ultimatum, even if there remained some rivalry-related reasons for maintaining support for the Taliban – indeed, the same reasons that drove support prior to 9/11. The American intervention, it should be clear, was a significant political shock, demanding a recalibration of standing policy for all regional actors. The decision at T2 reflects this reality.[14] Yet while the *policy* changed, the motivating rationale largely did not: Islamabad remained focused on preventing Indian influence in Afghanistan.

What, then, can these dynamics tell us about the decision at T4? Here again we see a policy shift, yet in keeping with T2, I argue – a consistent motivating rationale. The latter half of Reidel's summary is worth revisiting and emphasizing: *"There would be no role for India in the Afghan war."* Reidel meant this as a description of how the decision at T2 was made, but it could apply equally to the ongoing rationale through which an assessment of T3 – the actual American/international intervention – was filtered. As such, it is necessary to assess T3 itself: what aspects or dynamics of the intervention might have induced a policy shift at T4, assuming a rivalry-related motivation for Pakistani decision-making? We would expect to see aspects of the intervention, or developments associated with it, which might lead to increased (or at least the perception of increased) Indian influence or involvement in Afghanistan. Such developments would then trigger a re-evaluation in Islamabad, causing it to flip on the American intervention, given that the intervention might be producing the exact situation Pakistan's own participation was meant to exclude.

Keen on maintaining a light military footprint, as part of then-secretary of defense Donald Rumsfeld's vision of an agile, modern American military, the United States entered Afghanistan with a small contingent – "approximately 100 Central Intelligence Agency officers [and] 350 U.S. Special Forces soldiers" (Jones 2008, 7) – and used as its main

---

14 Or, more precisely, the *impending* American intervention is reflected in T2; American signalling following 9/11 was quite clear and there was little doubt on the part of any nation that the United States was sincere in its intention to intervene in Afghanistan. Note that Musharraf broadcast his desire to "save the Taliban" by forestalling the US invasion, even trying to convince Taliban leader Mullah Omar to hand over Osama bin Laden to the Americans (Omar, beholden to the Pashtun cultural practice of protecting "guests," steadfastly refused). These efforts failed, but this was clearly the preferred outcome for Pakistan, as it would have preserved the gains of the late 1990s by keeping the Taliban in power. Once American involvement was inevitable, however, the calculation became one of adjusting policy to reflect impending new realities.

fighting force the Northern Alliance (approximately 15,000 fighters). The United States thus took advantage of an already-existing enemy of the Taliban, essentially supercharging one side of an ongoing if low-boil civil conflict to alter decisively the political status quo in the country. Through the use of, in particular, air power and tactical strikes, the Americans were able to effectuate the collapse of the Taliban in less than three months. The Americans' decision to pursue what became known as the "Afghan Model" of warfare (support for an indigenous proxy force) was predicated on their own interests and the desire to overthrow the Taliban with as few US casualties as possible – in this, the model was strikingly effective (O'Hanlon 2002). Less consideration, by contrast, was given to the regional ramifications associated with intervening in this way, even as Islamabad explicitly lobbied against the empowerment of the Northern Alliance and exhorted the United States to pursue alternative options.

As noted, Indian and Pakistani involvement in Afghanistan during the 1990s came in the form of support for competing proxy forces: the mostly ethnic-Tajik Northern Alliance (India) and the almost entirely ethnic-Pashtun Taliban (Pakistan). Obviously, the US decision to side with the Northern Alliance was alarming for Islamabad; American involvement, given their military capacity, likely would prove decisive. Musharraf expressed anxiety that "the Northern Alliance ... would take over Afghanistan" (Woodward 2002, 260), but Pakistani concerns were ignored. Among Musharraf's early requests, for example, was that Pakistan be given time to form a "moderate Taliban" government and, at the very least, that the Northern Alliance not be the expeditionary force tasked with seizing and occupying Kabul (Rubin and Rashid 2008). Officially, the United States claimed that it did not order the Northern Alliance to enter Kabul, preferring a UN mandate for the capital with Northern Alliance forces stopped north of the city. Nonetheless, in early November 2001, as it became clear that Taliban forces were retreating from the capital to strongholds farther south, the Northern Alliance moved in and the Americans did not stop them. While cognizant of the promises that had been made[15] and aware of the complications that might arise from Tajik and Uzbek forces seizing a predominately Pashtun city, American calculations ultimately were driven by the desire to

---

15 In early November, as the Norther Alliance was making steady territorial gains moving south, President Bush assured Musharraf that he "fully [understood] your concern about the Northern Alliance" and that "we will encourage [them] to head south, across the Shamali Plains, but not into the city of Kabul" (quoted in Woodward 2002, 260–1).

achieve military objectives. Woodward (2002, 264), for example, reports that, for Secretary of Defense Rumsfeld, "the real question … was how will the taking of Kabul affect the mission of pursuing al Qaeda and other bad guys." Keeping promises to Pakistan was less of a priority.

What was an ancillary consideration for the United States was, by contrast, a central one for Pakistan. As Fair (2017, 139) summarizes: "the United States failed to honor its commitment to Musharraf to prevent the Northern Alliance from taking Kabul, unaware that Pakistan regarded the Northern Alliance as an Indian proxy. As Musharraf saw it, the United States had handed the keys of Kabul to his country's nemesis." Allowing the Northern Alliance to occupy territory in the north – their traditional seat of power and far from the Pakistan border – was one thing, but allowing them into the country's capital, potentially granting them central control of Afghanistan, was too much for the Pakistani leadership. Musharraf was "shocked" by what he referred to as a hostile "occupation" (Harding 2001). The reaction was not limited to the Pakistani president: "Privately, Pakistani diplomats admit they feel betrayed by their new allies in Washington, who failed to halt the alliance's advance" (Harding 2001). Hamid Gul, a former ISI chief, was even more pointed, accusing the Americans of "deceiving Pakistan" and suggesting that Musharraf "should do a lot of explaining" (quoted in Reddy 2002, 267). These sentiments likely were shared within the military and intelligence apparatuses. The United States and Northern Alliance leaders tried to mollify concerns by publicly insisting that a UN-backed multi-ethnic government was the desired administrative structure in Kabul (Moore 2001). The reality, however, was that the Northern Alliance was in control for the time being, with Taliban fighters pushed towards the mountainous regions near the Pakistan border.

The fall of Kabul marked a significant shift in the war: hostilities entered a new phase, away from larger battles towards guerilla-type hit-and-run engagements (a portent of things to come). The effectiveness of such tactics was augmented not only by the terrain in the south, but, additionally, by the porosity of the Afghanistan-Pakistan border. Many Taliban fighters retreated to the Pakistani side to recuperate, reorganize, and strategize future attacks (Behuria 2007; Yusuf 2014). It is the provision of these safe havens that many experts identify as Pakistan's first significant contribution to the new Taliban insurgency. By allowing Taliban leader Mullah Omar space to operate – it was later determined that Omar and much of the leadership had resettled in Quetta – and Taliban fighters avenues of retreat into territory off-limits to American airpower, Pakistan effectively undermined efforts to eradicate the Taliban as a fighting force in 2002. Over time, it also allowed them to gather renewed strength as an insurgency against US, international, and eventually newly constituted Afghan forces.

Officially, Pakistan maintained nominal support for what was now a major international coalition operating in Afghanistan, with the Pakistani military conducting antiterrorist and counterinsurgent operations in its northern areas along the border such as the Federally Administered Tribal Area (FATA), Balochistan, and the Northwest Frontier Province. Yet such operations were highly selective, drawing "clear distinction[s] between 'foreign' insurgents (predominately Uzbeks, Arabs and Chechens) and Taliban-aligned Pashtun fighters – the so-called 'good jihadis,' who could still potentially serve Pakistan's strategic interests" (Bird and Marshall 2011, 193) – this, despite "lavish" American aid designed to ensure Islamabad's genuine support for coalition priorities (194). Periodic arrests of Taliban leaders did occur, but such "crackdowns [were] limited in scope and … largely concerned with checking the autonomy of the Taliban leadership or satisfying external demands for greater Pakistani effort" (Nadiri 2014, 143). Sanctuary, training, and control: as the insurgency emerged, Pakistan played a significant role in gathering kindling, stoking flames, and causing it to spread.

In sum, what led to Pakistan's *volte face* at T4 in which it opted to support (indeed, help create) the new Taliban insurgency? My contention is that Pakistan's decision-making rationale was consistent during this period, and that it was the changing *circumstances* of the situation in Afghanistan that triggered the policy reversal. The decision at T2 (to end the existing relationship with the Taliban regime) was a challenging one. Musharraf faced opposition from the public as well as from high-ranking members of the military. Ultimately, the combination of a coercive threat from the United States and, even more important, the belief that resisting US demands would advantage India at Pakistan's expense, resulting in potential security threats in the form of Indian aggression, led Islamabad tentatively to support the American intervention. Yet, as we have seen, subsequent events led, not to the minimization of India's role in Afghanistan, but to the precise increase in Indian influence that Musharraf originally feared. The initial selection of the Northern Alliance as a proxy force was unwelcome in this regard – essentially a complete reversal of the "victory" Pakistan had achieved during the 1990s by installing its own preferred client in Kabul. Pakistan was clear in its demand that the Northern Alliance not be allowed to move into the south or to capture Kabul. As the Taliban slipped south away from American air power, they became the one force buffering a hostile Indian proxy from the Pakistani border.

Recall, also, that around this time New Delhi made its first significant pledges towards the reconstruction of Afghanistan. As detailed in chapter 5, India quickly became a major donor to the nascent, Northern Alliance–influenced, Bonn Conference–created regime in Kabul. Again, this was unwelcomed in Islamabad, further undermining its clear and stated position that there be "no role for India in the Afghan war." New Delhi's rapid move to open both old and new embassies and consulates (particularly in the south, near the border) likewise emphasized the extent to which India had a foothold in the new Afghanistan. Responding to these new circumstances, Islamabad not only offered sanctuary to retreating Taliban forces (reactivating old networks and relationships), but similarly provided active assistance and training. A new intervention in Afghanistan had begun: support for an insurgency against a new central government and its international (the United States and, shortly, NATO) backers. The same fears of Indian influence that drove the decision at T2 led to the decision at T4, even as the policy changed. The intervention that Pakistan conducted from 2002 onward was intended to balance against India and forestall strategic advantage from accruing to New Delhi, owing to the belief that any such advantage would lead to security challenges in the future.

Evidence in support of this contention is somewhat difficult to obtain, insofar as Pakistan's *official* position remained that of support for the Afghan government and the NATO/ISAF mission. Thus, unlike New Delhi, which could be open about its own intervention in the form of development activity, Islamabad denied its involvement and spoke more cryptically about potential justifications for its behaviour. Nonetheless, there exist snippets of information, in the form of reporting, interviews, and leaked classified material, that help to illustrate what Pakistan was doing in Afghanistan after 2003, and that provide insight into its motivations for such activity.

Pakistan's Support for the Insurgency

Establishing that Pakistan's top-down policy in Afghanistan was to support the Taliban is crucial for this case study. Islamabad, in fact, officially denied this involvement: in a terse exchange with regional expert Barnett Rubin at the Council on Foreign Relations in 2006, for example, Musharraf dismissed the notion that Pakistan was helping the Taliban. "We are not supporting [the] Taliban," he said. "We are not supporting anyone."[16] He went on to explicate "official" Pakistani policy: "We

---

16 For the full transcript, see Council on Foreign Relations (2006).

are totally neutral toward Afghanistan. We support the Bonn process. We support – actually, we are totally in support of President Karzai." If Pakistan were "neutral" – even more, if it actually had supported the Afghan government from 2002 onward, aligning it with India – it would not be possible to argue that some form of "balancing intervention" *against* India was taking place. As I show, however, the evidence is clear that Pakistan was not neutral in the manner Musharraf described, and indeed engaged in behaviour that directly undermined the Afghan government. As to the more equivocal possibility, which suggests that any support flowing from Pakistan to the Taliban was the product of lower-level (or retired) intelligence officials gone "rogue," rather than policy sanctioned by top-level decisionmakers, this too would be problematic for my argument. Had this been the case, the contention that Pakistan's intervention post-2001 was the product of broader, international factors such as rivalry would be suspect. It is therefore necessary to provide evidence not only that Pakistani operatives were involved in helping the Taliban, but further, that such activity was directed by the Pakistani leadership. This evidence is a necessary prelude to my argument that the rationale behind the intervention was international rivalry.

By 2003, insurgent training camps on the Pakistani side of the border had proliferated, abetted and often organized by ISI. Recruitment campaigns were widespread and aggressive, with the *madrassa* system (funded originally by Saudi Arabia going back decades) producing no shortage of available and committed jihadi graduates (Sirrs 2017). In Afghanistan, the attention had shifted to post-conflict reconstruction, with the United States and other international allies more or less convinced that the Taliban were a spent, defeated force. Any kinetic operations focused primarily on al-Qaeda and associated terrorist groups, a mission for which Pakistan remained a more or less reliable partner. As mentioned, subsequent events allow us to reinterpret evidence from this time as the seeds of an insurgency – supported by Pakistan – slowly taking root. At the time, however, it was generally believed that a widespread, long-term, organized guerilla insurgency was unlikely to persist in Afghanistan.[17]

---

17 Donald Rumsfeld announced the end of major combat operations in May 2003 (CNN 2003). Consider also the following description by Rhode and Sanger (2007): "Two years after the Taliban fell to an American-led coalition, a group of NATO ambassadors landed in Kabul, Afghanistan to survey what appeared to be a triumph … they thundered around the country in Black Hawk helicopters, with little fear for their safety … At a briefing from the United States Central Command, they were told that the Taliban were now a 'spent force.'"

Hard evidence of a Taliban revival emerged in 2004 (Coll 2018). Having simmered below boil, the security landscape in Afghanistan now changed drastically, from the "pockets of resistance" Rumsfeld dismissively mentioned in his end-of-combat-operations speech the year before to a recognized, and alarming, new reality of active, significant insurgency.

There are several reasons the insurgency might have ramped up at this point, beyond merely the natural momentum of the reorganization and recruitment activities begun earlier. First, the United States had largely shifted its focus to the war in Iraq. This left Islamabad (and other regional actors, including India) concerned about the American commitment and by extension the long-term prospects for governance and security in Afghanistan. If the United States left – and despite the now NATO-led ISAF mission, American departure effectively would undermine the potency of the international coalition – Pakistan wanted to be sure it could protect its long-standing security interests.[18] These interests would not be protected, Islamabad believed, by the Bonn-created government. Thus, the 2004 Afghan election that solidified Hamid Karzai as president potentially was related to the timing of the insurgency's efflorescence.[19] It is worth noting, finally, that 2004 also marked the beginning of the tenure of Lieutenant General Ashfaq Parvez Kayani as head of ISI. Brought in to replace the "moderate" Ehsan ul-Haq, Kayani would become, by many accounts, the architect of ISI's support for the insurgency. (In 2008 Kayani would succeed Musharraf as Chief of the Army, thus retaining an overall position of authority with respect to ISI and military operations vis-à-vis Afghanistan.) Kayani's appointment in 2004 reflected the anxiety produced by ongoing dynamics, each of which served to generate concern about the future of Afghanistan and Pakistan's ability to secure its own interests within that future.

Figure 2 shows the increase in insurgent attacks over the relevant period, while figure 3 graphs the number of fatalities that resulted.

---

18 Journalist and regional expert Carlotta Gall (2014, 77) reports: "By 2004, with the United States embroiled in the war in Iraq, Musharraf's generals began to think that the Americans would soon leave Afghanistan. The prospect gave them reason to strengthen links with Pakistan's main asset and former ally in Afghanistan, the Taliban."

19 According to Steve Coll (2018, 217), Afghan intelligence chief Amrullah Saleh believed the "consolidation of Karzai's government between 2003 and 2005 explained the timing of [the] Pakistani turn." "What made them switch?" Coll quotes Saleh as saying, "Parliamentary elections, presidential elections, Afghan consensus [that] we will make the new order work, and the growing, positive relationship of Afghanistan with India."

Figure 2. Number of Insurgent Attacks, by Year, Afghanistan, 2002–6

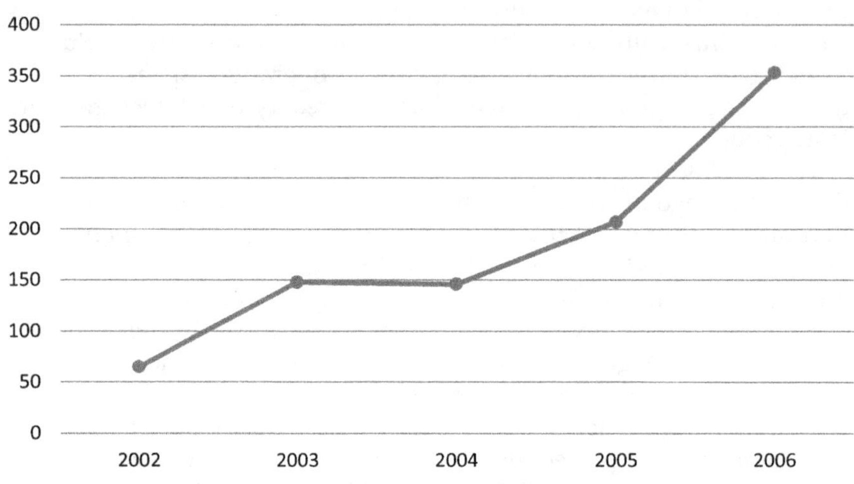

Source: Jones 2008.

Figure 3. Number of Fatalities from Insurgent Attacks, by Year, Afghanistan, 2002–6

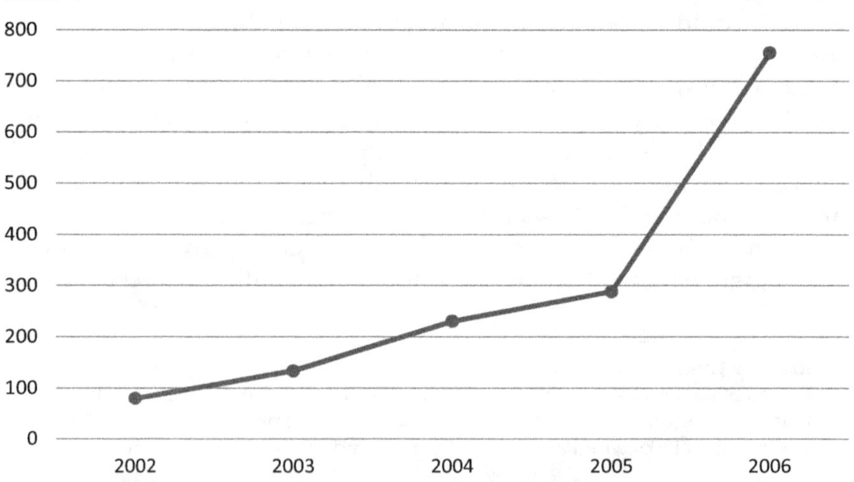

Source: Jones 2008, from the RAND-MIPT Terrorism Database (RAND n.d.). Jones states that the RAND-MIPT data are probably a conservative estimate of both attacks and fatalities "because most improvised explosive device and armed attacks were never reported in the press." The trends, nonetheless, are clear, with a steady increase in violence over the years 2002 to 2006.

Fair (2017, 136) summarizes that, "by 2005, with strong Pakistani support, the Afghan Taliban, along with support from the Waziristan-based Haqqani network, had launched an insurgent campaign against the US and ISAF missions."[20] In addition to sanctuary and recruiting, ISI helped "provide the Taliban with fuel, ammunition, and other logistical support, and they hold strategy meetings with the Taliban to discuss when to increase or ease up on operations" (Gall 2014, 129). By 2006, writes Sirrs (2017, 228), "the full impact of ISI's efforts to revive the Taliban was being felt inside Afghanistan, especially in the south. For the first time, Taliban forces were standing their ground, catching the NATO-led coalition by surprise." NATO/ISAF were forced to face up to this reality. Lieutenant General Michael Maples, then-director of the US Defense Intelligence Agency, offered the following summary to the US Congress in February 2006:

> In 2005, Taliban and other anti-coalition movement groups increased attacks by 20 per cent over 2004. Insurgents also increased suicide attacks almost four-fold, more than doubled improvised explosive devices attacks and increasingly used beheadings to terrorize the local population. This more active enemy will continue to negatively impact Afghan government and international efforts to create a stable Afghanistan. We judge insurgents now represent a greater threat to the expansion of Afghan government authority than at any point since late 2001, and will be active this spring. (United States 2006c)

That spring, in fact, the Taliban launched their largest offensive since 2001. Secretary of State Condoleezza Rice said at the time that "there was no doubt that people were surprized that the Taliban was able to regroup and come back in a large, well-organized force" (Rhode and Sanger 2007). In October 2006, NATO assumed security responsibilities for the entire country, largely as a response to the deteriorating security situation.

Publicly, the United States and its allies maintained the position that Pakistan was a crucial ally in Afghanistan – that year, the United States and Pakistan entered into a formal "strategic partnership" (see United States 2006b) – privately, frustration was beginning to mount as

---

20 The Haqqani network, an organization formed during the jihad against the Soviets, took its name from a *madrassa* in northern Pakistan; run by patriarch Jalaludin Haqqani and more recently his son Sirajuddin Haqqani, the group is a subset of, but nonetheless partially autonomous from, the broader Taliban movement. It is the organization in Afghanistan most closely linked to ISI. See Ruttig (2009).

evidence of ISI's activities accumulated. As a way of deflecting blame and justifying continued American financial and military support, blame was placed, as noted, on low-level "rogue" agents operating outside officially sanctioned channels (Johnson and Mason 2008; see also the discussions in Sirrs 2017; Waldman 2010). The "rogue ISI" hypothesis might have allowed high-level officials in both the United States and Pakistan to save face publicly, but was increasingly belied by evidence of sanctioned ISI complicity (see Guistozzi 2007; Jones 2010). By 2008,

> American and NATO intelligence [became] clearer, informed by harder evidence. It showed that Musharraf and Kayani had authorized deniable support to the [Taliban] movement, stopping short of weapons supply – the reporting showed that they were very cautious about directly providing money and weapons to the Taliban because they feared they could get caught and pay a price in the international system. Retired ISI officers, nongovernmental organizations, and other cutouts supplied the Taliban to reduce this risk. American intelligence reporting on individual, serving ISI case officers, who managed contacts with the Quetta Shura or the Haqqanis or Lashkar-e-Taiba, which fought in Kashmir, also showed that they were clearly in the Pakistan Army's chain of command. This reporting belied any "rogue ISI" hypothesis. (Coll 2018, 289)

This was not a problem that could be blamed on a renegade intelligence agency, unable to break pre-existing ties and beholden to Islamist sympathies in its lower ranks. Rather, the policy pursued by ISI during this time was the specific strategy coordinated by Kayani, Musharraf, and the top Pakistani leadership.

Interviews conducted by Matt Waldman (2010) provide some of the clearest, first-hand evidence of ISI's involvement in the insurgency. Speaking with active Taliban insurgents, high-level Taliban intermediaries, former Taliban commanders, and Afghan elders, he found evidence "that support to the Afghan insurgency is official ISI policy" (5). "Interviews strongly suggest that the ISI has representatives on the [Quetta] Shura," he writes, referring to the Taliban's leadership council, "either as participants or observers, and the agency is thus involved at the highest level of the movement" (6). "Every commander knows about the involvement of the ISI in the leadership," one Taliban commander said, "but we do not discuss it because we do not trust each other, and they are much stronger than us … Everyone sees the sun in the sky but cannot say it is the sun" (quoted, 6). Another opined that "all our plans and strategy [sic] are made in Pakistan and step by step it is brought to us, for military or other activities" (quoted, 10). A Taliban insurgent operating in Afghanistan's tumultuous south explained that "the ISI gives orders to the Taliban to attack road contractors, schools or aid workers. They tell our commander and he orders us. They say it is the Taliban's plan, we know it is their [ISI's] plan" (quoted, 12). Additional interviews highlight the continued porosity of the border, the provision of funding, munitions, and supplies, training and recruitment, and the special role of the Haqqani network.

In 2010, a cache of over 90,000 secret US intelligence files relating to the war in Afghanistan was released by WikiLeaks. Known collectively as the "Afghanistan War Logs" and published in conjunction with the *Guardian*, the *New York Times*, and *Der Spiegel*, the documents offered unique insight as to the on-the-ground realities of the NATO/ISAF campaign and the scope of the security challenge from 2004 to 2010. Among the more arresting revelations were the details of Pakistani involvement provided by the raw intelligence data (Walsh 2010). The documents are primarily intelligence reports about insurgent activity, threat assessments about potential attacks, accounts of meetings with prominent individuals and intelligence assets, and assessments of security challenges. Of course, these are American documents, detailing American intelligence and assessments – sometimes shared from and/or with other NATO and coalition partners or Afghanistan's National Directorate of Security – and therefore not "smoking gun" evidence of the kind that would, for example, connect the Pakistani military and ISI directly with the insurgency. Nonetheless, both the scope and level of specificity of the documents suggest the basic veracity of the accounts; details might err – an attack that did not occur, a speculation that was not borne out – but the broader picture of Pakistan's role is brought into focus. The documents corroborate the information contained in Waldman's (2010) interviews with current and former Taliban commanders and fighters. The provision of weapons, ammunition, and supplies, the coordination of attacks and the specification of targets, the broader control over strategy, the training at camps on the Pakistani side of the border, and the physical presence of ISI operatives embedded with, and fighting alongside, the Taliban. All of these claims are supported by the intelligence assessments contained in the War Logs release.[21]

This evidence can be added to other on-the-ground reporting and analysis conducted by journalists and regional experts. Carlotta Gall (2014) and Steve Coll (2018), in particular, have written exhaustively

---

21 See https://wardiary.wikileaks.org/iraq/diarydig.

researched books, drawing on years of experience and travel in the region, that concentrate on the issue of Pakistani support for the Taliban. Of this support, Gall (2014, 159) writes: "Pakistan denied all this. In every interview, officials insisted that they wanted a stable Afghanistan and were working to defeat terrorism. But Pakistan's actions tell a different story. Even as its militants at home were surging out of control, and the cost in lives and stability to Pakistan was becoming exorbitant, Pakistan's military leaders continued to pursue a policy of using the Taliban to attack the Afghan government and NATO forces in Afghanistan." As quoted previously, but worth revisiting now, Coll (2018, 667) calls the "failure to solve the riddle of ISI and to stop its covert interference in Afghanistan" the "greatest strategic failure of the … war."

The riddle eluded the internationally community for two decades. The year 2010 was the deadliest of the war in terms of coalition casualties, marking the culmination of a steady and unbroken increase since 2003, as the insurgency accelerated in size and scale (iCasualties.org n.d.). In 2011, Chairman of the Joint Chiefs of Staff Admiral Michael Mullen delivered stunning testimony to the US Congress. In discussing the ongoing security challenges in Afghanistan, Admiral Mullen explicitly identified Pakistan's role vis-à-vis the insurgency:

> A second, but no less worrisome, challenge we face is the impunity with which certain extremist groups are allowed to operate from Pakistani soil. The Haqqani network for one acts as a veritable arm of Pakistan's Internal Services Intelligence agency. With ISI support, Haqqani operatives planned and conducted that truck bomb attack [in Wardak province] as well as the assault on our embassy. We also have credible intelligence that they were behind the June 28 attack on the Intercontinental Hotel in Kabul and a host of other smaller, but effective operations. (United States 2011)

This was among the first times an American or NATO official had spoken in such direct terms, and certainly Mullen was the most high-profile to offer an assessment of this kind in public. His decision to do so likely derived from the frustration felt by the Americans and their allies as they considered the steady stream of intelligence regarding Pakistan's activities, the fallout out from the attacks Mullen mentions (and others), and the impregnable denialism of Pakistani officials.

Although the trend of coalition fatalities tapered after the peak in 2010, coinciding with a drawdown in overall troop levels, the security situation remained fraught in subsequent years. The ISAF was disbanded in 2014, as NATO's official combat operations came to a close. The decision to end the official combat phase was as much about war fatigue and political promises as it was about any discernible progress on the ground.[22] Subsequently, the United States and other partners were involved in Operation Resolute Support, or Resolute Support Mission (RSM), intended to train and assist Afghan security forces as they continued the fight against the Taliban and affiliated insurgent groups. As we now know, this arrangement ultimately was untenable. Over the final years of the mission, IED attacks became rampant[23] and the Taliban began retaking control of larger and larger swaths of territory. During this period, Pakistan's involvement with the insurgency continued; there is evidence, in particular, of Islamabad's attempting to control any embryonic negotiations between the Taliban and the Afghan government (along with US/NATO). Those Taliban who had been involved in, or attempted to initiate, negotiations absent Pakistani approval were, for example, subject to seizure and arrest, unlike more compliant counterparts (Fair 2017). This amounted to an effective veto on any reconciliation attempts. Finally, in August 2021, the Taliban defeated the ANSF and regained control of the country. The Taliban's summer offensive was aided, according to regional expert Jane Perlez (2021), by "a surge of new fighters" flowing across the border from sanctuaries in Pakistan, "waved [on]" by the Pakistani military to deliver a "final coup de grace" to Afghan forces and, by extension, the American and NATO countries that had trained them.

The Rivalry Explanation

Despite a general consensus on the part of US/NATO that Pakistan engaged in the behaviour described above, *dealing* with that behaviour remained the "riddle" that Coll (2018) describes, one that doggedly resisted solution and led in part to the "strategic failure" that culminated in August 2021. Gall (2014, 159) hints at the nature of this riddle, or puzzle, when she writes that "even as its militants at home

---

22 Even as the United States officially announced the end of combat operations, complete with optimistic appraisals and public pronouncements of improving security and positive trends, Lieutenant General Joseph Anderson, the departing US commander of forces in Afghanistan, could not hide his concerns: "The fact that we are in less places, the fact that there are less of us as a coalition, is obviously concerning" (quoted in Azam 2014).
23 According to a February 2018 UN report, 2016 and 2017 were the deadliest years for civilians, with most fatalities attributable to either suicide attacks or IEDs. See United Nations Assistance Mission in Afghanistan (2017).

were surging out of control" – that is, creating a major domestic security challenge – "and the cost in lives and stability to Pakistan was becoming exorbitant" – that is, both security costs and the negative consequences of instability more generally, including lost economic opportunities and even diplomatic isolation – "Pakistan's ... leader's continued to pursue a policy of using the Taliban to attack the Afghan government and NATO forces in Afghanistan." The implied question is: why did Pakistan continue to support an insurgency as the immediate costs of doing so rose and became, by dint of most outside observers, prohibitive?

Faced with such behaviour, many analysts have employed the language of "paranoia" and "obsession." Frederick Kagan (2012, 103), for example, argues: "Those in the Pakistani leadership who believe that India is up to no good in Afghanistan will always find 'proof' of their paranoia. The fear is irrational, and reality is almost irrelevant in addressing it." Vanda Felbab-Brown (2018) of the Brookings Institution writes of "Pakistan's paranoia of India's engagement in Afghanistan" in the context of a proposed increase in India's role post-2018. William Dalrymple (2013), for his part, describes General Kayani's "burning obsession" for "India's presence in Afghanistan." Fréderic Grare (2010, 17) talks about the "paranoia [that] feeds [Pakistan's] strategic outlook, hence the floating accusations of terrorism and sabotage, conspiracy theories regarding Indian consulates in Afghanistan, and allegations of Indian support for the Baloch and Wazir insurgencies." Dexter Filkins (2008), writing in the *New York Times*, suggests that "[t]he most common theory offered to explain Pakistan's continued contact with Islamic militants is the country's obsession with India ... Pakistan's officer corps remains obsessed by the prospect of Indian domination of Afghanistan should the Americans leave." The point is not to police the language analysts' and scholars' descriptions of Pakistani foreign policy – it is understandable that one might use "paranoid" as shorthand for Islamabad's cautious, constant, even obsessive focus on India – but rather the *implications of thinking about Pakistani foreign policy in this way.* Not only does it lead to quasi-fatalist positions with respect to policy options – as Kagan concludes, "reality is irrelevant in addressing" Pakistani perceptions, so why bother trying? – but also, from a theoretical point of view, it suggests that Pakistan's behaviour was either unsystematic and capricious, or that it was predicated on the personal failings/emotions and psychological pathologies of its leaders (for example, it is *Kayani's* "burning obsession" driving policy, the implication being that a different decision-maker might have had a different focus), or that of entire institutions

(ISI or the "officer corps"). If unsystematic, it is not subject to generalizable explanations; if psychological, it is subject to explanations at the individual level of analysis. I argue, by contrast, that Pakistan's behaviour is explicable through an appreciation of the international pressures associated with ongoing rivalry, and that it is generalizable to other instances of rivalry in the international system, irrespective of psychological or emotional factors associated with individual leaders or decisionmakers.

Pakistan's primary aim was (and is) to keep India out of Afghanistan and, perhaps more realistically, to minimize its influence as much as possible. Steve Coll (2018) recounts a meeting between Karzai and Kayani in 2010, as the possibility of negotiations with the Taliban was picking up momentum. According to Coll, Kayani suggested to Karzai that he had the power to rein in the Taliban: "The heart of Kayani's offer to Karzai was 'We can help you sort out the insurgency – we can turn it off,' as a NATO diplomat briefed on the discussion soon after described it. In exchange, *Pakistan would expect Karzai to 'end' – that was the word Kayani used, according to these accounts – Indian influence in Afghanistan*" (Coll 2018, 427, emphasis added). In other words, no role whatsoever for India. This was, of course, in keeping with Pakistan's position on Afghanistan going back decades: preventing Indian influence so as to preclude a security threat from the east *and* the west, a position tied to the history of the India-Pakistan relationship. Kayani himself declared in a speech in 2001: "Strategically, we cannot have an Afghan army on our western border which has an Indian mindset and capabilities to take on Pakistan" (quoted in Basit 2015). The implications of such a scenario were considered sufficient to warrant opposition to any and all Indian involvement in Afghanistan, particularly when Islamabad had comparatively lost its own influence, as its did following the Taliban's ouster in 2001. The stakes had become incredibly high – "existential," in the words of Pande (2016).

These concerns are similarly reflected in diplomatic cables sent from the American embassy in Islamabad to the State Department, in which US diplomats recount their conversations with Pakistani officials and offer assessments of Pakistani priorities in Afghanistan. It goes without saying that not all such statements – even those made in private, as most of the quoted statements were – can be taken at face value. Much is standard diplomatic obfuscation, the denial of any aggressive behaviour whatsoever, and the insistence that "Pakistan and the US had a convergence of interests" in Afghanistan, when their actions belied such a claim. Yet they are nonetheless illuminating for the picture they paint of Pakistani priorities. We see, for example, a clear emphasis on the Balochistan issue. Pakistani officials repeatedly pointed to perceived Indian support for rebels in the province:

> India was also providing support and cash to "feudal tribals" who were making trouble in Balochistan.[24]
>
> [T]he GOP [government of Pakistan] had evidence that a "proxy force" (i.e., India) was putting significant amounts of money into Balochistan.[25]
>
> Musharraf ... alluded to Indian support to the rebellious Bugti tribe, blaming both the Bugtis and Indian intelligence agencies for a recent series of fatal bombings in Quetta and telling Boucher that he has sigint [signals intelligence] to prove Indian complicity.[26]
>
> Ali added that "we all know" that India has "activities" in the region [of Balochistan].[27]
>
> He added that India would need to gain Pakistan's trust and indicated that reducing the Indian footprint in Afghanistan and halting Indian support of militants in Balochistan would be steps in the right direction.[28]

In the context of these concerns, much was made of the Indian consulates that had been established (or re-established) following 2001: "Musharraf began by discussing reports of Afghan-Indian intelligence operations against Pakistan. He cited the growing number of Indian consulates in Afghanistan and continued Indian involvement in adverse activities in Pakistan." In an otherwise "cordial" meeting between Afghan and Pakistani officials, friction arose due to the Pakistani side's inability to get past the issue of "India using Afghanistan as a base for nefarious operations in Balochistan and the Tribal Areas."[29] The question of the consulates, in particular, frustrated the Afghan government, insofar as

---

24 WikiLeaks, "President Musharraf expresses concern to Senator Hagel on his relationship with the US," 14 April 2006, online at https://wikileaks.org/plusd /cables/06ISLAMABAD6420_a.html.

25 WikiLeaks, "Prime Minister Aziz discusses challenges on the Afghan border and reviews request," 19 June 2006, https://wikileaks.org/plusd/cables/06ISLAMABAD11504_ a.html.

26 WikiLeaks, "President Musharraf determined to deal with border areas," 8 November 2006, https://wikileaks.org/plusd/cables/06ISLAMABAD21879_a.html.

27 WikiLeaks, "Codel Tierney meets with Pakistani Prime Minister Gilani," 17 November 2009, https://wikileaks.org/plusd/cables/09ISLAMABAD2769_a .html.

28 WikiLeaks, "Codel Kerry's meeting with PM Gilani," 19 February 2010, https:// wikileaks.org/plusd/cables/10ISLAMABAD399_a.html.

29 WikiLeaks, "Afghan ambassador on FM Spanta's June 23 visit to Islamabad," 27 June 2006, online at https://wikileaks.org/plusd/cables/06ISLAMABAD12211_a .html.

it was unable to "disabuse the GOP of its misimpression regarding the nature and extent of the official Indian presence in Afghanistan," insisting that only six, not the twelve that Pakistan alleged, "official Indian posts" were open in Afghanistan.[30] The Americans commented in an endnote that they were "not surprised that the 'Indian consulate' conspiracy took up much of [Afghan foreign minister] Spanta's visit [with Pakistani officials], as Pakistani interlocutors at every level subscribed to the theory."[31] In such assessments we see again why the word "paranoid" might be employed – or, indeed, "conspiracy theory," as was the case here – in describing Pakistan's position regarding Indian influence. Without question, Islamabad afforded the topic of Indian support for Balochi rebels an importance well above what Washington, Kabul, or certainly New Delhi believed appropriate or commensurate with realities on the ground.[32] Yet the depths of this perception among Pakistani officials – "interlocutors at every level subscribed to the theory" – suggests a systematic cause, a collective "paranoia" that cannot thereby be explained by what is conventionally meant by the term: non-rationality at the individual level.

It is important to note that, despite "frustration" regarding Pakistan's persistence on this point, it is not as though the claims are entirely baseless. Even Kagan (2012, 103) – who, as described above, believes "Pakistani perceptions of Indian intentions [in Afghanistan are] badly skewed" – writes that "India has … done just enough in Afghanistan to support Pakistani conspiracy theories … reports of Indian intelligence operatives in Afghanistan are frequent and credible enough to maintain Pakistani suspicions." Christine Fair (2010, 14), likewise observes with respect to Pakistan claims about the consulates: "anecdotal evidence suggests that, while Pakistan's most sweeping claims are ill-founded, Indian claims to complete innocence also are unlikely to be true." Avinash Paliwal (2017, 238–9) describes Indian involvement in Balochistan, including the relationship with Afghan intelligence through which such activity was made possible:

Soon after 2002 India began developing its covert infrastructure to develop what Indian officials called their "Baloch" and "Pashtun" cards. Afghanistan's intelligence agency, the National Directorate of Security

---

30 Ibid.

31 Ibid.

32 Musharraf did not reserve these talking points for behind closed doors, but also repeated them publicly following meetings with Afghan and American officials; see Gall (2006).

(NDS), then under Mohammad Arif Sarwari, who had an excellent rapport with India since the civil war years, was a strong ally. With Karzai's permission, Arif began dispatching NDS officers for training to India, unlocking new and heightened levels of intelligence cooperation. Arif's successor, Amrullah Saleh, also had a close relationship with [Indian officials]. Though various (serving and retired) Indian intelligence officers acknowledge this relationship, [former Assistant Director of the Joint Intelligence Committee at India's National Security Council Secretariat Benoy] Khare, who knew its nuts-and-bolts, is categorical that India remains "very close to the NDS." Though he denies that such links translate into joint offensive operations against Pakistan, the latter's allegation of a R&AW[*sic*]-NDS "nexus," more broadly if not on specific operations, is accurate.

In 2004, a major insurrection broke out in Balochistan, requiring the deployment of the Pakistani military. As Paliwal notes, while specific claims regarding the participation of Indian special "commandos" in the insurrection were likely "incorrect," "that the NDS chief [Amrullah] Saleh was closely engaged with the Baloch rebels as well as [Indian National Security Advisor M.K.] Narayanan was amply clear" (Paliwal 2017, 240). Pakistani concerns about Indian activity were not, therefore, completely unfounded, only "exaggerated," according to those – Washington, Kabul, New Delhi – inconvenienced by the claims. Of course, by standard measures this assessment of "exaggeration" is likely correct; for Pakistan, however, such exaggeration (or overwrought concern) was inevitable *in the context of rivalry* – which is to say, in the context of a decades-long conflictual relationship[33] squeezed by the imperatives for security and survival mandated by the international system.

That Indian activity seemed to occur in conjunction with the NDS (and therefore the Afghan government) was precise confirmation of Pakistani fears about what would occur were India to gain influence in Afghanistan post-2001. Unrest along the western border – requiring the deployment of conventional military forces away from the east – such as occurred in Balochistan in 2004, with violence continuing until a ceasefire in 2008, is the exact scenario Pakistan's Afghan policy had

---

33 Indian support for Balochi rebels stretches back to as early as the 1970s; of the
   period, an Indian intelligence official said "we gave them everything" (quoted in
   Paliwal 2017, 38).

been designed for decades to prevent. The belief was that an Afghanistan beholden to India would foment such unrest and/or allow India access to do it itself.[34] There was even concern, as the so-called Pakistani Taliban – an entity separate from the Afghan version and known also by the name Tehrik-e-Taliban – emerged in 2007 and took aim at the Pakistani state, that India, again through Afghanistan, was helping to stimulate instability inside Pakistan by supporting the group. "Under the old adage 'The enemy of my enemy is my friend,'" writes Coll (2018, 647), "there seemed scope for Afghan intelligence to cooperate with the Pakistani Taliban." Although Pakistani suspicions were strong despite a relative dearth of concrete evidence, there was just enough smoke to suggest fire. In 2013, Pakistani Taliban leader Latif Mehsud was in Afghanistan under the protection of the NDS, only to be snatched up by the United States (Mehsud allegedly had been involved in the failed 2010 Times Square bombing plot) and eventually handed over to Pakistani authorities (Bhatnagar and Mohan 2016). In 2017, a former Pakistani Taliban commander claimed that India's Research and Analysis Wing and the NDS "provided safe heavens [*sic*] to terrorist organizations in Afghanistan" (Zaidi 2017).[35] This was in addition to any classified intelligence Islamabad might have collected regarding such activities.[36] While many, correctly, saw the emergence of the Pakistani Taliban as blowback for the decades Pakistan had spent fostering Islamism in the region (see Ganguly and Kapur 2010), it was also true that the group's presence rekindled concerns regarding Pashtun separatism or, at the very least, the possibility of instability in Pashtun areas

---

34 In assessing "the Pakistan's government's own perception of its security requirements," a cable from September 2009 highlights "the perception of India as the primary threat to the Pakistani state that colors its perceptions of the conflict in Afghanistan and Pakistan's security needs. The Pakistani establishment fears a pro-India government in Afghanistan would allow India to operate a proxy war against Pakistan from its territory." See WikiLeaks, "Reviewing our Afghanistan-Pakistan strategy," 23 September 2009, https://wikileaks.org/plusd/cables/09ISLAMABAD2295_a.html.

35 The veracity of the confession has been challenged, however; see "Ehsanullah Esan's India claims and Pakistan's favorite narrative" (Zaidi 2017).

36 Reports from two Pakistan-based government-sponsored think tanks have made further claims regarding Indian involvement in Balochistan and FATA; see Kehtran (2017) and Wazir (2011). Both articles claim that Pakistani intelligence was in possession of concrete evidence of the Research and Analysis Wing's involvement in Balochistan and the tribal areas.

that might require military action.[37] Indeed, the Pakistani army was forced to undertake significant operations to quell the Pakistani Taliban, losing thousands of soldiers in the process (Siddiqa 2011). Whether in the form of support for Balochi rebels or for Tehrik-e-Taliban, Islamabad was concerned that India would leverage domestic groups against Pakistan, both because this specific tactic had been employed in the past (i.e., before 2001, and particularly in the mid-1970s) and because of associated fears of a potential two-front problem in any direct confrontation with India.

This latter fear is accentuated by an important consequence of rivalry: the belief that (another) conventional confrontation is possible, even likely. It is for this reason that Pakistan maintained its military's conventional posture, rather than adapting to counterinsurgency requirements that would have been helpful in dealing with domestic militant groups and terrorists such as the Pakistani Taliban. This refusal led to much criticism and confusion, in particular from the United States,[38] especially since domestic extremists appeared to represent a larger, more immediate threat to the Pakistani state. As Fair and Jones (2009, 162) summarize, "Pakistan prefers to retain its conventional focus against India and hesitates to adopt a counter-insurgency orientation, viewing such operations against internal threats as residing at the lower end of a conventional-conflict spectrum." And elsewhere: "The army is a conventional force primarily geared towards a conflict with India, a configuration which it prefers. In the early months of General Ashfaq Kayani's tenure as chief of army staff from the end of 2007, US officials were optimistic that Pakistan would formally adopt a counter-insurgency strategy. Since then, Kayani has frequently said that the army will not become

---

37 Many of the subgroups within the Pakistani Taliban are Punjabi, not Pashtun, but the group as a whole is most active in the northern areas, particularly Waziristan and FATA (now part of Khyber Pakhtunkhwa). In any event, the possibility of Pashtun nationalism – one of the driving forces behind Pakistani concerns regarding Afghanistan since partition – resurfaced in the context of greater instability along the border. There was (and is) a synergy between the Balochi insurgency and this dynamic; Ganguly and Howenstein (2009, 134) note the "alliance of northern Baluchis with tribes in FATA in an effort to form an ethnically Pashtun province in Pakistan." In this context, Islamabad would see Indian instigation along the border as extremely problematic.

38 Recall here Washington's consternation in the mid-1980s that much of its military aid went to equipment and planning directed towards India rather than the guerrilla fight against the Soviets. This pattern repeated itself post-2001. For example, Grare (2010, 18) points out that, of the first US$15 billion the United States "ostensibly [offered Pakistan] as reimbursement [for] expenses in the war on terror" US$4 billion was "spent on conventional equipment for its army and air force."

a counter-insurgency force; rather, the bulk of the army will remain deployed along the Indian border" (Fair and Jones 2009, 163). Again, this dogged refusal to adjust military posture elicits the perception that Pakistan is "obsessed" with the Indian threat, and, much like assessments of the Balochistan issue, this, in a vacuum, might be a fair characterization. Yet having fought multiple conventional wars with India in the past, Pakistan believes that it might have to do so again in the future (*experience* is a major part of its calculation); by this view, to abandon a posture that prepares it for such an eventuality would be derelict. For Pakistan, the prospect of such a conflict is existential,[39] underscoring the extent to which the India-focused orientation is unlikely to change. That it has survived decades of intense diplomatic pressure and billions upon billions of US military aid intended, essentially, to "buy" Pakistani compliance and support for the counterinsurgent, counterterrorist-focused US/NATO operation in Afghanistan is further evidence to this effect.[40]

To summarize, briefly, we can glean two basic dynamics at play with respect to Pakistan's intervention in Afghanistan in the form of its support for the Taliban insurgency. First, its goal was no role for India whatsoever in the country. Second, its concern regarding any failure to achieve this goal stemmed from the fear that Indian influence in Afghanistan would lead to destabilization along or near Pakistan's border. An Afghanistan in which India had a major role, up to and including close relationships with the Afghan military and security institutions – recall that many prominent Afghan security and intelligence officials were drawn from, or had connections with, the India-aligned Northern Alliance – would allow India to force Pakistan to divert military resources away from the east or, more nefariously, as part of a coordinated two-front offensive. Islamabad believed this destabilization activity was likely to occur, given the history of the relationship in which similar tactics had been employed and, perhaps even more important, *it had to assume such activity would occur* because it considered the implications potentially existential. In the context of a future conflict, to be faced by a "pincer-movement," with two hostile borders and therefore two fronts,

---

39 The perception can be linked to ISI behaviour in Afghanistan. As Sirrs (2017, 7) explains in his assessment of the intelligence agency, "[r]eflecting the siege mentality of its army master, ISI believes it is engaged in an *existential war for national survival* in the face of India's expanding military capabilities not to mention New Delhi's aspirations for great power status" (emphasis added).

40 Fair (2017, 140) estimates that since 2001 Pakistan has received approximately US$33 billion "in security and economic assistance as well as CSF [Coalition Support Funds] reimbursements."

would be devastating. Given the basic assumption that this conflict eventually would occur, it logically followed that preventing Indian influence in Afghanistan took on extreme importance.

Not only was Pakistan's strategy intended to undermine Indian influence in Afghanistan in a general sense, there is further evidence that India was the *specific* target of Pakistani efforts. As the Afghanistan War Logs demonstrate, for example, Indian assets and personnel frequently were singled out for attack: targeting the Indian embassy in Kabul and consulates in Kandahar, Jalalabad, Herat, Kandahar, and Mazar-e-Sharif; targeting an Indian road construction company and a telecommunications company; plots to kidnap Indian nationals, representatives, and diplomats; and standing offers of payment for the murder of Indian citizens in Afghanistan.[41]

Perhaps the most prominent incident was the 2008 attack on the embassy in Kabul, "allegedly directed by Pakistan's intelligence service," which killed fifty-eight and wounded dozens of others (Curtis 2012, 264). Evidence linking ISI to the operation is robust. Before the attack, "the National Security Agency intercepted communications between ISI officers and the Taliban indicating planning was under way for a big attack in Afghanistan" (Sirrs 2017, 238). Though unable to determine the target and thus prevent the bombing, "a cellphone found in the embassy wreckage enabled investigators to trace phone calls made by the perpetrators to an ISI officer in Peshawar" (238). The CIA and NDS both concluded that the attack had been coordinated by ISI through the Haqqani network, operating out of North Waziristan. As Steve Coll (2018, 308) summarizes, "[t]he strike was effectively an act of guerilla war by the Pakistan Army against [the] Indian military." Just fifteen months later, the embassy was attacked again, this time with seventeen killed and over seventy others wounded. The Afghan government stated its belief that this second attack "was planned and implemented from outside Afghan borders" by the same elements (namely, ISI) responsible for the 2008 bombing (Faiez and Magnier 2009). A major blast on 31 May 2017 killed over eighty in the international section of Kabul, near the Indian and German embassies. NDS once again blamed the Haqqani network and ISI for the bombing (Arnold 2017). Although it is unclear whether the Indian embassy was the explicit target, given the history it is not likely that the proximity of the blast was a coincidence.

In addition to the main embassy in Kabul, Indian consulates throughout Afghanistan were similarly subject to repeated attack, as shown in box 1.

---

41 See https://wardiary.wikileaks.org/iraq/diarydig.

Box 1. Attacks against the Indian Embassy and Consulates in Afghanistan, 2004–16

24 January 2006: attack on Indian consulate in Kandahar.

"In one of two related attacks, unknown perpetrators threw a hand grenade at the Indian consulate in Kandahar (Province), Afghanistan, but it exploded outside, causing no casualties. It was not reported whether or not there was property damage, and there were no reported claims of responsibility for the attack."

5 April 2006: attack on Indian consulate in Herat.

"An unknown number of unknown perpetrators detonated a bomb near the Indian consulate in the city of Herat, Afghanistan. No one was injured or killed in the blast. No group claimed responsibility for the attack."

13 December 2007: attack on Indian consulate in Jalalabad.

"Two improvised explosive devices were thrown outside the Indian consulate in the city of Jalalabad in eastern Afghanistan. There were no casualties or damage. Afghan Islamic Press reported that a similar incident was reported several days before. The Taliban was suspected in both attacks."

7 July 2008: attack on Indian embassy in Kabul.

"On Monday morning at 8:30, 58 were killed and 141 wounded when a suicide car bomber targeted the Indian Embassy in Kabul, Kabul province, Afghanistan. The suicide bomber detonated 220 pounds of explosives near a row of metal turnstiles outside the embassy gates after being denied access to enter the embassy. Seventeen students and four Indian nationals, in addition to dozens of Afghan men who line up every morning to apply for visas, were killed in the attack. Two diplomatic vehicles and several nearby shops were also damaged or destroyed in the blast. Although authorities held the Taliban responsible for the bombing attack, a spokesman for the Taliban's Zabihullah Mujahed group denied responsibility on 07/08/2008 on Tuesday to Agence France-Presse. No claim of responsibility was made for the incident."

8 October 2009: attack on Indian embassy in Kabul.

"On Thursday morning at about 0830, in Kabul, Afghanistan, a suicide bomber detonated his vehicle-borne improvised explosive device near the outer wall of the Indian Embassy, killing 12 police officers and civilians, injuring at least 83 police officers and civilians, and damaging the embassy, many vehicles, many residences, and many shops. The

Indian embassy was located near Afghanistan's Ministry of Interior, which was also damaged. The Taliban claimed responsibility."

3 August 2013: attack on Indian consulate in Jalalabad.

"Three assailants wearing explosives-laden vests attempted to ram their vehicle into the Indian Consulate in Jalalabad city, Nangarhar province, Afghanistan. Two assailants opened fire on the checkpoint guards and one assailant detonated a vest. Nine civilians and three assailants were killed and 22 other people were injured in the attack. No group claimed responsibility for the incident; however, the police commissioner attributed the attack to Lashkar-e-Taiba ... and the Haqqani Network."

13 March 2014: attempted attack on Indian consulate in Kandahar city.

"A suicide bomber attempted to detonate an explosives-laden vest at the Indian Consulate in Kandahar city, Kandahar province, Afghanistan. The assailant was killed and the explosives-laden vest was defused by authorities. No group claimed responsibility for the incident."

23 May 2014: attack on Indian consulate in Herat.

"Assailants opened fire on the Indian consulate in Herat province, Afghanistan. Three assailants were killed and two police officers were wounded in the attack. No group claimed responsibility for the incident; however, sources attributed the attack to Lashkar-e-Taiba (LeT) and the Taliban."

20 December 2015: attempted attack on Indian consulate in Jalalabad.

"A suicide bomber attempted to attack the Indian consulate in Jalalabad, Nangarhar province, Afghanistan. The assailant was detained before reaching his target and confessed to being a member of the Taliban."

3 January 2016: attack on Indian consulate in Mazar-e-Sharif.

"Assailants armed with rocket-propelled grenades ... and firearms attacked the Indian consulate in Mazari Sharif [*sic*] city, Balkh province, Afghanistan. Seven people, including a police officer, and all six assailants were killed and eight others were injured in the ensuing clash that lasted until January 5, 2016. No group claimed responsibility; however, sources attributed the attack to Jaish-e-Mohammad."

8 January 2016: attempted attack on Indian consulate in Herat.

"An explosives-laden vehicle was discovered and defused near the Indian consulate in Herat province, Afghanistan. No group claimed responsibility for the incident; however, one person was arrested in connection with the attempted attack."

2 March 2016: attack on Indian consulate in Jalalabad.

"A suicide bomber detonated an explosives-laden vehicle at the entrance of the Indian consulate in Jalalabad, Nangarhar, Afghanistan. Additional assailants stormed the consulate and opened fire. At least two people and four assailants were killed and 19 people were injured in the blast and ensuing clash; the victims included civilians and security force members. The Khorasan Chapter of the Islamic State claimed responsibility for the attack. Authorities also suspected Taliban involvement."

Source: National Consortium for the Study of Terrorism and Responses to Terrorism Global Terrorism Database.

Although not all attacks were as deadly or as well planned as the 2008 embassy bombing, the timeline in the box indicates a clear pattern of behaviour: the systematic targeting of Indian diplomatic installations. It is not possible to attribute ISI or Pakistani-complicity directly in each and every incident, but the known links between the Taliban/Haqqani network and the Pakistani intelligence agency (as made clear by the Afghanistan War Logs release) allow for a reasonable inference that the frequency of the attacks was partly due to ISI pressure, doubly so considering Islamabad's well-known objections to India's diplomatic presence, particularly in the south, and the belief that the consulates there were being used to help support Balochi and Pashtun rebels.

Diplomatic installations were not the only Indian targets during this time. Indian construction workers – recall that infrastructure development was a major feature of New Delhi's involvement in Afghanistan – also faced consistent security challenges, to the point that New Delhi cited the killings of Indian workers as proof that Pakistan was seeking to discourage India's presence in Afghanistan. In 2010, for example, a spate of terrorist attacks against Indians led Minister of External Affairs S.M. Krishna to declare that Indians had become "soft targets" in Afghanistan for terrorist organizations keen on derailing Indian-Afghan relations (*Hindustan Times* 2010). (Such concerns were also communicated extensively to the United States, as evidenced by the statements recorded in US diplomatic cables from New Delhi.) Although the Zaranj-Delaram road was comparatively short (approximately 215 kilometres), its construction road took four years, primarily due to security challenges and frequent attacks (129 Afghans were killed during construction, as well as six Indians) (*Hindu* 2009). In addition to attacks on road workers, the 26 February 2010 attack on the Hamid Guesthouse in

Kabul – for foreign workers and known to be popular with Indian doctors – resulted in eighteen casualties, nine of them Indian (Rubin 2010). In 2013, an ISI-directed Taliban plot to blow up the Salma Dam (now known as the India-Afghanistan Friendship Dam), another centrepiece of India's infrastructure efforts and at the time still under construction, was foiled by NDS (Bhatnagar and Mohan 2016; Ghanizada 2013). In 2017, a checkpoint near the dam was attacked by gunmen, killing ten policemen (*Times of India* 2017). In April 2012, the Afghan parliament – built by India – was one of a spate of targets in a large, coordinated Taliban attack (*BBC News* 2012).[42] The parliament was struck again in 2015 (Weaver 2015) and in 2017, when a bus leaving with government personnel exploded (Rasmussen 2017). (Of course, attacks on the Afghan parliament have meaning beyond the fact that the building was constructed by India, but it is nonetheless another piece of India's developmental assistance that encountered acts of sabotage and terrorism.) The purpose of such attacks, according to Bhatnagar and Mohan (2016, 96), was to "deter India … from investing in such projects in the future."

In addition to physical attacks, Pakistan attempted to limit Indian influence in other ways. It persistently denied India transit rights for trade with Afghanistan, for example, inducing great consternation in New Delhi, given the centrality of regional economic opportunities in India's broader quest for great power status. Despite clear incentives to cooperate on economic issues, Pakistan preferred to frustrate rather than facilitate Indian trade, transit, and investment. It was well positioned to do so, given that India lacks contiguity with Afghanistan and therefore cannot access the country directly. Which is not to say that Pakistan was completely and totally obstructionist – projects were implemented and moved forward, for example the TAPI pipeline and the Afghan-Pakistan Transit Trade Agreement (APTTA), signed in 2010, which was to allow Afghan products to transit Pakistan en route to India (but not vice versa). As discussed earlier, however, TAPI was famously delayed, and scepticism persisted even as the Afghan portion of the pipeline finally began construction in 2018 (Putz 2018). The APTTA, meanwhile, fell apart in 2017 as a result of Pakistan's refusal to extend reciprocal transit rights to India as part of the deal (Haidar 2017). Pakistan's obstinacy on the issue of transit rights forced India to pursue alternative trade routes, including the Chabahar sea port in Iran (*Express Tribune* 2017).

---

42 Of this set of attacks, Felbab-Brown (2016, 128–9) writes: "[T]he April 2012 attack against the Afghan parliament … while perpetrated by the Haqqani network, [has] been … linked by US intelligence officers to the ISI."

We see in this activity further evidence of Pakistan's goal to minimize and discourage India's presence in Afghanistan. Note also that, from Islamabad's point of view, the attacks on Indian assets were largely *reactive*, a response to perceived Indian aggression, either in fomenting instability on Pakistani territory or, more generally, in terms of New Delhi's attempts to cultivate greater influence in the country – for example, by opening the consulates in the first place and spending billions of dollars on infrastructure and investment. Most of the international community viewed India's presence positively. For Pakistan, however, in the context of rivalry, even putatively benign Indian behaviour was considered potentially aggressive. Rivalry, after all, is a condition of ongoing conflict. When considered in this light, the establishment of diplomatic outposts – which, as all governments know, double as intelligence gathering operations – just miles from the Pakistani border was inevitably alarming. More generally, India's growth potential in terms of linking through Afghanistan to Central Asia was viewed negatively in Pakistan because of the *implications* of Indian growth for the rivalry. India is not merely a "competitor" for regional influence and economic growth, a competition Pakistan has been losing spectacularly, but also an *adversary* in the precise sense of the term. Whatever the typical influence of absolute versus relative gains in generic international relationships,[43] it is logical to assume that relative gains matter in rivalry. This proposition is reflected in Pakistan's behaviour vis-à-vis India in Afghanistan.

Like India, Pakistan became increasingly concerned, particularly at the turn of the decade and shortly thereafter, about a potential US withdrawal from Afghanistan. This might seem counterintuitive, considering that the insurgency Pakistan fuelled and supported often took direct aim at the United States and the rest of the international presence. Yet the prospect of US and international withdrawal meant dealing with the reality of a post-US/NATO Afghanistan; in reality, both the Indian and Pakistani interventions were always about shaping this future, and both worried that a precipitous US pullout would leave it in a subordinate position. Shortly before his death, US Special Representative for Afghanistan and Pakistan Richard Holbrooke was tasked with crafting some type of negotiated power sharing end to the war. In the context of that effort, he flew to Pakistan to meet with General Kayani. "It was all India all the time," Holbrooke said of the meeting, "the Pakistanis see everything through the prism of India" (quoted in Coll 2018, 406). Holbrooke's

---

43 For an early overview of this consequential debate, see Powell (1991).

takeaway from the talks was that "the Pakistanis believe that if we leave [Afghanistan], the Indians are going to move in" (406). Sirrs (2017, 235) writes of the negotiation efforts at the time: "ISI was not going to allow any settlement that did not include Pakistani interests. At a minimum, those interests included resolving the Afghan-Pakistan border dispute, creating a pro-Pakistan … government in Kabul and sharply reducing the Indian presence in Afghanistan." Obviously, the Taliban themselves were not as committed to these positions, and some of the less hard-line elements of the insurgency likely would have entertained an agreement that maintained, for example, the influence of Tajiks and former Northern Alliance officials – indeed, to do so was a prerequisite of the talks then being initiated. The result, as mentioned, was that many of the Taliban who showed an interest in the negotiations were arrested in Pakistan, with such arrests amounting to a Pakistani veto.[44] Subsequent attempts at negotiation largely stalled. The 2011 strategic partnership agreement between India and Afghanistan reinforced, for Islamabad, the depth of their relationship, further eroding any Pakistani enthusiasm for negotiations that might have entrenched the Afghan regime. Following the 2014 presidential election, in which Ashraf Ghani succeeded Karzai, there was an attempt in Kabul to shift the relationship with Pakistan. Ghani went out of his way to cultivate good relations, sending Afghan troops to the border to aid the Pakistani military in operations against anti-Pakistan militants and suspending several weapons acquisition contracts with India (Boone 2015; Panda 2015). On the basis of this new goodwill, there were again talks of potential negotiations, this time with a seemingly more eager Islamabad (Ahmed and Goldstein 2015). These talks failed to materialize, however, and Ghani subsequently adopted a critical tone towards Pakistan, accusing Islamabad of coordinating terror attacks in Afghanistan in January 2018, and describing Pakistan as the "center of Taliban terrorism" (Constable 2018). As the Taliban gained ground, the prospects of negotiations continued to "fizzle," writes Christine Fair (2017, 140): "The reason for this is simple: Pakistan and its proxy, the Taliban, are winning. Why would they negotiate?" The prospect of impending US withdrawal reinforced Pakistan's resolve to maintain its activities in the furtherance of its objectives.

Taken as a whole, Pakistan's post-2001 intervention in Afghanistan was consistent with the expectations of rational rivalry. The initial

---

44 As one Pakistan official said with regard to such efforts: "We picked up [Taliban leader Abdul Ghani] Baradar and the others because they were trying to make a deal without us … We protect the Taliban. They are dependent on us. We are not going to allow them to make a deal with Karzai and the Indians" (quoted in Filkins 2010).

decision to cut ties with the Taliban was predicated on an assessment of what policy would minimize India's presence and influence in Afghanistan. The subsequent reversal, likewise, occurred as it became clear that the trajectory of the American intervention would not achieve this goal, but indeed its opposite: the United States' partnering with the Northern Alliance was crucial to this perception, given the latter's history. As India launched its own intervention in support of the new Afghan government – the establishment of a robust diplomatic presence (reopening old consulates, opening new ones), major aid and development assistance, including massive infrastructure projects, and extensive training of Afghan officials across a range of domains, all lubricated by close ties with former Northern Alliance officials now in government – Pakistan resorted to support for a re-emerging Taliban insurgency against the new regime in Kabul. Indeed, ISI was deeply involved in the *creation* of the insurgency through sanctuary, recruitment, training, and material support. Although it is difficult to establish a one-to-one causal relationship, available evidence suggests that, as India steadily increased its involvement in Afghanistan, the insurgency also escalated, pushed by Pakistani assistance. The eruption of a rebellion in Balochistan in 2004, Paliwal (2017) notes, was followed by direct attacks on Indian assets in Afghanistan; Islamabad believed that newly opened Indian consulates were supporting the Balochi rebels. Pakistan persisted in its efforts despite intense diplomatic pressure from the United States and the international community and in the face of genuine costs associated with the policy. The Pakistanis systematically targeted Indian interests, including diplomatic installations, infrastructure projects, and personnel (ISI, via the Haqqani network, allegedly had a standing US$15,000–$30,000 bounty on Indian nationals) in an attempt to discourage India's presence. As talk turned to potential negotiations with the Taliban, Islamabad ensured that no such negotiations could proceed without its approval, for fear that any deal might undermine its goal of an Afghan regime devoid of Indian influence; it was not, in other words, about getting the Taliban *in* so much as it was about keeping India *out*. Behind doors closed to both the United States and the Afghan government, Pakistani leaders repeated their concerns about India's presence. In one meeting with President Karzai, General Kayani essentially offered a quid pro quo: end India's role altogether, and Pakistan would rein in the insurgency. Much of this was apparently confirmed in 2015 by former president Musharraf in an interview with the *Guardian* newspaper, in which he intimated that Pakistan's support for the Taliban was retaliation against a Karzai government that had "helped India stab Pakistan in the back" (quoted in Boone 2015). Frustrated by what he saw as Karzai's deference to India – sending Afghan cadets to India rather than to Pakistan for military training, for example – Musharraf went on to say: "Obviously we were looking for some groups to counter this Indian action against Pakistan … That is where the intelligence work comes in. Intelligence being in contact with Taliban groups. Definitely they were in contact, and they should be" (quoted in Boone 2015). Musharraf's comments support the preceding analysis: Pakistan systematically attempted to exclude and minimize India's presence, largely in reaction to India's own intervention in Afghanistan. The *anticipated process* of leaving such an intervention unchecked involved potential future Indian aggression – specifically, the fomentation of instability along the Durand Line and the associated potential of a two-front conflict.

Possible Alternative Explanations

Of course, if Islamabad's decision to support the Taliban, and to engage in anti-Indian activity more generally, had been simply straightforwardly rational – which is to say, if Pakistan's post-2001 intervention had corresponded to an evaluation of costs and benefits – than the rivalry explanation offered here would be superfluous. It would not be necessary to construct a "theory of rivalry" to describe what could be explained by a more basic rationalist model. As explained in chapter 2, while the theory presented here is broadly, procedurally rational, it nonetheless deviates from conventional expectations about what constitutes rational behaviour on the part of a state. That Pakistan's behaviour did not conform to such expectations is, in fact, what drives so much confusion about its priorities in Afghanistan. Again and again, observers, whether academics, journalists, or officials outside of Pakistan, have pointed out that Pakistani behaviour ran against Islamabad's own interests. In the broadest sense, there is consensus that a *stable* Afghanistan *should be* desirable. As Fair (2008, 216) concludes, "it is clearly in Pakistan's interests to have a stable Afghanistan." Hanauer and Chalk (2012, 36) likewise suggest that "the India-centric approach of the ISI and military has directly undermined Pakistan's ability to achieve its broader national goals." This is a message US officials spent years trying to impart.[45]

---

45 In preparation for General Kayani's 2009 trip to Washington, for example, the directive from Islamabad to the State Department was: "The single biggest message Kayani should hear in Washington is that [Pakistani] support [for the Taliban] must end. It is now counterproductive to Pakistan's own interests." See WikiLeaks, "Scenesetter for General Kayani's visit to Washington," 19 February 2009, https://wikileaks.org/plusd/cables/09ISLAMABAD365_a.html.

It is also the source of the language noted earlier, in which Pakistan was described as "paranoid," "obsessed," or "neuralgic" in its focus on India as the driver of its Afghan policy. The rational rivalry explanation demonstrates how such terms are inaccurate insofar as there are systematic and predictable reasons behind the policy. Yet it also accounts for the confusion the policy elicits by explaining why more straightforward, obvious interests were sacrificed for rivalry-related reasons.

Specifically, Pakistan's Afghan policy undermined both its immediate security and its economic interests. The security dimension relates to the rise of Islamic militancy within Pakistan and the increasing threat Islamists pose to the Pakistani state. As mentioned, beginning as early as 2005 the tribal areas in the west and north saw the rise of Tehrik-e-Taliban (TTP), an offshoot of the Afghan Taliban with a distinct agenda related to challenging the central Pakistani government. The 2007 Red Mosque incident, in which members of the Pakistani Taliban seized control of the Lal Majid mosque in Islamabad and engaged in a stand-off with Pakistani security forces, demonstrated that the group's threat had expanded from the tribal areas to the capital itself, and by 2008 it was even threatening to take control of major cities such as Peshawar and Karachi (Iqbal and De Silva 2013). In contrast to the lacklustre counterinsurgency efforts against militants in Afghanistan, the Pakistani military engaged in an extended campaign against militants in its own country beginning in 2004. Over 120,000 troops were deployed in this effort, incurring extensive casualties (Weinbaum 2017). Bhatnagar and Mohan (2016, 89) note that "fatalities in Pakistan since 2003, as a result of terrorist violence, have exceeded 50,000 and nearly half of these are civilians and members of Pakistan's security forces"; as well, these deaths represent, in part, "massive blowback ... from [Pakistan's] policy of using violent nonstate actors." This conclusion is echoed elsewhere, as many consider Islamic militancy aimed at the Pakistani state as "chickens come home to roost" in the sense the Pakistan itself was responsible for cultivating such forces going back decades.

There are indeed more or less direct links between Pakistan's Afghan policy specifically and these new security challenges. Pakistan's "accommodation" of the Afghan Taliban, writes Nadiri (2014, 152), "has created the political space for more revisionist and internally focused forms of militancy to expand within Pakistan, threatening Pakistan's domestic security." Weinbaum and Harder (2008, 31) paint a similar picture:

Pakistan has seen growing challenges in recent years to its legitimacy and authority. These challenges have included a surge in militant Islamism, mounting provincial and tribal unrest, and the weakening of the institutional capacity of the state. All three are apparent in its western border areas, and can be traced in large measure to its Afghan policies. By indulging and supporting extremists as a tool to retain and hold influence in Afghanistan, Pakistan introduced changes that undermined its ability to maintain its writ within its own borders.

In 2004, a Pakistani observer remarked: "Today's Wanna [a city in Waziristan home to anti-Pakistan militants] is the creation of yesterday's Afghanistan … For the Pakistani state [TTP leader] Nek Mohammad represents its own creation" (quoted in Behuria 2007, 717). As Dalrymple (2013) colourfully summarizes, "the fear of being squeezed in an Indian nutcracker is so great that it has led ISI to take steps that put Pakistan's own security at risk."

And yet, even as the TTP gained ground in 2007 and 2008, controlling larger swaths of territory and threatening major population centres, Islamabad refused to end its support for militancy full stop, with the insistence on distinguishing between "good" (Afghan) and "bad" (Pakistani) Taliban inevitably fuelling both groups, given the synergy between them (Weinbaum 2017). Islamabad also failed to reorient its military capabilities towards counterinsurgency, as the United States and the international community had been urging for years. Its troops were "trained to fight a conventional war with India [and had] very limited capacity for effective counter-insurgency" (Weinbaum and Harder 2008, 33). Instead it continued to use American money to purchase military hardware geared towards India rather than for the counterinsurgency capabilities for which it was intended. Despite the clear and present danger of Islamism, Pakistani leaders remained focused on the state's long-standing international rival. There was a failure to recognize, Ganguly and Kapur (2010, 57) suggest, "that, despite past successes, the costs of supporting militancy [had come to] outweigh its benefits." In 2014, a string of major terrorist attacks in Pakistan – most prominently the massacre of 132 school children in Peshawar – seemed to shake Islamabad's calculus somewhat. A more concerted counterinsurgency campaign known as Operation Zarb-e-Azb ("strike of the Prophet's sword") was launched to eliminate the threat. Nonetheless, as Felbab-Brown (2016, 134) writes, "there are reasons to doubt how comprehensive and impartial the campaign's choice of militant targets has been. For one, the Pakistani military seems to have given the Afghan Taliban ample time to clear out from the territory and move into Afghanistan." Although the operation proved moderately successful in weakening the TTP – the public backlash following the Peshawar school attack also undermined support for the group – "the military has likely achieved only a temporary victory in Pakistan's long-term fight against extremism" (Weinbaum 2017, 46). The weakened TTP continued to mount major terrorist attacks throughout the country.

Key to resolving the issue of militancy more conclusively was Pakistan's policy in Afghanistan. A stable and effective Afghan military was necessary to eliminate the safe havens that TTP and other anti-Pakistan militants used to coordinate and plan attacks – in an ironic reversal of the long-standing reality of Afghan militants using territory in Pakistan for the same purposes. And yet, Pakistan continued to hedge, convinced that its ties with the Afghan Taliban and the campaign to destabilize Afghanistan were a necessary bulwark against Indian influence. As Weinbaum (2017, 52) concludes, "the continued patronizing of Afghan Taliban insurgents undermines chances for the kind of stable, unified Afghanistan that can ... be to Pakistan's advantage." Even though Islamic militancy likely constituted the most significant immediate threat, Pakistan remained concerned with the long-term threat from India.

This is a puzzle, according to Nadiri (2014, 155–6), insofar as one would not expect a rational actor "to accommodate the Afghan Taliban, particularly in light of the costs this accommodation has carried for Pakistani internal and external security." "Pakistan has departed from structural expectations of security-seeking behaviour," he argues, and "to explain this deviation" one must highlight "a set of domestic-level imbalances," including "organizational culture, domestic coalitions, and grassroots militancy [which combine] with external security considerations to explain Islamabad's risky and ultimately destabilizing choice to accommodate the Taliban after 2001" (Nadiri 2014, 168). I argue, by contrast, that domestic considerations are unnecessary for understanding the basic orientation of Pakistani policy. Rather, Pakistan's "risky behaviour" was a condition of the perceptions generated within rivalry: given the history of interactions between India and Pakistan and the consequent belief that future conflict is likely, Pakistan considers itself to be involved in an ongoing confrontation. This fundamentally alters its decision-making calculus: although Islamabad certainly recognizes that Islamic militancy is a threat – consider General Kayani's 2012 remarks in which he "described militancy in [the Federally Administered Tribal Area] as a grave security challenge confronting Pakistan" (Bhatnagar and Mohan 2016, 89) – it nonetheless continues to see India as the most significant security challenge. This belief is not a consequence of personal animosities, domestic politics, or even the organizational culture of the military-intelligence establishment, but rather the dynamics of rivalry and the pressures of the international system.

The other apparently puzzling feature of Pakistan's Afghan policy was the negative economic consequences of Afghanistan's destabilization. Weinbaum and Harder (2008, 27), for example, note that "Pakistan's commercial interests in Afghanistan require a stable neighbour." Obviously, Pakistan, like India, has economic interests in the region, including access to Central Asian energy and expanded markets for Pakistani goods. That India and Pakistan *share* economic interests had been held out as the basis for potential cooperation between Islamabad and New Delhi. This was the hope behind, for example, the 2011 "Silk Road" initiative spearheaded by the United States, which attempted "to entangle Afghanistan, Pakistan, India, and other regional actors in a web of economic interdependence and cooperative relations" (Felbab-Brown 2016, 137). The project created a forum for discussion – the Istanbul Process – which persists to this day, although the more comprehensive economic cooperation originally envisioned has failed to materialize. While bilateral trade with Afghanistan increased significantly after the fall of the Taliban in 2001 (when it stood at just US$25 million), it nonetheless remained significantly below its potential given the ongoing instability and security challenges that Pakistan had, in large measure, perpetuated with its policies (Fair 2008). Recall the example of the APTTA, which Islamabad effectively scuttled through its refusal to extend reciprocal transit rights to India. Pakistan continuously sacrificed its economic interests at the altar of rivalry, preferring instead to block and frustrate India rather than craft policies that might have improved its own, rather dreary, economic outlook (see Mangi 2018).

It is important to note that, much like the situation vis-à-vis security and the threat of domestic militants, Islamabad did not abandon its economic interests altogether; it engaged in development projects in Afghanistan, including offering over US$300 million in assistance, "most of which has been directed toward the construction of roads and railways that would connect Pakistan to the energy-rich [central Asian republics]" (Hanauer and Chalk 2012: 30). The TAPI pipeline, likewise, despite significant delays, continues to inch forward. Opportunities for expanded trade were pursued, and Pakistan remained keen to expand the bilateral relationship with Afghanistan in this regard. Yet to the extent there was a trade-off between economic opportunity and policies that might enhance Indian interests, Pakistan opted for obstructionism over cooperation. More broadly, it continued its support for the insurgency, and thereby undermined the stability that all agreed was a prerequisite for the maximization of potential economic gains. The "carrot" of such gains, however, was insufficiently appealing to alter behaviour. Again, this presents a conundrum for a standard rationalist explanation, particularly in conjunction with the security-related reasons to change course noted above. By contrast, this behaviour is consistent with the expectations of rivalry behaviour: prospective economic gains were simply overwhelmed by the exigencies of rivalry and the associated perceptions they engender – namely, the belief that India is an ongoing, potentially existential threat.

A final consideration to be addressed is the possibility that Pakistan's Afghan intervention was produced by *aggressive* anti-Indian designs. (This is the evaluation India itself formed.) There is no question that the Taliban insurgency helped to fuel Islamism in the region more broadly. There are clear synergies between the forces of extremism in Afghanistan and the Pakistani tribal regions on the one hand and in Kashmir on the other. This relationship was evident, for example, in the presence in Afghanistan of groups such as Lashkar-e-Taiba, which traditionally has focused on the Kashmir issue. It also remains true that Pakistan *does* harbour revisionist designs with respect to Kashmir, and thereby engages in behaviour that is aggressive, including supporting violence and terrorism intended to "bleed" India.[46] An Afghanistan that can serve as an incubator for such groups is helpful in this effort. The argument that Pakistan's Afghan policy was fundamentally defensive should not be taken as dismissing or denying such motivations. As was the case with respect to pre-2001 policy – support for the Taliban – however, the benefits associated with pursuing aggressive anti-Indian designs were *ancillary*; they were not the primary motivators for the intervention.

Assessing the Interventions

What does the Afghanistan case as a whole say about the influence of rivalry on interventions in civil conflicts? In fact, we have *two* cases for the purposes of comparison; Case 1: Indian intervention; Case 2:

---

46 During the course of the Afghan insurgency, there have been high-profile terrorist attacks in India proper, most notably those in Mumbai in 2008, in which ISI was strongly implicated. Conflict over Kashmir has similarly continued, with frequent violations of cease fires along the Line of Control and stops and starts in the official Composite Dialogue peace process between the countries.

Pakistani intervention. What are the implications of the within-case evidence and how do the two interventions compare?

Both countries were involved in Afghanistan before 2001, going back roughly to partition and the creation of modern-day India and Pakistan in 1947. This history is useful context for the post-2001 period, insofar as both India and Pakistan had standing policy in Afghanistan at the time of the American intervention. Before 2001, Afghanistan constituted a peripheral, although not insignificant, node in India-Pakistan relations – primary concerns were Kashmir, the rest of the border, East Pakistan, the development of nuclear weapons, etc. – with each pursuing its own interests through support of various regimes and domestic Afghan factions. New Delhi enjoyed the upper hand for the bulk of this period, given Afghan-Pakistani disputes about the parameters of the Durand Line and Pakistan's concerns regarding Afghan-supported Pashtun nationalism. This was reinforced as Afghanistan moved into the Soviet – and by extension Indian – orbit in the mid- and late 1970s. The period of the *mujahideen* resistance against the Soviet-backed communist government during the 1980s was particularly formative. The United States funnelled much of its support for the *mujahideen* through Pakistan, and Islamabad developed many of the techniques, networks, and expertise to support Islamic militants that became a standard piece of its foreign policy playbook. The communist government finally fell in 1992, initiating a brief period of intra-*mujahideen* conflict before the rise of the Taliban in the mid-1990s. When the Taliban seized power, Pakistan finally had a regime in Kabul that was anti-Indian. New Delhi, by contrast, supported the remaining anti-Taliban force in the country, the Northern Alliance, in what amounted to a low-boil but ongoing civil conflict.

The basic structure of this conflict was upended by American intervention in 2001. The United States selected the Northern Alliance as its local proxy, essentially supercharging the insurgents' campaign against the Taliban government through the use of overwhelming American air power. The Taliban were swiftly defeated, and Northern Alliance fighters triumphantly entered Kabul in November 2001. Shortly thereafter, the Taliban re-emerged as an anti-government insurgency, initiating a new period of civil war that persisted until 2021. In this period, India intervened on behalf of the Kabul government, while Pakistan intervened on the side of the insurgency. The decision-making tied to each of these interventions reflected *anticipated processes* regarding the consequences of *not* intervening. Both New Delhi and Islamabad evaluated the potential consequences of deferring to the other in terms of influence in Afghanistan.

For India, the opportunity associated with the overthrow of the Taliban – which had for years been the source of region-wide Islamic extremism and associated terrorism and violence in both Kashmir and India proper – was to consolidate a friendly Kabul regime, one that would enhance India's security vis-à-vis the ongoing Pakistani campaign to target India and, eventually, revise the status quo in Kashmir. The basis for this perception was the decades of Pakistani behaviour in which they attempted to achieve these goals.

For Pakistan, the overthrow of the Taliban represented the reversal of a perceived victory achieved in the 1990s – the consolidation of an Afghan regime absent Indian influence that would thereby not create security concerns along its western border. Initially, the American ultimatum either to join or resist their efforts in Afghanistan was filtered through the prism of this interest; Pakistan knew the Taliban were "gone" – although futile diplomatic efforts were made to forestall this outcome – and decided that joining with the United States and dropping support for the Taliban was the best means by which to minimize Indian involvement in the coming post-Taliban era. As the United States pursued its narrow security agenda, however, this calculation proved faulty: the empowering of the Northern Alliance essentially guaranteed significant Indian involvement, as did the composition of the transitional government, which quickly developed close diplomatic and economic ties to New Delhi. Reacting to this reality, Pakistan shifted gears, moving to support – in fact, to breathe life into – an embryonic Taliban revival. Again, the consequences of not doing so were considered too great, as an "encircling" India acting through an India-friendly Afghan regime presented the possibility of Indian-fuelled instability in the tribal area, including Balochi and potentially Pashtun separatism, and even a two-front situation in the case of conventional conflict. The basis of this perception was also the decades of experience in the relationship, in which India had engaged in such behaviour and, as evidenced particularly in 1971 but also in other conflicts, deployed military force to decisive effect.

Neither intervention was caused by emotional or psychological hatred (or "negative affect") as would be expected by the theory of rivalry (pathological rivalry) which emphasizes such dynamics. There is simply too little evidence to support such an explanation. The interventions were the product of broadly rational decision-making processes in which the consequences of alternatives were assessed. This was consistent across multiple leaders and administrations in both countries. The decisive consideration was long-term security given presumed future conflict in the context of ongoing rivalry. Both interventions were therefore fundamentally *defensive* in their orientation.[47] That said, the interventions were not strictly rational in the typical understanding of the term, insofar as there were obvious and immediate interests that *should* have produced different policies but failed to do so.

This contention is more difficult to prove in the Indian case, insofar as the economic, security, and rivalry pressures all pushed in more or less the same direction: towards intervention. Nonetheless, the intensity and scope of the intervention suggests rivalry concerns were decisive. The Pakistani case is clearer, as immediate economic/security interests contradicted rivalry interests, with the latter winning out, towards support for the insurgency. In this way, rivalry can be said to alter a state's basic preference structure with respect to its decision-making calculus; the weight of past experience is such that long-term assessments as to probable outcomes – specifically, that conflict is almost certain to occur – tilts preferences towards defensive policies. Although the content of these calculations differed for both India and Pakistan in the Afghanistan case in terms of what the relevant experiences were, what form concerns about the future took, and what the resulting policies looked like, the basic structure was the same. This structure, I argue, is the consequence of international rivalry, an appreciation of which is necessary for understanding and explaining what India and Pakistan did in Afghanistan post-2001. This explanation is superior to typical and widespread assessments of Indian and, in particular, Pakistani behaviour that implicitly or explicitly suggest that decision-making was beholden to "obsession" or "paranoia," or to unique domestic dynamics tied to organizational culture, domestic politics, public pressures, or religious and/or ethnic affiliations.

What are the implications of these findings for the generalizability of the rational theory of rivalry and its consequences for civil conflict intervention? First, and most fundamentally, it suggests that the findings *are* generalizable: because the theory does not rely on idiosyncratic

---

47 Again, this is not a comment on the *broader* intentions of either side. That is, I am not arguing that both India and Pakistan are "defensive" or "satisfied" states in general and that any security competition between them is merely a consequence of misperception. Rather, the specific interventions themselves are defensive. The consequences of rivalry – the experiences of conflict and the reputations for hostility that result – do of course promote cautious interpretations of present behaviour. Thus, one rival's intervention is viewed as aggressive by the other, reinforcing the import of one's own defensive intervention. But again, this (security-dilemma-like) dynamic is contained within the space of the intervention itself, and need not necessarily apply to the larger relationship. As mentioned, for example, one need not deny that Pakistan is revisionist and India status quo with respect to Kashmir.

explanations tied to particular leaders or more complex and contingent explanations linked to (potentially multiple) domestic variables, there is a greater likelihood that the basic dynamics at work can be found in other cases. Thus, other instances of civil conflict intervention also might be amenable to the rivalry explanation. Second, and relatedly, the consequences of rivalry can be considered quite powerful: in both the India and Pakistan cases, we see other, non-rivalry considerations basically overwhelmed by the dictates of rivalry. Thus, in exploring other rivalries in the international system, there is a good chance that whatever the particular circumstances at work and the potentially different bases of rivalry that might exist – ideological, religious, ethnic, positional, regional, etc. – the preference structure of rivalry that is created through multiple and ongoing interactions as filtered through the imperatives of the international system should be operative. Which is to say, cases that differ on multiple dimensions, with unique histories and circumstances, are nonetheless amenable to analysis through a single theoretical framework. The next several chapters engage this possibility through case studies of other civil conflict interventions involving international rivals.

Chapter Six

The Syrian-Israeli Rivalry and Intervention in Lebanon

As part of the broader Arab-Israeli rivalry, the relationship between Israel and Syria has been marked by repeated confrontation and war.[1] Three wars have been fought (in 1948, 1967, and 1973) along with numerous crises and disputes. Israel's territorial acquisitions in the Golan Heights during the 1967 war in particular have generated prolonged and enduring hostility, as Syria has consistently expressed its desire to re-establish pre-1967 borders. Following the Egypt-Israel Peace Treaty of 1979, Syria became Israel's primary antagonist in the region, its desire to revise the status quo tempered by an asymmetry in conventional military capabilities. As was the case in chapter 4 with respect to the India-Pakistan rivalry, these conflicts and crises are crucial to establishing the context

---

1 Although all historical writing is fraught with complexity and subject to potential biases related to the interpretation of documentary evidence – seminal contributions to the philosophy of history as an academic discipline include Collingwood ([1936] 2005); Carr (1961); and the essays collected in White (2010) – this is particularly true of historical interpretations of the Arab-Israeli conflict. An ongoing debate exists among historians about major aspects of the conflict, often – though not always – turning on which side – Arab or Israeli – is most culpable for perpetuating violence, with the "New Historians" challenging traditional – "Old" – scholars by introducing more evidence from the Arab perspective. See, for example, the discussions in Shlaim (2004); Slater (2002); and Karsh (1997). I attempt to avoid such controversies by offering a straightforward – to the extent this is possible – narrative of the series of events that constitute the ongoing Syrian-Israeli rivalry, eschewing judgment as to culpability while nonetheless addressing perceptions and intentions where appropriate. Obviously, the question of historiography cannot be sidestepped entirely, but the focus of this book on the cumulative effects of prolonged and ongoing conflict – the reality of which neither side of the debate contests – minimizes the centrality of such considerations. Further, the following historical narrative draws on accounts from both "Old" historians (such as Moshe Ma'oz and Itamar Rabinovich) and "New" (such as Benny Morris and Avi Shlaim).

in which the interventions of interest occurred. The rivalry reputations that informed threat assessments in 1975 were the product of repeated interactions in the preceding decades, leading to both specific and general attributions regarding likely future behaviour – a dynamic well captured by the quotation from Israeli Defense Force Chief of Staff (1974–8) Mordecai Gur that opens the book: the depth of experience for both states offered powerful evidence regarding what the other side was likely to do – its *disposition* – irrespective of what it insisted its actual intentions to be.

The Nature of the Rivalry

The identity of Israel as a Jewish state and the predominately Muslim character of the Arab nations arrayed against it, including Syria, mean that the Arab-Israeli conflict has an inescapable religious/ethnic dimension. The Palestinian issue at the centre of the dispute is fundamentally a question about the rights of an ethnic and religious miniority vis-à-vis the Jewish majority in Israel. For a nation like Syria, solidarity with the Palestinian cause is largely predicated on identification with its co-ethnics/co-religionists. Antagonism towards Israel, similarly, is often justified – particularly when appealing to the public or on the part of the public itself – in thinly veiled (if veiled at all) xenophobic and anti-Semitic terms. Israeli fears, likewise, are often justified by pointing out that, in a regional context, it is a relatively small Jewish population encircled by much larger Arab neighbours, while portions of the Israeli population engage in xenophobic rhetoric of their own. Yet as we will see, the driving consideration behind the Israeli-Syrian rivalry, specifically, is *territory*.

The creation of the State of Israel in 1948 immediately triggered a dispute over, first, the existence of the state at all; second, its ability to claim sovereignty over a patch of land in the former British Palestine; and, third, over the parameters of its borders. After the war in 1967, the territorial dimension would grow even more acute. The point is not to obscure the religious/ethnic component of the rivalry – indeed, the *genesis* of the territorial dispute is rooted in the perceived need for a distinct Jewish state and the unwillingness or inability of Palestinian Arabs to live as a minority within it. This led to the civil war in 1948, the subsequent Arab intervention, and the decades of conflict that have ensued. Which is to say, religion and ethnicity – and the emotions of hatred and hostility, which, unfortunately, commitment to these identities can often produce – are baked into the clay of the dispute; this is not a reality the present analysis is meant to deny. Rather, *once set in motion,* territory became the most salient dimension for Israeli and Syrian leaders and, as conflicts and disputes accumulated, the dynamics of rivalry became operative. Their rivalry is strikingly similar to the India-Pakistan rivalry in many ways: a political shock in the form of the creation of a new state[2] predicated on an ethnic/religious character; a subsequent war over the territorial parameters of the new state(s); continued dissatisfaction with the territorial status quo; and ongoing conflicts and confrontations. Like the India-Pakistan rivalry, the Syrian-Israeli rivalry is regional, territorial, *and* religious/ethnic. Also like the India-Pakistan case, these dimensions now operate through the logic of rivalry whereby past behaviour engenders the anticipation of future conflict.

Crises and Conflict, 1948–75

Space constraints preclude an exhaustive survey of Syrian-Israel relations between 1948 and 1975, but a brief summary of the major wars and crises during this period provides context for the perceptions that existed between the two states at the time intervention in Lebanon was considered.

Following civil war in British Palestine in 1947, the creation of the State of Israel in 1948 precipitated interstate conflict between the new Jewish entity and several of its Arab neighbours. Forces from Egypt, Transjordan, Syria, Lebanon, and Iraq, as well as smaller contingents from Saudi Arabia and Yemen, intervened in May 1948 to prosecute the Palestinian cause (Ilan 1996; Shlaim 2007). Several stages of fighting occurred – with intermittent truces and ceasefires – until armistice agreements were signed in 1949, bringing hostilities to a halt. The result of the war left Israel with more territory than had been envisioned by UN partition plans.

Towards the end of the conflict, Syria attempted to fortify and entrench its limited territorial gains by introducing additional troops to areas it controlled in what is now southern Lebanon, in order "to secure the Syrian flank against deep Israeli intrusion into Lebanon, which was outflanking the Syrian deployment from the west to the east" (Tal 2003, 426). Even at this incipient stage, then, the territory of southern Lebanon was recognized as important in strategic terms. Disagreements as to territorial dispensations in these and other areas along

---

2 Technically two states in the case of India and Pakistan, although the creation of Pakistan was akin to a secession from an already-existing Indian state.

the Syrian-Israeli border, particularly in the region of Lake Tiberias, coloured the conclusion of official hostilities and became the basis for subsequent "violent disputes and clashes which erupted periodically" between the two countries throughout the 1950s (Ma'oz 1995, 21). Thus, despite the relatively limited scope of direct Israeli-Syrian fighting during the 1948 war, the relationship between the two countries became "the most acrimonious" of all the bilateral relationships in the Arab-Israeli conflict (Rabinovich 2008, 177).

The literature on the 1967 Arab-Israeli war is voluminous, although the conflict itself was brief (it is referred to as the "Six Day War"), reflecting the extent to which the events of 5–10 June 1967 would reshape (quite literally) the landscape of the Middle East in their aftermath. (For useful overviews of the war, see Dupuy 1978; Louis and Shlaim 2012; Morris 2001; Oren 2002; Pollack 2002.) The impact of the conflict for Syria was devastating: a sweeping Israeli victory saw Syrian forces decimated and Israel in control of large swaths of new territory, including the Golan Heights. Much like the 1971 war between India and Pakistan, the lessons derived from the 1967 war would reverberate across subsequent decades.

Israeli forces were able to capture a large portion of the Golan Heights – roughly 1,250 square kilometres – before the war was ended through ceasefire agreement. The final Israeli position put them less than sixty kilometres – with clear sight lines, given the raised vantage point – from Damascus, presenting Syria with acute security concerns. According to Muslih (1993, 625–6): "From a geostrategic point of view, the Syrians consider the Golan a critical natural defense against Israel." Mount Hermon, in the northern part of the Golan, is of "exceptional strategic value because it offers a commanding position overlooking southern Lebanon, the Golan plateau, and much of southern Syria and northern Israel" (621). In addition to these objective strategic disadvantages, the very act of seizing the territory – in addition to the various border activities and incursions that had been a regular feature since 1948, and the initial expansion of Israel's borders in 1948 – reinforced Syrian perceptions that Israel was expansionist and willing to use force to achieve its goals. "As Syria saw it," writes Rabinovich (2008, 227), "Israel captured the Golan in a war of aggression, characteristic of an inherently expansionist and aggressive state." Of course, it is also true – and is at least part of, if not the major, reason behind the Israeli move in 1967 – that the Golan offered Syria significant offensive potential against Israel, looking down as it does on Israeli towns and settlements. Thus, there was a similarly defensive consideration for Israel; the pattern of Syrian behaviour up to and including the 1967 war suggested that ownership of the plateau translated into Syrian military activity from the heights.[3]

This situation, and the outcome of the 1967 war more broadly, led almost inexorably to the next major Arab-Israeli conflict in 1973. On 6 October – the day of Yom Kippur, hence the practice of referring to the conflict as the "Yom Kippur War" – Egyptian and Syrian forces launched a coordinated invasion of Israeli-controlled territory on the Sinai and in the Golan. The thrust was quickly reversed, as Israeli forces recaptured the Golan within a week, and actually pushed past the 1967 lines, drawing even closer to Damascus. Despite the reversal, and the similar outcome to that of the 1967 war, the respective moods in Jerusalem and Damascus were drastically different than they had been six years earlier. The aura of Israeli invincibility had been shattered by the early successes of the Syrian forces. The subsequent years were again characterized by periodic crises and clashes between the two rivals.

Israeli and Syrian Perceptions in 1975

The cumulative effect of rivalry up until the mid-1970s was to shape perceptions in Jerusalem and Damascus towards caution and pessimism. In offering an assessment of Israeli and Syrian perceptions in the lead-up to their respective interventions in Lebanon, I draw on the relevant secondary historical literature, memoirs, political biographies of decisionmakers, and archival sources. With respect to the latter, particularly illuminating are the reports and transcripts, available in US archives, of American – and specifically Henry Kissinger's – diplomatic efforts in the region from 1974 to 1976. It was the US secretary of state

---

3 In describing the Israeli position in late June 1967, Chairman of the US Joint Chiefs of Staff Earle Wheeler wrote to US Secretary of Defense Robert McNamara: "[S]olely on military considerations from the Israel point of view … Israel must hold the commanding terrain [in the Golan] east of the boundary of 4 June 1967 which overlooks the Galilee area. To provide a defense-in-depth, Israel would need a strip about 15 miles wide … inside the Syrian border [which] would give Israel control of the terrain which Syria has used effectively in harassing in the border area … This line would provide protection for the Israeli villages on the east bank of Lake Tiberias" ("Memorandum for the Secretary of Defense" 1984, 124). In his biography of Moshe Dayan, Shabtai Teveth (1972, 353) describes the minister of defense's attitude following the war: "As he had opposed the withdrawal from Sinai in 1957, Dayan now emphatically opposed the withdrawal of Israeli forces from Sharm el-Sheikh, in order to prevent a third blockade of the Straits of Tiran; from the Gaza Strip, to prevent its reverting to a convenient base for the Egyptian aggression against Israel; *and from the Golan Heights, so that the Syrians could not renew their bombardments of the settlements below.*"

who had been instrumental in crafting the disengagement agreement of 1974, and it was he who took steerage of subsequent negotiations for a more comprehensive peace deal. In order to massage such an agreement into existence, Kissinger and his team hosted visiting Arab and Israeli delegations in Washington and, particularly during the summer of 1975, "shuttled" back and forth from the various regional capitals (primarily Cairo, Jerusalem, and Damascus). In meetings with state leaders and top decisionmakers, perceptions were often relayed directly to Kissinger and his team.[4] What emerges from these and other sources is a sense of the strategic moment: both states remained wary of each other, citing their experiences over the preceding decades, and believing that renewed conflict was all but a foregone conclusion. Moreover, security concerns *mandated* that leaders consider present policy, including potential concessions and the character of any putative peace deals, in the context of this belief about future conflict.

Yitzhak Rabin became Israeli prime minister in June 1974. He describes the moment in his memoirs, and his challenges in the wake of the 1973 war: "Being prime minister is very different from being a candidate for the post. I was almost physically aware of the enormous weight of responsibility that I now bore. The wounds of the Israeli people were still fresh and painful after the recent war, and deep fissures undermined its faith in its leaders and government" (Rabin 1979, 242). With respect to the negotiations that concluded the war (these occurred as late as May 1974), he was cautious, even pessimistic: "The disengagement-of-forces agreement with Egypt – already being implemented – and a similar agreement with Syria signed three days before would stabilize the ceasefire on both fronts. *Yet no one had any doubts that these agreements were of limited duration*" (242, emphasis added). Which is to say, there was an apparently unanimous belief that hostilities would resume sooner or later. The priority, given such an assumption, was to "make a supreme effort to strengthen the IDF [Israel Defense Forces]" as "only a very powerful IDF could convince the Arab leaders that the only course open to them was political negotiations" (242). The belief that only a powerful deterrent could placate Damascus reflected the perception that Syria remained hostile. For Rabin and other Israeli leaders, this was the inescapable lesson not only of 1973, but of the entire

---

4 The caveat noted in chapter 4 with respect to Indian and Pakistani statements to US officials recorded in US diplomatic cables is of course also applicable here; it is nonetheless reasonable to assume that both Syrian and Israeli leaders had incentives to more or less accurately articulate their concerns and priorities, given the context of high-stakes peace negotiations and the fact they were being conducted in private.

history of the Syrian-Israeli relationship since 1948. As Ma'oz (1995, 141) summarizes:

> Rabin, like his predecessor, Golda Meir, and like most Israelis, continued to consider Syria as Israel's most implacable and dangerous foe, and the Golan Heights as a vital area for defending Galilee and Israel's main water resources. Nearly all Israeli Jews, including political and military analysts, did not perceive the Syrian 1973 offensive as being motivated by Syria's ambition to recover merely the Golan Heights, but rather as a war aimed at capturing parts of northern Israel and, given the opportunity, eliminating Israel altogether. These perceptions derived [partly] from the collective memory of Syrian active belligerency prior to the 1967 war.

For Israel, in other words, the effects of 1973 were again confirmation of Syrian aggression, mandating continued vigilance with respect to Israeli security and rendering any concessions in pursuit of peace difficult – even if, as Israeli leaders insisted, they were keen on such an outcome.

Rabin communicated such concerns to President Gerald Ford and Secretary of State Kissinger during a visit to Washington in 1975:

> We know we cannot achieve peace by military means; conditions do not allow this. It happened in 1949, in 1956, in 1967, in 1973 … We have no interest in war but have an interest in defending ourselves. Without being able to defend ourselves we will not survive. When we talk of peace, I mean by this our existence as a Jewish state with boundaries we can defend with their defenses – not to depend on others to send their own troops. That would be the end of us.
>
> …
>
> The Arabs stress total Israeli withdrawal to the pre-June 1967 lines, which we consider practically indefensible. In the past when they moved their troops, we either had to wait for the attack or pre-empt … So the problem for Israel as far as an overall settlement is concerned is not to be in a position that in a few years, whenever they move, we have to go to a pre-emptive war. The real fact that they can move near to our borders means that we would have to mobilize and they can destroy our economy by requiring total mobilization.
>
> …
>
> Therefore, in terms of the readiness of Israel for a final peace and the needs for Israel's security, the 1967 lines with respect to Egypt and Syria does not allow for security arrangements which are required for a small country of three million people against a composition of states who total

60 to 65 million. We are ready to try to achieve peace, but the gap on these three issues is wide. We have not sensed an Arab readiness to come close to the essentials of peace as we see them from our point of view.

...

Ben-Gurion said Israel can win 20 wars and it will not solve the problem; but the Arabs need to win only once and it would mean the end of Israel. (United States 1975e)

With respect to the Golan specifically, Rabin stressed that the movement of Israeli settlements to accommodate territorial concessions was not in and of itself the issue, but rather the implications for Israeli defence that such movements would produce: "It is not only a question of settlements. It is also the destruction of our defensive line which would have to be rebuilt and would take at least two or three years" (United States 1975e). Again, a belief that Syria was likely to attack in the future meant that maintaining defensive lines was not merely a preference but, from the Israeli point of view, a necessity; failure to do so "would mean the end of Israel" – its very survival was at stake.

This logic was comprehensively articulated by then-Israeli minister of foreign affairs Yigal Allon in an article published in the journal *Foreign Affairs* in 1976. Allon laid out the Israeli position with respect to its borders, offering direct insight into the rationale guiding Israeli foreign and defence policy at the time. Several apposite passages are included here:

[A] military defeat of Israel would mean the physical extinction of a large part of its population and the political elimination of the Jewish state. In highly realistic and clear terms, therefore, the Arab states can permit themselves a series of military defeats while Israel cannot afford to lose a single war. Nor does this reflect a historical trauma in any sense. *To lose a single war is to lose everything, and this is a most real and stark fact.* (Allon 1976, 39, emphasis added)

In essence, that Israel today still exists is due only to its success in maintaining such defensive strength. Without it, Israel would never have seen the light of day or would already have been eliminated in the first years of its existence. *Such were the Arab intentions, and it was fortunate that the Arab states had not the strength to realize them.* (39, emphasis added)

The polarized asymmetry between the size and intentions of the Arab states and those of Israel, and the extreme contrast in the anticipated fate of each side in the event of military defeat, obliges Israel to maintain constantly that measure of strength enabling it to defend itself in every regional conflict and against any regional combination of strength confronting it, without the help of any foreign army. *To our deep regret, this is the first imperative facing us, the imperative to survive. And I would venture to say every other state in our place would behave exactly as we do.* (40, emphasis added)

The purpose of defensible borders is thus to correct this weakness, to provide Israel with the requisite minimal strategic depth, as well as lines which have topographical strategic significance. (42)

In the northeastern sector, the 1949 line left Syria on the dominating Golan Heights, controlling the Huleh Valley and the Galilee Basin at their foothills, and including the sources of the Jordan River and the Sea of Galilee from which Israel draws a vital part of its water supply. *Moreover, after 1949 Syria not only repeatedly shelled the Israeli villages located at the Golan foothills but also attempted to divert the sources of the Jordan and thereby deprive Israel of a vital source of water. Even more important, the Golan Heights served in past wars as the most convenient base for the Syrian army to make swift and major attacks upon Galilee, ultimately aimed at the conquest of the entire northern part of our country.* (46, emphasis added)

While the strategic zone in the central sector is crucial to Israel's security, so, too, is a zone on the Golan Heights. *As past experience has demonstrated, a border not encompassing the Golan Heights would again invite the easy shelling of the villages below in the Huleh Valley, the Galilee Basin and eastern Galilee.* More important than the danger of renewed Syrian shelling and sniping at Israeli villagers and fishermen below, which is basically a tactical question, is that Israel needs an effective defense line on the Golan Heights for two cardinal strategic reasons: first, to preclude any new Syrian attempts to deny Israel its essential water resources and, second, to prevent a massive Syrian attack on the whole of Galilee, either independently or in coordination with other Arab armies on Israel's other frontiers. (48, emphasis added)

To sum up, there were numerous bitterly deficient points in the pre-1967 lines, and these proposals encompass minimal corrections to them required for an overall peace settlement. The necessity for these corrections is all the more apparent when it is realized that Israel not only faces the military strength of its contiguous neighbors, but may also have to face the combined strength of many other Arab countries. *This has already happened to no small extent in the 1973 war, when contingents from Iraq, Libya, Algeria, Saudi Arabia, Morocco, Jordan and other Arab countries participated in the fighting together with the armies of Egypt and Syria.* Thus, in a very practical sense, solid defense lines are indispensable to Israel in order to withstand the attacks of the entire Arab world. (49, emphasis added)

But just as peace itself is one of the prime elements of national security, so, too, is the ability to defend oneself a prime guaranty for the maintenance of peace. In view of the marked asymmetry existing between the war aims of those participating in the Arab-Israeli conflict, and in light of the unstable internal and regional relations among the Arab states, one should be especially careful to uphold these principles here; *this applies even more so to the case of Israel, for whom the threat of total obliteration is always present.* (51, emphasis added)

We see in these passages three consistent themes. First, that Israel's primary concern, at least as far as Allon is concerned, is *survival*, and that this concern derives from the conditions in which Israel finds itself, as is clear when Allon says that "every other state in our place would behave exactly as we do." Second, and relatedly, that Israel's appreciation of these conditions stems at least in part from past experiences; Allon highlights specific instances of Arab – indeed Syrian – aggression and also references the 1948, 1967, and 1973 wars. And, third, that Israel firmly anticipates renewed conflict. Taken together, these perceptions reinforce one another and mandate the type of policy – the use of force to maintain "defensible borders" – that Allon outlines.

On the Syrian side, similarly, perceptions were driven by the dynamics of rivalry. In a 9 March 1975 meeting with the Americans in Damascus, for example, President Hafez al-Asad said, apropos Israel and the future: "You know our view. Of course, we're not optimistic. *We think it will be inevitable that there will be another war*" (United States 1975a, emphasis added). A few days later, on 15 March, Asad tried to assure Kissinger of Syria's peaceful intentions, while expressing doubt that peace was possible, given Syrian impressions of Israeli intentions, as per an assessment of Israeli behaviour:

[A]s I said before, we are for peace. War cannot be a hobby for any sane person. I have emphasized this. Peace is that situation which preserves justice for human beings. Otherwise it would be surrender rather than peace. Open declarations before our people could never be a maneuver. We don't like maneuvering and our people wouldn't stand for it. We want peace. I say it all the time. It is my conviction that it is in Syria's interest. My talk of peace is for our people – not for Israel. Peace would be our gain. This is a matter of our conviction. *But Israeli behavior doesn't give us evidence the Israelis want peace.* (United States 1975c, emphasis added)

Asad maintained that Syria was willing to entertain peace with Israel, but that a return to pre-1967 borders – i.e., the return of the Golan Heights – was the *sine qua non* of any agreement. Given Israel's own attitudes, an agreement that included a return to the pre-1967 lines, including giving the Golan back to Syria, was unlikely. In a meeting with President Ford and Secretary Kissinger in Washington on 20 June 1975, Syrian Minister of Foreign Affairs Abd al-Halim Khaddam reiterated Damascus's concerns: "The Israeli attitude arouses our suspicion – for example, the new settlements and new construction; Israel says they won't withdraw" (United States 1975f).[5] Khaddam went on to lament the publication of a map "by the Labour Party [then the ruling party in Israel] showing the Golan, Gaza and the West Bank as part of Israel." Clearly the fear was that such a map reflected Israeli attitudes about its permanent hold on these areas, thus reinforcing Syrian perceptions with respect to Israel's expansionism and the futility of any peace talks to roll back Israel's existing territorial gains.

Ultimately, negotiations between Asad and Kissinger soured, as the Americans focused primarily on crafting an Egyptian-Israeli peace agreement – what would become the "Sinai II" disengagement agreement signed in September 1975 – that effectively isolated Syria. Asad was angered by this approach, believing it left Syria vulnerable. While Kissinger saw it as a way of precluding another Arab-Israeli war, "to Asad it sounded more like a death sentence for Syria, Jordan and the Palestinians who [without Egypt] would be … unable to present any credible check upon Israel's ambitions" (Seale 1990, 256). Patrick Seale (1990, 260–1), Asad's British biographer, continues: "The removal of Egypt, the largest and strongest of the Arab states, left the rest of the Arab world with a sharply heightened sense of insecurity. Who would now defend it? Who could act as a brake on Israel's expansion or deter it from striking at will?" Implicit in these anxieties is, of course, the presumption

---

5 Khaddam's remarks regarding the influence of public opinion are also worth noting here as potentially discrepant evidence with respect to my argument that public attitudes do not play a significant role in perpetuating international rivalry. Khaddam worries that acquiescing to certain Israeli moves "would give a bad impression in the Arab world." "We can't ignore public opinion," he says, as justification for Syrian resistance. Later, he reiterates this point, saying, "[w]e can't afford to ignore Arab public opinion. If Israel can't ignore the views of a few settlers on the Golan, how can we ignore the views of 100 million Arabs?" The argument that Syria's anti-Israel stance was and is partly driven by anti-Israeli sentiment both within Syria and in the Arab world more generally is well known. Without question, there is great hostility towards Israel among the various Arab populations in the region. On balance, however, such explicit references to the influence of public opinion are rare among Syrian decisionmakers. In this case, Khaddam appears to be using an appeal to the pressures of public opinion almost as a way of indicating that his "hands are tied" with respect to opposing Israel – i.e., that the Syrian leadership had no choice in the matter. This position is, of course, largely – though, it must be said, not entirely – undermined by the autocratic nature of the Syrian military regime.

that the Arab world would *need* defending – that, absent a "brake," Israel's expansion would proceed apace. Just as Damascus pointed to Egypt's role in previous conflicts as proof that its participation was vital, the experience of such conflicts – and Israel's associated reputation for aggression, in Syrian eyes – was the basis for the concern that without Egypt the Syrians would be additionally vulnerable *next time*.

Partly to offset this putatively increased vulnerability, Syria cultivated closer ties with the Palestine Liberation Organization (PLO) and turned towards other Arab neighbours, particularly Jordan and Lebanon. Rabinovich (2008, 183) describes the "special relationship which [Syria] was trying to forge with the PLO," while Ma'oz (1995, 154) notes the "special efforts" being made by Asad to create a "strategic alliance with Lebanon, Jordan, and the Palestinians." From the Syrian point of view, he continues, "such an alliance, it would seem, would be relatively easy to form and dominate [and would be] crucial to Syria's defensive/offensive system vis-à-vis Israel." Laurie Brand (1990, 23) labels this approach Asad's "Levant Security Doctrine," and suggests that "this concept of Syrian security became increasingly salient in the late 1970s, following the Egyptian-Israeli disengagement agreements that culminated in the Camp David accords." The possibility of a so-called Eastern Front against Israel – comprising Syria, Jordan, Lebanon, and Iraq – would play a role in how *both* Syria and Israel viewed the Lebanon crisis when it arose. As such, a more complete discussion of this dynamic is reserved for the later in the chapter. Here it is merely important to highlight how the pursuit of greater Arab solidarity in the north and east of Israel is consistent with the notion that, "once Egypt decided on a separate peace with Israel, Syria's security situation became very vulnerable" (Knudsen 2001, 223).

For Israel, also, the progress on peace with Egypt shifted its focus to the northern front. Suspicion vis-à-vis Egypt would persist, although tempered by institutional arrangements and the moderating influence of the United States, and the effective elimination of one major front in the Arab-Israeli conflict did not alleviate Israeli concerns about future conflict. Rather, Israeli leaders believed that Asad would stoke further conflict, perhaps even in an effort to derail Egyptian-Israeli negotiations. More broadly, the moves being made by Damascus did not go unnoticed, including the acceleration of Syrian-sponsored PLO attacks[6]

---

6 Then-Israeli minister of defense Shimon Peres (1995, 195) decried, in reference to such activities, the "scourge of cross-border terrorism [that] had to be confronted." In January 1975 Israel complained directly to the UN about PLO attacks emanating from Lebanon, specifically citing the role of "the Syrian sponsored and supported terror grouping 'As-Saiqa' [*sic*]" (Israel 1975).

and, in particular, the cultivation of closer ties with Jordan, Lebanon, and Iraq. In a meeting with Kissinger on 9 March 1975, Rabin raised the spectre of Asad's proposed "unified command" with the PLO, suggesting that such an arrangement would effectively provide Syria with tactical control over "Fatahland," the term used to refer to PLO territory in southern Lebanon (United States 1975a). Three days later, during a meeting on 12 March, Kissinger asked the Israelis whether they thought "war [was] a serious option" being contemplated by Asad. "The aim is to create a coalition," replied Peres, "[h]e will try, I think, to heat things [up] in Lebanon, in Fatahland … Asad is warming them up for the start of war" (United States 1975b). Later that summer, in a conversation with Kissinger on 22 August, Peres lamented: "let's face it, even if we shall have agreement with the Egyptians, terror will be continued by the PLO, which we shall have to take into account" (United States 1975g). These concerns, moreover, were tied to Syria's broader moves regarding an Arab coalition in the north and east: "We don't know exactly what will happen on the part of Syria, Iraq and Jordan. We are certainly uneasy about the new connections between [King] Hussein [of Jordan] and Asad, and how do you say, the rapprochement between Iraq and Syria creates a threatening band around Israel, which would include Lebanon, Syria, Iraq and Jordan. They are fortifying all along the frontiers, including Jordan" (United States 1975g). These new dynamics played a significant part in how Israeli leaders would approach the Lebanese issue over the coming years.

To summarize, Israeli and Syrian perceptions by the mid-1970s – following the 1973 war and in the lead-up to the civil war in Lebanon – were powerfully shaped by the dynamics of rivalry. For Israel, Syrian hostility was evident given over two decades of aggressive acts along the northern border. Past Syrian behaviour led to the inference that future war was overwhelming likely, and the existential implications of such a war mandated defensive policy, including the maintenance of the Israeli position on the Golan Heights. For Syria, the very fact that Israel was in possession of the Golan – as a consequence of the 1967 war – was proof that it was "an expansionist state seeking to dominate the region" (Rabil 2003, 45). For Damascus, past Israeli behaviour was confirmation of this belief, which likewise led to the inference that future Israeli aggression was almost certain. Given Israel's demonstrated military superiority – and the proximity of IDF troops to Damascus from their perch on the Golan – this too had existential implications. The result was a policy dedicated to recovering the Golan, rapaciously building the Syrian military, primarily through its relationship with the Soviet Union, and coordinating closer ties with Arab neighbours, particularly as Egypt negotiated peace with Israel.

This, then, is the context in which both states approached the developing situation in Lebanon in 1975.

Intervention in Lebanon

The Israeli and Syrian interventions in Lebanon took place between 1975 and 1985. This period includes the Lebanese civil war (1975–6) and the so-called Lebanon War (1982–5), which was triggered by direct Israeli intervention in Lebanon as part of Operation Peace for Galilee. More generally, the period is understood as a protracted Israeli-Syrian confrontation in Lebanon, occurring in the context of prolonged violence and domestic political turmoil in the country. The case is illuminating as a comparative exercise vis-à-vis the India-Pakistan rivalry and intervention in Afghanistan. As the following evidence makes clear, the facts of the case support the rational rivalry explanation. As was the case with India and Pakistan in Afghanistan, both Israel and Syria were primarily concerned about the potential implications for the broader rivalry than they were about the immediate outcome of the civil conflict and/ or political struggle in Lebanon. They pursued their intervention strategies in a manner that was predictable and rational from the perspective of ongoing, continuous rivalry and expectations about future conflict.

Lebanese Civil War (1975–6)

The civil war in Lebanon began in 1975, although its eruption was the culmination of long-simmering tension and conflict within a severely fragmented society. A distinct, predominately Christian community has existed on and around Mount Lebanon stretching back centuries; modern Lebanon, however, is a construct of the twentieth century, arising from the post–First World War collapse of the Ottoman Empire. In 1920, the British and French – pursuant to the Sykes-Picot agreement – divvied up the Middle East into separate spheres of influence and control. As part of its mandate, France created a new political entity, carving much of it from historical Syria, covering an area larger than Mount Lebanon and naming it "Greater Lebanon." In addition to the Maronite Christian communities of the Mount, this new entity included both Shia and Sunni Muslim minorities, as well as a community of Druze, an esoteric religion with elements of Islamic mysticism (Traboulsi 2007). Rising tensions between the various communities, as well as regional pressures related to the volatile geopolitics of the wider Middle East, led to periodic political crises – including one in 1958 that required US intervention (Gerges 1993) – until, as Rabinovich (1985, 43) describes, "[i]n the spring of 1975, the Lebanese political system finally collapsed

Map 2. Lebanon

Source: United Nations, Map No. 4282, January 2010.

under the persistent pressure of rival internal and external forces." The precipitating event of the war was the killing of a busload of Palestinians by Christian "Phalangist" forces on 13 April 1975, which triggered escalating reprisal attacks by Muslim and Christian forces. Violence was first concentrated in Beirut, but eventually spread along confessional lines across the country, culminating in a state of full civil war (Abraham 1996).

The specifics of the conflict are complex, and I do not engage in significant detail here; however, a brief summary helps to provide the context of the Israeli and Syrian interventions. Various factions and armed groups participated in the war, each with its own particular interests and grievances. Two broad camps, however, are typically identified. Under one umbrella were Christian/rightist forces, the largest group of which were Phalangist forces under the leadership of Pierre Gemayel. Also prominent in this camp were the so-called Tigers, the armed wing of the centre-right Free National Party, led by Camille Chamoun. The main opposing camp typically were identified as including Muslim/leftist groups, the largest of which was headed by Druze political leader Kamal Junblatt. Also prominent within this camp were armed factions of the socialist and communist political parties. In addition to these two main camps, two distinct Palestinian groups were involved, one dominated by Fatah and loyal to Yasir Arafat, and the other by al-Saiqa, a pro-Syrian guerilla force. The Palestinians were broadly sympathetic to the Muslim cause and often fought alongside them, but were not contesting for central control of Lebanon in the same way; rather, they were interested in maintaining the Palestinian presence in the south, and were effectively a foreign entity operating on Lebanese soil.[7] Finally, the Lebanese government itself was a separate actor; it remained nominally split between Christian and Muslim political leaders, and therefore attempted to remain neutral. The Lebanese Armed Forces (LAF), initially still under the government's control, included both Christian and Muslim factions. Virtually none of these alignments was to remain static over the course of the war – in particular, the LAF eventually split, the two factions aligning themselves with their co-religionists. Fighting lasted for eighteen months, culminating in a tenuous ceasefire agreement negotiated at a conference in Riyadh in October 1976. This outcome left the pro-government, Christian/rightist forces in the ascendancy under the guise of a new power-sharing agreement backed by the creation of an Arab Deterrent Force (ADF) meant to maintain stability. Although the ADF comprised contingents from several regional Arab powers, including Jordan and Saudi Arabia, the dominant force

---

7 For a discussion of the Palestinian role in the civil war, see Hudson (1978).

was Syrian, and Damascus exerted effective hegemony over the Lebanese government.

The period of the civil war described here clearly constituted an opportunity for intervention for both Syria and Israel. As with the India-Pakistan rivalry in Afghanistan, geographic proximity was a relevant consideration. As a regional rivalry, Israel and Syria were likely to be concerned with a proximate civil conflict destabilizing a neighbouring state and the potential implications for the dynamics of the rivalry itself. Lebanon is bordered by Israel to the south and Syria to the east, serving essentially as a buffer between the rivals on what would otherwise be an extended frontier – the two share a shorter contiguous border in the region of the Golan plateau. This dimension played significantly on the minds of Israeli and Syrian leaders; indeed, previous experience in the rivalry – during both major wars[8] and lower-level, intermittent crises[9] – suggested that Lebanese territory was strategically significant.

Syrian Intervention (1975–6)

Syria was the first to intervene, doing so initially at the diplomatic and political level by sending Foreign Minister Khaddam to Beirut in May 1975 in order to craft a political compromise at the cabinet level; a new power-sharing deal was instituted in late June, leading to a temporary abatement in violence (Dawisha 1980). Fighting renewed in late August, however, this time with the LAF entering the fray on the side of the Christian militias. Syria made another attempt at diplomatic peacemaking, but the crisis deteriorated out of control, and over the fall months the total collapse of the Lebanese state appeared increasingly likely.

Syria was also involved indirectly during this period, lending support to Palestinian groups that traditionally had acted as proxies for Syrian interests, particularly in southern Lebanon; such groups had been helpful vis-à-vis Israel, serving as both offensive assets and as a defensive bulwark across the Beqa Valley.[10] When these groups

---

8 In describing Syrian concerns regarding Lebanese territory, Muslih (1993, 626) observes that, "during the 1973 war, Israeli aircraft did try to outflank Syrian aircraft defenses through Lebanon."

9 In particular, from the Israeli point of view, the use of southern Lebanon as a launching pad for frequent Palestinian guerilla attacks against Israeli territory.

10 Rabinovich (2008: 247) argues that "Israel figure[d] prominently in Asad's assessment of Lebanon and the Lebanese arena," and that Asad's "original investment in Lebanon [in] the early 1970s [including cultivation of, and support for, the PLO] was conceived ... as part of the effort to 'organize' (in his biographer's language) Syria's Arab environment into a strategic asset vis-à-vis Israel."

appealed to Damascus for support in the conflict, Asad complied, supplying them with arms and ammunition, some of which passed from the Palestinians to the Muslim/leftist militias battling for control of Lebanon. In January 1976, when pro-government Christian forces threatened to overwhelm Palestinian and Muslim positions in Tripoli and Zahlé – the latter the capital city of the Beqa Valley governorate – "Damascus … dispatched two brigades of the Syrian-controlled PLA [Palestine Liberation Army]"[11] in order "to defend the Lebanese-Palestinian radical forces against Christian attacks" (Ma'oz 1995, 164). Yet Syria's position was not simply comprehensive support for the Muslim/leftist position. In March 1976, for example, Damascus directed the PLA as well as al-Saiqa to stall the advance of Muslim/ leftist forces on the presidential palace of Suleiman Franjieh (Dawisha 1980; for an analysis of this episode in terms of deterrence theory, see Harvey 1995).

The Syrian goals in this phase were to protect the Palestinians while forestalling the complete collapse of the Lebanese state. In this way, the initial period of Syrian involvement can be seen as continuation of a policy the original aim of which was related to rivalry with Israel: keeping a pliant force in southern Lebanon that could serve as an extension of Syrian military strategy along Israel's northern border. This was best achieved through the maintenance of the status quo; hence the diplomatic attempts to broker a political compromise, the support for the Palestinians and, by extension, Muslim/leftists to prevent the loss of the PLO position in the south and elsewhere – Christian/rightist forces largely blamed the PLO for destabilizing the country in the first place and wished to see it expelled from Lebanon – and finally the direction of Syrian-controlled Palestinian forces to prevent the overthrow of the Christian regime. According to Rabinovich (1985, 48), "Asad was determined to prevent both Lebanon's partition and a clear-cut victory by the radical revisionists and their Palestinian supporters." Fear of a collapsing Lebanese state related to concerns "about the [potential] military weakness of Lebanon, which in [Syria's] opinion was fraught with potential dangers for Syria in time of war with Israel" (Avi-Ran 1991, 7). Fear of a radical victory, by contrast, was based on the perception that it "would … probably provoke Israeli intervention on the side of the beleaguered Christians" (Rabinovich 1985, 48). Yet Damascus was not willing, at that point, either to support or to acquiesce to a decisive

---

11 The PLA was created in 1964 ostensibly to serve as the military wing of the PLO; however, it never actually came under PLO control but instead became a proxy force for various Arab governments, particularly Syria.

Christian victory. First, as mentioned, this would endanger the Palestinian groups Syria controlled, influenced, and relied upon. Second, a regime in Beirut totally in Christian control could "[opt] for closer cooperation with Israel" (Rabil 2003, 49). As Seale (1990, 276) summarizes, Asad "envisaged two possible outcomes, both equally horrendous: either the Maronites would set up a separate state, which would bring Israel in as its protector, or the radicals with Palestinian backing would beat the Maronites, which would bring Israel in as punisher." These realities left Syria with few options, and resulted in the delicately balanced – and sometimes contradictory – intervention that it pursued in the early months of the war.

As the conflict proceeded, however, it became clear that greater Syrian involvement would be needed to forestall the collapse of the Lebanese state. Frustrated with the perceived intransigence of the Muslim/leftist leader Junblatt, Damascus cut supplies to radical forces. Asad also directed the PLA and al-Saiqa to side definitively with status quo, pro-government forces. This meant Syrian-directed Palestinian forces attacking the regular PLO, a move which drew condemnation, not surprisingly, from across the Arab world. On 1 June 1976, approximately 30,000 regular Syrian troops moved into Lebanon in support of Christian forces (Weinberger 1986). In addition to attacks on the Muslim/leftist forces led by Junblatt, this also brought Syrian troops into direct conflict with Palestinians. The move was interpreted "as an astonishing, and to many a profoundly shocking, reversal of alliances ... [T]he lion of Arabism ... slaughtering Arabism's sacred cow" (Seale 1990, 285). Anti-Syrian protests broke out across the region, with some accusing Asad of participating in a secret US-Israeli plot to take control in Lebanon.

The practical effects of direct intervention were immediate, changing the tide of the conflict in favour of Christian forces that had been teetering on the edge of defeat. Intense fighting continued over the summer, but by mid-October the PLO-Muslim/leftist axis had largely been defeated and Christian Maronite control – backed by the Syrian army – reaffirmed in most of Lebanon. The Riyadh conference mentioned above set the parameters of a new constitutional arrangement, and legitimized the Syrian presence (they became the official "guests" of the Lebanese government) through the formation of the ADF, in which Syria was the dominant force, with funding from Saudi Arabia and Kuwait (Deeb 1980).

Much like the Pakistani decision to abandon its initial support for the American intervention in Afghanistan and the Bonn-created Afghan government by turning to support the Taliban insurgency,

Syria's *volte-face* – in terms of its abandonment of its traditional allies in favour of direct support for its Christian opponents – helps elucidate the logic underpinning Syrian policy. As in the Pakistani case, what at first appears an "astonishing reversal" in fact reflected a consistent rationale. As it was for Islamabad, Damascus's decision was fundamentally predicated on rivalry concerns. Asad's decision, argues Rabinovich (1985, 48), "was the product of a new Syrian foreign policy devised in the aftermath of and under the impact of the October War [of 1973]." Specifically, the policy was predicated on ensuring a "united" or "eastern" front against Israel by retaining influence in both Lebanon and Jordan, thus precluding the possibility of flanking Israeli attacks through either country. As Rabinovich implies, the lessons of previous wars – in 1973, but also, I would argue, in 1967 and 1948 – as well as the new regional realities post–Sinai II, shaped this policy as well as the intensity with which it was pursued. The decisive Syrian fear, as the war in Lebanon spiralled out of control in 1976, was that instability and, even worse, a PLO-backed Muslim/leftist victory, would invite Israeli intervention.

Such an intervention would have been disastrous for Syrian security, opening up a new potential front against Israel in the event of war. According to Avi-Ran (1991, 8): "The Syrians feared that in a war the Israeli forces might outflank the Golan Heights from the west via 'Fatahland' and the Bekaa Valley, or reach the Syrian industrial centers in the North (Homs, Hama) via the Bekaa." Weinberger (1986, 271) concurs, noting that officials in Damascus recognized that "Syria's line of defense was vulnerable to an Israeli attack across Lebanese territory directed at its 'soft western underbelly.'" As Patrick Seale documents, these concerns weighed heavily on Asad, who felt his "environment bristling with perils." "He could not allow the Lebanese crisis to rot," writes Seale (1990, 276), "the longer it continued, the greater Israel's opportunities. In his mind it was as clear as a mathematical formula." Rabil (2003, 51) summarizes the implications well:

> President Asad realized that he had to immediately intervene in order to prevent the military downfall of the Christian side. Israel would not stand idly by and witness the creation of a radical country, swarming with Palestinian militants, along its border. It would undoubtedly help the Maronites create their own state, thus establishing a permanent foothold in Lebanon. Israel could easily then use Lebanon to militarily outflank Syria's defenses. At this point, it becomes clear that the idea of Syrian intervention in Lebanon was born out of Asad's

strategic security needs rather than his ideological convictions about Greater Syria.[12]

Nor was this belief unique to Asad. "Syrian decision-makers" more generally, writes Dawisha (1980, 73) – including Foreign Minister Kaddam, Air Force and National Security Chief Naji Jamil, and Chief of Staff Hikmat Shihabi – "were convinced that the partition of Lebanon would give Israel the pretext to move into Southern Lebanon and occupy the area up to the Litani River." Such an outcome, the Syrians concluded, would "provide Israel with a new front in any future confrontation with Syria" and was therefore unacceptable (74).

The belief that Israel would seize an opportunity to intervene in Lebanon – even more important, the *fear* this induced in Damascus – was predicated on several factors. First, Israel had been involved with Christian forces during the civil war, meaning it had already flirted with an involvement that could be easily expanded. Second, again, the experience of previous wars had suggested that Israel recognized the strategic opportunities afforded by Lebanese territory – as when, in 1973, it used Lebanese air space to outflank Syrian air defences. Israeli raids into southern Lebanon, similarly, had been consistent features over the previous decade. And third, more generally, the vulnerability that an Israeli intervention would create – *in the context of expectations about future conflict* – mandated that Syria work to preclude such a possibility.

---

12 The mention of "Greater Syria" refers to the possibility that Syrian intervention
    was motivated by ethnic/religious/cultural identity factors. Historically, Syria was
    and is intimately connected with the Lebanese state and its people. As mentioned
    above, the creation of modern-day Lebanon occurred by incorporating territory of
    what had historically been considered "Greater Syria" into a new state centred on
    Mount Lebanon and the city of Beirut. Thus, many of the inhabitants of Lebanon – in
    particular, the Muslim communities in the north, south, and along the coast – identify
    to varying degrees with the Syrian nation. Politically, Asad's Ba'athist regime was
    keen to emphasize this relationship, making frequent references to Lebanon as
    part of "Greater Syria" and of the Lebanese people as "brothers" to their Syrian
    counterparts. In light of such comments, some have suggested that the motivation for
    intervention had something to do with ethnic or national solidarity, with the shared
    identities of the Syrian and Lebanese people. Rabinovich (1985, 53–4) dispatches
    this explanation effectively: "The need to justify and legitimize a controversial
    intervention and a controversial policy in Lebanon induced Asad and his regime to
    develop and emphasize themes that were either implicit or inconsequential during
    the early phases of Syria's intervention. Most notable among them was the notion of
    a Greater Syria ... Asad's decision to intervene in Lebanon was not made in order to
    implement that notion. But when the conflict with the Palestinians and the Lebanese
    left developed, this vision became useful to justify their subjugation."

Here we see clearly the effects of rivalry. Taken in isolation, it would be difficult to explain a costly intervention, one that drew intense criticism from the Arab world and even led to a *froideur* in the Syran-Soviet relationship – no small consideration given the extent of Soviet military patronage (Karsh 1991) – in which Syria abandoned and indeed attacked the Palestinians, its long-standing clients and allies (let alone its spiritual brethren and the core of the Arab cause). As mentioned, many in the Arab world were accordingly confused and outraged. Yet in the context of ongoing rivalry with Israel, the rationale behind the move is explicable. The overriding concern was the threat from Israel. Seale (1990) summarizes Asad's attitude to the criticism he faced with regard to the intervention: "From first to last Asad remained convinced that, whatever the outside pressures on him, his intervention had been tactically and morally correct and that he had been impelled by the highest principles. He had been forced to act by the blindness and ambition of men *who could not grasp the nature of his life-and-death struggle with Israel*" (288, emphasis added). It was this rationale, this preoccupation with the "life-and-death struggle with Israel" – established over the course of multiple wars and crises since 1948 – that guided Syrian policy throughout the 1975–6 period in Lebanon. Even as "changes in circumstances required changes in policy – from mediation and indirect intervention to direct military intervention and several changes of allies – Syrian goals remained constant throughout the war: to put an end to it in a way that would keep Lebanon from in any way enabling Israel to threaten Syria" (Jorum 2014, 61).

Again, the parallels with the Pakistan case are worth making explicit; in each instance, a *change* in policy reflected *consistent* preferences confronting new circumstances. In Afghanistan, Pakistan's initial decision to abandon the Taliban and support the American intervention was designed to minimize India's role and thereby preclude advantages from accruing to India that would threaten Pakistan in the future. Once the American intervention occurred, however, it became clear that India's role would be significant in the new Afghan state. Pakistan therefore reversed its decision and re-engaged with a Taliban insurgency that was taking aim at the Indian-supported Afghan government.

Israeli Intervention (1975–6)

In the years leading up to the civil war, Israel had conducted numerous raids into Lebanon in retaliation for Palestinian cross-border attacks and terrorist activities, and this practice continued once war broke out.[13] In terms of new involvement, however, Israel's activities remained relatively limited. Its interests in Lebanon were twofold at the time. First, there was a genuine identification with the Christian population as another non-Muslim religious minority in the region. Second, and much more important, there was the security issue related to the Palestinian threat. As mentioned above, the "scourge" of cross-border terrorism had become a major issue for Israeli leaders, particularly in the context of improving Egyptian-Israeli relations. Quelling such activities was a priority.

As a contiguous state, Israel was naturally concerned with instability in Lebanon. Ironically, however, given the PLO presence in the south and its relative autonomy from the Lebanese government, the outbreak of civil war did little – at first – to alter fundamentally the security situation for Israel. The Israelis were concerned with the safety of Christian communities, but were not prepared to commit fully to their protection or to intervene directly on their behalf.[14] Instead, Israel was focused on potential Syrian involvement. Weinberger (1986) summarizes Jerusalem's position effectively: "Israel's behaviour during the Lebanese Civil War was reactive to Syria. Israel was at first primarily concerned with the *direction* of Syrian alignments, fearing that Syrian support for traditional allies in Lebanon would strengthen the PLO's capabilities against Israel. Once Syria shifted alignments, Israel's main priority was to limit the *intensity* and geographic scope of Syria's military presence within range of Israel's northern border" (269, emphasis in original). This reference to "limiting the intensity and geographic scope" of intervention refers to the so-called red line agreement between Israel and Syria, explored in greater detail below. First it is important to note the limited Israeli intervention that followed from their apprehension regarding initial Syrian involvement.

This intervention took the form of aid and support to Christian forces. As mentioned, Israel did not identify sufficiently with the Christian cause to intervene more comprehensively, but recall that, during this initial phase, Syria had not yet gone beyond indirect intervention either. At this point, concerned only with the "direction" of Syria's aid to PLO-Muslim/leftist forces, Israel moved to balance Syrian efforts by offering aid to the Christian/rightist side. It did this through arms transfers

---

13 Primarily in the south, but also into Beirut itself, as on 13 April 1973 when Israeli commandos executed three Fatah leaders in their apartments (Dawisha 1980).

14 As Rabin (1979, 281) notes in his memoirs: "Israel felt a natural affinity to the Christian community of Lebanon, but under no circumstances could we undertake political or military responsibility for its fate."

and aid estimated to be worth about US$100 million (Weinberger 1986). Obviously, Israel had a preference for the Maronites over the Muslims, particularly given that the former shared Jerusalem's antagonistic view of the PLO. A Lebanese state controlled by Muslim/leftist forces was likely to offer even greater free rein to the Palestinians than was already the case, and would also certainly be closely aligned with Syria, exacerbating Israeli security concerns on both counts. The Israelis were well aware of the so-called Eastern Front strategy tying Syria together with Lebanon, Jordan, and Iraq, but unlike Damascus – which considered such Arab solidarity necessary for defence – Jerusalem saw it as a potential offensive threat. Israel's focus during this phase was primarily on southern Lebanon, which it considered to be in its legitimate sphere of influence. All told, however, Israeli involvement remained limited, meant primarily to offset Syrian contributions to PLO-Muslim/leftist forces and to retain the ability to retaliate against PLO attacks from south Lebanon.

As the prospect of direct Syrian intervention increased, however, Israeli interest became more acute. The prospect of Syrian troops arrayed along its northern border was not something Israel's leaders would tolerate. Rabin (1979) writes of the moment: "[I]t was clear that if the Syrian army occupied southern Lebanon, we would be forced to take pragmatic steps to push it back. Israel could not tolerate having Syrian troops stationed along *two* of her borders!" (280, emphasis in original). In fact, it seemed possible that a direct Syrian intervention could very well precipitate the very Israeli intervention it was designed to preclude. Jerusalem explicitly warned as much: "Through the United States, Israel made it clear to the Syrians that it considered the intervention of foreign armed forces in Lebanon a grave threat to its security, something that Israel would not allow to happen" (Rabil 2003, 51–2). Henry Kissinger (1999), as ever at the centre of Middle East developments at the time, describes his communications with Rabin on the issue: "In case of Syrian intervention, Israeli forces would occupy 'as quietly as they can' strategic positions in southern Lebanon." Damascus's use of the PLA and al-Saiqa in January 1976 was particularly alarming to Israel, which saw such activity as a probe by Syria and a portent of potential direct intervention. As Weinberger (1986, 282) describes, the Israeli response was clear: "Defense Minister Shimon Peres emphasized … that the presence of a large number of guerilla forces in Lebanon and the possible entry of the Syrian Army into Lebanon were two problems with direct repercussions for Israel's security. He warned that 'if Syria invades Lebanon, Israel will undertake the necessary defensive measures.'" Asad was aware of these threats, of course, and obviously did not wish to provoke an Israeli counterintervention that might bring on a direct conflict that he knew Syria was unlikely to win, and was the precise outcome his own forays into Lebanon were designed to prevent. This catch-22 was solved via a backchannel arrangement, brokered by the United States, which came to be known as the "red line" agreement. The specifics of this agreement are telling, and constitute solid evidence as to the priorities of both Israel and Syria in the Lebanese theatre. As such, it is worth exploring in detail.

The Red Line Agreement

The direct Syrian intervention that brought the Lebanese civil war to a close in October 1976 did not trigger the large-scale Israeli response that Israeli decisionmakers had threatened would occur in the event of Syrian troops deploying into Lebanon. Why? The answer is a tacit agreement reached between the rivals – with the United States as a partial architect and intermediary – that protected, at least initially, the core security concerns of each side. As described above, Syria's main concern was preventing the collapse of the Lebanese state lest Israel take advantage of such instability to move into Lebanon and exert control and influence over the country. Damascus saw the trajectory of the conflict heading in this direction, and therefore calculated that direct intervention was necessary to forestall such an outcome. On the Israeli side, the prospect of Syrian troops deployed in *southern* Lebanon was untenable. This would expand Israel's vulnerability to attacks on multiple fronts (at the very moment it believed it was reducing its vulnerability in the Sinai through negotiations with Egypt). Neither state, in other words, was driven primarily by offensive considerations, but rather by security concerns associated with the presence of its rival in Lebanon. Of course, it was very difficult to communicate these concerns directly, let alone arrive at any type of understanding, for precisely the reasons that the security concerns existed in the first place: mistrust and perceived hostile intentions.

Into this conundrum stepped Kissinger and the US diplomatic team. By going through the United States, Israel was able to communicate to Asad what would, and what would not, be acceptable in terms of Syrian intervention. This would allow Asad to move in and stabilize Lebanon without prompting an Israeli invasion. Over a period in the spring of 1976, messages were passed back and forth through the Americans, and the basic parameters of Israel's "red line" in Lebanon were established. These included a geographical dimension, but also stipulations as to the scope, scale, and intensity of Syrian activities, including what types of weapons systems could be introduced to certain areas. According to Israeli journalist Ze'ev Schiff, the deal had the following stipulations: "(1) The Syrian army would not enter southern Lebanon and would not cross a line starting south of Sidon, on the coast, and running east to Aysiya and from there towards the Syrian border; (2) the Syrian army in Lebanon would not be equipped with surface-to-air missile batteries; (3) and the Syrian army would not use its air force against the Christians in Lebanon" (quoted in Rabil 2003, 52). Because the agreement was unwritten, there are discrepancies as to what was actually included, so the above parameters cannot be considered definitive. In his memoirs, Kissinger, for example, simply writes of the deal that, "Israel would not tolerate movement of Syrian forces beyond an area of ten kilometers south of the Damascus-Beirut axis." Rabin (1979, 280), likewise, notes that the red line "was not marked out on any map," but that "we later made it clear that we meant a line running directly east from Sidon to the Lebanese-Syrian border." The Litani River is also often used as the de facto red line (see, for example, Ben-Yehuda and Sandler 2002; Ma'oz 1995; Mays 2004; Rabinovich 1985), which places it slightly farther south than the Sidon line. This discrepancy likely mirrors the fluidity of the line in practice, as circumstances changed and both sides continued to communicate through an intermediary.

In any event, the red line did result in Syria's entering Lebanon without the immediate looming threat of an Israeli countermove. The red line conditions were broadly respected by Damascus over the summer and fall of 1976, during which time, as described above, Syrian forces were able to effectuate a ceasefire and nominal end to the civil war. The restrictions associated with the red line, however, prevented this move from being decisive. Most significantly, given that Syrian forces were precluded from entering the south, the PLO continued to operate in that part of the country. As such, the October 1976 resolution to the war was not complete, and violence and instability continued in areas not open to Syrian intervention.

Here we see one of the striking features of the red line arrangement: Israel's policy amounted to a protective umbrella over a guerilla organization whose primary target was the Israeli state. Jerusalem was aware of the irony, but nonetheless preferred to keep Syria out of southern Lebanon rather than allow it in to subdue the PLO (Syria had, in fact, communicated its willingness to do as much). As Rabin (1979) writes: "[B]ecause the Syrians were prevented from moving south of the 'red line,' southern Lebanon became a haven for the terrorists. *We had foreseen such an eventuality and preferred it to Syrian military control of the area bordering our territory.* But that did not reduce the absurdity of the new situation: PLO terrorists, Israel's sworn foes, found asylum under an Israeli 'deterrence umbrella' intended against the Syrians" (280, emphasis added). In other words, the clear, ongoing, and demonstrable threat from Palestinian attacks was preferable to the *possible* threat from Syrian forces in control of areas along the border. This decision is bizarre in the context of immediate security interests, but explicable by reference to the long-term security calculus conditioned by international rivalry. As Weinberger (1986, 280) observes, "[i]*n the short term*, it was in Israel's interest to allow Syria to attack Palestinian positions in Lebanon; *in the long term*, however, a substantial Syrian presence in Lebanon could contribute to an effective Eastern Front strategy" (emphasis added). Israel was focused on the long term. Evron (2013) provides a useful overview of the logic at work: "Israel … faced a major dilemma which was also to recur later: to accept Syrian deployment in the south as a pacifying measure but that would allow the south to the turned into a Syrian military base. *Israeli suspicions of long-term Syrian intentions persisted, however, and Israel decided to maintain its opposition to* [Syrian deployment]" (56, emphasis added). Again, this decision constitutes striking evidence in support of the rivalry argument: a clear trade-off between immediate and visible security threats and a potential long-term threat, and the preference to protect against the latter as opposed to the former.

As Evron alludes to, this was a dilemma that would "recur" in the future – which is to say that the position of both Syria and Israel vis-à-vis the red line would not remain static. Following the civil war – again, ostensibly, although not definitively, ended in October 1976 – a new tenuous phase in the Lebanese crisis began. Syria, through the ADF, retained basic control of Lebanon north of the Litani River, while Israel continued to cultivate ties with Christian forces in the south. In other words, the respective Syrian and Israeli interventions in Lebanon continued.

Israel and Syria in Lebanon (1977–81)

The close of the Lebanese civil war did not end the broader Lebanese crisis. The underlying tensions in Lebanese society persisted, now supplemented by a de facto partition of the country into southern (Israeli) and northern (Syrian) spheres of influence. Nor were each state's activities confined to its particular zone. As Weinberger (1986, 286) describes: "Essentially, Syrian and Israeli policies were mirror images of each other. In northern and central Lebanon, Syria intervened directly while Israel offered covert assistance to the groups it favoured. Below the Litani River, Israel became progressively more actively involved while Syrian interference remained largely covert." In the south, protected by

Israel's deterrent umbrella vis-à-vis Syria, the PLO intensified its activities against Israel. Cross-border raids proliferated, leading to repeated Israeli reprisals and counterraids (Shilon, Zilberberg, and Sharett 2012).[15] This prompted Israel to enhance its defensive infrastructure along its northern border and to cultivate greater links with Christian communities and militias in southern Lebanon (Rabinovich 1985).

Yet even as the threat from the PLO intensified, Israel remained firm in its commitment to the principles of the red line, continuing to oppose the deployment of Syrian forces to quell instability. In January 1977, for example, Syrian troops entered the city of Nabatiya, some "seven kilometres to the south of the southernmost line of deployment of the Syrian force" (Avi-Ran 1991, 98) – which is to say, below Israel's geographical red line, by anyone's measure. "Israeli decision-makers" Evron (2013, 62) writes,

> were forced to confront once more … the trade-off between immediate current security and long-term basic security. It was understood that Syrian deployment along the border would probably diminish the threat of PLO activity. Indeed, one might add that in the view of Syria's cautious and controlled behaviour in the Golan Heights, Syrian deployment could have completely precluded terrorism from the north. On the other hand, Syrian might use its deployment in the south as an additional springboard for a conventional attack in Israel. Israel eventually decided to oppose the Syrian move very strongly.

The Nabatiye incident therefore reinforced the centrality of rivalry concerns for Israel; not only was long-term security preferred when Syrian intervention was being contemplated and the initial red line agreement crafted, but now, in the face of amplified PLO activity, it remained the priority.

At the same time, the tentative alliance of convenience between Christian/rightist forces and Syria began to crumble. Syrian forces had not withdrawn from Lebanon in 1976, instead staying on to ensure stability and maintain their influence and control over Beirut. Their presence increasingly worried the Maronites, who were "apprehensive that Syria intended to continue its control over Lebanon, attempting to

---

15 Some such reprisals included the movement of significant numbers of Israeli forces into Lebanese territory. In 1978, the IDF deployed troops into southern Lebanon as part of Operation Litani in response to the so-called Coastal Road Massacre in which a team of Palestinian guerillas penetrated into Israeli territory and killed thirty-eight Israeli citizens.

disarm the Christians of their heavy weapons and renewing its alliance with the PLO and the Lebanese left" (Ma'oz 1995, 167). Bashir Jumayyil, son of Maronite patriarch Pierre Jumayyil and an emerging leader of the dominant faction within the Christian alliance, sought to offset these concerns by cultivating closer ties with Israel. Indeed, Israel had continued its wartime policy of supplying Christian forces through seaports in the north; this practice intensified at Bashir Jumayyil's request (Zamir 1999). For Israel, support for the Christians was seen as a means to erode Syrian influence in Lebanon; the red line agreement notwithstanding, Syrian control over Lebanon remained a security threat. The goal of Jumayyil and the Christian front more broadly increasingly became the expulsion of Syrian forces from Lebanon, making them natural Israeli allies. Support for Christian forces in the north against Syria was mirrored by amplified support for, and even coordination with, Christians in the south against the PLO (Ma'oz 1995).

Recognizing that its control over Lebanon could never be consolidated absent a presence in the south, Syria undertook to cultivate ties with Muslim forces in the area, in part leading to a general rapprochement with its previously scorned Muslim-PLO allies (Rabinovich 1985; Shilon, Zilberberg, and Sharett 2012). Gradually, the situation between the Maronites and the Syrians deteriorated; in early 1978, fighting broke out, first in Beirut and then spreading elsewhere. The violence was stopped by both international and Israeli pressure: Israeli fighter jets flew over Beirut, and Jerusalem warned that it would not permit the "genocide" of Christians by Syrian forces (Ma'oz 1995). At the same time, the success of Egyptian-Israeli negotiations on a peace agreement were shifting Israel's attention more and more to the Lebanese theatre. There was an increased desire on the part of Jerusalem – now led by Menachem Begin's Likud government – to deal with the Palestinian issue and the threat emanating from Lebanon more broadly. Begin consequently expanded Israel's support for and cooperation with Jumayyil's forces in the north and Christian militias – in particular, the South Lebanon Army (SLA) led by Saad Haddad – in the south (Perlmutter 1987).

Partly as a result of this pressure, Syria chose to remove and reposition some of its forces in 1980. It ceded positions in Beirut and elsewhere to the PLO, but retained a presence along the Beirut-Damascus highway and concentrated remaining forces in the strategically important Beqa Valley, considered vital in any future conflict with Israel (Rabinovich 1985). The move further underscored the continued centrality of rivalry concerns with respect to Syria's presence in Lebanon; control over Lebanon was desirable but, in the face of significant opposition to

Syria's presence, the most important consideration remained the consolidation of defensive lines against a future Israeli attack.

These priorities were put to the test in the spring of 1981. In an attempt to link the Christian heartland to the Christian town of Zahlé, located in the Beqa Valley, Maronite forces moved into the area. The Christian-Israeli connection suggested the "possibility of Israeli troops or their Lebanese allies in the Beqa valley," and was therefore "most unsettling for Syria's leaders" (Rabinovich 1985, 116). O'Ballance (1998, 106), likewise, suggests that "Syria certainly did not want a [Maronite]-held Zahle bastion blocking the main highway from Damascus, Zahle being only ten miles from the Syrian border." As a result of these priorities, Syrian forces moved to expel the Maronites from the city. Fighting became intense, and Syria eventually employed combat helicopters to break the deadlock (Avi-Ran 1991). The introduction of such assets was a violation of the red line agreement; Israel responded by shooting down two Syrian helicopters on 28 April (O'Ballance 1998). The decision was a controversial one in Israel; several Israeli officials – including Deputy Minister of Defense Mordechai Tzipori – worried about being drawn into a war on the Christians' behalf (the move into Zahlé, after all, had been a Maronite decision). Yet Begin insisted that the protection of the Christians against aerial attack was necessary because Israel had publicly committed to such a position – failure to act would erode Israeli credibility vis-à-vis Syria and thereby invite further provocations, perhaps in southern Lebanon (Shilon, Zilberberg, and Sharett 2012). In response to Israel's downing of the helicopters, Syria introduced surface-to-air (SAM) missiles into Zahlé as well as "long-range missiles in Syrian territory along the Lebanese border" (Rabinovich 1985, 118). An Israeli plan to destroy the missile installations was stalled by inclement weather,[16] allowing for last-minute US negotiations that, although they failed to convince Asad to remove the missiles, delayed any Israeli action through the June 1981 Israeli elections. With the so-called missile crisis unresolved, the red line agreement crumbled, and conflict between Israel and Syria on Lebanese soil appeared increasingly likely. In July, increased Israeli-PLO fighting along the Israel-Lebanon border intensified; Israeli leaders now worried that Palestinian infrastructure could be protected by the umbrella provided by the newly installed

---

16 The moment again reflects the divergent perceptions of the two sides and the associated effects of rivalry. As Shilon, Zilberberg, and Sharett (2012) write, "[t]he deployment of batteries of anti-air missiles along the Beqaa Valley and Scud missiles near Damascus was meant mainly to warn Israel that it should avoid exacerbating the situation. *But Begin saw the deployment as a real threat*" (368, emphasis added).

Syrian missiles. A decision was therefore reached to enter south Lebanon to deal with the Palestinian threat more definitively, leading to the 1982 Lebanon war.

The Lebanon War (1982–5)

The collapse of the red line arrangement set the stage for the Israeli invasion of Lebanon in 1982. The roots of the war lay in the escalating crises described above, in particular the development of PLO infrastructure in the south and the simultaneous Syrian military presence in the adjacent Beqa Valley; the latter dynamic exacerbated Israeli fears not only of the PLO, which might be supported and protected by proximate Syrian forces, but also of a direct Syrian attack more generally (Rabinovich 1985).

The triggering event of the invasion was the attempted assassination of the Israeli ambassador in London by a Palestinian hit squad on 3 June 1982. The incident gave the Israeli leadership the political capital required to justify military action. Two days later, the Israeli cabinet approved "Operation Peace for Galilee," and on 6 June a "90,000-strong invasion force, combining armour, infantry and artillery, with substantial air and naval support" entered southern Lebanon (O'Ballance 1998, 113). The stated purpose of the operation was to push back the PLO and create a forty-kilometre buffer zone along the border, thereby putting Israeli territory out of range of Palestinian rocket and mortar attacks. This limited objective was swiftly achieved, but the IDF pushed beyond it. Three columns of Israeli troops advanced deeper into Lebanese territory, one along the coast towards Beirut, one in the central mountainous region towards the Beirut-Damascus highway, and another in the east down from the Golan towards the Beqa Valley. This last thrust put the IDF into direct conflict with Syrian forces (Bregman 2016).

Although outmatched in military hardware, the Syrians were able to slow the Israeli momentum until a ceasefire was reached – under international pressure – on 11 June. The ceasefire applied, however, only to the eastern sector and to Syrian and Israeli forces, and therefore did not extend to the PLO in the west and along the coast. On that front, Israel swept towards Beirut, reaching the outskirts of the capital by 13 June.[17] On 15 June, Israeli forces reached and captured portions of the Beirut-Damascus highway in the central sector, cutting off the PLO and

---

17 The Syrian-Israeli ceasefire had been extended to include the PLO on 12 June but quickly fell apart (Gabriel 1984).

a contingent of Syrian ADF troops in Beirut from Damascus. Approaching the city from two sides, the Israelis began what would become a seventy-three-day siege; by mid-August 1982 the initial, primary phase of the war had come to a close with an Israeli victory (Ma'oz 1995).

Israeli and Syrian behaviour in this phase is revealing of their respective priorities. First, the historical record is clear that the initial Israeli insistence that their war aims were limited to clearing the PLO from the south was disingenuous;[18] the intention was always to expand the conflict into other parts of Lebanon, including the central and eastern regions, and to eliminate or diminish the Syrian presence by destroying SAM installations and pushing Syrian troops from their positions in the Beqa Valley. The key question is why did Israel feel it necessary to initiate conflict with Syria in 1982?

Without attempting to adjudicate decisively between competing interpretations of the Israeli decision, one possibility is that Prime Minister Begin and his defence minister Ariel Sharon were driven by the desire to settle Israel's security issues in the context of a perceived ongoing – and growing – threat from the Syrian presence in Lebanon; this explanation is consistent with the general argument that rivalry considerations were relevant to Israeli decision-making in Lebanon throughout the 1975–85 period. If one considers, for example, the 1982 decision in the context of the breakdown of the red line agreement – and in particular the introduction of SAMs into the Beqa – it becomes less of a rash departure from hitherto limited involvement than a logical response to a deteriorating security situation within a protracted crisis. Recall that the entire *point* of the original red line agreement was to specify how Syria could *avoid* an Israeli invasion of Lebanon – which is to say, there was a standing threat of Israeli invasion if the agreement's conditions were violated. Syria quite clearly violated the red line by placing SAMs in the Beqa Valley. The Israeli move was consistent with the rationale that shaped the red line agreement in the first place.

As for Syria, it is clear that its response to the Israeli invasion reflected the unavoidable but reluctant defence of its vital Lebanese positions. Knudsen (2001, 225), for example, describes the 1982 war as "the conflict Asad did not want." As the IDF moved north, however, "there was no further Israeli pretence of avoiding combat with the Syrians nor room for doubt in Asad's mind that Israel aimed to destroy him. Now

---

18 These limited war aims had been explicitly laid out by Begin in the Knesset on 6 June, including the insistence that Israel wished to avoid conflict with Syria: "We do not want war with Syria. From this podium I call on President Asad to instruct the Syrian army not to attack Israel's soldiers" (quoted in Sucharov 2012, 94).

the question for him was: Would Sharon's armies surge forward to the Beirut-Damascus road, cutting off Syrian forces in Beirut and the mountains, or would they turn east and threaten Damascus itself?" (Seale 1990, 382). Given these perceptions, the Syrian forces dug in. Protecting their positions in the Beqa Valley and along the Beirut-Damascus highway was not about fighting for influence in Lebanon, but rather for the security and protection of the Syrian state itself.

The state of affairs in Lebanon after August–September 1982 represented a reversal of the previous situation: whereas before Israel had supported Christian forces against Syrian control in the north, now Syria endeavoured to undermine Israeli control through support for the PLO in and around Beirut. The period between 1983 and 1985 was defined by Syrian attempts to force the withdrawal of Israeli forces through a proxy campaign centred on support for the PLO, the Druze militia, and, increasingly, Shia guerillas, including Amal and the recently formed Iranian-backed Hezbollah. In January 1983, Syria once again introduced SAMs into the Beqa, and generally refortified its military positions in the east (O'Ballance 1998). Fighting continued in and around Beirut, while Israeli positions farther south came under repeated attack by Shia forces, leading to significant casualties. As a consequence, domestic Israeli support for the mission steadily eroded (Bregman 2016). Eventually, in early 1985, the decision was made to withdraw unilaterally, absent any final political deal or security arrangements with the Lebanese state. Israel did, however, create a ten-kilometre-wide security buffer along the Israel-Lebanon border, placing it under the control of the SLA, in order to protect itself from PLO and Shia attacks into Israeli territory (Ma'oz 1995).

Syria, meanwhile, moved to consolidate its position in Israel's wake. Through the Shia militias, in particular, Damascus was able to exert influence over the Lebanese government, crafting a political arrangement that protected the Syrian position throughout the country. The Amin government faltered, and the Maronite coalition saw its position erode in the face of challenges from the Shia and Druze militias. The 1985 Tripartite Agreement between the three warring factions (Christian, Shia, and Druze) reflected Syrian interests, specifying that "Lebanon cannot be allowed to be the gateway through which Israel may attack or threaten Syria" (quoted in Jorum 2014, 66). Though instability would continue in the years to come, the moment essentially reflected the end of Israeli and Syrian competition in Lebanon. Syria's presence in Lebanon would be further institutionalized in the 1989 Taif Agreement and again in 1991 in the Treaty of Brotherhood, Cooperation and Coordination. Full Syrian withdrawal from Lebanon would occur only in 2005, following the assassination of Lebanese politician Rafik Hariri and accompanying outrage from the Lebanese public, which blamed Damascus for the murder.

The behaviour of Israel and Syria during the reversal of the 1983–5 period provides further evidence of their respective priorities in Lebanon. Israel, having come to the cusp of control in Beirut – the high point of which was likely the election of Bashir Jumayyil – was reluctant to cede its gains. Only steadily decreasing domestic support for the occupation, combined with a confluence of events that eroded Israel's position – including Bashir's assassination and the international outcry following the massacres at the Sabra and Shatila refugee camps – led to its begrudging withdrawal. The cost of Israel's presence had become prohibitive. Yet its insistence that, as part of the May 1983 agreement, Syrian forces should similarly withdraw from Lebanon reflects Israel's desire to salvage the most important goal of the invasion. A failed attempt in 1984 to reach an agreement with Damascus – brokered through the United States – regarding mutual withdrawal similarly reflected this priority (Rabinovich 1985).

Syria, for its part, was more successful in achieving its aims. Rather than accept the outcome of the 1982 Israeli invasion, Damascus worked tirelessly to undermine it, supporting proxy forces against Israel in Beirut and other areas, including the south. Asad was clearly unwilling to allow the Israeli presence to go unchallenged. Syria similarly re-established its defensive positions in the Beqa Valley, consistent with previous policy in which a Syrian military presence in the area was considered vital for defence against potential Israeli attack. Yet the goal of Syria's policy during this period remained Israeli withdrawal, not gratuitous attacks for the sake of punishing its rivals. Rabinovich (1985, 191), for example, writes: "In 1983 and 1984 Syria's attitude toward the prospect of an Israeli departure from southern Lebanon had been the subject of debate and speculation. There were those who argued that Syria wanted Israel to remain and bleed further. Others held that for a small price Syria would be interested in having Israel leave southern Lebanon, particularly its eastern part. As it turned out, Syria was not asked in 1985 to pay any price *and for its part did not seek to obstruct Israel's departure*" (emphasis added). In other words, even as Israel found itself in a vulnerable position in the south, subject to repeated attacks – primarily from Syrian-backed Shia guerillas – the Syrian priority was expediting Israeli withdrawal, not bleeding them further. Similarly, the language in the 1985 Tripartite Agreement – indeed, as Jorum (2014, 66) notes, an "entire chapter" was devoted to security cooperation between Lebanon and Syria, with a heavy focus on the Israeli threat – reflects

Syria's continuing focus on Israel and the place of the Lebanese theatre in the context of the broader Syrian-Israeli rivalry. This is consistent with Syria's priorities throughout the 1975–85 period.

The Rivalry Explanation

In offering a general evaluation of Syrian and Israeli intervention in Lebanon in the context of rational rivalry, it is helpful to juxtapose this case with that of India-Pakistan. What do the similarities and differences between the two suggest with respect to the effects of rivalry on the decision to intervene in civil conflict? Are the observations of the India-Pakistan case reflected in the observations made in this chapter? Are there additional dynamics that may be theoretically relevant in the development of the Rational Rivalry explanation for civil war intervention? How compelling is this explanation, ultimately, for Syrian and Israeli intervention into Lebanon between 1975 and 1985?

I alluded above to several key similarities between the two cases: the creation of a state, a territorial dispute, recurring crises, multiple wars – all leading to the establishment of rivalry dynamics based on past experiences and the anticipation of future conflict. Both cases similarly involve regional rivalries with asymmetrical military capabilities and ethnic/religious dimensions. Interestingly, both rivalries also began in 1948, meaning the global geopolitical context was held constant. There are therefore multiple dimensions along which the cases are matched; as pathway cases, this can be beneficial insofar as the basic similarities should mean that the hypothesized causal mechanism is present and operating in the same way in both cases. Of course, the basic similarity does limit potential generalizability, but this concern is offset by the advantages of confirming the presence of the mechanism beyond the original case. This helps to refine our understanding of what rational rivalry looks like. Consistency across the cases does not definitively confirm the explanation or suggest that it is generalizable to all cases of rivalry interventions, but it does give us confidence that the proposed dynamics are real and therefore worth exploring in still additional cases.

There are, of course, important differences between the cases as well. This is largely unavoidable in the laboratory that is the real world, which makes it extremely difficult to match cases across all dimensions. Nonetheless, one benefit of the case study approach is its ability to deal with historical complexity; as such, it is possible to make reasoned assessments of how differences between cases affect the arguments being made and, additionally, how the new information can be leveraged for further theory development.

With respect to the development of rivalry over time, the attitudes and perceptions of each set of decisionmakers were remarkably consistent: Syrian decisionmakers were as convinced of Israel's aggression and expansionism as Pakistani decisionmakers were of India's. The same holds in a comparison of Israeli and Indian attitudes towards Syria and Pakistan, respectively. Both sets of rivals became convinced that the other side was intent on aggression, referencing past experience as support for the belief that future conflict was likely. Israel's seizure of the Golan Heights in 1967 was comparable in its effect on Syrian perceptions to the effect on Pakistan of the 1971 war: both wars involved the loss of considerable territory and corresponding anxiety about additional such defeats. The recurring mini-crises and intermittent clashes, often over disputed territory – the demilitarized zones and the Golan in the Syria-Israel rivalry, Kashmir and the Rann of Kutch in the India-Pakistan rivalry – similarly reflect a comparable conflict pattern. Of course, because one is comparing these perceptions across two *rivalries*, it is impossible to make any claims that such attitudes are unique to rivalries alone or that some variable other than recurring conflict is not driving the observed perceptions. The point, at this juncture, is not to make any causal or generalizable claim with respect to the relationship between recurring conflict and states' perceptions of intentions. Rather, it is simply to observe the similarity of perceptions across two cases in which I suggest that such perceptions were relevant to the decision to intervene in a civil conflict. The key consideration, ultimately, is that perceptions in the Syria-Israel rivalry on the cusp of intervention in Lebanon in 1975 were similar to those in the India-Pakistan rivalry in the lead-up to intervention in Afghanistan in 2001.

With respect to intervention itself, in the India-Pakistan case we observed that both states evaluated their interests in Afghanistan through the prism of a long-term strategic calculus; economic and immediate security interests were overridden by the desire to protect against potential security threats related to future conflict with their rival. For example, Pakistan sacrificed both the potential economic gains of a stable Afghanistan and the security gains of quelling Islamic militancy in favour of the perceived long-term benefit of using Islamic militancy to offset the strategic threat of an Afghanistan beholden to India. Though economic considerations were less prevalent with respect to the Lebanese crisis – neither Syria nor Israel appeared to sacrifice significant economic interests through its activities in Lebanon, save the inevitable economic disruption that instability and conflict produce – the security dimension was central. The most striking example is the Israeli articulation of their "red line" in southern Lebanon. This episode, and the trade-off it involved, is clear evidence that Israel was willing to sacrifice its immediate security in favour of protecting long-term security vis-à-vis its rival. The present and ongoing security threat from PLO cross-border terrorism – which was considerable, and a major issue for Israeli decisionmakers – was preferred to Syrian deployment in the south, which would have solved the PLO problem but presented a strategic disadvantage in a potential future conflict with Syria. It was this latter situation that Israel deemed intolerable. Similarly, during the Israeli invasion of 1982, Syrian positions in the Beqa Valley and along the Beirut-Damascus highway were challenged by superior Israeli military power. So important were these positions to the perceived defence of the Syrian state, however, that Damascus chose to dig in and fight the Israeli advance – at great cost – rather than pull back to Syrian territory. Relinquishing its position in Lebanon was unacceptable from the point of view of strategic vulnerability vis-à-vis Israel, which might use its control of either the Beqa or the Beirut-Damascus highway to launch a direct attack against Syrian territory. It was this larger possibility – the assumption and expectation of an Israeli attack "aimed to destroy" Syria, as Asad believed – that drove the decision to stay and fight in Lebanon, rather than any commitment to protect Lebanon itself.

In the India-Pakistan case, I argued that Pakistani and Indian support for their preferred proxies was less about shared aims – a desire to see a particular side "win" in the civil conflict in Afghanistan – than it was the utility the proxy could provide in pursuit of broader, rivalry-related aims. This was evident in India's relationship with the Northern Alliance in the 1990s, and particularly in Pakistan's support of the Taliban both before and after 2001. Rather than any shared Islamic, ideational, or ethnic identity, support was driven by functional goals. And yet, it is somewhat difficult to refute the possibility that shared identity played a role, because the fact remained that Pakistan, an explicitly Islamic state, was supporting Islamic militants. The shared-identity conundrum is present also in the Syrian-Israeli case. For one, there are those who argue that Israeli support for the Christians in Lebanon was driven, at least in part, by an identification with the Christian cause as a fellow non-Muslim community in the predominately Muslim region. Syrian support for the PLO – both in Lebanon and throughout the Arab-Israeli conflict – likewise is often linked to identity factors. And yet the Syrian case offers striking evidence to undermine the argument that such considerations drove their intervention in Lebanon. While the Syrians initially supported the PLO-Muslim side, they switched their support to the opposing Christian forces in early 1976, and indeed intervened decisively on the Christians' behalf. Later, they reverted again to the PLO.

This oscillating support is indicative of Syrian priorities; Damascus was concerned with its own interests in Lebanon – namely, preventing the collapse of the Lebanese state so as to forestall potential Israeli intervention – and did not immediately care *which* domestic faction allowed it to achieve its goals. Later, as Israeli influence on the Christian side increased, it was advantageous to support the PLO. Again, the shift was less about shared identity than about rivalry-related concerns.

The interventions in Afghanistan and Lebanon both occurred over an extended period, and both included changes in policy. Yet both also display a remarkable consistency in terms of the goals that were pursued. In Afghanistan, Pakistan's initial policy reversal reflects a consistent rationale confronted by changing circumstances. The priority was always to minimize Indian influence, even as the (perceived) best policy to achieve that priority shifted. The same holds true with respect to Israeli and Syrian behaviour in Lebanon. The Syrian policy reversal is logically consistent if their priority was preventing and mitigating Israeli involvement. Even the Israeli invasion of 1982 – an apparently brash departure from the cautious, defensive policy pursued in Lebanon up to that point – can be interpreted as a logically consistent response to changing circumstances. In the context of greater flexibility following rapprochement with Egypt and concern regarding the growing Syrian military presence in Lebanon, the decision can be seen as an Israeli attempt to forestall a future strategic threat, which is to say, again, was precisely the goal of previous Israeli policy vis-à-vis Lebanon. Indeed, the multiple phases of the Lebanese crisis between 1975 and 1985 provide even more detailed evidence of the consistent priorities and rationales of both Syria and Israel over the course of their interventions than the comparatively static Indian and Pakistani interventions in Afghanistan. As circumstances changed, new decision points arose. Each time, Israel and Syria adjusted according to a rationale consistent with rivalry concerns.

Chapter Seven

The US-Soviet Rivalry and Intervention in Angola

The US-Soviet rivalry emerged following the end of the Second World War, although its seeds had been germinating even as the countries fought on the same side against the German and Japanese.[1] Particularly after 1943, as it became increasingly clear that the allies, even if badly bloodied, would emerge victorious, manoeuvring began with an eye to the post-war international order. A series of conferences brought together the Americans, the Soviets, and the British to discuss, *inter alia*, the division of Europe. The Soviets were keen to maintain the territorial gains they had achieved by pushing back German forces. The Americans and the British, by contrast, wished to avoid a massive Soviet military presence in continental Europe. At the centre of these debates was Germany itself: which of the allies would control the country, and how could it be ensured that a resurgent Germany would not again threaten international peace? These initial disagreements were undergirded by deep ideological differences regarding the nature of political and

---

1 The historiography of the Cold War is voluminous, and it is well beyond the scope of this chapter to offer a comprehensive overview of the US-Soviet rivalry. Instead, I focus on those aspects of the Cold War relevant to an understanding of the *perceptions* of either side; these perceptions, after all, are fundamental to my theory regarding the motivation for intervention in Angola. In general terms, my reading of the Cold War is informed primarily by the "post-revisionist" approach. Led by historians such as John Lewis Gaddis and Melvyn P. Leffler, the post-revisionists challenge arguments as to either Soviet or American culpability (the "orthodox" and "revisionist" positions, respectively) and instead emphasize the conditions that rendered superpower confrontation more or less inevitable – although there is hardly consensus even within this camp, as the high-profile disagreements between Gaddis and Leffler demonstrate. In addition to the works directly cited, the contributions to the three volumes of the *Cambridge History of the Cold War*, edited by Leffler and Westad, were particularly helpful.

economic order and the trajectory of human history. Though no direct large-scale conflicts were to occur between the superpowers' respective military forces, the subsequent decades were defined by repeated crises, confrontations, and stand-offs. Both American and Soviet decisionmakers believed war was possible – at some juncture, even likely or inevitable – and considered the relationship in these terms. The ideological competition between capitalism and communism was viewed as essentially global and effectively zero sum for the balance of the Cold War. It is in this context that superpower involvement in the so-called Third World occurred. As states, particularly newly independent postcolonial nations, attempted to define and establish their political and economic systems, revolution and instability proliferated. For Washington and Moscow, the outcome of these disarticulations weighed heavily in the global struggle. The civil war in Angola is a case in point.

The Nature of the Rivalry

Central to the geopolitical struggle between the United States and the USSR was an ideological battle. For the Soviets, US foreign policy was invariably a function of monopolistic capitalism, the implications of which were most famously articulated by Lenin in 1917. As Soviet ambassador to the United States Nikolai Novikov expressed in a telegram to Moscow in 1946, "The foreign policy of the United States, which reflects the imperialist tendencies of American monopolistic capital, is characterized in the postwar period by a striving for world supremacy" (USSR 1946). This view was conventional wisdom among the Soviet leadership at the time.[2] Indeed, Garthoff (2015, 10–11) observes that, "by the fall of 1947, the Soviet evaluation of the main adversary [the United States] had hardened to a point at which even Novikov's analysis was regarded as too soft," and that "Soviet diplomatic and other analyses consistently stressed that America was preparing for military confrontation."

The Novikov telegram found its counterpart in the analysis of American diplomat George F. Kennan, who similarly linked Soviet intentions to the "original Communist thesis of a basic antagonism between the capitalist and Socialist worlds" (Kennan [1947] 2012, 119). Like Novikov's analysis, Kennan's writings on the "Sources of Soviet Conduct" – as

---

2 Soviet official Maxim Litvinov relayed to an American reporter in 1946 that "the ideological conception prevailing [in Moscow was] that conflict between the Communist and capitalist worlds is inevitable" (quoted in Garthoff 2015, 4).

his famous "X" article in *Foreign Affairs* was titled, as well as his "Long Telegram" from Moscow, which circulated in Washington – generally reflect post-war American belief regarding the nature, and intentions, of the Soviet regime. On both sides, the perceived incompatibility of the two ideological systems – and the assumed ideological motivations of the other state – generated assumptions about future behaviour. There could be no modus vivendi between the two camps; "antagonism" was "postulated" by the nature of the relationship itself – of course, just which side was responsible for such antagonism was a matter of disagreement.

Competing ideologies alone, however, were not sufficient to lock in the condition of rivalry. They were supplemented by tangible conflicts of interest manifest in the post-war distribution of power. Unlike Britain, which had been decimated by the war, the United States emerged post-1945 as an economic and military juggernaut. The Soviet Union had, for its part, experienced significant hardship as a consequence of the war,[3] but it too found its global position enhanced at war's end. With most of Europe in ruins, the world effectively had become bipolar: overwhelming economic and military power concentrated in two states. The implications of this structural distribution and its consequences for stability were (and are) the subject of much debate in the IR literature. In a general sense, however, this post-war distribution rendered it inevitable that Soviet and American decisionmakers would be concerned about the activities of the other side. This would have been true irrespective of their ideological incompatibilities even if, in reality, such incompatibilities compounded concerns about the future intentions of the other dominant power.

One final dimension of the rivalry is worth pointing out. Unlike the Indian-Pakistani dispute over Kashmir or the Israeli-Syrian conflicts over Palestine and the Golan Heights, the US-Soviet rivalry is not typically considered to have had a "territorial" dimension per se. There were no directly analogous disputes regarding pieces of land over which both sides claimed sovereignty – the two states were not contiguous, the Bering Strait notwithstanding. Yet, in practical terms, disagreements about the dispensation of post-war Germany and the borders of the Soviet Union in eastern Europe more generally, fulfilled much the same function. The Berlin blockade crisis of 1948, for example, involved confrontation over

---

3 In the words of Pechatnov (2010, 90): "The war losses of the USSR were staggering: the country lost at least 27 million people and about a quarter of its reproducible wealth; over 1,700 cities and towns were destroyed and more than 31,000 industrial enterprises demolished." He goes on to argue that given such losses "no wonder security concerns remained paramount in the Kremlin's thinking about the postwar world" (91).

Western (i.e., American) access to the German capital. Although the division of Germany into Western and Eastern political units constituted the creation of two ostensibly sovereign countries, in reality the demarcation was between the American and Soviet blocs, respectively. Each side, moreover, wished to see German reunification eventually occur on its terms. The German question, therefore, became the "front line" of the Cold War and the proximity of US and Soviet forces the subject of consistent concern and repeated crises over subsequent decades.

More broadly, the consequences of the Second World War were crucial in shaping the early parameters within which the rivalry subsequently emerged. Soviet penetration into eastern Europe occurred in the context of the war against Germany, yet the ensuing Soviet decision to *remain* in the territories it had captured transformed this thrust – in the eyes of the West – into hostile expansionism once the war ended. Potential Soviet control over the resources of continental Europe was alarming to the Americans precisely because of their experience of the Second World War, in which Germany had marshalled such resources to threaten American security. As a result, the lodestar of American strategic priorities post-1945 became the prevention of any such accumulation on the part of another state – a similar and related interest was operative with respect to Asia).[4] Germany was central to these fears: given its latent economic and military potential, a reconstituted and unified Germany within the Soviet bloc would be unacceptable. On the Soviet side, communist ideology specified the ineluctable hostility of the *capitalist* world. In this way, Leffler (2007) argues, the Great Patriotic War, as the Second World War is known in Russia, against capitalist Germany ultimately was considered part and parcel of a broader fight against capitalism, which, post-1945, took the form of the struggle against the United States, now the leader of the capitalist powers.[5] Moscow, too, was preoccupied with the possibility of German resurgence, but within the Western camp, and the consequent danger

---

4 See the discussion of US strategic priorities offered by Mearsheimer (2012). Leffler (2010, 77), for his part, argues that, in Washington, the "overriding priority was to keep the power centers of Europe and Asia outside the Soviet orbit and linked to the United States," and elsewhere that "their overriding priority was to prevent a totalitarian adversary from conquering or assimilating the resources of Europe and Asia and using them to wage war against the United States, *as the Axis powers had done during World War II*" (87, emphasis added).

5 Pechatnov (2010, 93) claims that "the wartime experience of cooperation did not change [Moscow's] basic Bolshevik view of the bourgeois allies as selfish and cunning hypocrites, anti-Soviet at heart," which led to "a belief in the need for the Soviet Union to gather strength for an inevitable new showdown."

posed by German military might, particularly in light of past German behaviour.[6]

In this way, the US-Soviet rivalry was much more complex than simply some combination of the ideological and structural dimensions typically foregrounded (for a discussion of the ideology-versus-power debate about the Cold War within IR, see Kramer 1999 and the response from Wohlforth 2000). There are also the dynamic consequences of the experiences of the Second World War and the initial disputes regarding the dispensation of post-war Germany. Again, much like the ethnic/religious dimension at the root of the India-Pakistan and Israel-Syria rivalries, the ideological dimension was an enabling condition for the US-Soviet rivalry: structural conditions were filtered through divergent and hostile ideological lenses, as were the events of the Second World War and the initial phases of the post-war era. This combination of factors created the condition of rivalry, locking in the perception on both sides that a long-term confrontation – one with existential security implications – was taking shape. Unpacking the precise mélange or formula with respect to the relative weight of each particular component – while a fascinating exercise in its own right – is unnecessary for present purposes. The point is to indicate the extent to which the US-Soviet rivalry shares core similarities with the other rivalries examined in this book, despite apparently significant differences at a more superficial level. The US-Soviet rivalry was global, not regional; ideological, not ethnic/religious; lacked an explicit territorial dispute; and was not initiated by a major direct war. And yet the internal dynamics of the rivalry look remarkably similar: the prevailing assumption became an expectation of future conflict, with attendant consequences for how each rival assessed its interests and the associated policies it pursued.

---

6 In 1962 Soviet leader Nikita Khrushchev offered a window into this preoccupation, telling American journalist Norman Cousins, "I can understand how Americans look at Germany somewhat differently than we do, even though you had to fight Germany twice within a short time. We have a much longer history with Germany ... We have a saying here: 'Give a German a gun, sooner or later he will point it at Russians' ... Of course we could crush Germany. We could crush Germany in a few minutes. But what we fear is the ability of an armed Germany to commit the United States by its own actions. We fear the ability of Germany to start a world atomic war. What puzzles me more than anything else is that the Americans don't realize that there's a large group in Germany that is eager to destroy the Soviet Union. How many times do you have to be burned before you respect fire?" (quoted in Leffler 2007, 163–4). In his evaluation of Stalin's strategic priorities in the post-war period, Mastny (1996, 43) suggests that, "instead of preparing to fight a German threat in the future, Moscow tried to preventively fend it off by advancing its scheme for a dependent Germany." Leng (2000, 43) notes that "Stalin had made it clear at Yalta that his first concern regarding Germany was that it remain too weak to challenge Soviet security."

Crises and Conflict, 1947–75

As mentioned, a key difference between the US-Soviet rivalry and the other rivalries discussed in this book is the lack of direct war: the two countries had not engaged each other in a major conventional conflict at any point prior to the civil conflict interventions of interest. This distinction has potential theoretical implications given the emphasis on past interactions as formative regarding expectations about the future; an absence of war in the past might soften or even preclude expectations about future direct conflict. That said, many of the same concerns present in the India-Pakistan and Israel-Syria rivalries were operative in the US-Soviet context as well. The initial point of conflict in the rivalry involved disagreement as to the dispensation of a particular piece of territory: control over a defeated Germany, and the Soviet presence in eastern Europe more broadly. Structurally, the two states were the dominant powers in a common sphere of competition, initially in central Europe and East Asia, then becoming global; in the India-Pakistan and Israel-Syria cases, by comparison, the rivalries were regional. Divergent ideological perspectives – according to which each side imputed implacably hostile motives to the other – formed an enabling condition analogous to the ethnic and religious foundations of the India-Pakistan and Israel-Syria relationships. The 1948 Berlin crisis involved military mobilization, and there was a general perception that war was likely in the short term, perhaps inevitable in the long. It is worth noting also that the *experience* of all-out war was strikingly fresh for each side, a lens through which both considered the German question: to acquiesce might mean a revanchist Germany, with all its latent industrial and military power, aligned with the other side. From this initial impasse subsequent crises arose, confirming perceptions that the other side was both aggressive and expansionist.

The Soviets quickly acquired nuclear weapons to match the American capability, meaning the effects of nuclear deterrence were established early in the rivalry, even if the logic was not immediately appreciable to the participants.[7] This dynamic likely mitigated escalation in several crises, keeping them tense stand-offs underscored by nuclear brinkmanship – for example, Berlin from 1958 to 1961 and Cuba in 1962. Yet the possibility of direct confrontation – the existential implications of which were now amplified by the nuclear dimension – remained

---

7 Both the Eisenhower administration and the Stalin regime believed the use of such weapons was acceptable, even advisable, in a potential conflict.

acute in the minds of decisionmakers. Additional crises took the form of indirect, proxy conflicts, as in Korea and the Middle East, which steadily extended the scope of the rivalry to global proportions, commensurate with the status of both states in the international distribution of power – a bipolar system in which the United States and USSR were overwhelmingly dominant.

What is particularly striking about this period is the extent to which "credibility" became the currency of confrontation: assessing the other side's and protecting one's own was a core concern as crises and confrontations accumulated. As Ball (1998, 115) points out, "[t]he nebulous concept of credibility came to be at the centre of American Cold War policies in the 1960s" – although the historical record suggests that leaders were concerned about it even earlier. Indeed, the concept has been criticized by a plethora of post–Cold War studies (for example, Hopf 1994; Mercer 1996; Press 2005; Tang 2005) in part because of the perceived "nebulosity" of its application during the US-Soviet rivalry. Putatively peripheral, marginal interests – such as the political ideology of the government in Vietnam or the sovereignty of South Korea – were accorded supreme importance by injecting an imperative to preserve American "credibility" vis-à-vis the Soviet Union. The work of Thomas Schelling was particularly influential in developing the logic of credibility in a theoretical framework; his book *Arms and Influence* ([1966] 2008) was quite explicitly a discussion of how credibility was implicated in, and important for, the US-Soviet relationship (see the discussion in Mitton 2015).

The development of the rivalry suggests that credibility was important both for *how* the two states responded from one crisis to the next – meaning that the reputation each state developed through its behaviour in particular crises was relevant for how the other side responded in subsequent confrontations; but also, and even more crucial in the present context, *why* they did so. We see, for example, that both the Americans and the Soviets made assessments about present credibility partly on the basis of past behaviour – as when Soviet threats over Berlin were deemed less and less credible because of its unenforced ultimatums in previous crises. We see additionally the extent to which both sides understood their relationship as one in which future crises and confrontations were certain: *the present crisis was always considered in the context of the next one.* This made it inevitable that concerns about credibility would be significant. Particularly – and this is crucial – because the perceived threat from the other side remained significant, even existential, a perception that persisted even as the relationship stabilized in central Europe and during the period of ostensible warming of relations characterized by détente. Indeed, this perception remained in place in 1975, as the competition for influence in the Third World, including Africa, became the active front of the rivalry.

US and Soviet Perceptions in 1975

By 1975, US and Soviet perceptions had shifted from where they stood in 1948. By the time intervention in Angola was being contemplated, neither country was as concerned about the *imminent* possibility of direct conflict as during the tense situation in Berlin in 1948 – or, for that matter, during the 1950–3 Korean War. Although the various crises had prevented the rivalry's senescence – tense moments and military mobilizations reminded respective leaders that conflict remained a possibility – the fact that none had spilled over into overt, large-scale engagement ultimately signalled that some measure of caution obtained in each capital. The perceived *source* of this caution, it is crucial to point out, was largely the deterrent effect each side believed its own military capabilities and manoeuvres exerted against the other. Which is to say, the basic assumption of antagonism remained in place, albeit coupled with the impression, built over the decades, that the enmity was not implacable or irrational, but rather could be tempered through the maintenance of credible resolve and counterforce.

This remained true in the period of so-called détente, which was still in effect in 1975, even as the Arab-Israeli war of 1973, the American involvement in Vietnam (as well as in Laos and Cambodia), and other Third World crises called into question each superpower's commitment to its principles. As Garthoff (2015) writes of the period, "Détente meant, of course, a relaxation of tensions but between two sides that remained counterposed in a systemic confrontation. Thus geopolitical competition continued, *and a return to greater tensions and even war remained possibilities* despite improved US-Soviet relations and formal agreements" (39, emphasis added). Indeed, the Soviet decision to pursue détente in the first place was predicated in part on continued apprehension about security tied to the possibility of an American attack.[8]

---

8 As Savranskaya and Taubman (2010, 142) point out, the Soviet military build-up that made détente possible was predicated on "the fear of a sudden attack brought on by 'inferiority' in armaments." The origins of détente more broadly, it is widely noted, lay in the perceived relative decline in US power vis-à-vis that of the Soviet Union. For Brezhnev, this meant he felt able to engage the United States as a strategic equal; for President Nixon and Henry Kissinger, it meant accommodating new geopolitical realities. In this way, détente was about structural adjustments within an adversarial relationship, not any genuine political rapprochement or softening of images of the other side. See Garthoff (1994); Hemmer (2015); Litwak (1984); Shulzinger (2010).

These dynamics continued to drive Soviet perceptions in the early and mid-1970s. One need only consider the tough negotiating position the Soviets adopted in the SALT I talks in 1969–72 to recognize that Moscow remained hypersensitive to shifts in the strategic balance which might endanger Soviet security in the future (see the discussions in Garthoff 1977; Kearns Jr. 2015; Payne 1980; Vigor 1986). Leffler's (2007) explanation of expanding Soviet defence expenditures in 1975–6 serves as a useful summation of the relevant prevailing attitudes: "Soviet officials believed the USSR was still the weaker nation ... Experience mandated vigilance against imperialist and fascist aggressors. History could recur. The Soviet Union could be attacked again" (254, emphasis added).

On the American side, assessments of the Soviet Union remained similarly cautious and pessimistic. A National Intelligence Estimate (NIE) from April 1972 projected that "for the foreseeable future" Soviet policy "will remain antagonistic to the West, especially to the US" (CIA 1972, 95). "Developments of recent years," the document states, "have given the USSR increased confidence in its security and strategic posture, in its capacity to engage its adversaries on favorable terms, and in the prospects for the long-term growth of its international influence. The Soviets have thus begun to pursue a more vigorous foreign policy and to accept deeper involvement in many world areas" (88). The estimate specifically mentions potential Soviet involvement in the Third World, stating that, "by virtue of [the Soviet Union's] acquisition in recent years of a greater capability to use its military forces in distant areas – a capability which is likely to continue to grow – Moscow may now believe its options in the Third World are expanding" (94).

There is evidence that such assessments were internalized by, and reflected the views of, the American leadership. Kissinger (1982), for example, wrote in his memoirs that his basic understanding of détente was the "managing of an adversarial relationship." This meant pursuing it in a way that advanced US interests vis-à-vis a presumed competitor. In a meeting with the Chinese in October 1975, for example, Kissinger explained that US policy with respect to the Arab-Israeli conflict had been designed precisely to "avoid ... settling it cooperatively with the Soviet Union." The policy of détente in general, he averred, was being "conduct[ed] ... as the best method for resisting Soviet expansionism" (United States 2007). Following meetings with Brezhnev in October 1974, Kissinger (1999) recounted his generally positive impressions of the Soviet leader, but nonetheless insisted that the realities of the relationship mandated circumspection – he worried, for example, what present developments would portend "ten years hence."

This, then, was the context in which the two superpowers contemplated the civil war in Angola in 1975. Perceptions on both sides were that (a) the relationship remained competitive and antagonistic, with the attendant threats to national security still acute; (b) as the situation in central Europe stabilized, the Third World had become the critical venue for the rivalry; and (c) each crisis in the rivalry was *connected* – as had been the case with respect to Korea, Vietnam, and the Middle East, the "peripheral" confrontations had important implications for the "core" considerations of Germany, central Europe, and the nuclear arms race.

Intervention in Angola

The Cold War is well known for the myriad "proxy wars" that occurred at seemingly all ends of the globe. From China in the late 1940s to Afghanistan during the late stages of the Cold War itself, the Soviets and Americans repeatedly intervened on opposing sides of ongoing conflicts. This phenomenon has elicited extensive study from a range of historical and social scientific perspectives. Aubone (2013) provides a useful summary of the political science related to, specifically, US interventions during the Cold War. Numerous studies – including Fordham (2008); Gent (2010); Lagon (1992); Mullenbach and Matthews (2008); Regan (2002); Rosenau (1968); Yarmolinsky (1968); and Yoon (1997) – emphasize the relationship with the USSR in their explanations of US interventions. "The common assumption," writes Aubone (2013, 287), "is that US intervention in civil conflicts during the Cold War was driven largely by the security concerns of containment and the motivation to be more powerful than its rival, the USSR" – in other words, rivalry considerations.

Here, I extend this research and connect it to a more generalized discussion of rivalry dynamics. I posit that the United States' behaviour was not unique, and that the Cold War in general was not *sui generis*. While perhaps exceptional in its scope and scale, the US-Soviet relationship nonetheless can be compared to other instances of international rivalry, including interventions in civil conflicts. Although the broader rivalry literature has treated the US-Soviet relationship as an example of the general concept, examinations of Cold War interventions have tended to consider such behaviour as more or less unique to that historical milieu. I argue, by contrast, that these interventions are part and parcel of general rivalry behaviour.

The Angolan Civil War

The precipitating cause of the civil war in Angola was the military coup in Portugal in 1974. The new regime in Lisbon announced a formal end to Portuguese colonialism in Africa. With official independence set for

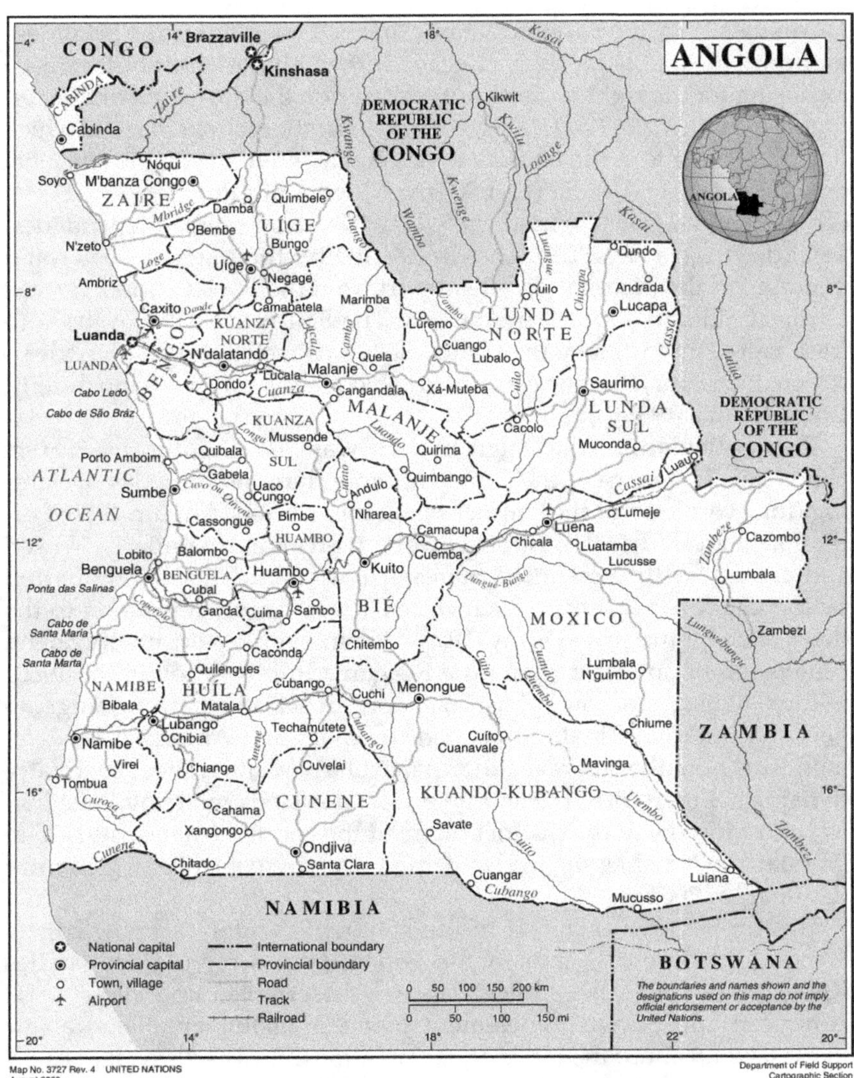

Map 3. Angola

Source: United Nations, Map No. 3727 Rev. 4, April 2008.

November 1975, the various factions that had been fighting Portuguese authority in Angola for over a decade turned against one another, each jockeying for the right to claim authority upon the departure of the Portuguese (Lockyer 2011). The three main domestic factions, each of which had played a role in the liberation movement, were the Frente Nacional de Libertaçào de Angola (FNLA), the Movimento Popular de Libertaçào de Angola (MPLA), and the Uniào Nacional para Independência Total de Angola (UNITA). The MPLA, led by the Marxist doctor and poet Agostinho Neto, received support from the Soviet Union, as well as direct aid and support from Cuba. The FNLA and UNITA, by contrast, were supported by the United States, as well as by South Africa – which, like Cuba, became directly involved in the conflict – and, briefly, China (Dunér 1985).

The particulars of the Angolan civil war are complex, as conflict ebbed and flowed over the course of more than two decades of fighting (for overviews of the conflict see Ebinger 1984; Marcum 1978; Porter 1984; Westad 2006). Superpower involvement, similarly, waxed and waned, with the United States at one point legislatively barred by the Clark Amendment – which itself was largely a reaction to the debacle in Vietnam; see Scott (1996) – from even covert involvement. (The resumption of aid under the Reagan administration in the 1980s marked a distinct second phase in American action regarding Angola.) Yet the initial machinations related to Soviet and American involvement are nonetheless revealing, particularly with respect to rivalry dynamics. I therefore concentrate on the decisions made by Washington and Moscow in the distinct phase of the conflict from early 1975 to February 1976, when the MPLA gained effective control of the country (Guimaraes 2001).

The US-Soviet dimension to the conflict is widely acknowledged. "Angola became the ante in the superpower sweepstakes," writes Klingshoffer (1980, 2), and despite some discernible important stakes,[9] American and Soviet involvement was less about tangible strategic interests than about the international relationship. The "broader issue," according to Garthoff (1994), "was not even clear at the outset, although the seeds of trouble were there: would one of the global powers see its interests damaged by the victory of a local contender supported by the

---

9 As Klingshoffer (1980, 73) describes, "Angola had tremendous economic potential as it is richly endowed with oil, diamonds, iron ore, phosphates, gold, copper, manganese, uranium and coffee. It can also be of great importance strategically as it possesses several excellent harbors and lies adjacent to the major Cape oil route from the Persian Gulf to Western Europe and the United States."

other power? What would it portend for the nature of the competition of the superpowers in the future? The stakes were not Angola itself, or even the influence the other side would gain from a victory of the faction it favoured. Rather the issue *became* the rules of competition under détente" (556–7, emphasis in original). Which is to say, the issue was the "rules" of US-Soviet interaction in the overall relationship, and what the ceding of influence in the Angolan conflict might portend for the future of the rivalry. An examination of the rationale and thought processes of each side is therefore apposite for the theory of rivalry intervention developed in this book.

Soviet Intervention in Angola

The Soviet decision to support the MPLA and intervene in Angola was part of a broader foreign policy emphasis on Africa emerging at the time. The realities of détente – and the US-Soviet relationship more broadly – in addition to rising competition with China, induced Moscow to pursue influence in the region. Africa was to Moscow a "blank sheet of paper," according to Guimaraes (2001, 161), having "little or no historical ties ... and yet by the mid-1970s [the Soviet Union] had developed a major presence in Africa." Despite putative affinity with the black African nations emerging from the oppressive colonial experience, Albright (1987, 3) suggests that "Moscow ... [dealt] with Africa as fundamentally an arena in which to further broad international objectives." The presence of a domestic Marxist force such as the MPLA accorded a natural avenue through which the Soviets could seek to influence political realities in Angola and the region more generally – similar efforts were ongoing in other African nations, including Mozambique, Guinea-Bissau, and South Africa.

Moscow agreed as early as 1970 to offer military hardware, logistical support, and political training to Neto and his followers (Westad 2006). Interestingly, this support was suspended in early 1974 (owing partly to infighting within the MPLA), but swiftly reinstated following the news of Chinese support for the FNLA (Garthoff 1994). Indeed, the influence of China's involvement on Soviet decision-making was significant – according to Garthoff (1994, 582), it was the "main element ... in the initial phase in 1974" owing to general Sino-Soviet competition for influence in the region occurring at the time (see also Gonzalez 1980). Leffler (2007, 255) suggests that, for Soviet Minister of Foreign Affairs Andrei Gromyko, "Chinese assistance to an opposing group" was a key motivating factor in the Soviet calculus at that stage (see also Legum 1976). Of course, the "main adversary" remained the United States, and concerns about potential US involvement played a role as well; the United States pledged US$300,000 to the FNLA over the summer of 1974, which reaffirmed the Soviet commitment to the MPLA (Garthoff 1994). Guimaraes (2001, 176) cites a Soviet academic, Alexei Vassiliev, who maintained that "the West has always been Moscow's principal adversary in the Third World and ... this was also the case in Angola." Certainly, as the conflict progressed and as China's role receded after Beijing decided to suspend aid to the FNLA and UNITA over concerns about South Africa's involvement on the same side, the US dynamic became more pronounced (Klingshoffer 1980).[10]

Soviet aid in the summer and fall of 1974 consisted largely of small-arms transfers, which helped significantly to increase the fighting capacity of the MPLA. In December that year, approximately 250 MPLA members were flown to Moscow for military training (Guimaraes 2001). In 1975, major arms transfers began and continued over the subsequent year, eventually totalling approximately US$200 million worth of hardware (Lockyer 2011). According to Westad (2006), an uptick in financial aid and arms transfers in September and October 1975 came in reaction to the United States' "extensive" resupply of the FNLA in August. Also at this time, Cuba's involvement began in earnest, with contingents of Cuban soldiers arriving to supplement MPLA forces – eventually over 30,000 Cuban troops would be deployed (George 2005). Although the Americans believed the Cubans were a direct Soviet proxy, archival evidence suggests that Havana initiated the move largely on its own as a way of bolstering its international revolutionary credentials (Guimaraes 2001). Nonetheless, once the Cubans were committed, Moscow became a facilitator, transporting Cuban troops via airlift and ultimately urging Havana to increase its efforts (Westad 2006).

In terms of the dynamics on the ground, the fall of 1975 was a key period, as 11 November, the date of official independence, loomed. Whichever faction was then ascendant could claim authority over the country. The FNLA and UNITA had secured significant outside support in their own right, largely matching the Soviet and Cuban contributions to the MPLA. South Africa had intervened with its own troops, offsetting the Cuban contingent and facilitating significant territorial gains

---

10 Even if the Chinese dynamic was dominant in the early stages, this simply underscores the interplay between overlapping rivalries in the international system: intervention in a civil war is triggered by one rival's involvement, which subsequently induces another rival to become involved.

for UNITA in the south.[11] As Lockyer (2011) points out, by this period the war had metastasized from a small-arms guerilla-style conflict to large-scale conventional warfare, almost entirely as a consequence of outside intervention.

When independence day arrived, the MPLA controlled the capital, and immediately declared itself the sovereign authority in Angola and was recognized by various communist states. Nonetheless, fighting continued against the FNLA in the north and UNITA in the south, with the latter buoyed by ongoing South African involvement. Crucially, the Clark Amendment's suspension of US aid in December 1975 crippled FNLA forces, which the MPLA pushed out of Angola and into Zaire (now Democratic Republic of Congo). The MPLA was then able to concentrate its efforts in the south, turning the tide there as well. By February 1976, owing largely to the Cuban presence and continued Soviet support – which, as "a response to American and Zairian aid to the FNLA" (Klingshoffer 1980, 26), had steadily increased throughout the conflict[12] – the MPLA effectively had won the civil war. The Organization of African Unity recognized Neto's government as the legitimate authority in Angola, inducing other nations around the world to follow suit.

The important question for our purposes is, why had Moscow considered this victory worthwhile? What, in other words, had been the motivating rationale behind the approximately US$300 million in total aid the Soviets had provided in the 1975–6 period? As mentioned, Angola seemed to be part of a new regional emphasis on Africa tied to Sino-Soviet and US-Soviet rivalry. As intervention was being contemplated, Westad (2006, 215) recounts, "KGB Deputy Chairman Viktor Chebrikov explained [to his superiors] that Angola and Guinea-Bissau had potential strategic importance for the Soviet Union, and that both the United States and China were trying to increase their influence with the liberation movements in these countries." Westad continues: "The main military intelligence bureau – GRU – reported that China was targeting countries and movements that already received aid from the Soviet Union. China, the GRU stressed, would use its resources to the

---

11 The geography of the conflict is relatively straightforward: the FNLA controlled territory mainly in the north, UNITA in the south, and the MPLA a band in the middle, including the capital, Luanda.

12 According to Klingshoffer (1980, 27–8), "[a]bout $30 million [in Soviet military aid] was sent from March through July [1975]; $80 million from August until mid-November; $90 million from mid-November until mid-January; and $100 million from mid-January until the termination of most fighting in mid-February."

maximum in order to attract African supporters, and could, within a few years, build its position to control large parts of Africa in a sort of loose coalition with the United States" (2006, 215). The mention of this last possibility is important: even the emphasis on Chinese involvement apparently was couched in relation to the United States, which remained the "main adversary." Once begun, moreover, the Soviet intervention was largely reactive to the American presence.

There were also, Guimaraes (2001) points out, tangible advantages offered by a potential presence in the country, including access to ports along Atlantic sea lanes used by Western shipping. Likewise, Soviet control over Angola would allow it to "make it more difficult for Western states to maintain their access to Angolan minerals and raw materials, particularly crude oil" (Klingshoffer 1980, 147). Naturally, this would also mean that the Soviets themselves would gain access to Angola's considerable resources. As discussed below, these possibilities were invoked by American officials as ostensible justifications for countering Soviet efforts, although in reality the Americans' rationale was not predicated on the immediate or specific stakes in play or on the direct consequences of Soviet control of Angolan resources or seaports. As for the Soviets, most analysts similarly recognize that such considerations were ancillary. The apparent confluence of political, ideological, force-projection, and economic motivations render it difficult to unpack the precise formula that pushed Soviet policy towards intervention. An "array of objectives" is said to have been in play (MacFarlane 1992, 2). And yet the broader context of rivalry not only helped to shape these underlying objectives – each of which found salience primarily in the context of superpower competition – but ultimately provided a galvanizing motivation that proved sufficient to trigger an intervention not explicable by reference to any specific domain of interests.

Interest in Africa, for example, was predicated on the development of the superpower rivalry. As Klingshoffer (1980, 149) explains, "on a world scale, the Soviet Union had experienced foreign policy setbacks in Chile and the Middle East and wanted to counter any Western moves in Angola." In the aftermath of the MPLA victory, moreover, a primary takeaway was the salutary effects successful Soviet intervention would produce elsewhere: "Recent memoirs and Moscow's own declassified documents show that the MPLA victory in Angola, together with Hanoi's victory in Vietnam, gave rise to unprecedented optimism in Soviet Third World policy – 'the world,' according to one of their high officials, 'was turning in our direction'" (Westad 2006, 241). This assessment is consistent with the observation that each superpower crisis ultimately was gauged as to its implications for *future* encounters; the assumption of continued hostility fundamentally altered assessments of present interests and priorities. Moscow knew, based on its experiences in the rivalry, that Washington would challenge it in the future. Given the underlying security threat tied to potential nuclear conflict, this mandated a concern over the global balance of power such that developments at the periphery – that is, a struggle for influence in Angola – was promoted to a vital strategic interest. This interest, moreover, had as much to do with the *perceptions* of resolve and credibility that could be won or lost in Angola as with the actual, tangible stakes in play there, such as access to naval ports or other modes of force projection.

Further evidence of the pre-eminence of rivalry considerations is found in the *development* of the Soviet intervention over time: the steady escalation and embrace and ultimate facilitation of Cuban involvement. This trajectory was clearly influenced by the American counterpresence (Guimaraes 2001). Noer (1993, 774) notes that Soviet aid increased dramatically as soon as Moscow became "convinced that America [was] now backing [Holden] Roberto [leader of the FNLA]" in early 1975. Having committed to Angola, in other words – largely as a consequence of China's involvement and the prospect of potential US-China cooperation in Africa – the US intervention amplified the Soviet motivation to ensure that the FNLA, the United States' preferred proxy, did not overrun the MPLA and deliver Angola to the Americans. Although the consequences of this outcome would not have been particularly damaging in immediate terms – the United States had, after all, enjoyed influence in Angola before 1975 through its relationship with Portugal, a NATO member – the perception that the USSR could be dissuaded and defeated by American counteraction would undermine perceptions of Soviet resolve with respect to other, future confrontations in the Third World. The long-term implications of such a loss would disadvantage the Soviets vis-à-vis the Americans, whom they still considered to be a grave security threat. In this way, the Soviet intervention in Angola can be linked to the fundamental security concerns that drive international rivalry by appreciating the interconnected nature of rivalry confrontations.

US Intervention in Angola

The US intervention in Angola began in July 1974, when the CIA started making secret payments to the FNLA (Guimaraes 2001). Until then, the American position had been to support the Portuguese regime, largely as a consequence of the access to naval bases on the Azores islands that accompanied positive US-Portuguese relations. Following the coup in Lisbon, however, and as it became clear that Portugal would relinquish control in Angola and that the Soviets were cultivating a relationship with the MPLA, the United States identified Roberto's FNLA as a potential proxy for its interests.[13] Nonetheless, aside from a few CIA payments, American involvement remained limited in the early phases of the war. This changed in January 1975, when a proposal for a payment of US$300,000 to the FNLA was approved by Secretary of State Kissinger (Davis 1978). "The US decision was a strong signal," writes Westad (2006, 222), "that Washington was more interested in keeping the MPLA out than in preserving the peace." The effect of the payment was to exacerbate violence by augmenting FNLA capabilities vis-à-vis the MPLA.[14] This involvement was ramped up again in the summer of 1975. "Intelligence on the growing Soviet involvement" led to the decision on 18 July to "help FNLA and UNITA win the Angolan civil war" (Westad 2006, 222).[15] From this point on, "the . . . operation became sizeable" (222). Nearly US$50 million eventually would be dispersed in the effort to "train, equip, and transport

---

13 There is evidence of a CIA connection to the FNLA earlier, in the 1960s, but whatever support was given was likely minimal, and tailed off in the early 1970s owing to explicit US support for the Portuguese position; National Security Study Memorandum 39, published in 1970, described the US belief that the "whites were here to stay" in southern Africa, referring to the regimes in Angola, South Africa, and Rhodesia (Zimbabwe) (Guimaraes 2001). See Lockwood (1974).

14 As Noer (1993, 774) explains, "in impoverished Angola … $300,000 was a major alteration of the balance of power."

15 Nathaniel Davis, Assistant Secretary of State for African Affairs at the time, wrote to Kissinger on 16 July that "the situation in Angola has importantly changed: We have evidence the Soviets are introducing more, heavier and more sophisticated weapons" (quoted in Davis 1978, 116). Interestingly, the thrust of Davis's memo was that, given the scope of Soviet involvement, American counteraction was likely to fail, and recommended the United States desist from further efforts to affect the situation in Angola. Kissinger reached the complete opposite conclusion, and used the intelligence on Soviet escalation to justify increased US involvement. Noer (1993, 775) describes Davis's rationale:

> Despite his involvement in U.S. covert activities in Chile, Davis saw intervention in Angola as wrong. He argued that the MPLA was militarily far superior to either of the other two groups and the United States could not bring the FNLA up to parity without massive aid and perhaps the direct use of American troops. Davis also warned that intervention might provoke South Africa to enter the struggle and Washington would be linked with the racist government in Pretoria. Finally, Davis contended that the Soviets and the Cubans would more than match any U.S. effort giving Angola the potential to escalate to a major power conflict. He urged Washington to work for a diplomatic solution in Angola based on a coalition government.

When the administration went the other way, Davis resigned in protest.

anti-MPLA troops" (222). The purpose, Westad suggests, was "to show that even after the Vietnam debacle, the United States could change events in the Third World according to its will" (222).

Nonetheless, the steady Soviet escalation combined with the Cuban intervention kept the MPLA largely on the front foot (Noer 1993). By November 1975, available CIA funds had been exhausted, and the Ford administration approached Congress with a request for an additional US$28 million (Garthoff 1994). News of the request was leaked to the *New York Times*, and subsequent articles revealed the extent of hitherto secret CIA involvement in the conflict. A public backlash ensued – support for overseas US involvement was at a low ebb given Vietnam – and a group in Congress led by Democratic senator Dick Clark proposed an amendment that would block further government funding for the effort. The amendment was fiercely debated in congressional hearings, but despite strident opposition from Kissinger and the administration, passed the Senate in December and was ratified by the House in January 1976. The Clark Amendment effectively ended large-scale US involvement in Angola. With American hands tied, the FNLA and UNITA were overwhelmed by the Soviet- and Cuban-backed MPLA – South Africa, for its part, had pulled its intervention in January, unwilling to continue absent US involvement – and fighting was over by February.

The motivation for US intervention is generally recognized as the US-Soviet rivalry. Historians and analysts almost universally ascribe Washington's decision-making – guided primarily by Kissinger – to the desire to block and counteract the Soviet intervention (see, for example, Marcum 1976; Westad 2006). Angola's intrinsic value – its raw materials and proximity to supply routes around the coast of Africa – was noted by the administration, but the expressed purpose of US policy was defended by its architects, in congressional hearings and elsewhere, in terms related to American credibility and resolve vis-à-vis the Cold War (this theme is picked up in greater detail below). "Angola was not strategically essential to the United States in an objective sense," writes Klingshoffer (1980, 78), "and acquired importance only within an adversary context." Senator Clark, in explaining his objections to his country's involvement, "pointed out that American strategic and economic interests in Angola were minimal and that ideological concern was not a major factor since the United States and China were on the same side" (78). Clark similarly derided what he saw as the mistaken US tendency to "counter the Soviets even if they have made a mistake or the area is not relevant to American interests" (79).

This perception that the United States was blindly committed to opposing Soviet influence – as if by rote – was shared by other critics of the Angola intervention; it was even the source of frustration among certain policy officials charged with implementing the policy. John Stockwell, a CIA official involved in the agency's African activities at the time, would later write a scathing account of what he considered blind American adventurism in the Third World, entitled *In Search of Enemies* (1978). Stockwell specifically criticized American involvement in Angola, noting that the MPLA had not been overtly hostile towards the United States, and that CIA action had frustrated rather than facilitated peace in the country. William Colby, then-CIA director, when asked in a congressional hearing why the United States was supporting the FNLA over other domestic factions, given that all were admittedly "leftists," could only muster: "Because the Soviets are backing the MPLA is the simplest answer" (quoted in Garthoff 1994, 576). Senator Clark, for his part, challenged the logic of the Angola policy during hearings before the Senate Subcommittee on African Affairs:

> We must certainly ask whether it is wise policy to react to Soviet actions anyplace in the world, whether it involves our strategic or economic interests or not. If we follow this policy, it means that … we are, indeed, the policeman of the world and that our policy is not an independent one, but rather a reactive one, determined by our adversary. In my judgement, the United States would be a more credible ally if we defined our own interests and did not become bogged down in conflicts of little real importance to us.

As part of the same hearings, the young Democratic senator Joseph Biden pointedly questioned Kissinger, wondering "if South Africa had been the one to take the role which Cuba and the Soviets have taken, we would not feel as compelled to be there, would we? Or any other country but the Soviet Union?" (United States 1976e, 33). The implication was that, if no tangible American interests were at stake – such that intervention would have been pursued *regardless* of who the other intervener might have been – why should the United States expend resources and commit itself to Angola? Pressing the secretary as to "what difference does it make" that the "Soviets exert influence on any part of the world other than Europe or Japan," Biden, clearly unpersuaded by the answers on offer – in which Kissinger refused to identify anywhere specific for fear of signalling a lack of resolve to the Soviets – quipped in parting that, "in private sometime I would like to find out whether there is any place in the whole wide world where it would not make any difference" (47).

What is interesting about this exchange and the points of view offered by Davis, Stockwell, and others – to say nothing of the lacklustre explanation offered by Colby – is the extent to which they mirror, in many ways, the observations that produce explanations of rivalry which foreground decision-making pathologies (psychological, emotional, or otherwise). The clear implication is that US policy was beholden to some misguided principle of automatic and unthinking opposition to any and all Soviet activity. (Posterity reinforces this observation, given that we now know, for example, that the loss of Angola did not fundamentally threaten US security; indeed, the Cold War would be won within two decades.) This is the basic criticism of the "domino theory" as applied to Southeast Asia, as well. Clark et al. concentrated in particular on the mismatch between American policy and the goal of "solving" the Angolan dispute. "Mr. Secretary," he wondered during Senate hearings, "is it credible for you to contend outside interference in Angola and Africa, while chastising the Congress for not allowing you to interfere as an outsider?" This was also, recall, the basic thrust of Stockwell's objections. Their misunderstanding[16] was focusing on the "local" conflict at the expense of the global one – US policy simply was not, despite genuflections in this direction for international public consumption, about maintaining peace in Africa or helping Angolans craft an "African solution" to the conflict. US policy therefore might have appeared to be callous and ill-conceived, but in reality was operating according to a logic dictated by concerns far removed from the local context: from 10,000 feet, it can be hard to see details on the ground.

It is unpacking this logic that is of interest here. Given that the record is quite clear regarding the Americans' purpose in Angola – the intervention was motivated, by most accounts, by a desire to counterbalance Soviet influence – it would be less useful to analyse the various alternative possibilities, be they immediate security imperatives, economic interests, or ideological affinities with a particular domestic faction.[17] Instead, we can better interrogate the causal mechanism – the

---

16 The misunderstanding was with respect to divining US motivations, not necessarily as a normative matter – indeed, a primary concern with the people fighting and dying on the ground hardly reflects "misunderstood" or mistaken priorities.

17 Each of these can, in fact, be dispatched rather quickly. The potential disruption of sea lanes around the African coast, which some suggested might be a threat to oil supply chains, did not, by all accounts, endanger vital US security interests – particularly given that passage via the Suez Canal was assured at the time. Nor were Angola's natural resources considered lucrative enough to justify a significant intervention. Finally, as noted earlier, the FNLA – though ostensibly anticommunist – was not a natural ideological ally; in fact, Kissinger quite clearly stated: "We do not favor any particular faction. We are not opposed to the MPLA per se, only to Cuban and Russian support and intervention" (United States 1976a).

anticipated process related to decision-making – if we examine the explanations offered by relevant decisionmakers as to *why* the need to counter the Soviet Union in Angola was so acute. In congressional hearings, public statements, and in meetings and communications behind closed doors, the Ford administration expressed the rationale behind the American counterintervention – in other words, an explanation considerably more complex than the "simple" one offered by William Colby is available. The point is not to vindicate Ford, Kissinger, or any other decisionmaker in the administration, or to argue that they were "right" with respect to the intervention's being in the national interest. Rather, by excavating the rationale on offer, we can assess whether the American decision was consistent with the explanation of rational rivalry. In so doing, we can demonstrate that the imperatives pushing the administration towards intervention were consistent across time and space, and that an explanation for the case is available through an understanding of these imperatives, as opposed to the idiosyncrasies of specific decisionmakers, the uniqueness of US grand strategy, or other factors that in some way insulate the case from the broader, systematic processes associated with international rivalry.

The underlying rationale articulated by the Ford administration for intervention in Angola was that unchecked Soviet intervention would undermine the future position of the United States in its ongoing struggle with the USSR; this competition continued to be thought of in existential terms, meaning that preventing any such disadvantage rose to the level of an acute national security interest. In a National Security Council Meeting on 22 December 1975, for example, Secretary of State Kissinger, with respect to US-Soviet relations (the main focus of the meeting was assessing the prospects of a SALT II agreement) observed that American strategic superiority was slowly disappearing, owing to recent crises and setbacks: "Looking back at the seven years I have been here, we have never had to manage a crisis under the current difficult conditions … The situation is changed, and this will present a real strategic problem, not only in a crisis, but in the way the Soviets throw their weight around. *This is one reason why Angola is so important; we don't want to whet the Soviet appetite"* (United States 1975h, 12, emphasis added).

The concern here is quite clearly with future Soviet behaviour. Failure in Angola meant trouble in the offing. In a conversation in early February with journalist Robert Kleiman of the *New York Times*, Kissinger similarly stressed that losing Angola to the Soviets had set a dangerous precedent and that, "if it happens again, then we are going to see massive erosion internationally" (United States 1975d). Around the same time, in a telephone exchange with Senator Jacob Javits, Kissinger dismissed Javits's concern as to whether a particular Soviet action had made a change in the "local" situation (i.e., on the ground in Angola); the question was beside the point, as indicated by Kissinger's reply: "I have no sense that it has. And even if it should make a local change *my concern is that will happen in the future*" (United States 1976c, emphasis added). The sense, ultimately, was that Soviet influence in Angola had marked an important episode in the enduring conflict – indeed, that its importance was *exclusive* to its position in this continuum – and that this conflict was implicated in, and would be influenced by, developments there. In a meeting with the Guyanese foreign secretary on 12 February, Kissinger stated that, "what is happening in Africa now means that we must become more active in Africa. It will become an area of great power rivalry."

Kissinger's appearance before the Senate subcommittee discussing the Angolan issue is particularly illuminative. In it, Kissinger welcomed the "opportunity to explain the global significance of what is now happening in Angola, the events that have brought us to this point, the US objectives *and the major consequences which can result*" (United States 1976f, 6). He emphasized the US imperative to "remain ... both strong and determined to use its strength when required" (6). "Any other course," he admonished, "will encourage the trends it seeks to accommodate; *a challenge not met today will tempt far more dangerous crises tomorrow*" (7, emphasis added). Specific reference was made to US experiences and the "history of the postwar period" in which "military aggression, direct or indirect, has frequently been successfully dealt with, but never in the absence of a local balance of forces" (7). In this way, Kissinger tied his preferred US policy in Angola to the crises of the preceding decades and the lessons derived from American resistance to perceived Soviet expansionism – e.g., in Berlin, where a strong West Germany was crucial to containment, or in Korea, where the communist advance south was repulsed. "And what conclusion will an unopposed superpower draw when the next opportunity for intervention beckons?" Kissinger asked, again invoking concern over future developments in the global rivalry. "The consequences" of backing down, he averred, "may well be far-reaching *and substantially more painful* than the course we have recommended" (8, emphasis added). These consequences partly related to American credibility, both with respect to allies and those other nations that relied on US security guarantees and also vis-à-vis the Soviet Union directly and its assessment of American resolve:

> The questions, then, come down to this: Do we really want the world to conclude that if the Soviet Union chooses to intervene in a massive way ... the United States will not be able to muster the unity or resolve

to provide even financial assistance? Can those faced with such a threat without hope of assistance from us be expected to resist? Do we want our potential adversaries to conclude that in the event of future challenges America's internal divisions are likely to deprive us of even minimal leverage over developments of global significance? (United States 1976f, 12)

The importance of American credibility, however, as discussed above, was in the context of the security threat emanating from the Soviet Union – which is to say, it was not simply crucial for its own sake, but given the assumption about future confrontations with the same adversary.[18] This is evident when Kissinger states that "what the United States does when confronted with a blatant challenge like Angola can be of great significance in shaping our future relations with the Soviet Union" (United States 1976f, 14). "A demonstration of a lack of resolve," he concludes, "could lead the Soviets to a great miscalculation, *thereby plunging us in a major confrontation which neither of us wants*" (14, emphasis added). We see here the evolution noted earlier whereby the United States no longer considered the Soviets to be rapaciously aggressive and intent on conflict, as was the case at the birth of the rivalry during the early crises in Berlin, but still posited a fundamental security concern regarding major, and possibly devastating, confrontation. This remained a powerfully motivating possibility.

Kissinger's exchanges with the various questioners during the hearings offer additional insight. Senator Clark questioned the logic of the Angola intervention given that "no strategic interest of the United States is affected," and expressed the associated concern that such a logic might commit the United States to action in each and every instance of Soviet activity worldwide. In response, Kissinger stressed that the policy did not represent a blanket commitment from the United States, pointing to other instances in Africa alone (e.g., Mozambique) where Soviet influence was tacitly accepted. The difference was in the scope of Soviet involvement, which included the transport of thousands of Cuban combat troops, and the projection of significant military power so far from Soviet territory.[19] Moreover, once committed, as the United

---

18 This is, in fact, the basic point Schelling makes in *Arms and Influence* ([1966] 2008), one that many of his current critics fundamentally misunderstand (see Mitton 2015).

19 Here Kissinger explains: "I would say that when Soviet military equipment appears on this massive scale and is backed by substantial military forces, that are, in effect, Soviet-controlled, then we have a problem in which any President, I would of think of either party, would have to ask himself what American security interests are" (United States 1976f, 26).

States had become by the time of the hearings, the implications of backing down were tied to future developments in the rivalry. Backing down, Kissinger explained, "would do two things: it would tell all countries outside of a traditional orbit that if that sort of pressure appears, they have no choice except to accommodate to the Soviets, and, second, it might tell the Soviet Union that even in areas of traditional concern of American security, our ability or willingness to react might be minimal" (United States 1976f, 26). The latter point is worth emphasizing. Here we see Kissinger connecting developments in Angola to "areas of traditional concern of American security" – a clear reference to "core" issues within the US-Soviet rivalry (e.g., central Europe, East Asia). Now, it might be that he was merely playing on fears that he hoped would persuade reluctant senators – that is, consciously distorting and exaggerating Angola's importance to core US security as a way of manipulating support for a preferred policy (even among his admirers, Kissinger's probity was never cast as a strength). Nonetheless, this contention is consistent with the expectation of rational rivalry.

These sentiments are reflected again in the above referenced exchange with Senator Biden. Pushing back against concerns that his preferred policy in Angola constitutes some kind of "Global Monroe Doctrine" (in the words of Biden), Kissinger clarifies: "[T]he dilemma is that if we say that anything else out of Europe or Japan is open to Soviet military action, then we will be inviting that very military action. That will sooner or later create an international situation in which the overall balance is so shifted against us that it will either require the most massive exertions and turn us into a military garrison, *or lead us into some sort of confrontation*. That is not a doctrine in my view. That is a reality" (United States 1976f, 45, emphasis added). And later, with respect to the "perception of reality" by which "anybody conducting foreign policy will have to be judged," Kissinger suggests that the key imperative "is if you take action at an early phase in the changes of equilibrium, you face a more ambiguous decision but a lesser investment. *You always have the choice of waiting while the threat becomes overwhelming.* In that case you will have gained inward assurance and *you will have to pay a much higher price*" (47, emphasis added). Here again we see the logic of rational rivalry at play: the prospect of future conflict is powerful enough to dictate and shape perceptions of a present crisis.

Finally, Kissinger supplied written responses to additional questions formulated by the subcommittee. One question wondered why, given the past successes by African nationalist movements in pushing out Soviet influence on their own (Mozambique is cited as an example), the United States could not simply rely on a similar outcome in Angola?

Kissinger acknowledged the "possibility" that such a scenario could recur, but countered that "this is no more than a hypothesis, which it is imprudent to count on to base our policy" (United States 1976f, 51). In other words, the *consequences* of being wrong were too severe, given that Soviet "success in this instance cannot but increase their own willingness to engage in such adventures in the future" (51).

One final exchange from these hearings is worth highlighting here, this time between Senator Biden and Deputy Secretary of Defense Robert Ellsworth. Biden again expresses frustration that administration officials seem to be applying what he calls a "worst case scenario" lens to the Angolan issue, connecting it to a broader, long-term security threat from the Soviet Union:

> I assume in your job that it is your responsibility to plan for the worst case scenario. That is what you are doing for us here, is it not? You are not at all certain that it is going to happen, but you must assume for your projections that that is a possibility of happening?
>
> In other words, since I have been a member of this committee, we, with regard to everything from Vietnam, the arms race, and everything in between in international relations, are presented with the worst case scenario all the time. We in this committee are told that we have to build based on that scenario, but seldom have we been confronted with specific information which would indicate that the probability [*sic*] that the worst case scenario will come to pass. (United States 1976f, 69)

One can certainly understand his frustration: from an outside perspective, the sensible thing likely would be to formulate policy by balancing objective "probabilities." Yet his question contains, in part, its own answer: it is indeed the "responsibility" of the administration to plan for the worst-case scenario. Further, given the weight of experience over the preceding decades and the scope of the threat associated with confrontation with the USSR, the worst-case scenario is considered probable *enough* to dictate policy. Ellsworth replies that, although it is difficult, the crafting of foreign and defence policy requires "looking into the future, *trying to be futurists and historians at the same time*." Which is to say, using history (past crises, confrontations, and associated reputations) to form expectations about future behaviour and future scenarios. As the continuity with respect to American foreign policy over the 1947–75 period demonstrates, moreover, this "responsibility" was felt, and acted upon, by both Democratic and Republican administrations.

This tension between outsiders and top decision-making officials is captured by Nathaniel Davis's (1978) account of the Angolan episode.

Davis resigned as Assistant Secretary of State for African Affairs when the administration pursued a policy he did not believe was calibrated to realities on the ground. Davis reflects on his disagreement with Kissinger over the matter:

> I hope I understand the depth of his conviction that it was dangerous to permit the Soviet Union to conclude that détente placed restraints only on America, and that the Third World was fair game, unlinked to the totality of our relationship. Both during the final weeks of the Vietnam War and during the Angolan crisis of 1975, *the Secretary and the President seem to have believed that it was better to roll the dice against the longest of odds than to abandon the competition against our greatest adversary.* The Secretary would freely acknowledge, I believe, that he saw Angola as part of the US-Soviet relationship, and not as an African problem. (Davis 1978, 123–4, emphasis added)

Indeed, Davis's assessment of Kissinger's and Ford's motivations is precisely accurate; his displeasure with those motivations was the product of his own responsibilities vis-à-vis African affairs. Davis himself recognizes as much when writes: "The strategic world overview of US policy is the responsibility of the President and the Secretary of State. Necessarily, my focus and argument had to be on a different level. The question I was principally addressing in my memos to the Secretary was whether covert intervention in Angola could work" (1978, 124). Davis's remit was the local, regional issue – the specifics and outcomes of the civil war itself and its ramifications for regional politics in southern Africa; the administration, on the other hand, was concerned with the totality of US foreign and defence policy. This disconnect resulted in strikingly different policy preferences that help clarify, in the final analysis, the logic according to which the latter was formulated.

The passing of the Clark Amendment therefore represents a significant episode in the history of US foreign policy, insofar as the discretion of the executive was challenged and curtailed by congressional action. The reaction from the administration was predictably hostile, and its statements to this effect are helpful in that they offer further insight into the rationale according to which it had justified intervention in Angola in the first place. To be forced to abandon Angola to the Soviets was, according to President Ford, "an abdication of responsibility" that would portend "the gravest consequences for the long term position of the United States" (quoted in Gaddis 2005, 179). Elsewhere, he was more concise, stating simply that Congress lacked "guts" (quoted in Noer 1993, 780). Kissinger himself was irate, calling it a "national disgrace" and opining that "Congress is now inflicting a defeat on the United States against the executive branch's better judgment. There must be something wrong with all the Congressmen who spend 10 minutes a day of [*sic*] these problems. It isn't a partisan matter either, this affects the whole posture of the United States" (United States 1976b). He expressed the belief that US credibility had been severely damaged, and that it might have consequences at the core of the US-Soviet rivalry:

> We are going to lose big. The President says to the Chinese that we're going to stand firm in Angola and two weeks later we get out ... The Department leaks that we're worried about a [Soviet] naval base and says it [Angola] is an exaggeration or aberration of Kissinger's. *I don't care about the oil or the base but I do care about the African reaction when they see the Soviets pull it off and we don't do anything. If the Europeans then say to themselves if they can't hold Luanda, how can they defend Europe?* The Chinese will say we're a country that was run out of Indochina for 50,000 men and is now being run out of Angola for less than $50 million. (quoted in Westad 2006, 245, emphasis added)

In a speech in March 1976, Kissinger reiterated these themes, arguing that, "if adventurism is allowed to succeed in local crises, an ominous precedent of wider consequences is set" (quoted in Garthoff 1994, 581). These statements reflect the general tenor of the executive's objection to the Clark Amendment: that it had grievously endangered the long-term security of the United States not only by forcing it out of Angola, but also by circumscribing the freedom of action necessary to respond fluidly and decisively to Soviet action. (Recall here the parameters of Kennan's original formulation of containment, with US responses at "constantly shifting geographical and political points.") Even more, this limit on American action was broadcast publicly to the Soviets and the rest of the world. It was a blow, in this regard, to US credibility – something that, as discussed above, was considered in the vital US interest to protect.

Subsequent assessments of Soviet intentions reflected these anxieties. As the October 1976 National Intelligence Estimate on "Soviet Policy in the Third World" concluded:

> The Soviets continue to regard insurgencies as instruments to advance their position, and will support such groups as the PLO and guerilla movements in southern Africa. We believe that Moscow will probably continue to act more boldly than in years past in support of liberation movements. Moscow's confidence has been bolstered by its current per-

ception of Western disinclination to counter Soviet activities in the Third World, its tested experience in supporting Cuban forces in Africa, and its improved military capabilities ... Soviet-Cuban cooperation in supporting a national liberation movement [in Angola] may be repeated [elsewhere] if suitable opportunities arise. (CIA 1976, 3)

Even with its hands effectively tied, the Ford administration did attempt to limit further Soviet gains in Africa as much as possible.[20] Interestingly, the subsequent Carter administration also became involved in Africa, countering Soviet influence in the conflict between Ethiopia and Somalia. Later, the Reagan administration restarted American involvement in Angola. It is beyond the scope of this volume to address the decision-making processes at work in these other cases, but they are instructive of a basic continuity across Democratic and Republican administrations.

The Rivalry Explanation

In offering a general evaluation of Soviet and American intervention in Angola in the context of rational rivalry, the effort is facilitated once again through comparing that case with those of India-Pakistan in Afghanistan and Israel-Syria in Lebanon. What do the similarities and differences say about the effects of rivalry on the decision to intervene in a civil conflict? What dynamics are potentially relevant to the development of the rational rivalry explanation for intervention in civil wars? How compelling is this explanation, ultimately, for Soviet and American intervention into Angola in 1975?

As mentioned at the outset of the chapter, the US-Soviet rivalry possessed several features which make it distinct from those of India-Pakistan and Israel-Syria. First and most fundamentally, it was a global rivalry between two superpowers, rather than a regional rivalry between two middle powers. Second, it was a rivalry between two states with nuclear capabilities (save a very limited timeframe at its

---

20 Kissinger for example told the National Security Council in April 1976 that "[w]e must keep our eye on the strategic concepts, our Africa policy is one thing but the surrogate Soviet action could come through North Viet Nam as well as Cuba. If this principle is accepted, it will be very dangerous for us. In time, there will be a real problem if the Cuban presence remains in Africa. In the period 1970–73 we successfully frustrated the Soviets in the Middle East so the Arabs finally had to turn towards us. We will try to identify with the aspirations of the black nations in Africa, but not in response to Cuban pressure" (United States 1976e).

outset), distinguishing it from the asymmetric nuclear rivalry between Israel and Syria, but matching the (rough) nuclear balance between India and Pakistan, at least at the time that the interventions of interest occurred. The enabling, or animating, condition between the Americans and Soviets was ideological – the perceived incompatibility between opposing modes of political and economic organization – rather than ethnic or religious. Unlike the India-Pakistan and Israel-Syria rivalries, no direct large-scale conflict had occurred between the United States and the USSR. Instead, despite tense direct stand-offs, primarily in central Europe, crises and confrontations prior to the Angola intervention were limited, often proxy, conflicts in which the states jockeyed for influence and position around the globe. Finally, unlike the India-Pakistan and Israel-Syria cases, in which the civil conflict was proximate, the US-Soviet intervention occurred at far remove from either's territory.

These differences present both challenges and opportunities for theory development. With respect to the former, the discrepancies represent potential confounding circumstances such that the outcome of interest – the decision to intervene in Angola – was in the US-Soviet case driven by factors present in that relationship but absent in the other rivalries. Which is to say, the circumstances influencing the specific decisions to intervene in Angola might not be comparable to the circumstances in the other two cases. One could argue, for example, that equating the decisions regarding Angola to those taken vis-à-vis Afghanistan and Lebanon is mistaken; these decisions are only superficially similar, grouped together according to a somewhat arbitrary concept of "civil conflict intervention," and not reflective of any underlying reality, given the differences described above: relative geographic proximity of the conflict to the interveners, ideological versus ethnic and religious motivations, etc. Ultimately, this possibility cannot be definitively overcome, but *confidence* that these differences are not operating in this way can be increased through logic and evidence. If the decision-making process, and accompanying rationale, can be shown to be consistent and similar across the cases *despite* these differences, it bolsters confidence that the differences in characteristics noted above did not drive the outcome.

Indeed, if it can be shown that the process leading to intervention is fundamentally consistent across cases that are dissimilar in significant respects, this would be solid evidence for my proposition. It also would increase the significance of that explanation by suggesting that it is scalable to a much larger set of potential cases. Whereas the theoretical leverage afforded by the move from the India-Pakistan case to the Israel-Syria case was minimal – while nonetheless important, representing a step beyond a single case – the move to the US-Soviet case greatly increases that leverage precisely because of the differences described above. It increases our confidence that the observations common to the India-Pakistan and Israel-Syria cases were not confounded by shared characteristics outside the parameters of the proposed theoretical explanation. Ultimately, the theory suggests that a common dynamic of "rivalry" links all three relationships, and that the influence of this dynamic results in behaviour that is consistent across them. Examining US and Soviet intervention in Angola is therefore useful as a pathway case, again not as a "most difficult" or "least likely" case – most observers linked US and Soviet decisions to intervene to the broader international relationship – but to help establish the actual process, the path, that *leads* from rivalry to intervention. Combined with the cases examined in previous chapters, moreover, the US-Soviet intervention demonstrates the way this pathway looks similar even as it traverses – metaphorically speaking – vastly different landscapes. Global as opposed to regional rivals; distant as opposed to proximate civil conflict; ideological as opposed to ethnic or religious; no direct contact as opposed to repeated direct conflict – despite all these differences, similar dynamics (rivalry) led to similar outcomes (offsetting civil conflict intervention).

Crucially, each crisis in the US-Soviet rivalry was linked in the minds of leaders to the broader relationship. There was a clear belief on both sides that the Cold War conflict was ongoing and certain to extend into the future. Leaders in Washington and Moscow remained concerned with long-term security and considered particular crises in this context. With respect to the decision to intervene in an ongoing civil war, moreover, we see the common influence of these rivalry dynamics. For the Americans and Soviets, the conflict in Angola carried minimal direct and immediate security, economic, or ideological interest. The Soviets had been developing a more proactive African policy – partly as a result of competition for influence with China – and did profess a desire to support Marxist revolutionary movements in the Third World. Yet the cultivation of such groups was itself motivated by the larger ideological struggle with the United States – and therefore implicated in the security competition of rivalry. Concern over Chinese gains, moreover, was also tied to the possibility of Sino-US collaboration against the USSR. Thus, the initial support for the MPLA was apparently influenced by rivalry concerns, although this argument is even stronger with respect to subsequent Soviet escalation, which came as a clear counterreaction to the US intervention. The American move, even more so, can be clearly linked to rivalry considerations. The logic expressed by the Ford administration – and in particular by Secretary of State Henry Kissinger – is entirely consistent with the expectations of rational rivalry: concern for the future, predicated on the past, driving present behaviour. The rational calculus for intervention was therefore reordered by rivalry dynamics, a decision that was roundly criticized – involvement in a distant African nation in which no vital US interests were immediately at stake – is made explicable absent reference to emotional, psychological, or other first- and second-image variables.

A final aspect of the US-Soviet case that warrants discussion – and that distinguishes it from the India-Pakistan and Israel-Syria cases – is the centrality of the concept of "credibility" in Cold War calculations. While the credibility of coercive (deterrent and compellent) threats was obviously still relevant in the interactions between Islamabad and New Delhi, and Jerusalem and Damascus, the *protection* of credibility as an *end unto itself* (that is, as a core vital interest) was not as pronounced in those relationships as it appeared to be between Washington and Moscow. As we have seen in all three cases, reputations for behaviour played a role in shaping rivalry perceptions, in terms of the specific tactics employed (for example, Pakistan's repeated use of militant Islamist proxies), comparative resolve and credibility between crises (as over Berlin and Cuba in the US-Soviet rivalry), and the general dispositions displayed (the Syrian perception that Israel is prone to seize and occupy territory). All of these factors constitute important information in an environment in which complete information – and therefore perfectly "accurate" knowledge – is impossible to obtain. In the US-Soviet rivalry, however, credibility (including reputation) became a fundamental stake; the Angola crisis itself was considered primarily in terms of its potential reputational consequences. One possible explanation for this dynamic is the combination of nuclear deterrence and global rivalry. In such a context, the prospect of direct conflict is circumscribed, while the competition plays out across the extended domain of various corners of the globe, *in which the common link is the identity of the two competitors.* Given that the dynamics of rivalry connect all these disputes together, each state becomes concerned that what happens in one crisis will have consequences elsewhere; knowing that the adversary will be the same, reputation and credibility become important tools for success in future encounters. This might explain why protecting credibility became such a vital concern during the Cold War.

Chapter Eight

Conclusion

In this book I have argued that international rivalry causes states to intervene in civil conflicts. The decision is basically defensive: given a history of conflict, states form perceptions about – assign specific and dispositional reputations to – rivals that generate expectations that future conflict is likely. Rivalry essentially "solves" the security dilemma, affording high certainty as to malign intentions. When confronted with whether or how to intervene in a civil conflict, these perceptions translate into concerns about long-term security. The condition of international anarchy, the requirement of self-help, and the (fundamental and logically primary) goal of security and survival mean these concerns are powerfully motivating. States worry that unchecked intervention by a rival might offer it an advantage by altering the status quo or in some other way shifting the general balance of power in the relationship. Intervention is seen as necessary to forestall these consequences.

Summary of Findings

The focus of the three case studies at the heart of this book is the process by which state leaders and decisionmakers chose to intervene in another country's civil conflict. In this process, I contend, rational rivalry is the mechanism that operated – that decisions were propelled by long-term security concerns vis-à-vis the rival in the context of anticipated future conflict.

To assess this argument, I gathered a range of evidence, including classified memoranda, meeting transcripts, telephone transcripts, government reports, diplomatic cables, official government releases, private statements, public statements, contemporary reporting, published interviews, memoirs of political leaders, and other direct evidence of the thought process, rationale, and justifications – both contemporaneous and post hoc – of decisionmakers regarding intervention. I additionally examined a significant body of secondary historical work on each case, both to inform the discussion of the history and development of the rivalry in the decades preceding intervention, and to offer additional insight into the interventions themselves. Finally, I considered indirect evidence pertaining to the timing, sequence, development, and scope of each intervention in order to assess logically what they reveal about the decision-making process, and the priorities and justifications for intervention that were implied.

Table 2 offers a summary and comparison of the cases along several key dimensions. Specifically, I note the key features of each case: the rivalry itself (its basis and history), the civil conflict in which intervention occurred (noting which side was supported by which rival), perceptions prior to intervention (key for understanding the context in which intervention was contemplated), and, finally, the rationale for intervention. Flowing from these considerations I identify six key take-aways from the case studies:

1. Rivalry Considerations Were Decisive in the Decision to Intervene

In general terms, the cases indicate that rivalry concerns were dominant in the minds of decisionmakers. Interventions were not the product of specific desires of leaders regarding particular outcomes related to the civil conflicts in which they occurred, or some easily identifiable balance of power and interests that produced a tipping point that caused specific interventions. The victory of the domestic faction (whether government or rebel) that a state supported was ancillary to the broader goal of offsetting the rival's interests and influence. Although the choice of which side to support was sometimes consistent with explanations based on affective linkage (as when the government of Muslim Pakistan supported the Islamist Taliban or the USSR supported the avowedly Marxist MPLA), at other times they were not (as when Syria intervened directly on behalf of the Christian-dominated Lebanese government or the US supported the broadly leftist FNLA). All choices, however, were logically consistent with the proposition that intervention was predicated on rivalry considerations.

2. The Choice of Which Faction to Support Was Ancillary to
  Rivalry Considerations

The choice of which domestic faction to support was determined by that faction's ability to service the intervener's broader aims regarding influence vis-à-vis its rival. India supported the post-2001 Afghan

Table 2. Case Summaries

Case	The Rivalry	The Civil Conflict	Perceptions Prior to Intervention	Rationale for Intervention
India-Pakistan (Afghanistan)	• Religious/ethnic • Partition of British India (1947) • First Kashmir War (1947) • Second Kashmir War (1965) • Bangladesh War (1971) • Partition of Pakistan • Kargil War (1999) • Border Crisis (2001–2)	• Afghanistan War (2001–21) • India: supports Afghan government • Pakistan: supports Taliban insurgency	• India: Pakistan is revisionist in Kashmir and antagonistic more broadly; Islamabad uses Islamist violence against India. • Pakistan: India is a powerful state fundamentally hostile to Pakistan's existence; New Delhi is willing to use decisive military force.	• India: prevent Afghan territory from hosting Pakistani-supported Islamist violence. • Pakistan: prevent Indian-friendly regime in Afghanistan, given strategic consequences in future war with India.
Israel-Syria (Lebanon)	• Religious/ethnic • First Arab-Israeli War (1948) • Six-Day War (1967) • Israeli seizure of Golan Heights • Yom Kippur War (1973)	• Lebanese civil war (1975–6) • Lebanon War (1982–5) • Israel: supports Christian forces • Syria: supports Muslim/PLO and Christian forces	• Israel: Syria is fundamentally hostile and committed to destruction of Israel. • Syria: Israel is expansionist and willing to use decisive military force.	• Israel: prevent Syrian control of southern Lebanon to preclude another front in next Arab-Israeli conflict. • Syria: prevent Israeli control of Lebanon to reduce strategic vulnerability on eastern flank in future conflict.
US-USSR (Angola)	• Ideological • End of Second World War (1945) • Partition of Germany • Berlin crises (1948, 1958, 1961) • Korean War (1950–3) • Cuban Missile Crisis (1962) • Vietnam War (1965–73)	• Angolan civil war (1975) • US: supports FNLA and UNITA • USSR: supports MPLA	• US: Soviet Union is an existential threat and committed to expanding its influence in Third World. • USSR: US is fundamentally hostile; strategic imbalance with US must be redressed.	• US: prevent Soviet influence in Angola to preserve US credibility in context of future Cold War confrontations. • USSR: prevent US and Chinese cooperation in southern Africa; expand influence in Third World to improve relative Soviet position in Cold War.

government because it represented an anti-Taliban, anti-Pakistan coalition, formed as it was by many former Northern Alliance members; Pakistan supported the Taliban precisely because it took aim at this Indian-influenced regime. Likewise, in Lebanon, Syria oscillated between supporting Christian and Muslim forces depending on which, at any given time, it believed provided a means to forestall Israeli influence and control in the country. The Israelis, for their part, made it clear that, while sympathetic to the Christian cause, they would not risk entanglement solely to support that side in the fight; support was offered instrumentally to push back against Syrian-controlled Muslim/PLO forces. In Angola, the United States selected the FNLA because, as was bluntly stated at the time, "the Soviets are backing the MPLA." We see across the cases, therefore, that international considerations trumped intrinsic interests in the outcome of the civil conflicts themselves.

3. The Decision to Intervene Was Fundamentally Defensive

The key question, of course, is what was the nature of these international considerations? Which is to say, what was the underlying strategic rationale that informed the decision to intervene? Here again the cases offer general support for the theory of rivalry intervention that I advance in this book. Decisionmakers on both sides justified their interventions primarily in *defensive* terms. India, having experienced an extended period of Pakistani control in Afghanistan via the Taliban government in the 1990s, saw an opportunity to forestall Pakistan's exploitation of Islamic militancy. Islamabad had long employed this tactic to attack and bleed India, primarily in Kashmir, and Pakistani influence (if not control) over Afghan territory had been helpful in these efforts. Pakistan saw potential Indian influence in Afghanistan as extremely threatening; the possibility of a two-front attack endangered Pakistan's very survival. More generally, the dispensation of Afghanistan was viewed primarily in military terms vis-à-vis potential future war with India, as in the concept of "strategic depth." For both Israel and Syria, Lebanese territory was directly implicated in military planning: the possibility of an Israeli swing through the Beqa Valley was at the forefront of Damascus's concerns, while the possibility of an additional front in a future Arab-Israeli war, which could also include Iraq and Jordan, focused Israeli concerns on southern Lebanon. Even the US and Soviet interventions in distant Angola were coloured by security anxieties. Moscow saw rising Chinese influence in southern Africa as a threat, both in its own right and in the context of potential US-China cooperation. Washington, for its part, considered its credibility to be at stake in Angola, the loss of which would have ramifications for future Soviet adventurism in the Third World and ultimately could invite crisis at the heart of the rivalry in central Europe. In each instance, therefore, states invoked defensive justifications for intervention, wary of the consequences of non-action for their long-term security.

4. The Decision to Intervene Was Not Conventionally Rational

In deciding to intervene, states were not operating according to a strict, conventional cost-benefit analysis of their immediate security and material interests – what might be considered the generic baseline for foreign policy analysis. Pakistan, for example, severely undermined its immediate security by creating conditions for domestic Islamist groups to challenge the Pakistani state. Yet, rather than fundamentally adjust course with respect to Afghanistan and reorient its military forces away from conventional conflict with India to a counterinsurgency posture in the tribal areas along the Afghan border, Islamabad maintained its support for the Taliban insurgency and kept its military geared towards India. Similarly, the clear and obvious economic benefits of a stable Afghanistan were insufficient to induce adjustment. In Lebanon, Israel refused to allow Syrian forces to move into the south in order to quell the PLO: the immediate and ongoing threat of terrorist attacks was acceptable as compared to the mere presence, and potential long-term threat, of Syrian forces along the Israeli border – in effect, Israel created a security umbrella against a militant group bent on its destruction. Syria, likewise, maintained a defensive position in the Beqa Valley, at great cost, when Israel forces moved into Lebanon in 1982, rather than retreat to Syrian territory. The basic logic appeared to be that defending Lebanese territory was akin to defending Syrian territory, because losing the former would allow Israel to threaten the latter – an advantage, Damascus believed, the Israelis inevitably would seize. Angola carried no significant material or immediate strategic (e.g., in terms of force projection) interest for either the United States or the USSR, yet both invested significant resources there. It is important to recognize that conventional cost-benefit calculations appear to have been violated, since several of the interventions – in particular, Pakistani involvement in Afghanistan and US involvement in Angola – have been discussed explicitly in terms of their purported "irrationality." They were "counterproductive" or "against the state's own interests," products of distorted, rather than deliberative, decision-making.

5. The Decision to Intervene Was Not "Pathological"

That decisions to intervene were "pathological" implies psychological and cognitive explanations that are characteristic of the approach I call pathological rivalry. In this view, states in rivalry operate according to a "negative-affect" calculus. Rather than operate according to which a cost-benefit calculus is employed to maximize gain, states take as their primary interest inflicting damage on their opponent. Harm to a rival is pursued even if it brings heavy costs. Pakistan, for example, attacks Indian interests in Afghanistan, and sacrifices its security and material interests to do so, due to its negative affect (essentially, hatred) towards India. Although I have not subjected this explanation to rigorous testing, given the evidentiary requirements associated with doing so, the case studies do not lend it much support even in passing. The available evidence indicates that leaders and policymakers typically offered justifications for their decisions, and proceeded deliberatively rather than capriciously. Of course, that reasoned justifications were offered does not preclude the possibility that underlying psychological biases associated with negative affect were operative; decisionmakers might be expected to couch their policies in national-interest terms – it is unlikely, for example, that a leader would say explicitly that a policy was being pursued simply to harm another state, irrespective of the costs. Without direct access to the thought processes of the relevant individuals, one can only assess the plausibility of competing explanations based on what they communicated to others and the availability of compelling evidence that other, more rationalist causal mechanisms and motivations were at play.

This leads to a second, more serious challenge to the proposed rational rivalry explanation: not that decision-making was predicated on blanket and naked hostility, but rather that the deliberative assessment of national interest was itself skewed by psychological/emotional biases fostered by decades of conflict and confrontation. In this formulation, leaders and policymakers overweighted the prospect of future conflict with a rival and conducted interventions to offset a rival's interests because of individual-level manifestations of bias. Individual decisionmakers were "paranoid" about their rival, seeing evidence of hostile intentions where they did not actually exist, interpreting all moves by the other side – even outwardly salutary ones – as duplicitous, and generally discounting any information that cut against the perception that the other side was a committed enemy. In many ways, this picture looks very much like that offered by the rational rivalry explanation. Indeed, much of the evidence in the case studies plausibly could be interpreted in this direction. The key to distinguish the two, however, is in assessing the *origin* of the relevant perceptions. Determining this source is vitally important because, depending on which level is emphasized – the individual (first image), societal (second image), or structural (third image) – the appropriate policy prescriptions will vary. An explanation predicated only on the individual level, for example, can end there with respect to its solution.

6. The Decision to Intervene Was Consistent with the Expectations of Rational Rivalry

The rational rivalry explanation situates the origins of rival perceptions, and the behaviours, such as intervention, that result from them at the level of the international relationship itself: specifically, the history of the interactions between two states, which generates reasonable expectations about future conflict and mandates defensive behaviour for security seekers. In each case study, I offered overviews of these conflict histories, noting the cumulative effect of confrontations over time not in *psychological* terms, but rather in *informational* terms vis-à-vis a broadly rational actor. We see the informational effects of past experiences in both specific and general (dispositional) references to past behaviour between rivals – for example, India's role in the separation of Bangladesh from Pakistan or Israel's seizure of the Golan Heights from Syria. As rivals assessed their security environment, these reputations were crucial for shaping expectations. Far from *discounting* relevant information, as the pathological rivalry approach would suggest, rivals appeared to credit their own experiences and the past behaviour of their opponent in their calculations, a move that the broader literature on reputations has established takes place in other situations – for example, in coercive diplomatic encounters. As in Schelling's "continuous negotiations," reputations become important. Particularly in the context of incomplete information, and the well-known logical reasons to discount so-called cheap talk, these rivalry reputations are crucial for calculating what a state is likely to do in the future.

It is possible that certain psychological biases constitute the microfoundations of a structural theory – that "paranoia" at the level of individual decisionmakers is prudence at the level of the state – but, if so, it is nonetheless important to recognize that the broader international explanation is logically prior to (and formative of) first- and second-image explanations. There are important implications for how one might address the perceptions that drive destabilizing – and potentially unnecessary – policies; recall that dual-sided or balancing interventions have been demonstrated to prolong and exacerbate civil conflicts. As argued, a psychological explanation risks situating solutions solely at the psychological level. With respect to rivalry, for example, one might stress the need to *overcome* psychological biases through the provision of *more* information; decisionmakers might be shown that their thought processes are in error and that a more "objective" assessment of the situation shows no reason to fear or plan for future confrontation with a rival. I am sceptical that such attempts would be successful: consider the US experience vis-à-vis Pakistan over the past several decades. Conversely, if one begins with the recognition that rivals' fears are predicated on largely inescapable consequences of the international environment and the dynamics of their relationship with each other, one might be able to mitigate those fears by addressing their source. (I return to this point in the discussion of policy implications, but the salient point for now is that it matters whether one situates the explanation for rivalry behaviour at one level of analysis over another.) The evidence presented in the case studies suggests that the best way to understand why rivals intervened when and where they did is by thinking about the pressures and imperatives states faced, and by thinking of them as broadly rational actors reacting to situations, not by focusing on the biases produced between the ears of individual leaders and decisionmakers. Rivalry is tragic, not ironic.

Theoretical Implications

The findings of this book should contribute to our understanding of the way in which international factors alter the dynamics of civil conflict. The literature has established that outside interventions often contribute to the length and intensity of violence in civil conflicts. Understanding how and why interventions occur is therefore necessary to address these damaging situations. Much extant work has focused on the characteristics of civil conflicts that invite or trigger intervention, yet it has also been noted that such interventions might occur for reasons "wholly unrelated to the civil war itself" (Balch-Lindsay and Enterline 2000, 620). I have demonstrated that certain third-parties intervene as an extension of international conflict; the circumstances of civil conflicts present challenges and opportunities for international relationships external to the country experiencing civil violence. These countries essentially become theatres for international confrontation and, as the Kikuyu proverb avers, "when elephants fight it is the grass that suffers." The goals and priorities of rival interveners tend towards stalemate as opposed to resolution, as each state is preoccupied with forestalling the interests of the other intervener, rather than advancing the interests of its preferred proxy.

By unpacking and explaining these motivations, I similarly hope to have advanced the study of intervention by offering a causal explanation of an established correlation. Balancing interventions are known to be more likely if one side is supported by a state engaged in rivalry (Findley and Teo 2006). My findings demonstrate how and why this is the case, and I have offered an explanation that links state perceptions in rivalry to a perceived need to offset, or balance, a rival's involvement.

In this way, I have offered an important contribution to the study of rivalry itself. Based on the recognition that conflicts between states are linked over time, rivalry scholars have demonstrated that certain international relationships operate differently than others – repeated conflict alters how states perceive and behave towards one another. From a quantitative point of view, these dyads account for a disproportionate amount of international conflict. Yet theoretical understandings of internal rivalry dynamics – how states engaged in rivalry behave, and what conditions/constraints the relationship places on the states involved – have suffered from imprecision. Psychological and emotional factors have blended with the consequences of strategic interaction. In general, rivalries have been characterized as deviations from conventional, rational decision-making. The literature has emphasized enmity, hatred, and hostility – often by invoking parallels or analogies with fraught interpersonal relationships between individuals. I have argued that rivalry is best understood as a distinctly international phenomenon between states – as in Carl Schmitt's friend/enemy distinction vis-à-vis his "concept of the political." This focus shifts the understanding of rivalry dynamics to the strategic interaction of states as broadly rational actors. Decision-making does indeed deviate from a conventionally rational baseline, but for reasons that are explicable by reference to the ongoing nature of such relationships under conditions of incomplete information and international anarchy. Rivalry approximates what Schelling termed a "continuous negotiation," in which the same two actors expect to confront each other again over time. Behaviour in the present is the product of past interactions and expectations regarding the future.

The arguments and findings I have presented are far from the final word on such considerations. As I have noted, the potential interrelation between the strategic/structural factors I have highlighted and the micro-foundational observations of cognitive psychology deserves further exploration. Nonetheless, I have offered a novel conceptualization of rivalry and expanded the empirical focus of rivalry research by focusing on behaviour other than direct war and conflict. Intuitively, if rivalry is recognized as a condition that obtains over time, it should have implications for state behaviour in the interval between direct crises. I have established that behaviour such as civil conflict intervention is explicable through an application of the rivalry lens. This is important because it folds rivalry into the theoretical explanation itself, rather than treating it merely as an exogenously defined variable or as a case-selection mechanism.

The thrust of my explanation for rivalry intervention involves the perceptions that rivals have of each other. The argument thus abuts debates about the perception of intentions between states more generally. By maintaining the focus on particular domains, I can make no definitive claims, but the findings do suggest a practical approach to unpacking this larger debate. I argue that, just as states have been categorized according to material power, regime type, and so on, so too can they be classified according to their *relationships* with each other. As Arnold Wolfers posited decades ago, dyads exist along a continuum between extreme enmity and extreme amity. When thinking about how states perceive each other's intentions, therefore, it might be useful to incorporate, at a theoretical level, what type of relationship the two states enjoy. Much of the literature on intentions specifies that assessing "adversaries" is particularly important, but it does not fold the implications of *being* adversaries into the analysis in an explicit way. As I have shown, the *condition* of rivalry appears to have independent effects on how states perceive each other's intentions. Instead of making general claims about how states perceive intentions, scholars might consider truncating their arguments to apply to specific types of relationships; such a move, moreover, would be consistent with the overall trend towards mid-level theorizing and away from grand, paradigmatic theory. Intuitively, this would also make sense with regards to relationships that are *not* antagonistic (i.e., closer to extreme amity on Wolfers' continuum). It is clear, for example, that the assessment of intentions operates differently between Canada and the United States than it does between India and Pakistan. There is some potential affinity to dyadic explanations of the democratic peace in this regard, in which expectations and perceptions between democracies operate differently than other types of international relationships.

Finally, the argument and findings of this book should contribute to the debate about the relevance of reputation in international relations. The categories of specific and general reputation are supplemented by the concept of rivalry reputation, which emphasizes the import of past behaviour and experience within an ongoing hostile relationship.

Rivals use past actions to assess the likelihood both of specific tactics and general dispositions and intentions. Even more, states come to see their own reputation as an important interest vis-à-vis a rival, knowing that present behaviour might affect future crises and confrontations. If rivalry is akin to continuous negotiation, this helps to explain Schelling's emphasis on reputation in *Arms and Influence* ([1966] 2008), a book very specifically about US-Soviet relations. Many of his critics (Hopf 1994; Mercer 1996; Press 2005) have argued – incorrectly in my view (Mitton 2015) – that Schelling's treatment of reputation is too broad. Yet as a conceptualization of reputation's relevance under certain conditions, Schelling's logic is consistent with the argument and evidence I have presented in this book. These findings also underscore an argument made elsewhere (Harvey and Mitton 2017), that the treatment of reputation in IR must move beyond a simplistic either/or (either it matters entirely or not at all) towards more nuanced questions of when, how, and why reputation matters in certain contexts and under certain conditions.

Policy Implications

The policy implications of the research findings presented in this book are grim, but important. As the United States and its NATO allies (including Canada) discovered over the course of their experience in Afghanistan, dissuading Pakistan from its support of the Taliban insurgency against the (Indian-supported) Afghan government proved extremely difficult. Massive diplomatic pressure and economic and military aid (and, later, the prospect that such aid could be suspended) failed to convince Islamabad to abandon its policy. This, even though its support for the Taliban seemed to undermine Pakistan's security and preclude significant opportunities for much-needed economic growth. Indeed, the United States and other NATO countries seemed to believe that, if only Islamabad would recognize its own national interests and pursue policy accordingly, it would discontinue an intervention that was playing a major role in exacerbating violence and instability in Afghanistan and the broader region. Implicit in such a belief was the assessment that Pakistan's policy was beholden to interests and priorities – whether of the military-intelligence apparatus or of Islamist elements within the government more generally – that skewed straightforward and broadly rational decision-making. The role of India was recognized, insofar as the Pakistani leadership, particularly in the military, was believed to be unduly "obsessed" with, and "paranoid" about, India's intentions. Again, such a priority was pathological, the product of deep-seated religious and ethnic hatreds, emotional and psychological antagonism stemming from previous military conflicts, and the bureaucratic and political interests of the military elite. American diplomats, following meetings and communications with their Pakistani counterparts, repeatedly expressed frustration and astonishment about the extent of Islamabad's focus on India.

As a consequence of such assessments, US and NATO policy persisted under the assumption that Islamabad had to be *convinced* to abandon its skewed priorities and recognize that its "true" (objective) interests lay in a stable Afghanistan if only its calculus could be adjusted and interfering interests reined in – if the decision-making process could be "uncaptured," as it were.[1] The carrots and sticks (mostly the former) the United States and its allies employed were designed to accomplish this goal. As for the "obsession" with India, some Western policymakers – for example, the late Richard Holbrooke – suggested that a resolution of the Kashmir dispute, the core issue in the India-Pakistan rivalry, might placate Pakistani concerns about Indian involvement in Afghanistan by warming the wider bilateral relationship.

As I have shown, however, Pakistan's decision-making calculus – its perception of its national interest and the means, the policy, by which that interest might be pursued – was less "pathological," less a deviation from the normal or regular, than oriented towards a set of concerns derived from the context of its rivalry with India. Pakistan's decision to intervene in Afghanistan by supporting the Taliban was a consequence of these priorities. This logic was consistent and predictable, not capricious. Rather than needing to be reminded of its own interests, therefore, Pakistan was in fact pursuing them, as far as Islamabad was concerned; Western exhortations to the contrary were always going to fall on deaf ears. As for a potential solution to Kashmir, the theory of rivalry I have developed in this book suggests that whatever the import of such a core conflict for establishing the condition of rivalry, once established the rivalry itself is perpetuated by concern about *future* confrontations. Thus there is no guarantee that, even in the unlikely event of a solution, the rivalry-related perceptions that drove policy in Afghanistan would be dispelled. Rivalry consists of, but is not reducible to, any particular issue or point of contention within it.

---

1 As observed in a 2015 "Lessons Learned" interview with a senior American official involved in the NSC's Strategy and Planning Process on Afghanistan, "[t]he Obama administration just thought if you just hang in there Pakistan will see the light" (quoted in Whitlock 2019).

The takeaway for US/NATO policy is that the *strength* of the Pakistani commitment to undermining Indian interests in Afghanistan was underestimated because the origin and source of that priority were misunderstood. Indian involvement in Afghanistan was always going to draw a response from Islamabad, and the extent to which Pakistan would commit itself to countering that influence was always going to be larger than outside observers (non-rivals) considered proportional. Likewise, India's significant contributions to reconstruction in Afghanistan were predictable, as was the persistence with which it maintained its interests there despite Pakistani pressure to withdraw. The prospects of mitigating Indian-Pakistani competition in Afghanistan consequently were quite low. My findings suggest that committed international rivals link the stakes of a civil conflict in which the enemy is engaged to the broader security competition – the *threat* – that exists at the international level. Commensurate with this perception, rivals accord high priority to protecting their interests in such conflicts.

These findings underscore the extent to which the international community should be aware of and appreciate the dynamics associated with potential rivalry interventions in civil conflicts. In the Afghanistan case, Musharraf's early concerns about the Northern Alliance could have been taken more seriously. Recognizing the pre-existing civil war situation, the United States and its allies might have opted to minimize tensions by remaining relatively neutral as to who would hold power in a post-Taliban era. A more purposeful Pakistani role in this regard, one that went beyond simply being a logistical source, might have been useful given its influence with the Taliban and Pashtuns more generally. It also might have alleviated Pakistani fears about strategic encirclement if India's proxy remained marginal, rather than central, to power structures in Afghanistan.

Particularly if rivalry exists at the regional level between two states in proximity to a civil war – contemporary examples are Syria and Yemen with respect to the Iranian-Saudi rivalry in the Middle East – there is a strong possibility that rivalry competition could be exported to such conflicts and, once operative, significantly exacerbate and prolong the violence. Even if such behaviour might undermine a state's security or economic interests by fostering regional instability, it should not be assumed that leaders will prioritize traditional interests and act accordingly. At the same time, interventions should not be attributed to ethnic or religious hatred or psychological or emotional hostility. Instead, by recognizing the strength of the rivalry-related calculus, predicated on long-term security concerns at the international level, it might be possible to craft policies to help mitigate rivals' perceived threat.

For example, in the early years of the Lebanon crisis (1975–85), the United States was able to function as an intermediary between Israel and Syria, leading to the establishment of a "red line" – essentially a division of the country into separate spheres of influence above and below the Litani River – which tempered violence for several years. Eventually, the agreement unravelled, owing largely to the roiling domestic situation in Lebanon. (One of the inescapable difficulties in dealing with rivalry competition in such settings is that it occurs against the backdrop of an ongoing conflict with its own dynamics.) Yet the tentative lesson is that the violence associated with rivalry interventions might be mitigated by policies that acknowledge and reflect the (rivalry-related) security concerns of the interveners.

Of course, the red-line arrangement took into consideration the specific circumstances of the Lebanese theatre and attendant Syrian and Israeli priorities – specifically, that the territory of Lebanon not become a staging ground for future military attack by the other side. The "division" or articulation of spheres of influence will not necessarily work in other circumstances – although the post-war East-West division of Germany is a somewhat analogous example. Crafting appropriate and effective policy with respect to any future civil conflict will require a deep appreciation of the specific histories and dynamics of the international rivalries in question. I have shown that rivals will pursue intervention vigorously, rather than concede influence to an opponent they anticipate facing in a future war. The key is understanding how powerful this motivation is for states engaged in an ongoing rivalry. Perhaps if American policymakers had analysed Indian and Pakistani involvement in Afghanistan by recalling their own experience from the Cold War – how the United States might have responded to the Soviets in similar circumstances – they might have better weighted the imperatives involved.

References

Abbas, H. 2014. *The Taliban Revival: Violence and Extremism on the Pakistan-Afghanistan Frontier*. New Haven, CT: Yale University Press.

Abraham, A.J. 1996. *The Lebanon War*. Westport, CT: Praeger Publishers.

Ahmed, A., and J. Goldstein. 2015. "Pakistanis try to nudge Taliban along the path to peace talks with Kabul." *New York Times*, 19 February. https://www.nytimes.com/2015/02/19/world/pakistan-tries-to-steer-taliban-along-path-to-peace-talks-in-afghanistan.html.

Ahmed, S. 1999. "Pakistan Nuclear Weapons Program: Turning Points and Nuclear Choices." *International Security* 23 (4): 178–204. https://doi.org/10.1162/isec.23.4.178.

Ahmed, S. 2000. "Security Dilemmas of Nuclear-Armed Pakistan." *Third World Quarterly* 21 (5): 781–93. https://doi.org/10.1080/014365900750011972.

Akcinaroglu, S., and E. Radziszewski. 2005. "Expectations, Rivalries, and Civil War Duration." *International Interactions* 31 (4): 349–74. https://doi.org/10.1080/03050620500303449.

Albright, D. 1987. *Soviet Policy toward Africa Revisited*. Washington, DC: Center for Strategic and International Studies.

Allon, Y. 1976. "Israel: The Case for Defensible Borders." *Foreign Affairs* 55 (1): 38–53. https://doi.org/10.2307/20039626.

Amin, S.M. 2000. *Pakistan's Foreign Policy: A Reappraisal*. Oxford: Oxford University Press.

Arnold, A. 2017. "Kabul bombing: Afghans blame Haqqani network and Pakistan." *Sky News*, 31 May. https://news.sky.com/story/kabul-bombing-afghans-blame-haqqani-network-and-pakistan-10900078.

Asian Times. 2001. "India seeks larger role." 28 November. http://www.atimes.com/ind-pak/CK28Df03.html.

Aubone, A. 2013. "Explaining US Unilateral Military Intervention in Civil Conflicts: A Review of the Literature." *International Politics* 50 (2): 278–302. https://doi.org/10.1057/ip.2013.1.

Avi-Ran, R. 1991. *The Syrian Involvement in Lebanon Since 1975*. Boulder, CO: Westview Press.

Aydin, A. 2010. "Where Do States Go? Strategy in Civil War Intervention." *Conflict Management and Peace Science* 27 (1): 47–66. https://doi.org/10.1177/0738894209352128.

Aydin, A., and P.M. Regan. 2012. "Networks of Third-Party Interveners and Civil War Duration." *European Journal of International Relations* 18 (3): 573–97. https://doi.org/10.1177/1354066111403515.

Azam, A. 2014. "Misgivings by US general as Afghan mission ends." *New York Times*, 9 December.

Bagchi, I. 2013a. "US-Taliban peace talks: Pakistan's political fortunes set to revive, India concerned." *Times of India*, 21 June. Online at https://timesofindia.indiatimes.com/india/US-Taliban-peace-talks-Pakistans-political-fortunes-set-to-revive-India-concerned/articleshow/20686702.cms.

Bagchi, I. 2013b. "Afghan peace talks: India voices concern." *Times of India*, 22 June. https://timesofindia.indiatimes.com/india/Afghan-peace-talks-India-voices-concern/articleshow/20704621.cms.

Bajpai, K. 1995. *Brasstacks and Beyond: Perception and Management of Crisis in South Asia*. New Delhi: Manohar.

Balch-Lindsay, D., and A.J. Enterline. 2000. "Killing Time: The World Politics of Civil War Duration, 1820–1992." *International Studies Quarterly* 44 (4): 615–42. https://doi.org/10.1111/0020-8833.00174.

Balch-Lindsay, D., A.J. Enterline, and K.A. Joyce. 2008. "Third-Party Intervention and the Civil War Process." *Journal of Peace Research* 45 (3): 345–63. https://doi.org/10.1177/0022343308088815.

Ball, S.J. 1998. *The Cold War: An International History, 1947–1991*. London: Arnold Publishers.

Basit, A. 2015. "Pakistan's Inextricable Role in Afghanistan's Future." In *Afghanistan After the Western Drawdown*, edited by R. Gunaratna and D. Woodall, 13–34. Lanham, MD: Rowman & Littlefield.

Basu, N. 2022. "Turkmenistan, Afghanistan push TAPI gas pipeline again but this is why India is being cautious." *Print*, 7 February. https://theprint.in/diplomacy/turkmenistan-afghanistan-push-tapi-gas-pipeline-again-but-this-is-why-india-is-being-cautious/823185/.

Basu, N., and R. Mishra. 2018. "India begins to get active on TAPI gas pipeline." *Business Line*, 23 January. https://www.thehindubusinessline.com/economy/policy/india-begins-to-get-active-on-tapi-gas-pipeline/article10048557.ece.

BBC News. 2006. "US 'threatened to bomb' Pakistan." 22 September. http://news.bbc.co.uk/2/hi/south_asia/5369198.stm.

BBC News. 2012. "Taliban strike across Afghanistan in 'spring offensive.'" 16 April. https://www.bbc.co.uk/news/world-asia-17719956.

Beach, D., and R.B. Pedersen. 2013. *Process-Tracing Methods: Foundations and Guidelines*. Ann Arbor: University of Michigan Press.

Bedi, R. 2001. "India joins anti-Taliban coalition." *Jane's 360*, 15 March. http://www.prop1.org/protest/2002/dick%20ochs/janes010315_1_n.shtml.

Behuria, A. 2007. "Fighting the Taliban: Pakistan at War with Itself." *Australian Journal of International Affairs* 61 (4): 529–43. https://doi.org/10.1080/10357710701684963.

Ben-Yehuda, H., and S. Sandler. 2002. *The Arab-Israeli Conflict Transformed: Fifty Years of Interstate and Ethnic Crises*. Albany: State University of New York Press.

Berntsen, G., and R. Pezzulo. 2005. *Jawbreaker: The Attack on Bin Laden and Al-Qaeda*. New York: Crown Publishers.

Bhatnagar, A., and C.R. Mohan. 2016. "India-Pakistan Relations and Regional Stability." In *Mapping Pakistan's Internal Dynamics: Implications for State Stability and Regional Security*. NBR Special Report 55. Seattle: National Bureau of Asian Research.

Bird, T., and A. Marshall. 2011. *Afghanistan: How the West Lost Its Way*. New Haven, CT: Yale University Press.

Boone, J. 2015. "Musharraf: Pakistan and India's backing for 'proxies' in Afghanistan must stop." *Guardian*, 13 February. https://www.theguardian.com/world/2015/feb/13/pervez-musharraf-pakistan-india-proxies-afghanistan-ghani-taliban

Brand, L.A. 1990. "Asad's Syria and the PLO: Coincidence or Conflict of Interests?" *Journal of South Asian and Middle Eastern Studies* 14 (2): 22–44.

Bregman, A. 2016. *Israel's Wars: A History since 1947*, 4th ed. New York: Routledge.

Burke, J. 2010. "Pakistan intelligence services aided Mumbai terror attacks." *Guardian*, 18 October. https://www.theguardian.com/world/2010/oct/18/pakistan-isi-mumbai-terror-attacks.

Business Standard. 2018. "India reiterates commitment to help in rebuilding stable Afghanistan." 27 March. http://www.business-standard.com/article/news-ians/india-reiterates-commitment-to-help-in-rebuilding-stable-afghanistan-118032701180_1.html.

Carment, D. and P. James. 1995. "Internal Constraints and Interstate Ethnic Conflict: Towards a Crisis-Based Assessment of Irredentism." *Journal of Conflict Resolution* 39 (1): 82–109. https://doi.org/10.1177/0022002795039001004.

Carment, D., and P. James. 1996. "Two-Level Games and Third-Party Intervention: Evidence from Ethnic Conflict in the Balkans and South Asia." *Canadian Journal of Political Science* 29 (3): 521–54. https://doi.org/10.1017/s0008423900008222.

Carment, D., P. James, and T. Zeynep. 2006. *Who Intervenes? Ethnic Conflict and Interstate Crisis*. Columbus: Ohio State University Press.

Carr, E.H. 1961. *What Is History?* Cambridge: Cambridge University Press.

Cheema, Z.I. 1996. "Pakistan's Nuclear Policies: Attitudes and Postures." In *Nuclear Non-Proliferation in India and Pakistan: South Asian Perspectives*, edited by P.R. Chari, P.I. Cheema, and Iftekharuzzaman. New Delhi: Monohar.

Chellaney, B. 2001/2. "Fighting Terrorism in Southern Asia: The Lessons of History." *International Security* 26 (3): 94–116. https://doi.org/10.1162/016228801753399736.

CIA (Central Intelligence Agency). 1972. "Soviet Foreign Policies and the Outlook for Soviet-American Relations." NIE–72. Langley, VA: Central Intelligence Agency Archives. https://www.cia.gov/library/center-for-the-study-of-intelligence/csi-publications/books-and-monographs/cias-analysis-of-the-soviet-union-1947-1991/nie_11_72.pdf.

CIA. 1976. "Soviet Military Policy in the Third World." NIE 11–10–76. Langley, VA: Central Intelligence Agency Archives. https://www.cia.gov/library/readingroom/docs/DOC_0000273313.pdf.

Clary, C. 2017. "Trump singled out India to do more in Afghanistan. That could easily backfire." *Washington Post*, 24 August. https://www.washingtonpost.com/news/monkey-cage/wp/2017/08/29/trump-singled-out-india-to-do-more-in-afghanistan-that-could-easily-backfire/?utm_term=.2338f7b8afef.

CNN. 2003. "Rumsfeld: Major combat over in Afghanistan." 1 May. http://www.cnn.com/2003/WORLD/asiapcf/central/05/01/afghan.combat/.

Cohen S. 2003. "India, Pakistan and Kashmir." In *India as an Emerging Power*, edited by S. Ganguly, 32–60. New York: Routledge.

Colaresi, M.P., K. Rasler, and W. Thompson. 2008. *Strategic Rivalries in World Politics: Position, Space and Conflict Escalation.* New York: Cambridge University Press.

Coll, S. 2018. *Directorate S: The CIA and America's Secret Wars in Afghanistan and Pakistan.* New York: Penguin Press.

Collier, P., A. Hoeffler, and M. Söderbom. 2004. "On the Duration of Civil War." *Journal of Peace Research* 41 (3): 253–73. https://doi.org/10.1177/0022343304043769.

Collingwood, R.G. [1936] 2005. *The Idea of History.* Oxford: Oxford University Press.

Constable, P. 2018. "Afghan president Ghani tells country that Pakistan was behind recent deadly attacks." *Washington Post*, 2 February. https://www.washingtonpost.com/world/afghan-president-ghani-tells-country-that-pakistan-was-behind-recent-deadly-attacks/2018/02/02/abcf4cda-082a-11e8-aa61-f3391373867e_story.html.

Council on Foreign Relations. 2006. "Pervez Musharraf." 25 September. https://www.cfr.org/event/pervez-musharraf.

Council on Foreign Relations. 2017. "A Conversation with Shahid Khaqan Abbasi." 20 September. https://www.cfr.org/event/conversation-shahid-khaqan-abbasi.

Crawford, N., S. Fiederlein, and S. Rzegocki. 2021. *Afghan Civilians*. Providence, RI: Watson Institute of International & Public Affairs. https://watson.brown .edu/costsofwar/costs/human/civilians/afghan.

Crescenzi, M. 2018. *Of Friends and Foes: Reputation and Learning in International Politics*. New York: Oxford University Press.

Cunningham, D.E. 2006. "Veto Players and Civil War Duration. *American Journal of Political Science* 50 (4): 875–92. https://doi.org/10.1111/j.1540 -5907.2006.00221.x.

Cunningham, D.E. 2010. "Blocking Resolution: How External States Can Prolong Civil War." *Journal of Peace Research* 47 (2): 115–27. https://doi .org/10.1177/0022343309353488.

Curtis, L. 2012. "The Reorientation of Pakistan's Foreign Policy toward Its Region." *Contemporary South Asia* 20 (2): 255–69. https://doi.org/10.1080 /09584935.2012.670205.

Dalrymple, W. 2013. *A Deadly Triangle: Afghanistan, Pakistan, and India*. Washington, DC: Brookings Institution.

Darnton, C. 2014. *Rivalry and Alliance Politics in Cold War Latin America*. Baltimore, MD: Johns Hopkins University Press.

Davis, N. 1978. "The Angola Decision of 1975: A Personal Memoir." *Foreign Affairs* 57 (1): 109–24. https://doi.org/10.2307/20040055.

Davis, Z. 2011. "Introduction." In *The India-Pakistan Military Standoff: Crisis Escalation in South Asia*, edited by Z. Davis, 1–16. New York: Palgrave Macmillan.

Dawisha, A. 1980. *Syria and the Lebanese Crisis*. New York: St Martin's Press.

Deeb, M. 1980. *The Lebanese Civil War*. New York: Praeger.

DiCicco, J. 2011. "Fear, Loathing, and Cracks in Reagan's Mirror Images: Able Archer 83 and an American First Step toward Rapprochement in the Cold War." *Foreign Policy Analysis* 7 (3): 253–74. https://doi.org/10.1111/j.1743 -8594.2011.00137.x.

Diehl, P. 1998. "Introduction: An Overview and Some Theoretical Guidelines." In *The Dynamics of Enduring Rivalries*, edited by P. Diehl. Urbana: University of Illinois Press.

Dixit, J.N. 2002. *India-Pakistan in War and Peace*. New York: Routledge.

Dobbins, J. 2008. *After the Taliban: Nation-Building in Afghanistan*. Washington, DC: Potomac Books.

Doyle, M.W., and N. Sambanis. 2000. "International Peacebuilding: A Theoretical and Quantitative Analysis." *American Political Science Review* 94 (4): 779–801. https://doi.org/10.2307/2586208.

Doyle, M.W., and N. Sambanis. 2006. *Making War and Building Peace: United Nations Peace Operations*. Princeton, NJ: Princeton University Press.

Dreyer, D.R. 2014. "Unifying Conceptualizations of Interstate Rivalry: A Min-Max Approach." *Cooperation and Conflict* 49 (4): 501–18. https://doi .org/10.1177/0010836713519980.

D'Souza, S.M. 2007. "India's Aid to Afghanistan: Challenges and Prospects." *Strategic Analysis* 31 (5): 833–42. https://doi.org/10.1080/09700160701662328.

D'Souza, S.M. 2014. "India, Afghanistan and the 'End Game'?" In *India's Grand Strategy: History, Theory, Cases*, edited by K. Bajpai, S. Basit, and V. Krishnappa, 376–411). London: Routledge.

Dunér, B. 1983. "The Many-Pronged Spear: External Military Intervention in Civil Wars in the 1970s." *Journal of Peace Research* 20 (1): 59–72. https://doi.org/10.1177/002234338302000106.

Dunér, B. 1985. *Military Intervention in Civil Wars: The 1970s*. New York: Palgrave Macmillan.

Dupuy, T.N. 1978. *Elusive Victory: The Arab-Israeli Wars, 1947–1974*. New York: Harper and Row.

Ebinger, C. 1984. *Foreign Intervention in Civil War: The Politics and Diplomacy of the Angolan Conflict*. Boulder, CO: Westview Press.

Economic Times. 2021. "Afghan territory must not be used for terrorism: Delhi dialogue on Afghanistan crisis." 11 November. https://economictimes.indiatimes.com/news/defence/afghan-territory-must-not-be-used-for-terrorism-delhi-dialogue-on-afghanistan-crisis/articleshow/87625831.cms.

Edelstein, D.M. 2002. "Managing Uncertainty: Beliefs about Intentions and the Rise of Great Powers." *Security Studies* 12 (1): 1–40. https://doi.org/10.1080/0963-640291906735.

Elbadawi, I., and N. Sambanis. 2002. "How Much Civil War Will We See? Explaining the Prevalence of Civil War." *Journal of Conflict Resolution* 46 (3): 307–34. https://doi.org/10.1177/0022002702046003001

Elias, B., ed. 2007a. "Document 17." National Security Archive Electronic Briefing Book 227. 14 August. https://nsarchive2.gwu.edu/NSAEBB/NSAEBB227/17.pdf.

Elias, B., ed. 2007b. "Pakistan: 'The Taliban's Godfather'?" National Security Archive Electronic Briefing Book 227. 14 August. https://nsarchive2.gwu.edu//NSAEBB/NSAEBB227/index.htm.

Evron, Y. 2013. *War and Intervention in Lebanon: The Israeli-Syrian Deterrence Dialogue*. New York: Routledge.

Express Tribune. 2017. "Afghanistan no longer depends on Pakistan for transit trade: Abdullah Abdullah." 16 November. https://tribune.com.pk/story/1560010/3-afghanistan-no-longer-depends-pakistan-transit-trade-abdullah-abdullah/.

Faiez, M.K., and M. Magnier. 2009. "Taliban claims responsibility for Kabul embassy attack." *Los Angeles Times,* 9 October. http://articles.latimes.com/2009/oct/09/world/fg-afghanistan-bomb.

Fair, C. 2004. *The Counterterror Coalitions: Cooperation with Pakistan and India*. Santa Monica, CA: RAND.

Fair, C. 2008. "Pakistan's Relations with Central Asia: Is Past Prologue?" *Journal of Strategic Studies* 31 (2): 201–27. https://doi.org/10.1080/01402390801940344.

Fair, C. 2010. *India in Afghanistan and Beyond: Opportunities and Constraints*. New York: Century Foundation.

Fair, C. 2011. "Under the Shrinking US Security Umbrella: India's End Game in Afghanistan." *Washington Quarterly* 34 (2): 179–92. https://doi.org /10.1080/0163660x.2011.562461.

Fair, C. 2012. "The US-Pakistan Relations after a Decade of the War on Terror." *Contemporary South Asia* 20 (2): 243–53. https://doi.org/10.1080/09584935.2 012.670204.

Fair, C. 2014. *Fighting to the End: The Pakistan Army's Way of War*. New York: Oxford University Press.

Fair, C. 2017. "Pakistan's Deadly Grip on Afghanistan." *Current History* 116 (789): 136–41. https://doi.org/10.1525/curh.2017.116.789.136.

Fair, C., and S. Jones. 2009. "Pakistan's War Within." *Survival* 51 (6): 161–88. https://doi.org/10.1080/00396330903465204.

Fearon, J.D. 1997. "Signaling Foreign Policy Interests: Tying Hands versus Sinking Costs." *Journal of Conflict Resolution* 41 (1): 68–90. https://doi.org /10.1177%2F0022002797041001004.

Fearon, J.D. 2007. "Fighting rather than Bargaining." In *Annual Meetings of the American Political Science Association* 4.

Felbab-Brown, V. 2016. "Pakistan's Relations with Afghanistan and Implications for Regional Politics." In *Mapping Pakistan's Internal Dynamics: Implications for State Stability and Regional Security*, 123–40. Seattle: National Bureau of Asian Research.

Felbab-Brown, V. 2018. "Order from chaos: Why Pakistan supports terrorist groups, and why the US finds it so hard to induce change." Washington, DC: Brookings Institution. https://www.brookings.edu/blog/order-from -chaos/2018/01/05/why-pakistan-supports-terrorist-groups-and-why-the -us-finds-it-so-hard-to-induce-change/.

Filkins, D. 2008. "Right at the edge." *New York Times*, 7 September.

Filkins, D. 2010. "Pakistanis tell of motive in Taliban leader's arrest." *New York Times*, 22 August. https://www.nytimes.com/2010/08/23/world/asia/23taliban.html.

Findley, M.G., and T.K. Teo. 2006. "Rethinking Third-Party Interventions into Civil Wars: An Actor-Centric Approach." *Journal of Politics* 68 (4): 828–37. https://doi.org/10.1111/j.1468-2508.2006.00473.x.

Florea, A. 2012. "Where Do We Go from Here? Conceptual, Theoretical, and Methodological Gaps in the Large-N Civil War Research Program." *International Studies Review* 14 (1): 78–98. https://doi.org/10.1111/j.1468-2486.2012.01102.x.

Fordham, B.O. 2008. "Power or Plenty? Economic Interests, Security Concerns, and American Intervention." *International Studies Quarterly* 52 (4): 737–58. https://doi.org/10.1111/j.1468-2478.2008.00524.x.

Fortna, V.P. 2004. "Does Peacekeeping Keep Peace? International Intervention and the Duration of Peace after Civil War." *International Studies Quarterly* 48 (2): 269–92. https://doi.org/10.1111/j.0020-8833.2004.00301.x.

Frantz, D. 2001. "A nation challenged: Supplying the Taliban." *New York Times*, 8 December. https://www.nytimes.com/2001/12/08/world/nation -challenged-supplying-taliban-pakistan-ended-aid-taliban-only-hesitantly.html.

Fuhrmann, M., and T.S. Sechser. 2014. "Signaling Alliance Commitments: Hand-Tying and Sunk Costs in Extended Nuclear Deterrence." *American Journal of Political Science* 58 (4): 919–35. http://www.jstor.org/stable /24363534.

Gabriel, R.A. 1984. *Operation Peace for Galilee: The Israeli-PLO War in Lebanon.* New York: Farrar, Straus and Giroux.

Gaddis, J.L. 2005. *The Cold War.* New York: Penguin Books.

Gall, C. 2006. "Musharraf vows to aid Afghanistan in fighting Taliban." *New York Times*, 7 September.

Gall, C. 2014. *The Wrong Enemy: American in Afghanistan 2001–2014.* New York: Houghton Mifflin Harcourt.

Ganguly, S. 1999. "India: Policies, Past and Future." In *India and Pakistan: The First Fifty Years*, edited by S. Harrison, P. Kreisberg, and D. Kux. Washington, DC: Woodrow Wilson Center Press.

Ganguly, S. 2001. *Conflict Unending: India-Pakistan Tensions since 1947.* New York: Columbia University Press.

Ganguly, S., and N. Howenstein. 2009. "India-Pakistan Rivalry in Afghanistan." *Journal of International Affairs* 63 (1): 127–40.

Ganguly, S., and P. Kapur. 2009. "The Sorcerer's Apprentice: Islamist Militancy in South Asia." *Washington Quarterly* 33 (1): 47–59. https://doi.org/10.1080 /01636600903418686.

Ganguly, S., and P. Kapur. 2010. *India, Pakistan and the Bomb: Debating Nuclear Stability in South Asia.* New York: Columbia University Press.

Garthoff, R. 1977. "Negotiating SALT." *Wilson Quarterly* 1 (5): 76–85.

Garthoff, R. 1994. *Détente and Confrontation: American-Soviet Relations from Nixon to Reagan*, rev. ed. Washington, DC: Brookings Institution Press.

Garthoff, R. 2015. *Soviet Leaders and Intelligence: Assessing the American Adversary during the Cold War.* Washington, DC: Georgetown University Press.

Geller, D.S. 2005. "The India-Pakistan rivalry: Prospects for War, Prospects for Peace." In *The India-Pakistan Conflict: An Enduring Rivalry*, edited by T.V. Paul, 80–102. New York: Cambridge University Press.

Gent, S.E. 2007. "Strange Bedfellows: The Strategic Dynamics of Major Power Military Interventions." *Journal of Politics* 69 (4): 1089–102. https://doi .org/10.1111/j.1468-2508.2007.00609.x.

Gent, S.E. 2010. "External Threats and Military Intervention: The United States and the Caribbean Basin." *Peace Economics, Peace Science, & Public Policy* 16 (1): 1–31. https://doi.org/10.2202/1554-8597.1195.

George, A., and A. Bennett. 2005. *Case Studies and Theory Development in the Social Sciences.* Cambridge, MA: MIT Press.

George, E. 2005. *The Cuban Intervention in Angola, 1965–1991*. New York: Frank Cass.

Gerges, F.A. 1993. "The Lebanese Crisis of 1958: The Risks of Inflated Self-Importance." *Beirut Review* 5: 83–113.

Ghanizada. 2013. "Attack on major water dam foiled in Herat province of Afghanistan." *Kharma Press*, 31 March. https://www.khaama.com/attack-on-major-water-dam-foiled-in-herat-province-of-afghanistan-1528/.

Glaser, C.L. 2010. *Rational Theory of International Politics: The Logic of Cooperation and Competition*. Princeton, NJ: Princeton University Press.

Gleditsch, N.P., E. Melander, H. Urdal, and T.D. Mason. 2016. "Introduction: Patterns of Armed Conflict since 1945." In *What Do We Know about Civil War*, edited by T.D. Mason and M.S. McLaughlin, 15–32. Lanham, MD: Rowman & Littlefield.

Gleditsch, K.S., I. Salehyan, and K. Schultz. 2008. "Fighting at Home, Fighting Abroad: How Civil Wars Lead to International Disputes." *Journal of Conflict Resolution* 52 (4): 479–506. https://doi.org/10.1177/0022002707313305.

Goertz, G., and P. Diehl. 1995) "The Initiation and Termination of Enduring Rivalries: The Impact of Political Shocks." *American Journal of Political Science* 39 (1): 30–52. https://doi.org/10.2307/2111756.

Goertz, G., and P. Diehl. 2001. *War and Peace in International Rivalry*. Ann Arbor: University of Michigan Press.

Goertz, G., P. Diehl, and D. Saeedi. 2005. "Theoretical Specifications of Enduring Rivalries: Applications to the India-Pakistan Case." In *The India-Pakistan Conflict: An Enduring Rivalry*, edited by T.V. Paul, 27–54. New York: Cambridge University Press, 2005.

Gonzalez, E. 1980. "Cuba, the Soviet Union, and Africa." In *Communism in Africa*, edited by D. Albright. Bloomington: Indiana University Press.

Grare, F. 2010. "Pakistan." In *Is a Regional Strategy Viable in Afghanistan?* edited by A. Tellis and A. Mukharji , 17–26. Washington, DC: Carnegie Endowment for International Peace.

Grove, A.K. 2007. *Political Leadership in Foreign Policy: Manipulating Support across Borders*. New York: Palgrave Macmillan.

Guardian. 2006. "The Afghan interim government: who's who." 6 December. https://www.theguardian.com/world/2001/dec/06/afghanistan1.

Guardian. 2010. "Afghanistan war logs: Pakistan allegedly offering money for money for assassination of Indian road workers." 25 July. https://www.theguardian.com/world/afghanistan/warlogs/7BE93069-2219-0B3F-9FC8ADDCFCCA9F38.

Guimaraes, F.A. 2001. *The Origins of the Angolan Civil War: Foreign Intervention and Domestic Political Conflict*. New York: Palgrave Macmillan.

Giustozzi, A. 2007. "War and Peace Economies of Afghanistan's Strongmen." *International Peacekeeping* 14 (1): 75–89. https://doi.org/10.1080/13533310601114285.

Gulick, E.V. 1955. *Europe's Classical Balance of Power: A Case History of the Theory and Practice of One of the Great Concepts of European Statecraft*. Ithaca, NY: Cornell University Press.

Gurr, T., and R. Duvall. 1973. "Civil Conflict in the 1960s: A Reciprocal Theoretical System with Parameter Estimates." *Comparative Political Studies* 6 (2): 135–69. https://doi.org/10.1177/001041407300600201.

Gurt, M. 2018. "Leaders launch start of Afghan section of TAPI gas pipeline." *Reuters*, 23 February. https://www.reuters.com/article/us-turkmenistan-afghanistan-gas-pipeline/leaders-launch-start-of-afghan-section-of-tapi-gas-pipeline-idUSKCN1G70PU.

Haidar, S. 2017. "India turns down Pak offer of talks on transit trade to Afghanistan." *Hindu*, 28 October. http://www.thehindu.com/news/national/india-turns-down-pak-offer-of-talks-on-transit-trade-to-afghanistan/article19941006.ece.

Hanauer, L., and P. Chalk. 2012. *India's and Pakistan's Strategies in Afghanistan: Implications for the United States and the Region*. Santa Monica, CA: RAND Corporation, Center for Asia Pacific Policy. https://www.rand.org/content/dam/rand/pubs/occasional_papers/2012/RAND_OP387.pdf.

Hanif, M. 2009. "Indian Involvement in Afghanistan: Stepping Stone or Stumbling Block to Regional Hegemony?" GIGA Working Papers 68. Hamburg: German Institute of Global and Area Studies. https://core.ac.uk/download/pdf/6862936.pdf.

Harding, L. 2001. "Musharraf shocked by 'occupation.'" *Guardian*, 14 November. https://www.theguardian.com/world/2001/nov/14/pakistan.afghanistan1.

Harrison, S.S. 2006. "Is Pakistan friend or foe?" *Los Angeles Times*, 5 September. http://articles.latimes.com/2006/sep/05/opinion/oe-harrison5.

Harvey, F.P. 1995. "Deterrence Theory Revisited: A Progress Report." *Canadian Journal of Political Science* 28 (3): 403–36. https://doi.org/10.1017/s0008423900006673.

Harvey, F.P., and J. Mitton. 2017. *Fighting for Credibility: US Reputation and International Politics*. Toronto: University of Toronto Press.

Heger, L., and I. Salehyan. 2007. "Ruthless Rulers: Coalition Size and the Severity of Civil Conflict." *International Studies Quarterly* 51 (2): 385–403. https://doi.org/10.1111/j.1468-2478.2007.00456.x.

Hemmer, C. 2015. *American Pendulum: Recurring Debates in US Grand Strategy*. Ithaca, NY: Cornell University Press.

Hersh, S.M. 2002. "The Getaway." *New Yorker*. January. https://www.newyorker.com/magazine/2002/01/28/the-getaway-2.

Hindu. 2009. "India hands over strategic highway to Afghanistan." 23 January. https://www.thehindu.com/todays-paper/India-hands-over-strategic-highway-to-Afghanistan/article16358624.ece.

Hindustan Times. 2010. "Indians in Afghanistan are soft targets: Krishna."
Hindustan Times. 21 March. http://www.hindustantimes.com/india-news
/indians-in-afghanistan-are-soft-targets-krishna/article1-521567.aspx.

Hindustan Times. 2015. "Modi inaugurates new Afghan parliament built by
India in Kabul." 25 December. https://www.hindustantimes.com/india
/modi-in-kabul-pm-meets-ghani-to-in%ADaugurate-afghan-s-parl
-building/story-wua2CtN8gj4IQsRnmNknHM.html.

Hindustan Times. 2017. "No Indian troops in Afghanistan: Sitharaman after
talks with US defence secretary." 26 September. https://www
.hindustantimes.com/india-news/no-indian-troops-will-be-deployed
-in-afghanistan-says-defence-minister-nirmala-sitharaman/story
-JfYy5AzBKMFsDlwgTPW1GN.html.

Hironaka, A. 2005. *Neverending Wars: The International Community, Weak States,
and the Perpetuation of Civil War.* Cambridge, MA: Harvard University Press.

History Commons. n.d. "Context of 'September 19, 2001: Pakistani President
Musharraf tells his country he still supports the Taliban, refuses to condemn
al-Qaeda.'" http://www.historycommons.org/context.jsp?item=
a091901urduspeech.

Hopf, T. 1994. *Peripheral Visions: Deterrence Theory and American Foreign Policy
in the Third World, 1965–1990.* Ann Arbor: Michigan University Press.

Hopf, T. 2010. "The Logic of Habit in International Relations." *European Journal of
International Relations* 16 (4): 539–61. https://doi.org/10.1177/1354066110363502.

Hudson, M.C. 1978. "The Palestinian Factor in the Lebanese Civil War." *Middle
East Journal* 32: 261–78.

Hussain, R. 2005. *Pakistan and the Emergence of Islamic Militancy in Afghanistan.*
Burlington, VT: Ashgate Publishing.

Huth, P.K. 1996. "Enduring Rivalries and Territorial Disputes, 1950–1990."
Conflict Management and Peace Science 15 (1): 7–41. https://doi.org
/10.1177%2F073889429601500102.[BN17]

Huth, P.K. 1997. "Reputations and Deterrence: A Theoretical and Empirical
Assessment." *Security Studies* 7 (1): 72–99. https://doi.org/10.1080
/09636419708429334.

iCasualties.org. n.d. "Operation Enduring Freedom." http://icasualties.org
/OEF/ByYear.aspx

Ilan, A. 1996. *The Origin of the Arab-Israeli Arms Race.* London: Macmillan.

India. 2001. "Lok Sabha, Unstarred Question No. 1686 28/11/2001." New
Delhi. http://164.100.47.194/Loksabha/Questions/QResult15.aspx?
qref=33384&lsno=13.

India. 2002. Ministry of External Affairs. "Statement on areas of cooperation
between India and Afghanistan on reconstruction and rehabilitation in post
conflict Afghanistan." New Delhi, 27 February. http://www.mea.gov.in
/Speeches-Statements.htm?dtl/5767/Statement_on_Areas_of_Cooperation_

between_India_and_Afghanistan_on_Reconstruction_and_Rehabilitation
_in_post_conflict_Afghanistan.

India. 2009. Ministry of External Affairs. *India and Afghanistan: A Development Partnership*. New Delhi. https://www.mea.gov.in/Uploads /PublicationDocs/176_india-and-afghanistan-a-development-partnership.pdf.

India. 2011a. Ministry of External Affairs. "Address by EAM at International Afghanistan Conference in Bonn. 5 December. http://www.mea.gov.in /Speeches-Statements.htm?dtl/13912/Address_by_EAM_at_International _Afghanistan_Conference_in_Bonn.

India. 2011b. Ministry of External Affairs. "PM's Statement prior to His Departure for Afghanistan." New Delhi, 11 May. http://www.mea.gov.in /Speeches-Statements.htm?dtl/358/PMs_statement_prior_to_his _departure_for_Afghanistan.

India. 2012. Ministry of External Affairs. "Opening Remarks by External Affairs Minister at the Joint Media Interaction during the Visit of Foreign Minister of Afghanistan." 1 May. http://mea.gov.in/incoming-visit-detail .htm?19679/Opening+Remarks+by+External+Affairs+Minister+at+the+Joint+ Media+Interaction+during+the+visit+of+Foreign+Minister+of+Afghanistan.

India. 2015. Ministry of External Affairs. "India-Afghanistan Relations." New Delhi, 15 June. http://www.mea.gov.in/Portal/ForeignRelation /Afghanistan_2015_07_20.pdf.

India. 2018. Ministry of External Affairs. "Foreign Secretary's Visit to Afghanistan." New Delhi, 28 February. http://www.mea.gov.in/press -releases.htm?dtl/29523/Foreign_Secretarys_visit_to_Afghanistan.

Indus Water Treaty. 1960. https://siteresources.worldbank.org/INTSOUTHASIA /Resources/223497-1105737253588/IndusWatersTreaty1960.pdf.

Iqbal, K., and S. De Silva. 2013. "Terrorist Lifecycles: A Case Study of Tehrik-e-Taliban Pakistan." *Journal of Policing, Intelligence and Counter Terrorism* 8 (1): 72–86. https://doi.org/10.1080/18335330.2013.789599.

Israel. 1975. Ministry of Foreign Affairs. "60 Israel's complaints to the United Nations on continued attacks from Lebanon – 19 and 22 January 1975." http://www.mfa.gov.il/MFA/ForeignPolicy/MFADocuments/Yearbook2 /Pages/60%20Israel-s%20complaints%20to%20the%20United%20 Nations%20on%20co.aspx.

Jackson, P.T. 2011. *The Conduct of Inquiry in International Relations: Philosophy of Science and its Implications for the Study of World Politics*. New York: Routledge.

Jackson, V. 2016. *Rival Reputations: Coercion and Credibility in US-North Korea Relations*. New York: Cambridge University Press.

Jaspal, Z. 2011. "Understanding the Political-Military Context of the 2002 Military Standoff: A Pakistani Perspective." In *The India-Pakistan Military Standoff: Crisis Escalation in South Asia*, edited by Z. Davis, 53–65. New York: Palgrave Macmillan.

Jervis, R. 1976. *Perception and Misperception in International Politics*. Princeton, NJ: Princeton University Press.

Jervis, R. 1978. "Cooperation under the Security Dilemma." *World Politics 30* (2): 167–214. https://doi.org/10.2307/2009958.

Jervis, R. 2002. "Signaling and Perception: Drawing Inferences and Projecting Images." In *Political Psychology*, edited by K.R. Monroe, 293–312. New York: Psychology Press.

Johnson, T., and C. Mason. 2008. "No Sign until the Burst of Fire: Understanding the Pakistan-Afghanistan Frontier." *International Security* 32 (4): 41–77. https://doi.org/10.1162/isec.2008.32.4.41.

Jones, S.G. 2008. "The Rise of Afghanistan's Insurgency." *International Security* 32 (4): 7–40. https://doi.org/10.1162/isec.2008.32.4.7.

Jones, S.G. 2010. *In the Graveyard of Empires: America's War in Afghanistan*. New York: W.W. Norton.

Jorum, E.L. 2014. *Beyond Syria's Borders: A History of Territorial Disputes in the Middle East*. New York: I.B. Tauris.

Joshi, S. 2010. "India's Af-Pak Strategy." *RUSI Journal* 155 (1): 20–9. https://doi.org/10.1080/03071841003683393.

Kagan, F.W. 2012. "A Case for Staying the Course." In *Afghan Endgames: Strategy and Policy Choices for American's Longest War*, edited by H. Rothstein and J. Arquilla, 97–114. Washington, DC: Georgetown University Press.

Kapur, P. 2011. "Peace and Conflict in the Indo-Pakistani Rivalry: Domestic and Strategic Causes." In *Asian Rivalries: Conflict, Escalation, and Limitations on Two-level Games*, edited by S. Ganguly and W. Thompson, 61–78. Stanford, CA: Stanford University Press.

Karnad, B. 2009. "Habit of Free-riding." *India Seminar*. http://www.india-seminar.com/2009/599/599_bharat_karnad.htm.

Karsh, E. 1991. *Soviet Policy towards Syria since 1970*. New York: Palgrave Macmillan.

Karsh, E. 1997. *Fabricating Israel's History: The New Historians*. London: Frank Cass.

Kathman, J.D. 2011. "Civil War Diffusion and Regional Motivations for Intervention." *Journal of Conflict Resolution* 55 (6): 847–76. https://doi.org/10.1177/0022002711408009.

Kearns Jr., D.W. 2015. *Great Power Security Cooperation: Arms Control and the Challenge of Technological Change*. Lanham, MD: Lexington Books.

Kehtran, M.S. 2017. "Indian Interference in Balochistan: Analysing Evidence and Implications for Pakistan." *Strategic Studies* (Institute of Strategic Studies Islamabad) 37 (3): 112–25.

Kennan, G.F. [1947] 2012. "The Sources of Soviet Conduct." In G.F. Kennan, *American Diplomacy: Sixtieth-Anniversary Expanded Edition*, 113–34. Chicago: University of Chicago Press.

Kenoyer, J.M. 1991. "The Indus Valley Tradition of Pakistan and Western India." *Journal of World Prehistory* 5 (4): 331–85. https://doi.org/10.1007/bf00978474.

Kertzer, J.D. 2016. *Resolve in International Politics.* Princeton, NJ: Princeton University Press.

Kiesow, I., and N. Norling. 2007. "The Rise of India: Problems and Opportunities." Institute for Security and Development Policy, 1 January. http://isdp.eu/publication/rise-india-problems-opportunities/.

Kissinger, H. 1982. *Years of Upheaval.* New York: Little, Brown and Company.

Kissinger, H. 1999. *Years of Renewal.* New York: Simon & Schuster.

Klinghoffer, A.J. 1980. *The Angolan War: A Study in Soviet Policy in the Third World.* Boulder, CO: Westview Press.

Knudsen, E.L. 2001. "The Syrian-Israeli Political Impasse: A Study in Conflict, War and Mistrust." *Diplomacy and Statecraft* 12 (1): 213–34. https://doi.org/10.1080/09592290108406196.

Kramer, M. 1999. "Ideology and the Cold War." *Review of International Studies* 25 (2): 539–76. https://doi.org/10.1017/s0260210599005392.

Kydd, A. 2005. "In America We (Used to) Trust: US Hegemony and Global Cooperation." *Political Science Quarterly* 120 (4): 619–36. http://www.jstor.org/stable/20202601.

Lagon, M.P. 1992. "The International System and the Reagan Doctrine: Can Realism Explain Aid to 'Freedom Fighters'?" *British Journal of Political Science* 22 (1): 39–70. https://doi.org/10.1017/s000712340000034x.

Lahore Declaration. 1999. http://www.satp.org/satporgtp/countries/india/document/papers/lahore_declaration.htm.

Laskar, R. 2018. "India will provide 4 Mi-24 choppers to Kabul, says Afghan envoy." *Hindustan Times*, 27 March. https://www.hindustantimes.com/world-news/india-will-provide-4-mi-24-choppers-to-kabul-says-afghan-envoy/story-HGvDXi8b6D0fTT8unBwPMO.html.

Lebow, R.N., and J.G. Stein. 1989. "Rational Deterrence Theory: I Think, Therefore I Deter." *World Politics* 41 (2): 208–24. doi:10.2307/2010408.

Leffler, M.P. 2007. *For the Soul of Mankind: The United States, the Soviet Union, and the Cold War.* New York: Farrar, Strauss and Giroux.

Leffler, M.P. 2010. "The Emergence of an American Grand Strategy, 1945–1952." In *Cambridge History of the Cold War Volume I: Origins,* edited by M.P. Leffler and O.A. Westad, 67–89. New York: Cambridge University Press.

Legum, C. 1976. *After Angola: The War over Southern Africa.* New York: Africana Publishing.

Lemke, D., and P. Regan. 2004. "Intervention as Influence." In *The Scourge of War: New Extensions on an Old Problem,* edited by P. Diehl, 145–68. Ann Arbor: University of Michigan Press.

Leng, R.J. 2000. *Bargaining and Learning in Recurring Crises: The Soviet-American, Egyptian-Israeli, and Indo-Pakistani Rivalries*. Ann Arbor: University of Michigan Press.

Levy, J.S. 1992. "An Introduction to Prospect Theory." *Political Psychology* 13 (2): 171–86. https://www.jstor.org/stable/3791677.

Levy, J.S. 1997. "Prospect Theory, Rational Choice, and International Relations." *International Studies Quarterly* 41 (1): 87–112. https://www.jstor .org/stable/2600908.

Levy, J., and W. Thompson. 2010. *The Causes of War*. London: Wiley & Sons.

Linebarger, C., and A. Enterline. 2016. "Third Party Intervention, Duration, and Civil War Outcomes." In *What Do We Know about Civil Wars?* edited by T.D. Mason and S.M. Mitchell, 93–108. Lanham, MD: Rowman & Littlefield.

Lippert, K. 2015. *War Plan Red: The United States' Secret Plan to Invade Canada and Canada's Secret Plan to Invade the United States*. New York: Princeton Architectural Press.

Litwak, R.S. 1984. *Détente and the Nixon Doctrine: American Foreign Policy and the Pursuit of Stability, 1969–1976*. New York: Cambridge University Press.

Lockwood, E. 1974. "National Security Study Memorandum 39 and the Future of United States Policy toward Southern Africa." *Issue: A Journal of Opinion* 4 (3): 63–72. https://doi.org/10.1017/s0047160700007514.

Lockyer, A. 2011. "Foreign Intervention and Warfare in Civil Wars." *Review of International Studies* 37 (5): 2337–64. https://doi.org/10.1017/s0260210510001488.

Louis, W.R., and A. Shlaim, eds. 2012. *The 1967 Arab-Israeli War: Origins and Consequences*. New York: Cambridge University Press.

Lupton, D.L. 2020. *Reputation for Resolve: How Leaders Signal Determination in International Politics*. Ithaca, NY: Cornell University Press.

MacFarlane, S.N. 1992. "Soviet-Angolan Relations. 1975–1990." Occasional Paper, National Council for Soviet and East European Research. https:// www.ucis.pitt.edu/nceeer/1992-1006-5550009-2-MacFarlane.pdf.

Mahoney, J. 2000. "Path Dependence in Historical Sociology." *Theory and Society* 29 (4): 507–48. https://doi.org/10.1023/a:1007113830879.

Majumder, S. 2017. "Why has India's Punjab fallen into the grip of drug abuse?" *BBC News*, 2 February. http://www.bbc.com/news/world-asia -india-38824478.

Maley, W. 2002. *The Afghanistan Wars*. London: Palgrave Macmillan.

Mangi, F. 2018. "Pakistan's economy goes from bad to worse as growth seen slowing." *Bloomberg*, 13 May. https://www.bloomberg.com/news /articles/2018-05-13/pakistan-s-economy-seen-slowing-for-first-time-in-six -years.

Ma'oz, M. 1995. *Syria and Israel: From War to Peacemaking*. New York: Oxford University Press.

Marcum, J. 1976. "Lessons of Angola." *Foreign Affairs* 54 (3): 407–25. https://doi.org/10.2307/20039585.

Marcum, J. 1978. *The Angolan Revolution, Volume II: Exile Politics and Guerilla Warfare (1962–1976)*. Cambridge, MA: MIT Press.

Mason, T.D., and P. Fett. 1996. "How Civil Wars End: A Rational Choice Approach." *Journal of Conflict Resolution* 40 (4): 546–68. https://doi.org/10.1177/0022002796040004002.

Mason, T.D., J.P. Weingarten Jr, and P.J. Fett. 1999. "Win, Lose, or Draw: Predicting the Outcome of Civil Wars." *Political Research Quarterly* 52 (2): 239–68. https://doi.org/10.1177%2F106591299905200201.

Mastny, V. 1996. *The Cold War and Soviet Insecurity: The Stalin Years*. New York: Oxford University Press.

Mays, T. 2004. *Historical Dictionary of Multinational Peacekeeping*. Lanham, MD: Scarecrow Press.

McCarthy, R. 2002. "Dangerous game of state-sponsored terror that threatens nuclear conflict." *Guardian*, 25 May. https://www.theguardian.com/world/2002/may/25/pakistan.india.

McDermott, R. 2004. *Political Psychology in International Relations*. Ann Arbor: University of Michigan Press.

McDermott, R. 2017. "Emotions in Foreign Policy Decision Making." *Oxford Research Encyclopedia of Politics*. https://doi.org/10.1093/acrefore/9780190228637.013.418.

McManus, R.W. 2017. *Statements of Resolve: Achieving Coercive Credibility in International Conflict*. New York: Cambridge University Press.

McNab, R.M., and E. Mason. 2007. "Reconstruction, the Long Tail and Decentralisation: An Application to Iraq and Afghanistan." *Small Wars & Insurgencies* 18 (3): 363–79. https://doi.org/10.1080/09592310701674234.

Mearsheimer, J.J. 1995. "A Realist Reply." *International Security* 20 (1): 82–93. https://doi.org/10.2307/2539218.

Mearsheimer, J. 2001. *The Tragedy of Great Power Politics*. New York: W.W. Norton.

Mearsheimer, J. 2012. "Introduction." In G.F. Kennan, *American Diplomacy: Sixtieth-Anniversary Expanded Edition*, xii–xliii. Chicago: University of Chicago Press.

"Memorandum for the Secretary of Defense." 1984. *Journal of Palestine Studies* 13 (2): 122–6. https://doi.org/10.1525/jps.1984.13.2.00p0015i.

Mercer, J. 1996. *Reputation and International Politics*. Ithaca, NY: Cornell University Press.

Michael, G.J. 2015. "Who's Afraid of Wikileaks? Missed Opportunities in Political Science Research." *Review of Policy Research* 32 (2): 175–99. https://doi.org/10.1111/ropr.12120.

Midlarsky, M.I., ed. 1989. *Handbook of War Studies*, vol. 1. Boston: Unwin Hyman.

Mitchell, C.R. 1970. "Civil Strife and the Involvement of External Parties." *International Studies Quarterly* 14 (2): 166–94. https://doi.org/10.2307/3013515.

Mitton, J. 2015. "Selling Schelling Short: Reputations and American Coercive Diplomacy after Syria." *Contemporary Security Policy* 36 (3): 408–31. https://doi.org/10.1080/13523260.2015.1091573.

Mohan, C.R. 2006. "India and the Balance of Power." *Foreign Affairs* 85 (4): 17–34. https://doi.org/10.2307/20032038.

Moore, O. 2001. "Northern Alliance calls for UN role in Afghanistan." *Globe and Mail*, 13 November. https://www.theglobeandmail.com/report-on-business/northern-alliance-calls-for-un-role-in-afghanistan/article20934549/.

Morgenthau, H.J. 1967. "To Intervene or Not to Intervene." *Foreign Affairs* 45 (3): 425–36. https://doi.org/10.2307/20039247.

Morris, B. 2001. *Righteous Victims: A History of the Zionist-Arab Conflict, 1881–2001.* New York: Vintage.

Mullen, R.D. 2017. "India in Afghanistan: Understanding Development Assistance by Emerging Donors to Conflict-Affected Countries." *Policy Brief.* Washington, DC: Stimson Center.

Mullenbach, M.J. 2001. "Third-Party Interventions in Intrastate Disputes in the Twentieth Century." PhD diss., University of Arizona.

Mullenbach, M.J., and G.P. Matthews. 2008. "Deciding to Intervene: An Analysis of International and Domestic Influences on United States Interventions in Intrastate Disputes." *International Interactions* 34 (1): 25–52. https://doi.org/10.1080/03050620701878835.

Murray, M. 2019. *The Struggle for Recognition in International Relations: Status, Revisionism, and Rising Powers.* New York: Oxford University Press.

Musharraf, P. 2001. "Address to People of Pakistan." 19 September. http://web.archive.org/web/20080511213354/http://www.americanrhetoric.com/speeches/pakistanpresident.htm.

Musharraf, P. 2006. *In the Line of Fire: A Memoir.* New York: Simon & Schuster.

Muslih, M. 1993. "The Golan: Israel, Syria, and Strategic Calculations." *Middle East Journal* 47 (4): 611–32.

Nadiri, K.H. 2014. "Old Habits, New Consequences: Pakistan's Posture toward Afghanistan since 2001." *International Security* 39 (2): 132–68. https://doi.org/10.1162/isec_a_00178.

Noer, T.J. 1993. "International Credibility and Political Survival: The Ford Administration's Intervention in Angola." *Presidential Studies Quarterly* 23 (4): 771–85. https://doi.org/10.1163/2468-1733_shafr_sim230130095.

O'Ballance, E. 1998. *Civil War in Lebanon, 1975–92.* New York: Springer.

Ogden, C. 2011. "International 'Aspirations' of a Rising Power." In *Handbook of India's International Relations*, edited by D. Scott, 3–13. London: Routledge.

Ogden, C. 2013. "Tracing the Pakistan-Terrorism Nexus in Indian Security Perspectives: From 1947 to 26/11." *India Quarterly* 69 (1): 35–50. https://doi.org/10.1177/0974928412472102.

O'Hanlon, M. 2002. "A Flawed Masterpiece." *Foreign Affairs* 81 (3): 47–63. https://doi.org/10.2307/20033162.

O'Loughlin, J. 2016. "The Perils of Self-Censorship in Academic Research in a Wikileaks World." *Journal of Global Security Studies* 1 (4): 337–45. https://doi.org/10.1093/jogss/ogw011.

Oren, M. 2002. *Six Days of War: June 1967 and the Making of the Modern Middle East.* New York: Oxford University Press.

Paliwal, A. 2017. *My Enemy's Enemy: India in Afghanistan from the Soviet Invasion to the US Withdrawal.* New York: Oxford University Press.

Panda, A. 2015. "Who's negotiating with the Taliban anyway?" *Diplomat*, 20 February. https://thediplomat.com/2015/02/whos-negotiating-with-the-taliban-anyway/.

Pande, A. 2016. "Pakistan's worst nightmare?" *Hudson Institute*, 5 September. https://www.hudson.org/research/12808-pakistan-s-worst-nightmare.

Pant, H.V. 2010. "India in Afghanistan: A Test Case for a Rising Power." *Contemporary South Asia* 18 (2): 133–53. https://doi.org/10.1080/09584931003674984.

Pant, H.V. 2012. *India's Changing Afghanistan Policy: Regional and Global Implications.* Strategic Studies Institute. http://ssi.armywarcollege.edu/pdffiles/pub1141.pdf.

Pant, H.V. 2016. *Indian Foreign Policy: An Overview.* Manchester, UK: Manchester University Press.

Parashar, S. 2011. "Govt worried over Af fallout, hasty US troop withdrawal." *Times of India*, 6 May. https://timesofindia.indiatimes.com/india/Govt-worried-over-Af-fallout-hasty-US-troop-withdrawal/articleshow/8164854.cms.

Parashar, S. 2013. "In change of stance, India supports talks with Taliban." *Times of India*, 3 July. https://timesofindia.indiatimes.com/india/In-change-of-stance-India-supports-talks-with-Taliban/articleshow/20884297.cms.

Paris, R. 2013. "Afghanistan: What Went Wrong?" *Perspectives on Politics* 11 (2): 539–48. https://doi.org/10.1017/s1537592713000911.

Pattanaik, S.S. 2012. "India's Afghan Policy: Beyond Bilateralism." *Strategic Analysis* 36 (4): 569–83. https://doi.org/10.1080/09700161.2012.689527.

Paul, T.V. 2005. "Causes of the India-Pakistan Enduring Rivalry." In *The India-Pakistan Conflict: An Enduring Rivalry*, edited by T.V. Paul, 3–24. New York: Cambridge University Press.

Payne, S.B. 1980. *The Soviet Union and SALT.* Cambridge, MA: MIT Press.

PBS Frontline. n.d. "Filling the Vacuum: The Bonn Conference." https://www.pbs.org/wgbh/pages/frontline/shows/campaign/withus/cbonn.html.

Pearson, F. 1974a. "Foreign Military Intervention by Large and Small Powers." *International Interactions* 1 (4): 273–8. https://doi.org/10.1080/03050627408434412.

Pearson, F. 1974b. "Geographic Proximity and Foreign Military Intervention." *Journal of Conflict Resolution* 18 (3): 432–60. https://doi.org/10.1177/002200277401800304.

Pechatnov, V.O. 2010. "The Soviet Union and the World, 1944–1953." In *Cambridge History of the Cold War Volume I: Origins*, edited by M.P. Leffler and O.A. Westad, 90–111. New York: Cambridge University Press.

Perlez, J. 2021. "The real winner of the Afghan war? It's not who you think." *New York Times*, 7 October. https://www.nytimes.com/2021/08/26/world/asia/afghanistan-pakistan-taliban.html.

Perlmutter, A. 1987. *The Life and Times of Menachem Begin*. New York: Doubleday.

Pollack, K. 2002. *Arabs at War: Military Effectiveness, 1948–1991*. Lincoln: University of Nebraska Press.

Porter, B.D. 1984. *The USSR in Third World Conflicts: Soviet Arms and Diplomacy in Local Wars 1945–1980*. Cambridge: Cambridge University Press.

Powell, R. 1991. "Absolute and Relative Gains in International Relations Theory." *American Political Science Review* 85 (4): 1303–20. https://doi.org/10.2307/1963947.

Press, D. 2005. *Calculating Credibility: How Leaders Assess Military Threats*. Ithaca, NY: Cornell University Press.

Price, G. 2013. "India's Policy towards Afghanistan." *Asia ASP 2013/14*. London: Chatham House. https://www.chathamhouse.org/sites/default/files/public/Research/Asia/0813pp_indiaafghanistan.pdf.

Print. 2017. "Talk Point: What More Can India Do in Afghanistan without Provoking Pakistan?" 26 October. https://theprint.in/talk-point/talk-point-can-india-afghanistan-without-provoking-pakistan/13467/.

Putz, C. 2018. "TAPI moves into Afghanistan, Taliban promise to protect the project." *Diplomat*, 27 February. https://thediplomat.com/2018/02/tapi-moves-into-afghanistan-taliban-promise-to-protect-the-project/.

Rabil, R.G. 2003. *Embattled Neighbors: Syria, Israel and Lebanon*. Boulder, CO: Lynne Rienner.

Rabin, Y. 1979. *The Rabin Memoirs*. Boston: Little, Brown.

Rabinovich, I. 1985. *The War for Lebanon, 1970–1985*. Ithaca, NY: Cornell University Press.

Rabinovich, I. 2008. *The View from Damascus: State, Political Community and Foreign Relations in Twentieth-Century Syria*. Elstree, UK: Vallentine Mitchell.

Raghavan, S. 2009. "A Coercive Triangle: India, Pakistan, the United States, and the Crisis of 2001–2002." *Defence Studies* 9 (2): 242–60. https://doi.org/10.1080/14702430902921486.

Raghavan, V.R. 2001. "Limited War and Nuclear Escalation in South Asia." *Nonproliferation Review* 8 (3): 82–98. https://doi.org/10.1080/10736700108436865.

Rajagopalan, R. 1999. "Neorealist Theory and the India-Pakistan Conflict II." *Strategic Analysis* 22 (10): 1525–36. https://doi.org/10.1080/09700169908458901.

Rajghatta, C. 2002. "Musharraf brought region to brink of nuclear war." *Times of India*, 16 May. https://timesofindia.indiatimes.com/Musharraf-brought-region-to-brink-of-nuclear-war/articleshow/10012966.cms.

RAND. n.d. *Database of Worldwide Terrorism Incidents.* https://www.rand.org/nsrd/projects/terrorism-incidents.html

Rashid, A. 2001. "Intelligence team defied Musharraf to help Taliban." *Telegraph*, 10 October. https://www.telegraph.co.uk/news/worldnews/asia/pakistan/1359051/Intelligence-team-defied-Musharraf-to-help-Taliban.html.

Rashid, A. 2009. *Descent into Chaos: The US and the Disaster in Pakistan, Afghanistan, and Central Asia.* London: Penguin.

Rasler, K. 1983. "Internationalized Civil War: A Dynamic Analysis of the Syrian Intervention in Lebanon." *Journal of Conflict Resolution* 27 (3): 421–56. https://doi.org/10.1177/0022002783027003002.

Rasmussen, S.E. 2017. "Taliban bombings kill at least 30 people near Afghan parliament." *Guardian*, 10 January. https://www.theguardian.com/world/2017/jan/10/taliban-bombings-kill-people-near-afghan-parliament-kabul.

Reddy, L.R. 2002. *Inside Afghanistan: End of the Taliban Era?* New Delhi: APH Publishing.

Regan, P. 1996. "Conditions of Successful Third-Party Intervention in Intrastate Conflicts." *Journal of Conflict Resolution* 40 (2): 336–59. https://doi.org/10.1177%2F0022002796040002006.

Regan, P. 2000. *Civil Wars and Foreign Powers: Outside Intervention in Intrastate Conflict.* Ann Arbor: University of Michigan Press.

Regan, P. 2002. "Third-Party Interventions and the Duration of Intrastate Conflicts." *Journal of Conflict Resolution* 46 (1): 55–73. https://doi.org/10.1177/0022002702046001004.

Regan, P. 2009. "Civil War and Territory? Drawing Linkages between Interstate and Intrastate War." *International Interactions* 35 (3): 321–9. https://doi.org/10.1080/03050620903084844.

Regan, P., and A. Aydin. 2006. "Diplomacy and Other Forms of Intervention in Civil Wars." *Journal of Conflict Resolution* 50 (5): 736–56. https://doi.org/10.1177/0022002706291579.

Regan, P., R.W. Frank, and A. Aydin. 2009. "Diplomatic Interventions and Civil War: A New Dataset." *Journal of Peace Research* 46 (1): 135–46. https://doi.org/10.1177%2F0022343308098408.

Reidel, B. 2011. *Deadly Embrace: Pakistan, America, and the Future of the Global Jihad.* Washington, DC: Brookings Institution Press.

Renshon, J. 2009. "When Public Statements Reveal Private Beliefs." *Political Psychology* 30 (4): 649–61. https://doi.org/10.1111/j.1467-9221.2009.00718.x.

Renshon, J. 2010. "Stability and Change in Belief Systems: The Operational Code of George W. Bush from Governor to Second Term President." In *Rethinking Foreign Policy Analysis: States, Leaders, and the Microfoundations of Behavioral International Relations*, edited by S.G. Walker, A. Malici, and M. Schafer, 170–88. New York: Routledge.

Rhode, D., and D. Sanger. 2007. "How the 'good war' in Afghanistan went bad." *New York Times*, 12 August.

Rohlfing, I. 2012. *Case Studies and Causal Inference*. London: Palgrave Macmillan.

Rosato, S. 2015. "The Inscrutable Intentions of Great Powers." *International Security* 39 (3): 48–88. https://doi.org/10.1162/ISEC_a_00190.

Rosenau, J.N. 1964. *International Aspects of Civil Strife*. Princeton, NJ: Princeton University Press.

Rosenau, J.N. 1968. "The Concept of Intervention." *Journal of International Affairs* 22 (2): 165–76.

Rosenau, J.N. 1969. "Intervention as a Scientific Concept." *Journal of Conflict Resolution* 13 (2): 149–71. https://doi.org/10.1177/002200276901300201.

Roy, S. 2017. "India steps up development partnership with Afghanistan." *Indian Express*, 12 September. http://indianexpress.com/article/india/india-steps-up-development-partnership-with-afghanistan-4839291/.

Rubin, A.J. 2010. "Guesthouses used by foreigners in Kabul hit in deadly attacks." *New York Times*, 26 February. https://www.nytimes.com/2010/02/27/world/asia/27kabul.html.

Rubin, B., and A. Rashid. 2008. "From Great Game to Grand Bargain: Ending Chaos in Afghanistan and Pakistan." *Foreign Affairs* 87 (6): 30–44.

Rubin, M. 2015. *Dancing with the Devil: The Perils of Engaging Rogue Regimes*. New York: Encounter Books.

Ruttig, T. 2009. "The Haqqani Network as an Autonomous Entity." In *Decoding the New Taliban: Insights from the Afghan Field*, edited by A. Giustozzi, 57–88. London: Hurst & Company.

Saikal, A. 2004. *Modern Afghanistan: A History of Struggle and Survival*. London: I.B. Tauris.

Salehyan, I. 2009. "Kinship and Diasporas in International Affairs by Yossi Shain." *Political Science Quarterly* 124 (2): 383–5. https://doi.org/10.1002/j.1538-165X.2009.tb01902.x.

Salehyan, I., K.S. Gleditsch, and D.E. Cunningham. 2011. "Explaining External Support for Insurgent Groups." *International Organization* 65 (4): 709–44. https://doi.org/10.1017/s0020818311000233.

Sathasivam, K. 2005. *Uneasy Neighbors: India, Pakistan, and US Foreign Policy*. New York: Ashgate.

Savranskaya, S., and W. Taubman. 2010. "Soviet Foreign Policy, 1962–1975." In *Cambridge History of the Cold War Volume II: Crises and Détente*, edited by M.P. Leffler and O.A. Westad, 134–57. New York: Cambridge University Press.

Schelling, T. 1960. *The Strategy of Conflict*. Cambridge, MA: Harvard University Press.

Schelling, T. [1966] 2008. *Arms and Influence*. New Haven, CT: Yale University Press.

Schmitt, C. [1928] 2007. *The Concept of the Political*. Chicago: Chicago University Press.

Schweller, R.L. 1996. "Neorealism's Status-Quo Bias: What Security Dilemma?" *Security Studies* 5 (3): 90–121. https://doi.org/10.1080/09636419608429277.

Scott, J.M. 1996. *Deciding to Intervene: The Reagan Doctrine and American Foreign Policy*. Durham, NC: Duke University Press.

Seale, P. 1990. *Asad: The Struggle for the Middle East*. Berkeley: University of California Press.

Sharma, D.P. 2001. "Harkat's presence negligible in J&K." *Times of India*, 1 October. https://timesofindia.indiatimes.com/india/Harkats-presence-negligible-in-JK/articleshow/1276462486.cms.

Sharma, R. 2011. "India's Relations with Afghanistan." In *Handbook of India's International Relations*, edited by D. Scott, 107–17. New York: Routledge.

Shilon, A., D. Zilberberg, and Y. Sharett. 2012. *Menachem Begin: A Life*. New Haven, CT: Yale University Press.

Shlaim, A. 2004. "The War of the Israeli Historians." *Annales* 59 (1): 161–7.

Shlaim, A. 2007. "Israel and the Arab Coalition in 1948." In *The War for Palestine: Rewriting the History of 1948*, edited by E. Rogan and A. Shlaim, 79–103. Cambridge: Cambridge University Press.

Shore, Z. 2014. *A Sense of the Enemy: The High Stakes History of Reading Your Enemy's Mind*. New York: Oxford University Press.

Shulzinger, R.D. 2010. "Détente in the Nixon-Ford Years, 1969–1976." In *Cambridge History of the Cold War Volume II: Crises and Détente*, edited by M.P. Leffler and O.A. Westad, 373–94. New York: Cambridge University Press.

Siddiqa, A. 2011. "Pakistan's Counterterrorism Strategy: Separating Friends from Enemies." *Washington Quarterly* 34 (1): 149–62. https://doi.org/10.1080/0163660x.2011.538362.

Sipress, A., and S. Mufson. 2001. "America lines up support for strike: Pakistan pressured to aid any reprisal." *Washington Post*, 13 September. https://www.highbeam.com/doc/1P2-459236.html.

Sirrs, O. 2017. *Pakistan's Inter-Services Intelligence Directorate: Cover action and internal operations*. New York: Routledge.

Slantchev, B.L. 2005. "Military Coercion in Interstate Crises." *American Political Science Review* 99 (4): 533–47. https://doi.org/10.1017/S0003055405051865.

Slater, J. 2002. "Lost Opportunities for Peace in the Arab-Israeli Conflict: Israel and Syria, 1948–2001." *International Security* 27 (1): 79–106. https://doi.org/10.1162/016228802320231235.

Spector, L.S. 1984. *Nuclear Proliferation Today*. Cambridge, MA: Ballinger.

Stein, J.G. 1985. "Detection and Defection: Security 'Regimes' and the Management of International Conflict." *International Journal* 40 (4): 599–627. https://doi.org/10.1177/002070208504000403.

Stein, J.G. 2013. "Threat Perception in International Relations." In *The Oxford Handbook of Political Psychology*, 2nd ed., edited by L. Huddy, D.O. Sears, and J.S. Levy, 363–94. New York: Oxford University Press.

Stockwell, J. 1978. *In Search of Enemies: A CIA Story*. New York: W.W. Norton.

Sucharov, M.M. 2012) *The International Self: Psychoanalysis and the Search for Israeli-Palestinian Peace*. Albany: State University of New York Press.

Swami, P. 2011. "The Roots of Crisis: Post-Kargil Conflict in Kashmir and the 2001–2002 Near War." In *The India-Pakistan Military Standoff: Crisis Escalation in South Asia*, edited by Z. Davis, 19–52. New York: Palgrave Macmillan.

Syed, B.S. 2016. "Ghani's call for India joining transit trade rejected." *Dawn*, 11 September. https://www.dawn.com/news/1283445.

Tadjbakhsh, S. 2011. *South Asia and Afghanistan: The Robust India-Pakistan Rivalry*. Oslo: Oslo Peace Research Institute.

Tal, D. 2003. *War in Palestine 1948: Strategy and Diplomacy*. New York: Routledge.

Taliaferro, J. 2000/01. "Security Seeking under Anarchy: Defensive Realism Revisited." *International Security* 25 (3): 128–61. https://doi.org/10.1162/016228800560543.

Taliaferro, J. 2004. *Balancing Risks: Great Power Intervention in the Periphery*. Ithaca, NY: Cornell University Press.

Tang, S. 2005. "Reputation, Cult of Reputation, and International Conflict." *Security Studies* 14 (1): 34–62. https://doi.org/10.1080/09636410591001474.

Tanha, F. 2015. "Substation supplying electricity to 3 provinces built in Parwan." *Pajhwok Afghan News*, 29 November. https://www.pajhwok.com/en/2015/11/29/substation-supplying-electricity-3-provinces-built-parwan.

Teveth, S. 1972. *Moshe Dayan*. London: Weidenfeld and Nicolson.

Thies, C.G. 2008. "The Construction of a Latin American Interstate Culture of Rivalry." *International Interactions* 34 (3): 231–57. https://doi.org/10.1080/03050620802469872.

Thompson, W. 1995. "Principal Rivalries." *Journal of Conflict Resolution* 39 (2): 195–223. https://doi.org/10.1177/0022002795039002001.

Thompson W.R., and D.R. Dreyer. 2011. *Handbook of International Rivalries*. Washington, DC: CQ Press.

Thornton, T.P. 1999. "Pakistan: Fifty Years of Insecurity." In *India and Pakistan: The First Fifty Years*, edited by S. Harrison, P. Kreisberg, and D. Kux. Washington, DC: Woodrow Wilson Center Press.

Tilemma, H.K. 1989. "Foreign over Military Intervention in the Nuclear Age." *Journal of Peace Research* 26 (2): 179–95. https://doi.org/10.1177/0022343389026002006.

Times of India. 2001. "India, Russia reject moderate Taliban." 20 October. https://timesofindia.indiatimes.com/india/India-Russia-reject-moderate -Taliban/articleshow/2028360379.cms.

Times of India. 2012. "Taliban attack checkpost near India-made dam in Afghanistan, kill 10 policemen." 25 June. https://timesofindia.indiatimes. com/world/south-asia/taliban-attack-india-made-dam-in-afghanistan-kill -10-policemen/articleshow/59309625.cms

Timmons, H. 2012. "Can India 'Fix' Afghanistan?" *New York Times*, 7 June. https://india.blogs.nytimes.com/2012/06/07/can-india-fix-afghanistan/.

Tisdall, S. 2011. "India may pay heavily in future for supporting the Karzai regime." *Guardian*, 5 October. https://www.theguardian.com/world/2011 /oct/05/india-regret-supporting-karzai-afghanistan?INTCMP=SRCH.

Traboulsi, F. 2007. *A History of Modern Lebanon*. Ann Arbor, MI: Pluto Press.

United Nations. 2001. "Pakistan: Statement by His Excellency General Pervez Musharraf, President of the Islamic Republic of Pakistan at the Fifty Sixth Session of the United Nations General Assembly." 10 November. http:// www.un.org/webcast/ga/56/statements/011110pakistanE.htm.

United Nations Assistance Mission in Afghanistan. 2017. *Afghanistan: Protection of Civilians in Armed Conflict Annual Report 2017*. https://www.ohchr.org /Documents/Countries/AF/ProtectionCiviliansAnnualReport2017.pdf.

United Nations Special Programme for the Economies of Central Asia. 2016. "Strengthening Trade and Economic Ties between Afghanistan and Central Asia." https://www.unece.org/fileadmin/DAM/SPECA/documents /ecf/2016/Session_I_Background_paper_1_English.pdf.

United States. 1975a. "Memorandum of Conversation Sunday March 9, 1975." Kissinger Reports on USSR, China, and Middle East Discussions (Box 3 – March 7–22, 1975 – Kissinger's Trip – Vol. 1 (2)). Gerald R. Ford Presidential Library Digital Collections. https://www.fordlibrarymuseum.gov/library /document/0331/1553950.pdf.

United States. 1975b. "Memorandum of Conversation March 12, 1975." Kissinger Reports on USSR, China, and Middle East Discussions (Box 3 – March 7–22, 1975 – Kissinger's Trip – Vol. 1 (6)). Gerald R. Ford Presidential Library Digital Collections. https://www.fordlibrarymuseum.gov/library /document/0331/1553954.pdf.

United States. 1975c. "Memorandum of Conversation March 15, 1975." Kissinger Reports on USSR, China, and Middle East Discussions (Box 3 – March 7–22, 1975 – Kissinger's Trip – Vol. 1 (9)). Gerald R. Ford Presidential Library Digital Collections. https://www.fordlibrarymuseum.gov/library /document/0331/1553957.pdf.

United States. 1975d. "NSC Meeting, 6/27/1975." Gerald R. Ford Presidential Library Digital Collections. https://www.fordlibrarymuseum.gov/library /document/0312/1552391.pdf

United States. 1975e. "Memorandum of Conversation Wednesday, June 11, 1975." Gerald R. Ford Presidential Library Digital Collections. https:// www.fordlibrarymuseum.gov/library/document/0314/1553116.pdf.

United States. 1975f. "Memorandum of Conversation Friday, June 20, 1975." Gerald R. Ford Presidential Library Digital Collections. https://www .fordlibrarymuseum.gov/library/document/0314/1553132.pdf.

United States. 1975g. "Memorandum of Conversation August 22, 1975." Kissinger Reports on USSR, China, and Middle East Discussions (Box 4 – August 21 – September 1, 1975 – Sinai Disengagement Agreement – Vol. I (1)). Gerald R. Ford Presidential Library Digital Collections. https://www .fordlibrarymuseum.gov/library/document/0331/1553968.pdf.

United States. 1975h. "NSC Meeting, 12/22/1975." Gerald R. Ford Presidential Library Digital Collections. www.fordlibrarymuseum.gov /library/document/0312/1552396.pdf.

United States. 1976a. Department of State. "Memorandum of Conversation, January 3, 1976, Secretary's Meeting with Jamaican Prime Minister and Other Officials." Document No. C17827946. https://foia.state.gov /searchapp/DOCUMENTS/1-FY2012/F-2006-01366/DOC_0C17827946 /C17827946.pdf.

United States. 1976b. Department of State. "TELCON, Congressman Mahon /Secretary Kissinger, January 14, 1976." Document No. 0000D705. https:// foia.state.gov/searchapp/DOCUMENTS/kissinger/0000D705.pdf.

United States. 1976c. Department of State. "TELCON, Senator Javits/Secretary Kissinger, January 31, 1976." Document No. 0000D712. https://foia.state .gov/searchapp/DOCUMENTS/kissinger/0000D712.pdf.

United States. 1976d. Department of State. "TELCON, Sec. Kissinger/Robert Kleiman, 2/6/76." Document No. 0000BE34. https://foia.state.gov /searchapp/DOCUMENTS/kissinger/0000BE34.pdf.

United States. 1976e. "NSC Meeting, 4/7/1976." Gerald R. Ford Presidential Library Digital Collections. https://www.fordlibrarymuseum.gov/library /document/0312/1552402.pdf.

United States. 1976f. Senate. Committee on Foreign Relations. "Angola: Hearings before the Subcommittee on African Affairs, Ninety-Fourth Congress, Second Session on US Involvement in Civil War in Angola." 29 January; 3, 4, 6 February. https://babel.hathitrust.org./cgi/pt?id=purl.3275 4074746417;view=1up;seq=6;size=150.

United States. 2006a. Department of the Interior. United States Geological Survey. "Assessment of Undiscovered Petroleum Resources of Northern Afghanistan, 2006." https://pubs.usgs.gov/fs/2006/3031/pdf/FS-3031.pdf.

United States. 2006b. Office of the Press Secretary. "Joint Statement on United States-Pakistan Strategic Partnership." 4 March. https://georgewbush -whitehouse.archives.gov/news/releases/2006/03/20060304-1.html.

United States. 2006c. Defense Intelligence Agency. "Current and Projected National Security Threats to the United States, Lieutenant General Michael D. Maples, US Army, Director, Defense Intelligence Agency, Statement for the Record, Senate Armed Services Committee, 28 February 2006." https://fas.org/irp/congress/2006_hr/022806maples .pdf.

United States. 2007. "Foreign Relations of the United States." Document 121. 1969–1976, Volume XVIII, China, 1973–1976, edited by D.P. Nickles and E.C. Keefer. Washington, DC: US Government Printing Office. https://history .state.gov/historicaldocuments/frus1969-76v18/d121.

United States. 2011. Senate. Armed Services Committee. "Hearing to Receive Testimony on the US Strategy in Afghanistan and Iraq." 22 September. https://www.armed-services.senate.gov/imo/media/doc/11-70%20-%20 9-22-11.pdf.

USSR. 1946. "Telegram from Nikolai Novikov, Soviet Ambassador to the US, to the Soviet Leadership." 27 September. AVP SSSR, f. 06. op. 8, p. 45, p. 759. History and Public Policy Program Digital Archive. *Mezhdunarodnaya Zhizn'* 11 (1990): 148–54, trans. G. Goldberg. http://digitalarchive.wilsoncenter. org/document/110808.

Valeriano, B. 2012. *Becoming Rivals: The Process of Interstate Rivalry Development*. New York: Routledge.

Vasquez, J.A. 1996. "Distinguishing Rivals That Go to War from Those That Do Not: A Quantitative Comparative Case." *International Studies Quarterly* 40 (4): 531–58. https://doi.org/10.2307/2600890.

Vasquez, J.A. 2009. *The War Puzzle Revisited*. Cambridge: Cambridge University Press.

Vasquez, J.A., and M. Henehan. 2001. "Territorial Disputes and the Probability of War, 1816–1992." *Journal of Peace Research* 38 (2): 123–39. https://doi.org /10.1177/0022343301038002001.

Vasquez, J.A., and C. Leskiw. 2001. "The Origins and War Proneness of Interstate Rivalries." *Annual Review of Political Science* 4: 295–316. https:// doi.org/10.1146/annurev.polisci.4.1.295.

Vigor, P.H. 1986. *The Soviet View of Disarmament*. New York: Palgrave Macmillan.

Waldman, M. 2010. *The Sun in the Sky: The Relationship between Pakistan's ISI and Afghan Insurgents*. Cambridge, MA: Harvard University, Kennedy School of Government.

Waldman, M. 2013. "System Failure: The Underlying Causes of US Policy-Making Errors in Afghanistan." *International Affairs* 89 (4): 825–43. https:// doi.org/10.1111/1468-2346.12047.

Walsh, D. 2010. "Afghanistan war logs: Clandestine aid for Taliban bears Pakistan's fingerprints." *Guardian*, 25 July. https://www.theguardian.com /world/2010/jul/25/pakistan-isi-accused-taliban-afghanistan.

Walter, B. 2002. *Committing to Peace: The Successful Settlement of Civil Wars.* Princeton, NJ: Princeton University Press.

Waltz, K. 1959. *Man, the State, and War.* New York: Columbia University Press.

Waltz, K. 1979. *Theory of International Politics.* Reading, PA: Addison-Wesley.

Ward, S. 2017. *Status and the Challenge of Rising Powers.* New York: Cambridge University Press.

Wazir, M.M.K.W. 2011. "Geopolitics of FATA after 9/11." *IPRI Journal* 11 (1): 59–76.

Weaver, M. 2015. "Afghanistan parliament attacked by Taliban suicide bomber and gunmen." *Guardian*, 22 June. https://www.theguardian.com/world/live/2015/jun/22/afghanistan-parliament-attack-live-updates.

Weinbaum, M. 2017. "Insurgency and Violent Extremism in Pakistan." *Small Wars & Insurgencies* 28 (1): 34–56. https://doi.org/10.1080/09592318.2016.1266130.

Weinbaum, M., and J. Harder. 2008. "Pakistan's Afghan Policies and Their Consequences." *Contemporary South Asia* 16 (1): 25–38. https://doi.org/10.1080/09584930701800370.

Weinberger, N. 1986. *Syrian Intervention in Lebanon: The 1975–76 Civil War.* New York: Oxford University Press, 1986.

Wendt, A. 1999. *Social Theory of International Politics.* New York: Cambridge University Press.

Westad, O.A. 2006. *The Global Cold War: Third World Interventions and the Making of Our Times.* New York: Cambridge University Press.

White, H. 2010. *The Fiction of Narrative: Essays on History, Literature, and Theory, 1957–2007.* Baltimore: Johns Hopkins Press.

Whitlock, C. 2019. "Stranded without a strategy." *Washington Post*, 9 December. https://www.washingtonpost.com/graphics/2019/investigations/afghanistan-papers/afghanistan-war-strategy/.

Wirsing, R.G. 2003. *Kashmir in the Shadow of War: Regional Rivalries in a Nuclear Age.* New York: M.E Sharpe.

Wirsing, R.G. 2007. "In India's Lengthening Shadow: The US-Pakistan Strategic Alliance and the War in Afghanistan." *Asian Affairs: An American Review* 34 (3): 151–72. https://doi.org/10.3200/aafs.34.3.151-172.

Wittmeyer, A. 2013. "What went wrong in Afghanistan?" *ForeignPolicy.com*, 4 March. http://foreignpolicy.com/2013/03/04/what-went-wrong-in-afghanistan/.

Wohlforth, W.C. 2000. "Ideology and the Cold War." *Review of International Studies* 26 (2): 327–31. https://doi.org/10.1017/s0260210500003272.

Wolak, P. 2014. "Foreign Military Interventions in Civil Conflicts, 1946–2002." PhD diss., University of Maryland.

Wolfers, A. 1962. *Discord and Collaboration: Essays on International Politics.* Baltimore: Johns Hopkins Press.

Wolpert, S. 2010. *India and Pakistan: Continued Conflict or Cooperation?* Berkeley: University of California Press.

Woodward, B. 2002. *Bust at War*. New York: Simon & Schuster.

Yarhi-Milo, K. 2014. *Knowing the Adversary: Leaders, Intelligence, and Assessment of Intentions in International Relations*. Princeton, NJ: Princeton University Press.

Yarhi-Milo, K. 2018. *Who Fights for Reputation: The Psychology of Leaders in International Conflict*. Princeton, NJ: Princeton University Press.

Yarmolinsky, A. 1968. "The Atlantic Alliance." *Survival* 11 (2): 57–62.

Yoon, M.Y. 1997. "Explaining U.S. Intervention in Third World Internal Wars, 1945–1989." *Journal of Conflict Resolution* 41 (4): 580–602. https://doi.org/10.1177/0022002797041004005.

Yusuf, M. 2014. "Introduction." In *Pakistan's Counterterrorism Challenge*, edited by M. Yusuf, 1–14. Washington, DC: Georgetown University Press.

Zaidi, M. 2017. "RAW providing safe haven to Pakistani Taliban chief, says breakaway faction spokesman." *Hindu*, 26 April. https://www.thehindu.com/news/international/raw-providing-safe-haven-to-pakistani-taliban-chief-says-ehsanullah-ehsan-breakaway-faction-spokesman/article18221720.ece.

Zamir, M. 1999. "From Hegemony to Marginalism: The Maronites of Lebanon." In *Minorities and the State in the Arab World*, edited by O. Bengio and G. Ben-Dor, 111–28. Boulder, CO: Lynne Rienner.

Index